Frommer's

Toronto

2005

by Hilary Davidson

SO-BCZ-367

Here's what the critics say about Frommer's:

"Amazingly easy to use. Very portable, very complete."
—Booklist

"Detailed, accurate, and easy-to-read information for all price ranges."
—Glamour Magazine

"Hotel information is close to encyclopedic."
—Des Moines Sunday Register

"Comprehensive and includes information about the many festivals—from beer to literature—that Toronto hosts each year."
—The Washington Post

WILEY

Wiley Publishing, Inc.

About the Author

Toronto native **Hilary Davidson** now calls New York City home, thanks to her persuasive Manhattan-born husband, Daniel. She is a contributing editor at *Chatelaine* magazine and writes for *American Archaeology, Fitness, Martha Stewart Weddings, Executive Traveler, Wedding Bells, Discover,* and *Pages.* She is also a contributor to *Frommer's Canada.* She can be reached at hcdavidson@yahoo.com.

Published by:

Wiley Publishing, Inc.

111 River St.
Hoboken, NJ 07030-5774

ISBN 0-7645-7530-9

Editor: William Gibson
Production Editor: Ian Skinnari
Cartographer: Roberta Stockwell
Photo Editor: Richard Fox
Production by Wiley Indianapolis Composition Services

Front cover photo: The CN Tower in reflection
Back cover photo: Admiring the Toronto skyline

For information on our other products and services or to obtain technical support, please contact our Customer Care Department within the U.S. at 800/762-2974, outside the U.S. at 317/572-3993 or fax 317/572-4002.

Wiley also publishes its books in a variety of electronic formats. Some content that appears in print may not be available in electronic formats.

Manufactured in the United States of America

5 4 3 2 1

Contents

List of Maps

Acknowledgments

Many thanks to my terrific editors, Myka Carroll Del Barrio and William Gibson, whose talent, wit, and good sense made working on this book a pleasure. Thanks are also owed to the rest of the Frommer's team, who worked their usual magic in transforming a manuscript into a book. I am also grateful to my mother, Sheila Davidson, who is always ready to help but never makes me feel guilty for taking advantage of her highly skilled—yet unpaid—labor. I owe a heartfelt thanks to my husband, Dan, whose sense of humor and tireless enthusiasm carried me throughout this project. Finally, deepest thanks to my wonderful friends in Toronto who are always so generous in sharing their observations and opinions.

An Invitation to the Reader

In researching this book, we discovered many wonderful places—hotels, restaurants, shops, and more. We're sure you'll find others. Please tell us about them, so we can share the information with your fellow travelers in upcoming editions. If you were disappointed with a recommendation, we'd love to know that, too. Please write to:

Frommer's Toronto 2005
Wiley Publishing, Inc. • 111 River St. • Hoboken, NJ 07030-5774

An Additional Note

Please be advised that travel information is subject to change at any time—and this is especially true of prices. We therefore suggest that you write or call ahead for confirmation when making your travel plans. The authors, editors, and publisher cannot be held responsible for the experiences of readers while traveling. Your safety is important to us, however, so we encourage you to stay alert and be aware of your surroundings. Keep a close eye on cameras, purses, and wallets, all favorite targets of thieves and pickpockets.

Other Great Guides for Your Trip:

Frommer's Canada

Frommer's Montréal & Québec City

**Frommer's Nova Scotia, New Brunswick
& Prince Edward Island**

Frommer's Ottawa with Kids

Frommer's Toronto with Kids

Frommer's Star Ratings, Icons & Abbreviations

Every hotel, restaurant, and attraction listing in this guide has been ranked for quality, value, service, amenities, and special features using a **star-rating system.** In country, state, and regional guides, we also rate towns and regions to help you narrow down your choices and budget your time accordingly. Hotels and restaurants are rated on a scale of zero (recommended) to three stars (exceptional). Attractions, shopping, nightlife, towns, and regions are rated according to the following scale: zero stars (recommended), one star (highly recommended), two stars (very highly recommended), and three stars (must-see).

In addition to the star-rating system, we also use **seven feature icons** that point you to the great deals, in-the-know advice, and unique experiences that separate travelers from tourists. Throughout the book, look for:

Finds	Special finds—those places only insiders know about
Fun Fact	Fun facts—details that make travelers more informed and their trips more fun
Kids	Best bets for kids and advice for the whole family
Moments	Special moments—those experiences that memories are made of
Overrated	Places or experiences not worth your time or money
Tips	Insider tips—great ways to save time and money
Value	Great values—where to get the best deals

The following **abbreviations** are used for credit cards:

AE	American Express	DISC	Discover	V	Visa
DC	Diners Club	MC	MasterCard		

Frommers.com

Now that you have the guidebook to a great trip, visit our website at **www.frommers.com** for travel information on more than 3,000 destinations. With features updated regularly, we give you instant access to the most current trip-planning information available. At Frommers.com, you'll also find the best prices on airfares, accommodations, and car rentals—and you can even book travel online through our travel booking partners. At Frommers.com, you'll also find the following:

- Online updates to our most popular guidebooks
- Vacation sweepstakes and contest giveaways
- Newsletter highlighting the hottest travel trends
- Online travel message boards with featured travel discussions

What's New in Toronto

Toronto—or "Hollywood North," as some wags would have it—is brimming with energy these days. Here's a quick look at what's happening now.

PLANNING YOUR TRIP   If you're flying to Toronto from the U.S., the longstanding choices have been **Air Canada** (www.aircanada.com), which code-shares with United, and American Airlines (www.aa.com). But there will be some new discount options starting in the fall of 2004: **WestJet** (www.westjet.com) will begin service between Toronto and San Francisco, Los Angeles, and Phoenix. Another budget, **JetsGo** (www.jetsgo.com), operates flights to Toronto from New York, Los Angeles, Las Vegas, and Orlando.

Toronto's **Pearson International Airport** has opened a spacious new terminal that's about at stunning as an airport can be. It will eventually replace the gloomy Terminals 1 and 2. In the meantime, try to ignore the messy rerouting of traffic at the airport. See "Orientation" in chapter 3 for complete details on transportation from the airport to downtown Toronto.

WHERE TO STAY   Toronto's most stylish new inn is the **Drake Hotel,** 1150 Queen St. W. (© **416/531-5042;** www.thedrakehotel.ca), which was immediately embraced by the city's arts community. Perched on the western end of the newly gentrified West Queen West neighborhood (also known as the Art & Design District), part of the Drake's appeal is its rags-to-riches pedigree (formerly a flophouse, it was rescued and transformed by a C$6-million renovation). The rooms are tiny but ergonomically designed and affordable (about C$139–C$249/US$97–US$174 per night).

The Drake has a yoga studio and a massage room, but if you're looking for a full-service spa, there are many to choose from. Some of the very best spas in the city are located in hotels, such as the **Victoria Spa** at the InterContinental, the **Stillwater Spa** at the Park Hyatt, and the **Elizabeth Milan Hotel Day Spa** at the Fairmont Royal York (see "Spas & the City" in chapter 6 for details). The new **Pantages,** 200 Victoria St. (© **866/852-1777**), hasn't opened its spa at press time.

WHERE TO DINE   One of the best pieces of news on the foodie front is that chef Jamie Kennedy is back with a new restaurant. Kennedy, who lost his old restaurant at the Royal Ontario Museum because of its extensive renovations, has opened the **Jamie Kennedy Wine Bar** at 9 Church St. (© **416/362-1957**). The cooking is sublime, the wines are well chosen, and the prices are surprisingly low.

Other new notables include **Oliver & Bonacini Café & Grill** at Bayview Village, 2901 Bayview Ave. (© **416/590-1300**) which offers familiar meat-and-potatoes fare with a gourmet twist uptown; the **Holt Renfrew Café,** 50 Bloor St. W. (© **416/922-2223**), for gourmet sandwiches made with bread flown in fresh from the Poilane bakery in Paris (all the better to keep your strength up while shopping, my dears); and **350 Fahrenheit,**

467 Bloor St. W. (© **416/929-2080**) for food specifically designed for people on diets ranging from South Beach to Atkins. See chapter 5 for full reviews.

WHAT TO SEE & DO Some Toronto museums are renovating and expanding so that they can show off more of their fantastic collections. The most notable are the **Royal Ontario Museum (ROM)** and the **Art Gallery of Ontario (AGO)** which are both staying open throughout the year but with a limited number of galleries. The **George R. Gardiner Museum of Ceramic Art** will be closed for much of the year. The new settings, designed by the likes of **Frank Gehry** (AGO) and **Daniel Libeskind** (ROM), promise to be stunning.

There are, however, some wonderful smaller galleries that visitors shouldn't miss. The University of Toronto boasts two of the best: the **University Art Centre** (© **416/978-1838**), which has an impressive collection of Byzantine art; and the **Justina M. Barnicke Gallery at Hart House** (© **416/978-8398**), which features both Group of Seven paintings and works by contemporary artists. Another don't-miss spot is the **Museum of Contemporary Canadian Art**, which will have moved into its new home at 952 Queen St. W. by the time you read this. For complete details, see chapter 6.

WALKING TOURS The **University of Toronto** has one of the most beautiful campuses in the world. It's not just locals who think so: U of T has been used by film crews for countless movies, including *Good Will Hunting*. The university is currently engaged in a multiyear **Open Space Master Plan** (www.utoronto.ca/openspace) to make its buildings and landscape even more stunning. But because it's a public institution, everyone can walk onto its campus and into many of its architectural gems. The new walking tour begins on p. 164.

SHOPPING The Canadian dollar is still anemic, which is a boon to U.S. and overseas shoppers. Not that you should need further inducement to stop in at the unique local shops, including only-in-Toronto spots like **Fashion Crimes** and **Girl Friday** (for women's fashions), **Boomer** and **Eza Wear** (for men's), **Boudoir** (for vintage clothing, accessories, and decorative items), and **Mabel's Fables** (for children's books and toys). If you only have a short time to shop while you're in town, turn your sights to **West Queen West,** an up-and-coming neighborhood where you'll find independent clothing boutiques, housewares shops, and antiques boutiques. See chapter 8 for details.

AFTER DARK Toronto's rock-'n'-roll institution, **El Mocambo,** is back yet again (fans of this venue, which has featured everyone from the Rolling Stones to Liz Phair, know that its openings and closings are legendary). Glamorous new bars and clubs, such as **Laide, Cobalt, Sutra,** and **Lobby** have opened up around town. **The Drake Hotel** is popular with Toronto residents for its performance space, The Underground, as well as its ground-floor lounge and rooftop bar. See chapter 9 for complete details.

SIDE TRIPS The **Niagara** region just keeps getting better. Not only did several of its vintners win gold medals in 2004 international competitions, but the renowned **Shaw Festival** is more vibrant that ever (the Shaw was originally dedicated to performing works written during George Bernard Shaw's lifetime, but in 2004 it extended its reach to contemporary works). Another excellent option is the **Muskoka** region, just 90 minutes away from Toronto. Its Golf Trail—a series of challenging courses—is a unique experience. See chapter 10 for complete details.

1

The Best of Toronto

Chances are that even if you've never set foot in Toronto, you've seen the city a hundred times over. Known for the past decade as "Hollywood North," Toronto has stood in for international centers from European capitals to New York—but rarely does it play itself. Self-deprecating Torontonians embody a paradox: Proud of their city's architectural, cultural, and culinary charms, they are unsure whether it's all up to international snuff.

After spending a single afternoon wandering around Toronto, you might wonder why this is a question at all. The sprawling city boasts lush parks, renowned architecture, and excellent galleries. There's no shortage of skyscrapers, particularly in the downtown core. Still, many visitors marvel at the number of Torontonians who live in houses on tree-lined boulevards that are a walk or a bike ride away from work.

Out-of-towners can see the fun side of the place, but Torontonians aren't so sure. They recall the stuffiness of the city's past. Often called "Toronto the Good," it was a town where you could walk down any street in safety, but you couldn't get a drink on Sunday.

Then a funny thing happened on the way through the 1970s. Canada loosened its immigration policies and welcomed waves of Italians, Greeks, Chinese, Vietnamese, Jamaicans, Indians, Somalians, and others, many of whom settled in Toronto. Political unrest in Québec drove out Anglophones, many into the waiting arms of Toronto. The city's economy flourished, which in turn gave its cultural side a boost.

Natives and visitors alike enjoy the benefits of this rich cultural mosaic. More than 5,000 restaurants are scattered across the city, serving everything from simple Greek souvlakia to Asian-accented fusion cuisine. Festivals such as Caribana and Caravan draw tremendous crowds to celebrate heritage through music and dance. Its newfound cosmopolitanism has made Toronto a key player on the arts scene, too. The Toronto International Film Festival in September and the International Festival of Authors in October draw top stars of the movie and publishing worlds. The theater scene rivals London's and New York's.

Toronto now ranks at or near the top of any international urban quality-of-life study. The city has accomplished something rare, expanding and developing its daring side while holding on to its traditional strengths. It's a great place to visit, but watch out: You might just end up wanting to live here.

1 Frommer's Favorite Toronto Experiences

- **Taking in the Art Galleries and Boutiques on West Queen West:** The stretch of Queen that runs west of Bathurst Avenue is also known as the "Art & Design District" with good reason. This is the new home of the Museum of Contemporary Canadian Art; it's also the neighborhood to visit for cutting-edge style. See chapter 6.

Metropolitan Toronto

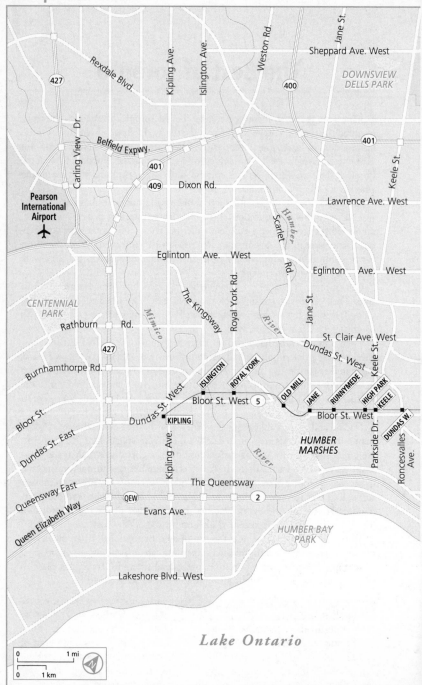

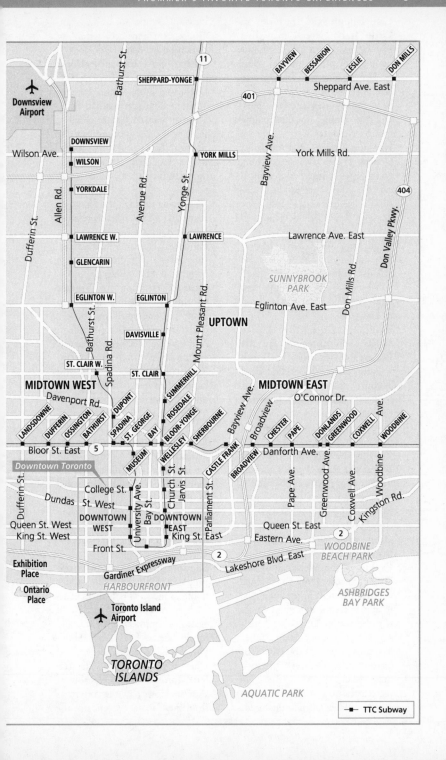

- **Cafe Hopping at Trattorias in Little Italy:** Several magazines have zeroed in on this neighborhood as one of the *haute*-est spots in North America. Trendy, yes, but it's also a fun area for stopping by the many cafes and wine bars, and for dining on outstanding food. See chapter 5.

- **Hanging Out at Harbourfront Centre:** There's always something going on—the International Festival of Authors, art exhibits, cultural celebrations, and the Toronto Music Garden, just to name a few. See p. 119.

- **Picnicking on Centre Island:** Hop on the ferry and escape to the islands. From across the water, you'll see the city in a whole new light. See The Toronto Islands on p. 125.

- **Swinging from the Henry Moore Sculptures at the Art Gallery of Ontario:** The British sculptor Henry Moore so loved Toronto that he bestowed his greatest works on this museum. Kids have been known to swing from the gigantic works in front of the gallery. See p. 125.

- **Viewing the City from the Roof Bar at the Park Hyatt:** Unfortunately, the famous CN Tower gives you a better view of Niagara Falls than it does Toronto itself. To truly appreciate the city's beautiful architecture, there's no better spot than the Roof. See p. 217.

- **Exploring the Wonders of the World at the Ontario Science Centre:** You don't have to be a tyke to appreciate the amazing interactive displays about biology, ecology, and technology. See p. 130.

- **Visiting the University of Toronto Art Centre:** This intimate gallery is one of the city's secret treasures. Visit it for the special exhibits (such as the recent Picasso Ceramics) or for the stunning permanent collection of Byzantine art. See p. 135.

- **Taking in a Game at SkyDome or the Air Canada Centre:** SkyDome is home base for the Toronto Blue Jays baseball team. The Air Canada Centre is where the Maple Leafs (hockey) and the Raptors (basketball) play. Torontonians love their teams and come out to support them in droves. See p. 143.

- **Wandering through the Riverdale Farm:** In case you need more proof that Toronto is a very green city, it has a working farm in its midst. Cows, sheep, pigs, goats, and other critters call it home. See p. 148.

- **Treasure Hunting for Vintage Clothing in Kensington Market:** How can one small area have a dozen vintage-clothing vendors? And how do they keep prices low and quality good? Haphazard Kensington Market is a joy for bargain hunters. See "Walking Tour 1: Chinatown & Kensington Market" in chapter 7 and p. 196 in chapter 8.

- **Listening to a Concert at the Toronto Music Garden:** This serene space was codesigned by cellist Yo-Yo Ma, and it's intended to invoke Bach's First Suite for Unaccompanied Cello. It's easy on the eye, but the best time to come here is for a summertime concert. Pure bliss. See chapter 7.

- **Shopping (or Window-Shopping) in Chic Yorkville:** Once home to the city's bohemian community, Yorkville is an enclave of exclusive shops, art galleries, and upscale cafes. See "Great Shopping Areas" in chapter 8.

- **Checking Out Local Theater:** Sure, Toronto likes its blockbuster shows. However, the offerings from the CanStage Company, the

Tarragon Theatre, and the Lorraine Kimsa Theatre for Young People are innovative and consistently excellent, too. See "The Performing Arts" in chapter 9.

- **De-stressing in a Day Spa:** Toronto is home to some of the best day spas on the continent, including the Victoria Spa, the Stillwater Spa, and the Estée Lauder Spa. See "Spas & the City" in chapter 6.

- **Busting a Gut at a Comedy Club:** Maybe it's something in the water: Toronto has produced more than its share of top-notch comedians, including the shagadelic Mike Myers, Jim Carrey, Dan Aykroyd, and the late John Candy. Check out local talent or international stand-up stars at one of the many comedy clubs. See "The Club & Music Scene" in chapter 9.

- **Day-Tripping for Festivals and Falls:** Niagara-on-the-Lake is Ontario's wine country, and home of the Shaw Festival; it's less than a half-hour drive away from Niagara Falls. Picturesque Stratford has its own theater festival. See "Stratford" and "Niagara-on-the-Lake & Niagara Falls" in chapter 10.

2 Best Hotel Bets

- **Best Historic Hotel:** The (gloved) hands-down winner is **Le Royal Meridien King Edward,** 37 King St. E. (© **800/543-4300**), which was built in 1903 and in the past few years has been restored to its former glory. The lobby, with its pink marble columns and ornate frescoes, has seen the crème de la crème of society trot through over the years. In the 1960s, the Beatles holed up in the King Eddy while 3,000 fans stormed the lobby. See p. 64.

- **Best for a Romantic Rendezvous:** The **Park Hyatt Toronto,** 4 Avenue Rd. (© **800/233-1234**), has it all: a beautifully renovated Art Deco building, top-notch service, and one of the best views in the city from the rooftop terrace lounge. This is the place to relax and let yourself be pampered. See p. 68.

- **Best for Making Guests Feel Part of the Community:** The **Drake Hotel,** 1150 Queen St. W. (© **416/531-5042**) fosters a sense of community by hosting music events, literary readings, and countless other festivities. If you hate feeling like a tourist, this hotel is for you. See p. 62.

- **Best for Tech-Lovers:** The **SoHo Metropolitan Hotel,** 318 Wellington St. W. (© **800/668-6600**), makes the best use of technology I've ever seen at a hotel. It's as if the designers compiled a list of all of the most frustrating aspects about staying in a hotel room and resolved to fix them. And they succeeded! See p. 58.

- **Best for Families:** The **Delta Chelsea,** 33 Gerrard St. W. (© 800/243-5732), is a longtime family favorite, and in 2003 it further enhanced its standing by introducing the Family Fun Zone, which includes a playroom with live bunnies and fish, a video arcade, and a waterslide. It also offers children's programs, a daycare center, and kid-friendly restaurants. There are two pools, one for tykes and one for adults, and many rooms have refrigerators or kitchenettes. See p. 61.

- **Best for Business Travelers:** The **Metropolitan Hotel,** 108 Chestnut St. (© **416/977-5000**), is just a few minutes from the Financial

District, and its amenities are competitive with those of its pricier competitors. Features include a 24-hour business center and in-room amenities such as fax/modem hookups, large work desks, and cordless two-line phones. The restaurants, Hemispheres and Lai Wah Heen, are favorite sites for business lunches. See p. 59.

- **Best Moderately Priced Hotel:** Given the location and amenities, it's hard to beat the **Delta Chelsea,** 33 Gerrard St. W. (© 800/243-5732), for price. Close to the Eaton Centre, Chinatown, and the Financial District, its double rooms start at C$129 (US$90) per night. See p. 61.

- **Best Budget Accommodations: Victoria University,** 140 Charles St. W. (© 416/585-4524), rents out its student residences from mid-May to late August. It's in an excellent location, with simple rooms and great facilities, including tennis courts and a pool. All this for C$67 (US$47) a night. See p. 72.

- **Best Service:** At **The Sutton Place Hotel,** 955 Bay St. (© 800/268-3790), ask and you shall receive. The high staff-to-guest ratio means that there's always someone around to do your bidding. You also won't lack attention at the **Four Seasons Hotel Toronto,** 21 Avenue Rd. (© 800/268-6282), or the **Park Hyatt Toronto,** 4 Avenue Rd. (© 800/233-1234). See p. 69, 68, and 68.

- **Best Hotel Dining:** The prize goes to **Senses,** 318 Wellington St. W. © 416/961-0055, at the **Metropolitan SoHo** for its divine combination of delicious fare, sensuous setting, and impeccable service. Close runners-up are the Hilton Toronto's very grand dining room, **Tundra** (© 416/860-6800); the Fairmont Royal York's new offering, **Epic** (© 416/860-6949); and the Park Hyatt's restaurant, **Annona** (© 416/924-5471). See p. 91, 88, 89, and 102.

- **Best Gay-Friendly Hotel:** Everyone comes to the **Clarion Hotel & Suites Selby,** 592 Sherbourne St. (© 800/387-4788). In a Victorian building in a predominantly gay neighborhood, this hotel draws gay, lesbian, and straight travelers with Belle Epoque style and individually decorated rooms. See p. 69.

- **Best for a Stylish Stay:** The **Hôtel Le Germain,** 30 Mercer St. (© 866/345-9501), one of Toronto's new boutique hotels, is a stunner, with its dramatic design and lots of artwork in public and private spaces alike (even the elevators!). See p. 58.

- **Best for Travelers with Disabilities:** The **Fairmont Royal York,** 100 Front St. W. (© 800/441-1414), looks monolithic but it pays a lot of attention to accessibility. The adaptations accommodate wheelchair users, the visually impaired, and the hearing impaired. See p. 59.

3 Best Dining Bets

- **Best New Restaurant:** 2004 saw some stiff competition for the title, with lots of new restaurants opening for business, but the winner is **Jamie Kennedy Wine Bar,** 9 Church St. (© 416/362-1957).

The combination of unforgettable cooking and stellar service is hard to resist. See p. 99.

- **Best for a Business Lunch:** A sure bet is **Canoe Restaurant & Bar,** in the Toronto Dominion

Tower, 66 Wellington St. W. (☎ 416/364-0054), a see-and-be-seen spot for local and visiting power brokers. See p. 86.

- **Best for a Celebration:** The atmosphere at **Blowfish Restaurant & Sake Bar,** 668 King St. W. (☎ 416/860-0606), is lively every night. The mix of the glamorous dining room, fine sushi, and a cool crowd gives the restaurant its edge. See p. 89.

- **Best for a Romantic Dinner:** I'm the first to admit that I'm biased, but the **Rosewater Supper Club,** 19 Toronto St. (☎ 416/214-5888), is my idea of perfect romance (this restaurant was where my husband proposed to me). Relax and let the pampering begin. See p. 98.

- **Best Decor: Monsoon,** 100 Simcoe St. (☎ 416/979-7172), has an award-winning interior design by Toronto firm Yabu Pushelberg. The brown-on-black setting vies for attention with the impressive kitchen. Upstart **Rain,** 19 Mercer St. (☎ 416/599-7246), is easy on the eye, but good luck getting in—even pop diva Nelly Furtado couldn't do it. See p. 87 and 91.

- **Best View:** Forget the obvious choice (**360 Revolving Restaurant,** in the CN Tower, 301 Front St. W.). Instead, dine at **Scaramouche,** 1 Benvenuto Place (☎ 416/961-8011), which has a far more elegant perspective. Its floor-to-ceiling windows overlook the downtown skyline. See p. 87 and 112.

- **Best Wine List:** The international selection **Centro,** 2472 Yonge St. (☎ 416/483-2211), is hard to beat. The basement is a wine bar with Italian, Californian, and Australian vintages by the glass; upstairs, the dining room boasts more than 600 bottles from around the world. Prices range from C$32 (US$22) into four figures. See p. 111.

- **Best Bistro:** Bistros often do well with comfort foods, but **Biff's,** 4 Front St. E. (☎ 416/860-0086), serves up modern takes on classic dishes; its setting goes beyond comfortable to luxury. See p. 97.

- **Best Italian: Il Posto Nuovo,** 148 Yorkville Ave. (☎ 416/968-0469), serves fine modern Italian cuisine in elegant digs—and the efficient, knowledgeable waitstaff makes everyone feel at home. See p. 102.

- **Best Portuguese:** Standing alone on Italian-dominated College Street, **Chiado,** 484 College St. (☎ 416/538-1910), serves modern Portuguese cuisine. The seafood is flown in daily. See p. 89.

- **Best Greek:** The cooking at **Pan on the Danforth,** 516 Danforth Ave. (☎ 416/466-8158), will convince you that Pan really was the god of food. This is Greek cuisine updated with panache. See p. 109.

- **Best Out-of-Towner:** Talk about catching on like wildfire—the new restaurant **Wildfire,** at Taboo Resort in the Muskoka region (☎ 705/687-2233), is a work of art. Give yourself over to the genius chef by having one of the 4-, 5-, or 11-course tasting menus. See p. 251.

- **Best People-Watching:** Across from the Sutton Place Hotel is **Bistro 990,** 990 Bay St. (☎ 416/921-9990), where everyone in Toronto but me has made a celebrity sighting. (I'm too busy enjoying the delicious food.) See p. 101.

- **Best Value:** First prize goes to **Brassaii,** 461 King St. W. (☎ 416/598-4730), a stylish bistro with excellent food, top-notch service, and wallet-friendly prices. It's open for breakfast, lunch, and dinner. An honorable mention

The Best of Toronto Online

How did anyone ever plan a trip without the help of the Internet? It's hard to imagine now, given the wealth of information available online. But not all sites are created equal, so before you get ensnared in the Web, point and click on these gems.

- **Toronto.com** (www.toronto.com) boasts articles on arts and culture as well as a hotel directory, restaurant reviews, community news, and events listings. One of its best features is its extensive use of photographs.
- **City of Toronto** (www.city.toronto.on.ca) is the official municipal guide to Toronto, a straightforward source of practical information peppered with profiles of fun places to visit and announcements of festivals, free concerts, kids' events, and more.
- **Girl Talk Toronto: A Mini City Guide** (www.journeywoman.com/girltalk/toronto.html) runs the gamut from the serious (transit safety) to the frivolously fun (the best places to shop for shoes). This user-friendly site also highlights arty spots, off-the-beaten-path attractions, and the best places for brunch, all from a female perspective.
- **Green Tourism Association** (www.greentourism.on.ca) is an excellent resource for eco-friendly travelers. There's information about car-free transportation, outdoor activities and sports, and healthy dining.
- *Toronto Life* (www.torontolife.com) has extensive restaurant listings, as well as links for events, activities, and nightlife.
- *Toronto Star* (www.thestar.com) includes everything from theater and concert reviews to local news and weather conditions.

goes to **Messis,** 97 Harbord St. (© **416/920-2186**), which has been a training ground for some of the best chefs in Toronto. See p. 97 and 105.

- **Best for Kids: Millie's Bistro,** 1980 Avenue Rd. (© **416/481-1247**), is a family favorite with sunny dining rooms and a special children's menu. A more casual choice would be the deli-style **Shopsy's** (33 Yonge St.; © **416/365-3333**). See p. 112 and 101.
- **Best Steak House: Barberian's,** 7 Elm St. (© **416/597-0335**), has boosted the level of protein in Torontonians' diets since 1959. It also serves great martinis and

desserts, but what everyone comes here for is the meat. See p. 85.
- **Best Pizza:** A cubbyhole-size eatery in midtown, **Serra,** 378 Bloor St. W. (© **416/922-6999**), makes thin-crust pizzas laden with gourmet ingredients. See p. 107.
- **Best Sushi: Hiro Sushi,** 171 King St. E. (© **416/304-0550**). Chef Hiro Yoshida offers up classically prepared sushi as well as a few unique specialties. But there is competition from **Blowfish Restaurant & Sake Bar,** 668 King St. W. (© **416/860-0606**). See p. 98 and 89.
- **Best Afternoon Tea:** A very tough call. Afternoon tea in the lobby

lounge at the **Le Royal Meridien King Edward,** 37 King St. E. (© **416/863-3131**), has been called the most authentic English tea, and it is divine. But I am partial to the phenomenal lavender-and-rose-infused Rooibos Provence tea that you'll find at **Annona** at the Park Hyatt, 4 Avenue Rd. (© **416/924-5471**). See p. 64 and 102.

- **Best Alfresco Dining:** The lovely patio at **Biff's,** 4 Front St. E. (© **416/860-0086**), is just about perfect. Set well back from the street, it affords terrific people-watching possibilities. See p. 97.
- **Best If You Have Only One Meal in Toronto and Price Is No Object:** While I hate to go along with the crowd, the common wisdom is on the money with **North 44,** 2537 Yonge St. (© **416/487-4897**). Simply put: Great food, great staff, great setting. See p. 111.
- **Best If You Have Only One Meal in Toronto and Price *Is* an Object:** Look no further than **Brassaii,** 461 King St. W. (© **416/598-4730**). For all of the

reasons listed above under "Best Value." See p. 92.

- **Best Chinese: Lai Wah Heen,** at the Metropolitan Hotel, 110 Chestnut St. (© **416/977-9899**), serves deluxe Cantonese and Szechuan specialties, including a variety of shark's fin soups and abalone dishes. It features several good-value prix-fixe specials at lunch and dinner. See p. 90.
- **Best Brunch:** Who needs bacon and eggs when you can have *torta rustica* with layers of ricotta, mozzarella, leeks, peas, and smoked trout? This and other glamorous offerings are available at **Agora,** at the Art Gallery of Ontario, 317 Dundas St. W. (© **416/977-0414**). See p. 88.
- **Best Desserts:** It's a tie. Dufflet Rosenberg bakes up a storm at **Dufflet Pastries,** 787 Queen St. W. (© **416/504-2870**). You'll find her name on the dessert list at some of the city's top restaurants. And then there's the **Senses Bakery,** 2 Queen St. E. (© **416/364-7303**). Resistance is futile. See "Sweet Treats: Toronto's Dessert Cafes" on p. 220.

2

Planning Your Trip to Toronto

Whether you're traveling on a whim or charting your course months in advance, it's important to do some planning to make the most of your trip. You may already be asking how you'll get there and how much it will cost. There are many different sides of Toronto, so you'll need to figure out what kind of trip you want to take. This chapter will help you find the answers.

1 Visitor Information

FROM NORTH AMERICA

The best source for Toronto-specific information is **Tourism Toronto, Metro Toronto Convention & Visitors Association,** 207 Queens Quay W., Suite 590, Toronto, ON M5J 1A7 (© **800/363-1990** from North America, or 416/203-2600; www.toronto tourism.com). Call before you leave and ask for the free information package, which includes sections on accommodations, sights, and dining. Better yet, visit the website, which includes all of the above plus up-to-the-minute events information.

For information about traveling in the province of Ontario, contact **Tourism Ontario,** P.O. Box 104, Toronto, ON M5B 2H1 (© **800/ ONTARIO** or 416/314-0944; www. ontariotravel.net), or visit the travel center in the Eaton Centre on Level 1 at Yonge and Dundas streets. It's open Monday through Friday from 10am to 9pm, Saturday from 9:30am to 6pm, and Sunday from noon to 5pm.

Canadian consulates in the United States do not provide tourist information. They will refer you to the offices above. Consular offices in Buffalo, Detroit, Los Angeles, New York, Seattle, and Washington, D.C., deal with visas and other political and immigration issues.

FROM ABROAD

The following consulates can provide information or refer you to the appropriate offices. Consult Tourism Toronto (see "From North America," above) for general information. For a list of Canadian consular offices around the world, visit **www.dfait-maeci.gc. ca/world/embassies/cra-en.asp**.

U.K. and Ireland: The **Canadian High Commission,** MacDonald House, 1 Grosvenor Sq., London W1X 0AB (© **0207/258-6600;** fax 0207/258-6333).

Australia: The **Canadian High Commission,** Commonwealth Avenue, Canberra, ACT 2600 (© **02/6273- 3844**), or the **Consulate General of Canada,** Level 5, Quay West, 111 Harrington St., Sydney, NSW 2000 (© **02/9364-3000**). The consulate general also has offices in Melbourne and Perth.

New Zealand: The **Canadian High Commission,** 3rd floor, 61 Molesworth St., Thomdon, Wellington (© **04/473-9577**).

South Africa: The **Canadian High Commission,** 1103 Arcadia St., Hatfield 0083, Pretoria (© **012/ 422-3000**). The commission also has offices in Cape Town and Johannesburg.

2 Entry Requirements & Customs

ENTRY REQUIREMENTS

Only a passport is required for entry into Canada—no visas or proof of vaccinations are necessary. Canadian airports have been screening travelers for SARS, but this is done via a non-invasive thermal scan.

Safeguard your passport in an inconspicuous, inaccessible place like a money belt and keep a copy of the critical pages with your passport number in a separate place. If you lose your passport, visit the nearest consulate of your native country as soon as possible for a replacement.

FOR U.S. RESIDENTS Whether you're applying in person or by mail, you can download passport applications from the U.S. State Department website at **http://travel.state.gov**. For general information, call the **National Passport Agency** (© 202/647-0518). To find your regional passport office, either check the U.S. State Department website or call the **National Passport Information Center** (© 900/225-5674); the fee is 55¢ per minute for automated information and $1.50 per minute for operator-assisted calls.

FOR U.K. RESIDENTS To pick up an application for a standard 10-year passport (5-year passport for children 15 and under), visit your nearest passport office, major post office, or travel agency or contact the **United Kingdom Passport Service** at © 0870/521-0410 or search its website at www.ukpa.gov.uk. The UKPS also offers an online application option (you'll still need to send in documents and photographs by post).

FOR RESIDENTS OF IRELAND You can apply for a 10-year passport at the **Passport Office,** Setanta Centre, Molesworth Street, Dublin 2 (© 01/671-1633; http://foreignaffairs.gov.ie).

Children under age 3 can get a 3-year passport; youths from 3 to 17 can get a 5-year passport. You can also apply at 1A South Mall, Cork (© 021/272-525). Passport applications are available at all Garda stations and at most post offices.

FOR AUSTRALIAN RESIDENTS The Australian Passports Bill 2004 was introduced to Parliament in late June 2004, so check with the **Australian Passport Information Service** at © 131-232, or visit the government website at www.passports.gov.au for the latest details. At the time of this writing, you can pick up an application from your local post office or any branch of Passports Australia, or you can make an online application, but you must schedule an interview at the passport office to present your application materials.

FOR NEW ZEALAND RESIDENTS You can pick up a passport application at any New Zealand Passports Office or download it from their website. Contact the **Passports Office** at © 0800/225-050 if you are calling from inside New Zealand (dial © 04/474-8100 if you're not), or log on to www.passports.govt.nz.

CUSTOMS
WHAT YOU CAN BRING INTO CANADA

Most customs regulations are generous, but they get complicated when it comes to firearms, plants, meat, and pets. Fishing tackle poses no problem (provided the lures are not made of restricted materials—specific feathers, for example), but the bearer must possess a nonresident license for the province or territory where he or she plans to use it. You can bring in free of duty up to 50 cigars, 200 cigarettes, and 200 grams of tobacco, provided you're at least 18 years of age. You are also allowed 40 ounces (1.14ml) of liquor or 1.5 liters of wine as long as you're of age in the province you're visiting (19 in Ontario). There are no restrictions on what you can take out. But if you're thinking of bringing Cuban cigars back to the United States, beware—they can be confiscated, and you could face a fine.

For a clear summary of **Canadian** rules, visit the website of the **Canada Border Services Agency,** at **www.cbsa-asfc.gc.ca.** The CBSA allows you to download documents directly; you can also order printed copies to be delivered to you. You can also call © **800/959-2221** from Canada or the U.S., or 204/983-3500 from abroad.

WHAT YOU CAN TAKE HOME

Returning **U.S. citizens** who have been away for at least 48 hours are allowed to bring back, once every 30 days, $800 worth of merchandise duty-free. You'll be charged a flat rate of 4% duty on the next $1,000 worth of purchases. Be sure to have your receipts handy. On mailed gifts, the duty-free limit is $200. With some exceptions, you cannot bring fresh fruits and vegetables into the United States. For specifics on what you can bring back, download the invaluable free pamphlet *Know Before You Go* online at **www.customs.gov.** (Click on "Travel," and then click on "Know Before You Go.") Or contact **U.S. Customs and Border Protection,** 1300 Pennsylvania Ave. NW, Washington, DC 20229 (© **877/287-8867**) and request the pamphlet.

U.K. citizens returning from a non-E.U. country have a customs allowance of: 200 cigarettes; 50 cigars; 250 grams of smoking tobacco; 2 liters of still table wine; 1 liter of spirits or strong liqueurs (over 22% volume); 2 liters of fortified wine, sparkling wine, or other liqueurs; 60cc (ml) perfume; 250cc (ml) of toilet water; and £145 worth of all other goods, including gifts and souvenirs. People under 17 cannot have the tobacco or alcohol allowance. For more information, contact **HM Customs & Excise** at © **0845/010-9000** (from outside the U.K., 020/8929-0152), or consult their website at www. hmce.gov.uk.

The duty-free allowance for **Australian citizens** is A$400 or, for those under 18, A$200. You can bring in 250 cigarettes or 250 grams of loose tobacco, and 1,125 milliliters of alcohol. If you're returning with valuables you already own, such as foreign-made cameras, you should file form B263. A helpful brochure available from Australian consulates or Customs offices is *Know Before You Go.* For more information, call the **Australian Customs Service** at © **1300/363-263,** or log on to www.customs.gov.au.

The duty-free allowance for **New Zealand** is NZ$700. Citizens over 17 can bring in 200 cigarettes, 50 cigars, or 250 grams of tobacco (or a mixture of all three if their combined weight doesn't exceed 250g); plus 4.5 liters of wine and beer, or 1.125 liters of liquor. New Zealand currency does not carry import or export restrictions. Fill out a certificate of export, listing the valuables you are taking out of the country; that way, you can bring them back without paying duty. Most questions are answered in a free pamphlet available at New Zealand consulates and Customs offices: *New Zealand Customs Guide for Travellers, Notice no. 4.* For more information, contact **New Zealand Customs,** The Customhouse, 17–21 Whitmore St., Box 2218, Wellington (© **04/473-6099** or 0800/428-786; www.customs. govt.nz).

3 Money

CURRENCY

Canadians use **dollars** and **cents,** but with a distinct advantage for U.S. visitors—during the first six months of 2004, the Canadian dollar was fluctuating between 71¢ and 78¢ in U.S. money, give or take a couple of points' daily variation (in 2003, it was hovering between 65¢ and 70¢). In effect, your American money gets you 25% to 30% more the moment you exchange it for local currency. Because the nominal prices of many goods are roughly on par with those in the United States, the difference is real, not imaginary. Sales taxes are higher, though you should be able to recoup at least part of them (see "Taxes" under "Fast Facts: Toronto," in chapter 3).

Paper currency comes in $5, $10, $20, $50, and $100 denominations. (The $1,000 bill is being phased out.) Coins come in 1-, 5-, 10-, and 25-cent, and 1- and 2-dollar denominations. The gold-colored $1 coin is a "loonie"—it sports a loon on its "tails" side—and the large gold-and-silver-colored $2 coin is a "toonie." If you find these names somewhat, ah, colorful, just remember that there's no swifter way to reveal that you're a tourist than to say "one-dollar coin."

It's a good idea to exchange at least some money—just enough to cover airport incidentals and transportation to your hotel—before you leave home, so you can avoid the less-favorable rates you'll get at airport currency exchange desks. Check with your local American Express or Thomas Cook office or your bank. American Express cardholders can order foreign currency over the phone at ✆ **800/807-6233.**

It's best to exchange currency or traveler's checks at a bank, not a currency exchange, hotel, or shop.

ATMs

The easiest and best way to get cash away from home is from an ATM (automated teller machine). The **Cirrus** (✆ **800/424-7787;** www. mastercard.com) and **PLUS** (✆ **800/ 843-7587;** www.visa.com) networks span the globe; look at the back of your bank card to see which network you're on, then call or check online for ATM locations at your destination. Be sure you know your personal identification number (PIN) before you leave home and be sure to find out your daily withdrawal limit before you depart. Also keep in mind that many banks impose a fee every time a card is used at a different bank's ATM, and that fee can be higher for international transactions (up to $5 or more) than for domestic ones. On top of this, the bank from which you withdraw cash may charge its own fee.

TRAVELER'S CHECKS

Traveler's checks are something of an anachronism from the days before the ATM made cash accessible at any

---

Tips Spending American Cash

If you spend American money at Canadian establishments, you should understand how the conversion is calculated. Many times, especially in downtown Toronto, you'll see a sign at the cash register that reads U.S. CURRENCY 50%. This 50% is the "premium," which means that for every U.S. greenback you hand over, the cashier will consider it $1.50 Canadian. For example, for a $15 tab you need pay only $10 in U.S. currency.

The Canadian Dollar, the U.S. Dollar & the British Pound

The prices quoted in this guide are in Canadian dollars, with the U.S. equivalent in parentheses. The exchange rate we've used is $1.40 Canadian to $1 American. The conversion rate for the British pound is $2.20 Canadian. For the most up-to-date exchange rates, visit **www.xe.com/ucc**.

Here's a quick table of equivalents:

C$	US$	UK£
1.00	0.70	0.45
5.00	3.50	2.25
10.00	7.00	4.50
20.00	14.00	9.00
50.00	35.00	22.50
80.00	56.00	36.00
100.00	70.00	45.00

time. However, keep in mind that you will likely be charged an ATM withdrawal fee if the bank is not your own, so if you're withdrawing money every day, you might be better off with traveler's checks—provided that you don't mind showing identification every time you want to cash one.

You can get traveler's checks at almost any bank. **American Express** offers denominations of $20, $50, $100, $500, and (for cardholders only) $1,000. You'll pay a service charge ranging from 1% to 4%. You can also get American Express traveler's checks over the phone by calling ℭ **800/221-7282;** Amex gold and platinum cardholders who use this number are exempt from the 1% fee.

Visa offers traveler's checks at Citibank locations nationwide, as well as at several other banks. The service charge ranges between 1.5% and 2%; checks come in denominations of $20, $50, $100, $500, and $1,000. Call ℭ **800/732-1322** for information. AAA members can obtain Visa checks without a fee at most AAA offices or by calling ℭ **866/339-3378. MasterCard** also offers traveler's checks. Call ℭ **800/223-9920** for a location near you.

Foreign currency traveler's checks are useful because they're accepted at locations such as bed-and-breakfasts where dollar checks may not be, and they minimize the amount of math you have to do at your destination. American Express, Visa, and MasterCard all offer checks in Canadian dollars.

If you choose to carry traveler's checks, be sure to keep a record of their serial numbers separate from your checks in the event that they are stolen or lost. You'll get a refund faster if you know the numbers.

CREDIT CARDS

Credit cards are a safe way to carry money, they provide a convenient record of all your expenses, and they generally offer good exchange rates. You can also withdraw cash advances (often with an astronomical interest rate) from your credit cards at banks or ATMs, provided you know your PIN. If you've forgotten yours, or didn't even know you had one, call the number on the back of your credit card and ask the bank to mail it to you—it usually takes 5 to 7 business days. Your credit card company will likely charge a commission (1% or 2%) on every foreign purchase you

What Things Cost in Toronto	US$
Taxi from the airport to downtown	33.00
Subway/bus from the airport to downtown	6.80
Local telephone call	0.17
Double at the Park Hyatt (very expensive)	158.00–349.00
Double at the Delta Chelsea (moderate)	90.00–238.00
Double at Victoria University (inexpensive)	46.00
Two-course lunch for one at Stork on the Roof (moderate)*	15.00
Two-course lunch for one at Kalendar (inexpensive)*	10.60
Three-course dinner for one at North 44 (very expensive)*	50.40
Three-course dinner for one at Brassaii (moderate)*	28.30
Three-course dinner for one at the Rivoli (inexpensive)*	16.30
Pint of beer	3.50
Coca-Cola	1.00
Cup of coffee	1.00
Roll of ASA 1100 Kodacolor film, 36 exposures	5.40
Admission to the Royal Ontario Museum	6.80
Movie ticket at a Silver City multiplex	7.50
Ticket for the Royal Alexandra Theatre	17.00–85.00

Includes tax and tip, but not wine.

make, but don't sweat this small stuff; for most purchases, you'll still get the best deal with credit cards when you factor in things like ATM fees and higher traveler's check exchange rates.

Some credit card companies recommend that you notify them of any impending trip abroad so that they don't become suspicious when the card is used numerous times in a foreign destination and your charges are blocked. Even if you don't call your credit card company in advance, you can always call the card's toll-free emergency number if a charge is refused—a good reason to carry the phone number with you. But perhaps the most important lesson here is to carry more than one card with you on your trip; a card might not work for any number of reasons, so having a backup is the smart way to go.

WHAT TO DO IF YOUR WALLET IS LOST OR STOLEN

Be sure to block charges against your account the minute you discover a credit card has been lost or stolen; almost every credit card company has an emergency toll-free number to call. They may be able to wire you a cash advance off your credit card immediately, and in many situations they can deliver an emergency credit card in a day or two. The issuing bank's toll-free number is usually on the back of your credit card—though of course, if your card is gone, that won't help you unless you recorded the number elsewhere.

Citicorp Visa's U.S. emergency number is ✆ **800/336-8472.** American Express cardholders and traveler's check holders should call ✆ **800/221-7282.** MasterCard holders should call ✆ **800/307-7309.** Otherwise, call the toll-free number directory at ℭ **800/555-1212.**

After you've contacted your credit card company, be sure to file a police report. Odds are that if your wallet is gone, the police won't be able to recover it for you. However, it's still worth informing the authorities. Your credit card company or insurer may require a police report number or record of the theft.

If you need emergency cash over the weekend when all banks and American Express offices are closed, you can have money wired to you via **Western Union** (ℭ **800/325-6000;** www.westernunion.com).

Identity theft or fraud are potential complications of losing your wallet, especially if you've lost your driver's license along with your cash and credit cards. Notify the major credit-reporting bureaus immediately; placing a fraud alert on your records may protect you against liability for criminal activity. The three major U.S. credit-reporting agencies are **Equifax** (ℭ **800/766-0008;** www.equifax.com), **Experian** (ℭ **888/397-3742;** www.experian.com), and **TransUnion** (ℭ **800/680-7289;** www.transunion.com). For more information about identity theft and how to protect yourself, check the Federal Trade Commission's website at **www.ftc.gov** or www.consumer.gov/idtheft.

Finally, if you've lost all forms of photo ID, call your airline and explain the situation; they might allow you to board the plane if you have a copy of your passport or birth certificate and a copy of the police report you've filed.

4 When to Go

THE CLIMATE

Paris may be most delightful in springtime, but Toronto is truly sublime in the fall. It's my favorite time of year for a number of reasons: The climate is brisk but temperate, the skies are sunny, the countless city parks are a riot of color, and the cultural scene is in full swing. Another great time to see the city—if you don't mind some snow—is December, with nonstop holiday festivities. I can also make strong arguments for visiting in spring or summer, when the city's many gardens are blooming and the calendar is full of festivals. However, I do feel it's my duty to warn you away in January: The temperature can be unbearably cold, and there's less to do.

Never mind what the calendar says; these are Toronto's true seasons: **Spring** runs from late March to mid-May (though occasionally there's snow in mid-Apr); **summer,** mid-May to mid-September; **fall,** mid-September to mid-November; **winter,** mid-November to late March. The highest recorded temperature is 105°F (41°C); the lowest, –27°F (–33°C). The average date of first frost is October 29; the average date of last frost is April 20. The windblasts from Lake Ontario can be fierce, even in June. Bring a light jacket or cardigan.

HOLIDAYS

Toronto celebrates the following holidays: New Year's Day (Jan 1), Good Friday and Easter Monday (Mar or Apr), Victoria Day (Mon following the third weekend in May), Canada Day (July 1), Simcoe Day (first Mon

Toronto's Average Temperatures °F (°C)

	Jan	Feb	Mar	Apr	May	June	July	Aug	Sept	Oct	Nov	Dec
High	30 (1)	31 (1)	39 (4)	53 (12)	64 (18)	75 (24)	80 (27)	79 (26)	71 (22)	59 (15)	46 (8)	34 (1)
Low	18 (8)	19 (7)	27 (3)	38 (3)	48 (9)	57 (14)	62 (17)	61 (16)	54 (12)	45 (7)	35 (2)	23 (5)

Tips   Don't Forget the Sunscreen

Because of Canada's image of a land of harsh winters, many travelers don't realize that summer can be scorching. "The UV index goes quite high, between 7 and 10, in Toronto," says Dr. Patricia Agin of the Coppertone Solar Research Center in Memphis. "It's the same as in New York, Boston, Chicago, or Detroit." A UV index reading of 7 can mean sunburn, so don't forget to pack your sunscreen and a hat, especially if you're planning to enjoy Toronto's many parks and outdoor attractions.

in Aug), Labour Day (first Mon in Sept), Thanksgiving (second Mon in Oct), Remembrance Day (Nov 11), Christmas Day (Dec 25), and Boxing Day (Dec 26).

On Good Friday and Easter Monday, schools and government offices close; most corporations close on one or the other, and a few close on both. Only banks and government offices close on Remembrance Day (Nov 11).

TORONTO CALENDAR OF EVENTS

January, February, March, and April are dominated by trade shows, such as the International Boat and Automobile shows, Metro Home Show, Outdoor Adventure Sport Show, and more. For information, call **Tourism Toronto** (© **800/363-1990** or 416/203-2600; www.torontotourism.com).

January

Winterlicious, citywide. Baby, it's cold outside, but Toronto's restaurants really know how to heat things up. More than 100 of the city's finest eateries offer prix-fixe lunch menus for C$20 (US$14) and dinner menus for C$30 (US$21). Reservations must be made directly with participating restaurants; see **www.toronto.ca/special_events/ wintercity** for a complete listing. January 28 through February 10.

February

Chinese New Year Celebrations, downtown. 2005 is the year of the Rooster. Festivities include traditional and contemporary performances of Chinese opera, dancing, music, and more. For **Harbourfront** celebration information, call © **416/973-3000** or visit www.harbourfront.on.ca; for **SkyDome,** call © **877/666-3838** or check www.skydome.com. The New Year starts on February 9.

Winterfest, Nathan Phillips Square, Yonge and Eglinton, and Mel Lastman Square. This 3-day celebration spreads over three neighborhoods. It features ice-skating shows, snow play, midway rides, performances, ice sculpting, arts-and-crafts shows, and more. For information, call © **416/338-0338** or visit www.city. toronto.on.ca. Usually around Valentine's Day.

Toronto Festival of Storytelling, Harbourfront. Now in its 27th year, this event celebrates international folklore, with 60 storytellers imparting legends and fables from around the world. For information, call © **416/973-3000** or check www.harbourfront.on.ca. Last weekend of February.

March

Canada Blooms, Metro Toronto Convention Centre. At this time of year, any glimpse of greenery is welcome. There are 2.5 hectares (6 acres) of indoor garden and flower displays, seminars with green-thumb experts, and competitions. For information, call © **416/593-0223** or visit www.canadablooms.com. Usually the second week of March.

St. Patrick's Day Parade, downtown. Toronto's own version of the classic Irish celebration. For information, call ☎ **416/487-1566.** March 17.

April

Blue Jays Season Opener, SkyDome. Turn out to root for your home-away-from-home team. For information, call ☎ **416/341-1000** or visit www.bluejays.ca; for tickets, which usually aren't too hard to get, call ☎ **888/654-6529.** Mid-April.

The Shaw Festival, Niagara-on-the-Lake, Ontario. This festival presents the plays of George Bernard Shaw and his contemporaries. Call ☎ **416/690-7301** or 905/468-2172, or visit www.shawfest.com. Mid-April through October.

Sante—The Bloor-Yorkville Wine Festival, Yorkville. This 4-day gourmet event brings together award-winning Ontario vintages, food by top-rated chefs, and live jazz. For information, call ☎ **416/504-3977.** Last weekend in April.

May

Milk International Children's Festival, Harbourfront. This is a 9-day celebration of the arts for kids—from theater and music to dance, comedy, and storytelling. For information, call ☎ **416/973-3000** or visit www.harbourfront.on.ca. Usually starts on Mother's Day (second Sun in May).

The Stratford Festival, Stratford, Ontario. Featuring a wide range of contemporary and classic plays, this festival always includes several works by Shakespeare. Call ☎ **800/567-1600** or 416/364-8355 or check www.stratford-festival.on.ca. Early May through October.

Doors Open Toronto, citywide. This weekend event invites city residents and visitors alike to tour some of Toronto's architectural marvels. Some of the more than 150 participating buildings aren't normally open to the public, and all are free of charge. Call ☎ **416/205-2670** or check out www.doors open.org. Late May.

June

Harbourfront Reading Series, Harbourfront. Now in its 31st year, this festival celebrates the best of Canadian literature. Some of the writers who have previously appeared include Anne Michaels, Barbara Gowdy, and the late great Timothy Findley. Participating authors read from their most recent works. For information, call Harbourfront at ☎ **416/973-3000;** for tickets, call ☎ **416/973-4000** or go to www.harbourfront.on.ca. Readings go on through most of June.

North by Northeast Festival, citywide. Known in the music biz as NXNE, the 3-day event features rock and indie bands at 28 venues. For information, call ☎ **416/469-0986** or visit www.nxne.com. June 9 through June 11.

Toronto International Festival Caravan, citywide. This popular 9-day event is North America's largest international festival. It features more than 40 themed pavilions, craft demonstrations, authentic cuisine, and traditional dance performances by 100 cultural groups. For information, call ☎ **416/977-0466.** Usually the third and fourth weekends of June.

Symphony of Fire, Ontario Place. This international fireworks competition is set to music and draws 2 million people to the waterfront. Six shows take place, on several Saturdays and Wednesdays. For information, call ☎ **416/442-3667;** for tickets for waterfront seating, call ☎ **416/870-8000.** Mid-June through July.

Taste of Little Italy, College Street between Euclid and Shaw streets. Restaurants, craftspeople, musicians, and other performers put on displays during this 2-day festival for the whole family. For information, call © 416/531-9991. Mid-June.

International Dragon Boat Festival, Centre Island. More than 160 teams of dragon-boaters compete in the 2-day event, which commemorates the death of the Chinese philosopher and poet Qu Yuan. For information, call © 416/598-8945 or visit www.dragonboat.com. Third weekend in June.

Pride Week & Pride Parade, citywide. Celebrating Toronto's gay and lesbian community, Pride Week features events, performances, symposiums, and parties. It culminates in an extravagant Sunday parade, one of the biggest in North America. For information, call © 416/92-PRIDE or 416/927-7433, or visit www.pridetoronto.com. Late June.

Downtown Jazz Festival, citywide. Sponsored by tobacco giant du Maurier until 2003, when federal legislation prohibited the company from further involvement, the future of this Toronto tradition looked shaky. Fortunately TD Canada Trust has stepped in as sponsor of this 10-day festival that showcases international artists playing every jazz style—blues, gospel, Latin, African, traditional—at 60 venues. For information, check out **www.tojazz.com.** Late June.

July

Canada Day Celebrations, citywide. July 1, 2005, marks the nation's 138th birthday. Street parties, fireworks, and other special events celebrate the day. For information, contact Tourism Toronto (© 800/363-1990 or 416/203-2600; www.torontotourism.com). Weekend of July 1.

Summerlicious, citywide. It's just like January's Winterlicious event, except that you can dine al fresco. The prix-fixe menus (C$20/US$14 for lunch and C$30/US$21 for dinner) are the best deal around. Reserve directly with each restaurant; see **www.toronto.ca/special_events/streetfest** for a complete list. First two weeks of July.

The Fringe—Toronto's Theatre Festival, citywide. More than 90 troupes participate in this 10-day festival of contemporary and experimental theater. Shows last no more than an hour. For information, call © 416/534-5919 or visit www.fringetoronto.com. First week of July.

Celebrate Toronto Street Festival, Yonge Street. First staged in 1998, this block party is set up along the world's longest street, and it plays out over a three-day weekend. The festivities are set up in five areas (usually Yonge's intersections with Dundas St., Bloor St., St. Clair Ave., Eglinton Ave., and Lawrence Ave.), and include live music, jugglers and stilt-walkers, amusement park rides for kids, and plenty of food. Visit **www.toronto.ca/special_events** for a listing of performers and events. Mid July.

Great Canadian Blues Festival, Harbourfront Centre. Toronto shows that it's got soul in this 3-day festival of Canada's best blues musicians. In case the rhythm isn't enough to catch you, the Blues Festival coincides with a lip-smacking barbecue fest, also at Harbourfront. For information, call Harbourfront at © 416/973-3000; for tickets, call © 416/973-4000 or visit www.harbourfront.on.ca. Second weekend in July.

Molson Indy, the Exhibition Place Street circuit. One of Canada's major races on the IndyCar circuit. Away from the track, you'll find live music and beer gardens. For information, call ☎ **416/922-7477** or visit www.molsonindy.com. Third weekend in July.

Caribana, citywide. Toronto's version of Carnival transforms the city. It's complete with traditional foods from the Caribbean and Latin America, ferry cruises, picnics, children's events, concerts, and arts-and-crafts exhibits. Call ☎ **416/465-4884** for more information or check www.caribana.com. Late July through early August.

August

Festival of Beer, Fort York. More than 70 major Ontario breweries and microbreweries turn out for this celebration of suds. There's also a wide selection of food from local restaurants and live music of the blues, swing, and jazz persuasions. For information, call ☎ **416/698-7206.** First weekend in August.

Canadian National Exhibition, Exhibition Place. One of the world's largest exhibitions, this 18-day extravaganza features midway rides, display buildings, free shows, and grandstand performers. The 3-day Canadian International Air Show (first staged in 1878) is a bonus. Call ☎ **416/393-6000** for information or visit www.theex.com. Mid-August through Labour Day.

Tennis Masters Canada/Rogers AT&T Cup, National Tennis Centre at York University. These two international tennis championships (the former is for men, the latter for women) are important stops on the pro tennis tour. They attract players such as Sampras, Agassi, Seles, and the Williams sisters. In 2005, the women play in Toronto and the men in Montréal. In 2006, they'll alternate. For information,

call ☎ **416/665-9777** or visit www. tenniscanada.com. Mid- to late August.

September

Toronto International Film Festival, citywide. The stars come out for the second-largest film festival in the world. More than 250 films from 70 countries are shown over 10 days. For information, call ☎ **416/968-FILM** or log on to www.e.bell.ca/filmfest. Early September.

PGA Tour Canadian Open, Glen Abbey Golf Club, Oakville. Canada's national golf tournament (☎ **905/844-1800**) has featured the likes of Greg Norman and Tiger Woods in recent years. It's almost always held at Glen Abbey, though Montréal played host in 1997. First or second weekend of September.

Word on the Street, Queen Street West between Simcoe Street and Spadina Avenue. This street fair celebrates the written word with readings, discounted books and magazines, and children's events. Other major Canadian cities hold similar events on the same weekend. For information, call ☎ **416/504-7241.** Last weekend in September.

Muskoka Autumn Studio Tour, Muskoka region, Ontario. This year marks the 27th anniversary of this 2-day arts festival, which invites travelers to visit the studios of local artists and craftspeople. For information, check out **www.muskoka.com/tour**. Late September.

October

Oktoberfest, Kitchener–Waterloo, about 1 hour from Toronto. This famed 9-day drinkfest features cultural events plus a pageant and parade. For information, call ☎ **519/570-4267** or visit www.oktoberfest.ca. Mid-October.

International Festival of Authors, Harbourfront. This renowned 11-day literary festival is the most prestigious in Canada. It draws more than 100 authors from 25 countries to perform readings and on-stage interviews. Among the literary luminaries who have appeared are Salman Rushdie, Margaret Drabble, Thomas Kenneally, Joyce Carol Oates, A. S. Byatt, and Margaret Atwood. For information, call Harbourfront at ✆ **416/973-3000;** for tickets, call ✆ **416/973-4000** or visit www.harbourfront.on.ca. Third weekend of October.

Toronto Maple Leafs Opening Night, Air Canada Centre. Torontonians love their hockey team, so securing a ticket will be a challenge. For information, call ✆ **416/216-1700;** for tickets, call ✆ **416/872-5000** or visit www.toronto mapleleafs.com. Mid-October.

The Old Clothing Show & Sale, Exhibition Place. Everything from Jazz Age flapper frocks to Austin Powers–like '60s suits, all under one roof. For information, call ✆ **416/410-1310.** Third weekend of October.

November

Royal Agricultural Winter Fair and Royal Horse Show, Exhibition Place. The 12-day show is the largest indoor agricultural and equestrian competition in the world. Displays include vegetables and fruits, crafts, farm machinery, livestock, and more. A member of the British royal family traditionally attends the horse show. Call ✆ **416/393-6400** or check www. royalfair.org for information. Mid-November.

Santa Claus Parade, downtown. A favorite with kids since 1905, it features marching bands, floats, clowns, and jolly St. Nick. American visitors are usually surprised that the parade's in November, but it's better than watching Santa try to slide through slush. For information, call ✆ **416/249-7833** or visit www.city.toronto. on.ca. Third Sunday of November.

One-of-a-Kind Craft Show & Sale, Exhibition Place. More than 400 craft artists from across Canada display their unique wares at this 11-day show. For information, call ✆ **416/960-3680** or visit www. oneofakindshow.com. Last weekend in November through early December.

Cavalcade of Lights, Nathan Phillips Square. During this holiday celebration, lights decorate trees in and around Nathan Phillips Square, parties and performances take over the skating rink, and ice sculptures decorate the square. Visit **www.city.toronto.on.ca** for more information. Late November through December 31.

Canadian Aboriginal Festival, SkyDome. More than 1,500 Native American dancers, drummers, and singers attend this weekend celebration. There are literary readings, an arts-and-crafts market, and traditional foods. Call ✆ **519/751-0040** or visit www.canab.com. Last weekend in November.

December

First Night Toronto and New Year's Eve at City Hall. First Night is an alcohol-free family New Year's Eve celebration. A button (C$8/ US$5.60) admits you to a variety of musical, theatrical, and dance performances at downtown venues. In Nathan Phillips Square and in Mel Lastman Square in North York, concerts begin at around 10pm to usher in the countdown to the new year. Visit **www.city.toronto.on.ca** for more information. December 31.

Moments **Jump Up!**

One of the undisputed highlights of summer in Toronto is the annual Caribana festival. Created in 1967 as a community heritage celebration to tie in with Canada's centennial, Caribana has become North America's largest street festival, drawing more than a million visitors from North America, Britain, and the Caribbean each year. Originally based on Trinidad's Carnival, the festival now draws on numerous cultures—Jamaican, Guyanese, Brazilian, and Bahamian, to name a few—for its music, food, and events.

During the 2 weeks that it runs, you will see the influence of Caribana around the city. It starts with a bang (literally, as there are steel drums involved) at Nathan Phillips Square in front of Toronto City Hall, with a free concert that features calypso, salsa, and soca music. In the days that follow, there are boat cruises, dances, and concerts; the King and Queen Extravaganza, which showcases some of the most amazing costumes you could hope to see; and an arts festival. The highlight is the Caribana Parade, which brings together masquerade and steel-drum bands, dancers, and floats in a memorable feast for all the senses. This is one party you just can't miss.

5 Travel Insurance

Check your existing insurance policies and credit card coverage before you buy travel insurance. You may already be covered for lost luggage, canceled tickets, or medical expenses. The cost of travel insurance varies widely, depending on the cost and length of your trip, your age, health, and the type of trip you're taking.

TRIP-CANCELLATION INSURANCE Trip-cancellation insurance helps you get your money back if you have to back out of a trip, if you have to go home early, or if your travel supplier goes bankrupt. Allowed reasons for cancellation can range from sickness to natural disasters to the State Department declaring your destination unsafe for travel. (Insurers usually won't cover vague fears, though, as many travelers discovered who tried to cancel their trips in October 2001 because they were wary of flying.) In this unstable world, trip-cancellation insurance is a good buy if you're getting tickets well in advance—who knows what the state of the world, or of your airline, will be in 9 months? Insurance policy details vary, so read the fine print—and especially make sure that your airline or cruise line is on the list of carriers covered in case of bankruptcy. For information, contact one of the following insurers: **Access America** (© 866/807-3982; www.accessamerica.com); **Travel Guard International** (© 800/826-4919; www.travelguard.com); **Travel Insured International** (© 800/243-3174; www.travelinsured.com); and **Travelex Insurance Services** (© 888/457-4602; www.travelex-insurance.com).

MEDICAL INSURANCE Most health insurance policies cover you if you get sick away from home—but check, particularly if you're insured by an HMO. With the exception of certain HMOs and Medicare/Medicaid, your medical insurance should cover medical treatment—even hospital care—abroad. However, most out-of-country hospitals make you pay your bills up front, and send you a refund after you've returned home and filed the necessary paperwork. And in a worst-case scenario, there's the high cost of emergency evacuation. If you require additional medical insurance, try **MEDEX International** (© **800/527-0218** or 410/453-6300; www.medexassist.com) or **Travel Assistance International** (© **800/821-2828;** www.travelassistance.com); for general information on services, call the company's Worldwide Assistance Services, Inc., at © **800/777-8710**).

LOST-LUGGAGE INSURANCE On international flights (including U.S. portions of international trips), baggage is limited to approximately $9.07 per pound, up to approximately $635 per checked bag. If you plan to check items more valuable than the standard liability, see if your valuables are covered by your homeowner's policy, get baggage insurance as part of your comprehensive travel-insurance package, or buy Travel Guard's "Bag-Trak" product. Don't buy insurance at the airport, as it's usually overpriced. Be sure to take any valuables or irreplaceable items with you in your carry-on luggage, as many valuables (including books, money, and electronics) aren't covered by airline policies.

If your luggage is lost, immediately file a lost-luggage claim at the airport, detailing the luggage contents. For most airlines, you must report delayed, damaged, or lost baggage within 4 hours of arrival. The airlines are required to deliver luggage, once found, directly to your house or destination free of charge.

6 Health

While Toronto has excellent doctors and some fine hospitals, it's common sense to prepare for the trip as you would for any other. In the spring of 2004, some U.S. news outlets printed articles asking whether SARS would reappear in Toronto. It didn't, and to get a sense of just how overblown the city's unhealthy reputation was, see "The SARS Story" on page 26.

BEFORE YOU GO
If you worry about getting sick away from home, consider purchasing **medical travel insurance** and carry your ID card in your purse or wallet. In most cases, your existing health plan will provide the coverage you need. See the section on travel insurance above for more information.

If you suffer from a chronic illness, consult your doctor before your departure. For conditions like epilepsy, diabetes, or heart problems, wear a **Medic Alert identification tag** (© 800/825-3785; www.medicalert.org), which will immediately alert doctors to your condition and give them access to your records through Medic Alert's 24-hour hot line.

Pack **prescription medications** in your carry-on luggage, and carry prescription medications in their original containers, with pharmacy labels—otherwise they won't make it through airport security. Also bring along copies of your prescriptions in case you lose your pills or run out. Don't forget an extra pair of contact lenses or prescription glasses. Carry the generic name of prescription medicines, in case a local pharmacist is unfamiliar with the brand name.

Contact the **International Association for Medical Assistance to Travelers (IAMAT)** (© **716/754-4883,** or 416/652-0137 in Canada; www.iamat.org) for tips on travel and health concerns and lists of local doctors. If you get sick, consider asking your hotel concierge to recommend a local

The SARS Story

SARS hit Toronto hard in 2003, though not in the way most people think. The tourism industry was devastated by the World Health Organization warning against travel to the city, and by the many conferences and performances that were canceled in its wake. While Toronto was undoubtedly the hardest-hit city outside of Asia, the SARS outbreak was limited to health-care facilities. Not a single person picked it up at a restaurant, at the theater, on the subway, or in any other spot a visitor might frequent.

This is a drawn-out way of saying that the SARS story in Toronto was blown completely out of proportion. It's one of the safest cities you could visit in North America. And while the famous folks who canceled their trips got the media attention, many stars came to Toronto despite the SARS hysteria. These levelheaded luminaries include Colin Farrell, Sophia Loren, Gene Hackman, Ray Romano, and Amy Tan. In 2004, people in the tourism business launched a major campaign to get travelers back to Toronto, and their efforts largely succeeded.

doctor—even his or her own. You can also try the emergency room at a local hospital; many have walk-in clinics for emergency cases that are not life-threatening. You may not get immediate attention, but you won't pay the high price of an emergency room visit.

7 Specialized Travel Resources

FOR TRAVELERS WITH DISABILITIES

Toronto is a very accessible city. Curb cuts are well made and common throughout the downtown area; special parking privileges are extended to people with disabilities who have special plates or a pass that allows parking in "No Parking" zones. The subway and trolleys are not accessible, but the city operates **Wheel-Trans,** a special service for those with disabilities. Visitors can register for this service. For information, call © **416/393-4111** or visit www.city.toronto.on.ca/ttc.

The **Community Information Centre of Metropolitan Toronto,** 425 Adelaide St. W., at Spadina Avenue, Toronto, ON M5V 3C1 (© **416/392-0505**), may be able to provide limited information and assistance about social-service organizations in the city. It does not have specific accessibility information on tourism or hotels. It's available weekdays from 8am to 10pm, and weekends from 10am to 10pm.

Other organizations that offer assistance to travelers with disabilities include **MossRehab** (www.moss resourcenet.org), which provides a library of accessible-travel resources online; the **Society for Accessible Travel and Hospitality** (© 212/447-7284; www.sath.org; annual membership fees $45 adults, $30 seniors and students), which offers a wealth of travel resources for all types of disabilities and informed recommendations on destinations, access guides, travel agents, tour operators, vehicle rentals, and companion services; and the **American Foundation for the Blind** (© 800/232-5463; www.afb.org), which provides information on traveling with Seeing Eye dogs.

FOR SENIORS

Mention the fact that you're a senior when you make your travel reservations. Some hotels and many city attractions grant senior discounts; bring a form of photo ID.

Members of **AARP,** 601 E St. NW, Washington, DC 20049 (© **800/ 424-3410** or 202/434-2277; www. aarp.org), get discounts on hotels, airfares, and car rentals. AARP offers members a wide range of benefits, including *AARP The Magazine* and a monthly newsletter. Anyone over 50 can join.

Also look into the fun courses offered in the Toronto region at incredibly low prices by **Elderhostel** (© **877/426-8056;** www.elderhostel. org). Elderhostel arranges study programs for those 55 and over (and a spouse or companion of any age); many courses include airfare, accommodations in university dormitories or modest inns, meals, and tuition.

Another great resource is **Wired Seniors** (www.wiredseniors.com). Travelers ages 50 and over will appreciate this site, which lists accommodations and tours geared toward mature visitors (click on "Senior Friendly Web Sites" and enter "Toronto" in the search box). The discounts section (in "Seniors Discount Mall") lists special savings and deals.

FOR FAMILIES

The family vacation is a rite of passage for many households, one that in a split second can devolve into a *National Lampoon* farce. But in Toronto, a city that boasts a plethora of family-friendly sites, such as the Ontario Science Centre, Paramount Canada's Wonderland, Harbourfront, and the Toronto Zoo, you'll find that a family trip really can offer something for everyone.

For more suggestions on family and kid-oriented entertainment in Toronto, see "Frommer's Favorite Toronto Experiences" in chapter 1 and "Especially for Kids" in chapter 6. If you're already in town, pick up a copy of *Toronto Families,* a free magazine produced by the publishers of *Today's Parent* (an award-winning national magazine). You can also check it out online at www.torontofamilies.ca.

Other helpful features in this guide include "Family-Friendly Hotels" (p. 66) and "Family-Friendly Restaurants" (p. 94). Chapter 8, the "Shopping" chapter includes great suggestions for children's clothes and toys, and Indigo Books Music & More (p. 181) often offers events for kids. For even more tips, pick up a copy of *Frommer's Toronto with Kids.*

Familyhostel (© **800/733-9753;** www.learn.unh.edu/familyhostel) takes the whole family, including kids ages 8 to 15, on moderately priced domestic and international learning vacations. Lectures, field trips, and sightseeing are guided by a team of academics.

You can find good general vacation advice on the Internet from sites like the **Family Travel Network** (www.family travelnetwork.com); **Traveling Internationally with Your Kids** (www.travel withyourkids.com), a comprehensive site offering sound advice for long-distance and international travel with thefamilytravelfiles.com), which offers an online magazine and a directory of off-the-beaten-path tours and tour operators for families.

FOR STUDENTS

The key to securing discounts and other special benefits is to arm yourself with an **International Student Identity Card (ISIC),** which offers substantial savings on rail passes, plane tickets, and entrance fees. It also provides you with basic health and life insurance and a 24-hour help line. The card is available for $22 from **STA Travel** (© **800/781-4040** in North America, or visit www.statravel. com for other countries), the biggest student travel agency in the world. If you're no longer a student but are still under 26, you can get a **International Youth Travel Card (IYTC)** for the same price from the same people, which entitles you to some discounts. **Travel CUTS** (© **800/667-2887** or 416/614-2887; www.travelcuts.com) offers similar services for U.S. and Canadian residents.

If you'd like to meet other students, you've come to the right place. Toronto has several major colleges in addition to the sprawling **University of Toronto.** The largest university in Canada, with more than 50,000 students (41,000 full-time), the University of Toronto offers many year-round activities and events that any visitor can attend—lectures, seminars, concerts, and more. U of T Day is usually celebrated in the middle of October. The university holds an open house for the community and celebrates with a children's fair and the annual homecoming football game and parade. Call © **416/978-8342** for more information, call 416/978-5000 for campus tours, or visit www.utoronto.ca.

FOR WOMEN

Journeywoman (www.journeywoman. com) is a lively travel resource. The website has message boards and a huge library of articles, which includes a "GirlTalk Guide" to Toronto. There's also a free monthly e-mail newsletter.

Women Welcome Women World Wide (5W) (© **203/259-7832;** www. womenwelcomewomen.org.uk) works to foster international friendships by enabling women of different countries to visit one another (men can come along on the trips; they just can't join the club). It's a big, active organization,

with more than 3,000 members from all walks of life in some 70 countries. *Safety and Security for Women Who Travel,* by Sheila Swan Laufer and Peter Laufer (Travelers' Tales, Inc.), offers common-sense advice and tips on safe travel.

FOR GAY & LESBIAN TRAVELERS

Toronto is a member of the Big Four, the term for the North American cities with the largest gay communities (the others are San Francisco, New York, and Chicago). For the city's large gay population, estimated at about 250,000, community life is centered north and south of the intersection of Church and Wellesley streets, an area known as the Gay Village, but gay-friendly establishments aren't limited to one neighborhood. One of Toronto's most celebrated events is Pride Week in June (see "Toronto Calendar of Events," page 19). Also, Toronto has become a popular spot for gay and lesbian couples to marry; see "Wedded Bliss for Gay & Lesbian Couples," page 29 for details.

Gay and lesbian travelers can pick up a copy of the biweekly *Xtra!* It's available free at many bookstores, including the **Glad Day Bookshop,** 598A Yonge St., second floor (© **416/961-4161;** www.gladday.com). To read *Xtra!* before you get to town, log in to www.xtra.ca. You can also sign up for its Toronto e-mail list with information about local events and breaking news stories.

Another resource is **Gay Toronto** (www.gaytoronto.com), which lists gay-friendly restaurants, bars, night-clubs, guesthouses, travel agencies, and other businesses and organizations. The **Gay Toronto Tourism Guild** has a website with event links at www.gaytorontotourism.com. The

Wedded Bliss for Gay & Lesbian Couples

Niagara Falls used to be one of the most popular places to honeymoon, but Toronto today is one of the most in-demand wedding destinations. After same-sex marriage became legal in Ontario in 2003, gay and lesbian couples flocked to the city to marry. (The June Pride Week celebrations in 2003 and 2004 included many newlywed couples.)

If you want to get married in Toronto, it's pretty simple: Go with your partner to the Registrar General's office at 900 Bay St. (at Wellesley), bring ID (including your passport and birth certificate), pay a small fee, and the marriage license will be yours; there's no residency requirement. See **www.city.toronto.on.ca** for details and an application form that you can download. For help organizing a wedding beyond the confines of City Hall, check out the wedding planner pages at www.toronto.com. One company that specializes in planning same-sex weddings is **Pride Weddings** (℗ 888/418-1188; www.prideweddings. com). While many wedding ceremonies are being conducted at the **Toronto Civic Wedding Chambers,** 100 Queen St. W. (℗ 416/363-0316), couples are increasingly choosing to wed elsewhere. One popular place is the **Metropolitan Community Church of Toronto** (℗ 416/406-6228; www.mcctoronto.com), which has been very active in the battle for same-sex marriage rights.

daily news website **www.365gay.com** features Toronto travel information.

The International Gay & Lesbian Travel Association (IGLTA) (℗ **800/ 448-8550** or 954/776-2626; www. iglta.org) is the trade association for the gay and lesbian travel industry, and offers an online directory of gay- and lesbian-friendly travel businesses.

8 Planning Your Trip Online

SURFING FOR AIRFARES

The "big three" online travel agencies, **Expedia.com, Travelocity.com,** and **Orbitz.com** sell most of the air tickets bought on the Internet. (Canadian travelers should try Expedia.ca, Travelocity. ca, or Destina.ca; U.K. residents can go for Expedia.co.uk and Opodo.co.uk.) Each has different business deals with the airlines and may offer different fares on the same flights, so it's wise to shop around. Expedia and Travelocity will also send you **e-mail notification** when a cheap fare becomes available to your favorite destination. Of the smaller travel-agency websites, **Side-Step** (www.sidestep.com) has gotten the best reviews from Frommer's authors. It's a browser add-on that purports to "search 140 sites at once," but in reality only beats competitors' fares as often as other sites do.

Also remember to check **airline websites,** especially those for low-fare carriers, whose fares are often misreported or simply missing from travel-agency websites. Even with major airlines, you can often shave a few bucks from a fare by booking directly through the airline and avoiding a travel agency's transaction fee. But you'll get these discounts only by **booking online:** Most airlines now offer online-only fares that even their phone agents know nothing about. For the websites of airlines that fly to and from your destination, go to "Getting There," later in this chapter.

Great **last-minute deals** are available through free weekly e-mail services provided directly by the airlines. Most of these are announced on Tuesday or Wednesday and must be purchased online. Most are only valid for travel that weekend, but some can be booked weeks or months in advance. Sign up for weekly e-mail alerts at airline websites or check mega-sites that compile comprehensive lists of last-minute specials, such as **Smarter Living** (www. smarterliving.com). For last-minute trips, **site59.com** in the U.S. and **lastminute.com** in Europe often have better deals than the major-label sites.

If you're willing to give up some control over your flight details, use an **opaque fare service** like **Priceline** (www.priceline.com; www.priceline. co.uk for Europeans) or **Hotwire** (www.hotwire.com). Both offer rock-bottom prices in exchange for travel on a "mystery airline" at a mysterious time of day, often with a mysterious change of planes en route. The mystery airlines are all major, well-known carriers—and the possibility of being sent from Philadelphia to Toronto via Tampa is remote; the airlines' routing computers have gotten a lot better than they used to be. But your chances of getting a 6am or 11pm flight are pretty high. Hotwire tells you flight prices before you buy; Priceline usually has better deals than Hotwire,

but you have to play their "name our price" game (however, Priceline now also offers non-opaque service as well). If you're new at this, the helpful folks at **BiddingForTravel** (www.bidding fortravel.com) do a good job of demystifying Priceline's prices. Priceline and Hotwire are great for flights within North America and between the U.S. and Europe. But for flights to other parts of the world, consolidators will almost always beat their fares.

SURFING FOR HOTELS

Shopping online for hotels is much easier in the U.S., Canada, and certain parts of Europe than it is in the rest of the world. If you try to book a Chinese hotel online, for instance, you'll probably overpay. Also, many smaller hotels and B&Bs—especially outside the U.S.—don't show up on websites at all. Of the "big three" sites, Expedia offers a long list of special deals and "virtual tours" or photos of available rooms so you can see what you're paying for (a feature that helps counter the claims that the best rooms are often held back from bargain-booking websites). **Travelocity** posts unvarnished customer reviews and ranks its properties according to the AAA rating system. Also reliable are **Hotels.com** and **Quikbook. com**. An excellent free program, **TravelAxe** (www.travelaxe.net), can help you search multiple hotel sites at once, even ones you may never have heard of. Another booking site, **Travelweb** (www.travelweb.com), is partly owned by the hotels it represents (including

---

Tips Air Canada CyberDeals

One site that's particularly worth checking out is **Air Canada** (www. aircanada.ca). On Wednesday, it offers deeply discounted flights to Canada for that weekend. You need to reserve on Wednesday or Thursday to fly on Friday (after 7pm only) or Saturday (all day) and return on Monday or Tuesday (all day). Once you register with Air Canada's Web Specials page, you'll receive an e-mail every Wednesday about available discounts.

Frommers.com: The Complete Travel Resource

For an excellent travel-planning resource, we highly recommend **Frommers.com** (www.frommers.com). We're a little biased, of course, but we guarantee that you'll find the travel tips, reviews, monthly vacation giveaways, and online-booking capabilities thoroughly indispensable. Among the special features are our popular **Message Boards,** where Frommer's readers post queries and share advice (sometimes even our authors show up to answer questions); **Frommers.com Newsletter,** for the latest travel bargains and insider travel secrets; and **Frommer's Destinations Section,** where you'll get expert travel tips, hotel and dining recommendations, and advice on the sights to see for more than 3,500 destinations around the globe. When your research is done, the **Online Reservations System** (www.frommers.com/book_a_trip) takes you to Frommer's preferred online partners for booking your vacation at affordable prices.

the Hilton, Hyatt, and Starwood chains) and is therefore plugged directly into the hotels' reservations systems—unlike independent online agencies, which have to fax or e-mail reservation requests to the hotel, a good portion of which get misplaced in the shuffle. More than once, travelers have arrived at the hotel, only to be told that they have no reservation. To be fair, many of the major sites are undergoing improvements in service and ease of use, and Expedia will soon be able to plug directly into the reservations systems of many hotel chains—none of which can be bad news for consumers. In the meantime, it's a good idea to **get a confirmation number** and **make a printout** of any online booking transaction.

Priceline and Hotwire are even better for hotels than for airfares; with both, you're allowed to pick the neighborhood and quality level of your hotel before offering up your money. Priceline's hotel product even covers Europe and Asia, though it's much better at getting luxury lodging for moderate prices than at finding anything at the bottom of the scale. *Note:* Hotwire overrates its hotels by one star.

SURFING FOR RENTAL CARS

For booking rental cars online, the best deals are usually found at rental-car company websites, although all the major online travel agencies also offer rental-car reservations services. Priceline and Hotwire work well for rental cars, too; the only "mystery" is which major rental company you get, and for most travelers the difference between Hertz, Avis, and Budget is negligible.

9 The 21st-Century Traveler

INTERNET ACCESS AWAY FROM HOME

Travelers have any number of ways to check their e-mail and access the Internet on the road. Of course, using your own laptop—or even a PDA or electronic organizer with a modem—gives you the most flexibility. But even if you don't have a computer, you can still access your e-mail and even your office computer from cybercafes.

WITHOUT YOUR OWN COMPUTER

It's hard nowadays to find a city that *doesn't* have a few cybercafes. Although there's no definitive directory for cybercafes—these are independent businesses, after all—three places to start looking are at **www.cybercaptive. com**, **www.netcafeguide.com**, and **www.cybercafe.com**. See also "Internet Access" under "Fast Facts: Toronto" in chapter 3.

Aside from formal cybercafes, most **youth hostels** nowadays have at least one computer you can use to get onto the Internet. And most **public libraries** across the world offer Internet access free or for a small charge. Avoid **hotel business centers,** which often charge exorbitant rates.

To retrieve your e-mail, ask your **Internet Service Provider (ISP)** if it has a Web-based interface tied to your existing e-mail account. If your ISP doesn't have such an interface, you can use the free **mail2web** service (www. mail2web.com) to view and reply to your home e-mail. For more flexibility, you may want to open a free, Web-based e-mail account with **Yahoo! Mail** (http://mail.yahoo.com). (Microsoft's Hotmail is another popular option, but Hotmail has severe spam problems.) Your home ISP may be able to forward your e-mail to the Web-based account automatically.

If you need to access files on your office computer, look into a service called **GoToMyPC** (www.gotomypc. com). The service provides a Web-based interface for you to access and manipulate a distant PC from anywhere—even a cybercafe—provided your "target" PC is on and has an always-on connection to the Internet (such as with Road Runner cable). The service offers top-quality security, but if you're worried about hackers, use your own laptop rather than a cybercafe to access the GoToMyPC system.

WITH YOUR OWN COMPUTER

Major Internet Service Providers (ISPs) have **local access numbers** around the world, allowing you to go online by simply placing a local call. Check your ISP's website or call its toll-free number and ask how you can use your current account away from home, and how much it will cost.

If you're traveling outside the reach of your ISP, the **iPass** network has dial-up numbers in most of the world's countries. You'll have to sign up with an iPass provider, who will then tell you how to set up your computer for your destination(s). For a list of iPass providers, go to **www.ipass. com** and click on "Reseller Locator." Under "Select a Country" pick the country that you're coming from, and under "Who is this service for?" pick "Individual." One solid provider is **i2roam** (𝄐 **866/811-6209** or 920/ 235-0475; www.i2roam.com).

Wherever you go, bring a **connection kit** of the right power and phone adapters, a spare phone cord, and a spare Ethernet network cable. The electrical current is the same as in the United States—110 volts, 50 cycles AC.

Most business-class hotels throughout the world offer dataports for laptop modems, and a few thousand hotels in North America and Europe now offer high-speed Internet access using an Ethernet network cable. You'll have to bring your own cables either way, so **call your hotel in advance** to find out what the options are. Many business-class hotels in the U.S. also offer a form of computer-free Web browsing through the room TV set. We've successfully checked Yahoo! Mail and Hotmail on these systems.

If you have an 802.11b/**Wi-fi** card for your computer, several commercial companies have made wireless service available in airports, hotel lobbies, and coffee shops, primarily in the U.S.

Online Traveler's Toolbox

Veteran travelers usually carry some essential items to make their trips easier. Following is a selection of online tools to bookmark and use.

- **Visa ATM Locator** (www.visa.com), for locations of PLUS ATMs worldwide, or **MasterCard ATM Locator** (www.mastercard.com), for locations of Cirrus ATMs worldwide.
- **Intellicast** (www.intellicast.com) and **Weather.com** (www.weather.com). Gives weather forecasts for Toronto and other cities around the world.
- **Mapquest** (www.mapquest.com). This best of the mapping sites lets you choose a specific address or destination, and in seconds, it will return a map and detailed directions.
- **Universal Currency Converter** (www.xe.com/ucc). See what your dollar or pound is worth in more than 100 other countries.
- **Travel Warnings** (http://travel.state.gov/travel_warnings.html, www.fco.gov.uk/travel, www.voyage.gc.ca, www.dfat.gov.au/consular/advice). These sites report on places where health concerns or unrest might threaten American, British, Canadian, and Australian travelers. Generally, U.S. warnings are the most paranoid; Australian warnings are the most relaxed.

T-Mobile Hotspot (www.t-mobile.com/hotspot) serves up wireless connections at more than 1,000 Starbucks coffee shops nationwide. **Boingo** (www.boingo.com) and **Wayport** (www.wayport.com) have set up networks in airports and high-class hotel lobbies. IPass providers (see above) also give you access to a few hundred wireless hotel lobby setups. Best of all, you don't need to be staying at the Four Seasons to use the hotel's network; just set yourself up on a nice couch in the lobby. Unfortunately, the companies' pricing policies are Byzantine, with a variety of monthly, per-connection, and per-minute plans.

Community-minded individuals have also set up **free wireless networks** in major cities around the world. These networks are spotty, but you get what you (don't) pay for. Each network has a home page explaining how to set up your computer for their particular system; start your explorations at **www.personaltelco.net/index.cgi/Wireless Communities**.

USING A CELLPHONE

The three letters that define much of the world's **wireless capabilities** are GSM (Global System for Mobiles), a big, seamless network that makes for easy cross-border cellphone use throughout Europe and dozens of other countries worldwide. In the U.S., T-Mobile, AT&T Wireless, and Cingular use this quasi-universal system; in Canada, Microcell and some Rogers customers are GSM, and all Europeans and most Australians use GSM.

If your cellphone is on a GSM system, and you have a world-capable phone such as many (but not all) Sony Ericsson, Motorola, or Samsung models, you can make and receive calls across much of the globe, from Andorra to Uganda. Just call your wireless operator and ask for "international roaming" to be activated on your account. Unfortunately, per-minute charges can be high—usually $1 to $1.50 in Western Europe and up to $5 in places like Russia and Indonesia.

World-phone owners can bring down their per-minute charges with a bit of trickery. Call up your cellular operator and say you'll be going abroad for several months and want to "unlock" your phone to use it with a local provider. Usually, they'll oblige. Then, in Toronto, pick up a cheap, prepaid phone chip at a mobile phone store and slip it into your phone. (Show your phone to the salesperson, as not all phones work on all networks.) You'll get a local phone number in Toronto—and much, much lower calling rates.

Otherwise, **renting** a phone is a good idea. While you can rent a phone from any number of overseas sites, including kiosks at airports and at car-rental agencies, we suggest renting the phone before you leave home. That way you can give loved ones your new number, make sure the phone works, and take the phone wherever you go. But phone rental isn't cheap: You'll usually pay $40 to $50 per week, plus airtime fees of at least a dollar a minute. Be sure to shop around.

Two good wireless rental companies are **InTouch USA** (© 800/872-7626; www.intouchglobal.com) and **Roadpost** (© 888/290-1606 or 905/272-5665; www.roadpost.com). Give them your itinerary, and they'll tell you what wireless products you need. InTouch will also, for free, advise you on whether your existing phone will work overseas; simply call © 703/222-7161 or go to http://intouchglobal.com/travel.htm.

10 Getting There

BY PLANE

Wherever you're traveling from, always shop the airlines and ask for the lowest fare. You'll have a better chance of landing a deal if you're willing to be flexible about when you arrive and leave.

You may be able to fly for less than the standard advance (APEX) fare by contacting a ticket broker or consolidator. These companies, which buy tickets in bulk and sell them at a discount, advertise in the Sunday travel sections of major city newspapers. You may not be able to get the lowest price they advertise, but you're likely to pay less than the price quoted by the major airlines. Tickets purchased through a consolidator are often nonrefundable. If you change your itinerary after purchase, chances are you'll pay a stiff penalty.

FROM THE U.S. Canada's only national airline, **Air Canada** (© 888/247-2262; www.aircanada.ca), operates direct flights to Toronto from most major American cities and many smaller ones. It also flies from major cities around the world and operates connecting flights from other U.S. cities.

There are also a couple of discount Canadian carriers servicing select routes. One is **JetsGo** (www.jetsgo.com; bookings are made online, but if you need help with the process call © 866-448-5888), which operates flights to Toronto from New York, Los Angeles, Las Vegas, and Orlando. **WestJet** (© 888-WEST-JET or www.westjet.com) will begin service between Toronto and San Francisco, Los Angeles, and Phoenix in the fall of 2004.

Among U.S. airlines, **American** (© 800/433-7300; www.aa.com) has daily direct flights from Chicago, Dallas, Miami, and New York. **United** (© 800/241-6522; www.united.com) has direct flights from Chicago, San Francisco, and Washington (Dulles); it's a code-share partner with Air Canada. **US Airways** (© 800/428-4322; www.usairways.com) operates directly into Toronto from a number of U.S. cities, notably Baltimore, Indianapolis, Philadelphia, and Pittsburgh. **Northwest** (© 800/225-2525;

www.nwa.com) flies direct from Detroit and Minneapolis. **Delta** (© **800/221-1212;** www.delta.com) flies direct from Atlanta and Cincinnati.

FROM ABROAD   There's frequent service (direct and indirect) to Toronto from around the world.

Several airlines operate from the United Kingdom. **British Airways** (© **0845/773-3377;** www.ba.com) and **Air Canada** (© **08705/247-226**) fly direct from London's Heathrow airport. Air Canada also flies direct from Glasgow and Manchester.

In Australia, **Air Canada** (© **02/9286-8900**) has an agreement with Qantas and flies from Sydney to Toronto, stopping in Honolulu. From New Zealand, **Air Canada** (© **09/379-3371**) cooperates with Air New Zealand, scheduling on average three flights a week from Auckland to Toronto, via Honolulu, Fiji, or both.

From Cape Town, South Africa, **Delta** (© **011/482-4582** in South Africa) operates via New York; **Air Canada** (© **011/875-5800**) via Frankfurt; and **South African Airways** (© **021/254-610;** www.saa.co.za) via Miami or New York. Several airlines fly from Johannesburg, including **British Airways** (© **011/441-8600**) via Heathrow and **South African Airways** (© **011/333-6504**) via Miami or New York.

GETTING THROUGH THE AIRPORT

With the federalization of airport security, security procedures at U.S. airports are more stable and consistent than ever. Generally, you'll be fine if you arrive at the airport **2 hours** before an international flight; if you show up late, tell an airline employee and you'll probably be whisked to the front of the line.

Bring a **current, government-issued photo ID** such as a driver's license or passport; you'll need to show it at the security checkpoint, and your ID at the ticket counter or the gate. (Children under 18 do not need photo IDs for domestic flights, but the adults checking in with them need them.)

Security lines are getting shorter, but some doozies remain. If you have trouble standing for long periods of time, tell an airline employee; the airline will provide a wheelchair. Speed up security by **not wearing metal objects** such as big belt buckles or clanky earrings. If you've got metallic body parts, a note from your doctor can prevent a long chat with the security screeners. Keep in mind that only **ticketed passengers** are allowed past security, except for folks escorting disabled passengers or children.

Federalization has stabilized **what you can carry on** and **what you can't.** The general rule is that sharp things are out, nail clippers are okay, and food and beverages must be passed through the X-ray machine—but security screeners can't make you drink from your coffee cup. Bring food in your carry-on rather than checking it, as explosive-detection machines used on checked luggage have been known to mistake food (especially chocolate, for some reason) for bombs. Travelers in the U.S. are allowed one carry-on bag, plus a "personal item" such as a purse, briefcase, or laptop bag. Carry-on hoarders can stuff all sorts of things into a laptop bag; as long as it has a laptop in it, it's still considered a personal item. The Transportation Security Administration (TSA) has issued a list of restricted items; check its website (www.tsa.gov) for details.

The TSA has phased out **gate check-in** at all U.S. airports. Passengers with e-tickets and without checked bags can still beat the ticket-counter lines by using **electronic kiosks** or even **online check-in.** Ask your airline which alternatives are available, and if you're using a kiosk, bring the credit card you used to book the ticket. If you're checking bags, you will still be able to use most airlines' kiosks; again call your airline for up-to-date information. **Curbside check-in** is also a good way to avoid lines, although a few airlines still ban curbside check-in entirely; call before you go.

Airport screeners may decide that your checked luggage needs to be searched by hand. You can now purchase luggage locks that allow screeners to open and relock a checked bag if hand-searching is necessary. Look for Travel Sentry–certified locks at luggage or travel shops and Brookstone stores (you can buy them online at www.brookstone.com). These locks, approved by the TSA, can be opened by luggage inspectors with a special code or key. For more information on the locks, visit www.travelsentry.org. If you use something other than TSA-approved locks, your lock will be cut off your suitcase if a TSA agent needs to hand-search your luggage.

FLYING FOR LESS: TIPS FOR GETTING THE BEST AIRFARE

Passengers sharing the same airplane cabin rarely pay the same fare. Travelers who need to purchase tickets at the last minute, change their itinerary at a moment's notice, or fly one-way often get stuck paying the premium rate. Here are some ways to keep your airfare costs down.

- Passengers who can book their ticket **long in advance,** who can **stay over Saturday night,** or who **fly midweek** or **at less-trafficked hours** will pay a fraction of the full fare. If your schedule is flexible, say so, and ask if you can secure a cheaper fare by changing your flight plans.
- You can also save on airfares by keeping an eye out in local newspapers for **promotional specials**

or **fare wars,** when airlines lower prices on their most popular routes. You rarely see fare wars offered for peak travel times, but if you can travel in the off-months, you may snag a bargain.

- Search **the Internet** for cheap fares (see "Planning Your Trip Online," earlier in this chapter).
- **Consolidators,** also known as bucket shops, are great sources for international tickets, although they usually can't beat the Internet on fares within North America. Start by looking in Sunday newspaper travel sections; U.S. travelers should focus on the *New York Times, Los Angeles Times,* and *Miami Herald.* For less-developed destinations, small travel agents who cater to immigrant communities in large cities often have the best deals. *Beware:* Bucket shop tickets are usually nonrefundable or rigged with stiff cancellation penalties, often as high as 50% to 75% of the ticket price, and some put you on charter airlines with questionable safety records.

Several reliable consolidators are worldwide and available on the Net. **STA Travel** (© 800/781-4040; www.statravel.com) is now the world's leader in student travel, thanks to their purchase of Council Travel. It also offers good fares for travelers of all ages. **Flights. com** (© 800/TRAV-800; www. flights.com) started in Europe and has excellent fares worldwide. **Air Tickets Direct** (© 800/778-3447; www.airticketsdirect.com) is based in Montréal and leverages the currently weak Canadian dollar for low fares; it'll also book trips to places that U.S. travel agents won't touch, such as Cuba.

- Join **frequent-flier clubs.** Accrue enough miles, and you'll be rewarded with free flights and elite

Travel in the Age of Bankruptcy

Airlines go bankrupt, so protect yourself: **Buy your tickets with a credit card,** as the Fair Credit Billing Act guarantees that you can get your money back from the credit card company if a travel supplier goes under (and if you request the refund within 60 days of the bankruptcy). **Travel insurance** can also help, but make sure it covers against "carrier default" for your specific travel provider. And be aware that if a U.S. airline goes bust mid-trip, a 2001 federal law requires other carriers to take you to your destination (albeit on a space-available basis) for a fee of no more than $25, provided you rebook within 60 days of the cancellation.

status. It's free, and you'll get the best choice of seats, faster response to phone inquiries, and prompter service if your luggage is stolen, your flight is canceled or delayed, or if you want to change your seat. You don't need to fly to build frequent-flier miles—**frequent-flier credit cards** can provide thousands of miles for doing your everyday shopping.

BY TRAIN

Amtrak's "Maple Leaf" service links New York City and Toronto via Albany, Buffalo, and Niagara Falls. It departs daily from Penn Station. The journey takes 11¾ hours. From Chicago, the "International" carries passengers to Toronto via Port Huron, Michigan, a 12½-hour trip. Note that these lengthy schedules allow for extended stops at customs and immigration checkpoints at the border. Both trains arrive in Toronto at Union Station on Front Street, 1 block west of Yonge Street, opposite the Fairmont Royal York Hotel. The station has direct access to the subway.

To secure the lowest round-trip fares, book as far in advance as possible, and try to travel midweek. Seat availability determines price levels; the earlier you book, the more likely you are to land a lower fare. Sample fares (for use as guidelines only), depending on seat availability: from New York, US$65 to US$99 one-way or US$130 to US$198 round-trip; from Chicago, US$98 one-way, US$108 to US$196 round-trip. Prices do not include meals. Always ask about the availability of discounted fares, companion fares, and any other special tickets. Call **Amtrak** at ✆ **800/USA-RAIL** or 800/872-7245, or visit www.amtrak.com.

BY BUS

Greyhound (✆ **800/231-2222;** www.greyhound.com) is the only bus company that crosses the U.S. border. You can travel from almost anywhere in the United States. You'll arrive at the Metro Coach Terminal downtown at 610 Bay St., near the corner of Dundas Street.

The bus may be faster and cheaper than the train, and its routes may be more flexible if you want to stop along the way. Bear in mind that it's more cramped, toilet facilities are meager, and meals are taken at somewhat depressing rest stops.

Depending on where you are coming from, check into Greyhound's special unlimited-travel passes and discount fares. It's hard to provide sample fares because bus companies, like airlines, are adopting yield-management strategies, causing prices to change from day to day.

BY CAR

Crossing the border by car gives you a lot of options—the U.S. highway system leads directly into Canada at 13 points. If you're driving from Michigan, you'll enter at Detroit–Windsor (I-75 and the Ambassador Bridge) or Port Huron–Sarnia (I-94 and the Bluewater Bridge). If you're coming from New York, you have more options. On I-190, you can enter at Buffalo–Fort Erie; Niagara Falls, N.Y.–Niagara Falls, ON; or Niagara Falls, N.Y.–Lewiston. On I-81, you'll cross the Canadian border at Hill Island; on Route 37, you'll enter at either Ogdensburg–Johnstown or Rooseveltown–Cornwall.

From the United States you are most likely to enter Toronto from the west on Highway 401 or Highway 2 and the Queen Elizabeth Way. If you come from the east via Montréal, you'll also use 401 and 2.

Here are approximate driving distances to Toronto: from Boston, 11km (565 miles); Buffalo, 155km (96 miles); Chicago, 859km (533 miles); Cincinnati, 806km (500 miles); Detroit, 379km (235 miles); Minneapolis, 1,564km (970 miles); New York, 797km (494 miles).

Be sure you have your driver's license and car registration if you plan to drive your own vehicle into Canada. It isn't a bad idea to carry proof of automobile liability insurance, either.

If you are a member of the American Automobile Association (AAA), the **Canadian Automobile Association (CAA)** Central Ontario Branch in Toronto (© **416/221-4300;** www.caa.ca) provides emergency road service.

11 Packages for the Independent Traveler

Before you start your search for the lowest airfare, you may want to consider booking your flight as part of a travel package. Package tours are not the same thing as escorted tours. Package tours are simply a way to buy the airfare, accommodations, and other elements of your trip (such as car rentals, airport transfers, and sometimes even activities) at the same time and often at discounted prices—kind of like one-stop shopping. Packages are sold in bulk to tour operators—who resell them to the public at a cost that usually undercuts standard rates.

One good source of package deals is the airlines themselves. Most major airlines offer air/land packages, including **American Airlines Vacations** (© 800/321-2121; www.aavacations.com), **Delta Vacations** (© 800/221-6666; www.deltavacations.com), **Continental Airlines Vacations** (© 800/301-3800; www.coolvacations.com), and **United Vacations** (© 888/854-3899; www.unitedvacations.com). Several big **online travel agencies**—Expedia.com, Travelocity.com, Orbitz.com, Site59.com, and Lastminute.com—also do a brisk business in packages. If you're unsure about the pedigree of a smaller packager, check with the **Better Business Bureau** in the city where the company is based, or go online at www.bbb.org. If a packager won't tell you where it's based, don't fly with them.

Travel packages are also listed in the travel section of your local Sunday newspaper. Or check ads in the national travel magazines such as *Arthur Frommer's Budget Travel Magazine, Travel & Leisure, National Geographic Traveler,* and *Condé Nast Traveler.*

Package tours can vary by leaps and bounds. Some offer a better class of hotels than others. Some offer the same hotels for lower prices. Some offer flights on scheduled airlines, while others book charters. Some limit your choice of accommodations and travel days. You are often required to make a large payment up front. On the plus side, packages can save you money, offering group prices but allowing for independent travel. Some even let you add on a few guided excursions or escorted day trips (also at prices lower than if you booked them yourself) without booking an entirely escorted tour.

Before you invest in a package tour, get some answers. Ask about the **accommodations choices** and prices for each. Then look up the hotels' reviews in a Frommer's guide and check their rates for your specific dates of travel online. You'll also want to find out what **type of room** you get. If you need a certain type of room, ask for it; don't take whatever is thrown your way. Request a nonsmoking room, a quiet room, a room with a view, or whatever you fancy.

Finally, look for **hidden expenses.** Ask whether airport departure fees and taxes, for example, are included in the total cost.

12 Recommended Reading

Though it hasn't always played itself in the movies (doubling often as other major cities instead), Toronto does have quite a literary legacy to call its own. It's the hometown of authors Margaret Atwood, Michael Ondaatje, and media theorist and writer Marshall McLuhan. Famous for saying "The medium is the message," McLuhan's works include *Understanding Media: The Extensions of Man,* and *War & Peace in the Global Village.* There's also a volume called *The Essential McLuhan* to consider if you're a fan.

Atwood's *The Robber Bride* pays homage to her hometown with a story that covers three decades of life in the city. Some of her other novels, such as *The Edible Woman, Cat's Eye,* and *The Blind Assassin* also use Toronto as a backdrop. Her futuristic 2003 novel *Oryx and Crake* isn't set in any recognizable place, but it's such a brilliant read that it deserves a mention anyway. *In the Skin of a Lion* by Michael Ondaatje, the celebrated author of *The English Patient,* is a moving love story that brings the city's landmarks to life. Carol Shields, who died in 2003, set her final novel *Unless* in Toronto's streets.

Another notable novel is *Cabbagetown* by Hugh Garner, the story of the fight to survive in a Toronto slum in the 1930s. (Cabbagetown was famous as the largest Anglo-Saxon slum in North America.) For those more interested in possible futures than the past, there's an Afrofuturist/sci-fi novel called *Brown Girl in the Ring* by Nalo Hopkinson. Some other books to consider: *Noise* and *How Insensitive* by Russell Smith; *Headhunter* by Timothy Findley; *The Origin of Waves* by Austin Clarke; and *Lost Girls* by Andrew Pyper. (While you're at it, you might want to pick up the Booker Prize–winning *Life of Pi* by Yann Martel and *Martin Sloane* by Michael Redhill; while not set in Toronto, these novels are by local authors.)

If you're interested in architecture, an especially good read is *Emerald City: Toronto Revisited,* by John Bentley Mays. *Emerald City* explores all of Toronto's special places, from the majesty of Casa Loma to the colorful bedlam of Kensington Market. Speaking of craziness, another nonfiction book to check out is *In the Mad Water: Two Centuries of Adventure and Lunacy at Niagara Falls* by T. W. Kriner. Finally, travel writer Jan Morris is always a delight to read, and her book *O Canada! Travels in an Unknown Country* is no exception.

3

Getting to Know Toronto

Toronto is a wonderful city in which to get lost. Start anywhere in the downtown core and walk in any direction for no more than 15 minutes. You'll see eclectic modern buildings side by side with neo-Gothic and Art Deco architecture, catch a fair glimpse of the city's ethnic spectrum, and walk right into a pleasing patch of greenery.

This is a happy coincidence because the layout and organization of the city mean you *will* almost certainly get lost at least once during your stay. Streets have names, not numbers, and they have a crazy-making habit of changing their monikers as they go along. In Midtown, the must-see Avenue Road, for example, turns into Queen's Park Crescent and then into University Avenue as you head south, and into Oriole Parkway if you go north. My best advice: Relax and enjoy the ride. In this chapter, you'll find information on the highways, byways, and services that make Toronto tick.

1 Orientation

ARRIVING
BY PLANE

Most flights arrive at **Pearson International Airport,** in the northwest corner of Metro Toronto, approximately 30 minutes from downtown. The trip usually takes 10 to 15 minutes longer during the weekday morning rush (7–9am) and evening rush (4–7pm). A few (mostly commuter) flights land at the **Toronto Island Airport,** a short ferry ride from downtown.

Pearson serves more than 50 airlines. In 2004 its long-awaited **new terminal** opened up. As promised, it's a beautifully designed space that's light-years away from gloomy **Terminal 1** and ugly **Terminal 2** (© 416/247-7678 for both), the two depressing terminals that it's supposed to replace (as of press time, they were still in use). The other terminal is the **Trillium Terminal 3** (© 416/776-5100). This airy, modern facility has moving walkways, a huge food court, and many retail stores. For general airport information, including the Lost & Found department, call the Greater Toronto Airport Authority at © 416/776-3000 (www.gtaa.com).

To get from the airport to downtown, take Highway 427 south to the Gardiner Expressway East. A **taxi** costs about C$43 (US$30). A slightly sleeker way to go is by flat-rate **limousine,** which costs around C$50 (US$35). Two limo services are **Aaroport** (© 416/745-1555) and **AirLine** (© 905/676-3210). You don't need a reservation. Most first-class hotels run their own **hotel limousine** services; check when you make your reservation.

The convenient **Airport Express bus** (© 905/564-6333) travels between the airport, the bus terminal, and major downtown hotels—the Westin Harbour Castle, Fairmont Royal York, The Sheraton Centre Toronto, and the Delta Chelsea—every 20 minutes, from 4:55am to 12:55am, with one extra run around 2:30am. The adult fare is C$13 (US$9.10) one-way, C$22 (US$15.40) round-trip; children under 11 accompanied by an adult ride free. There is also a **GO Transit bus** (© 416/869-3200) that at press time is picking up passengers at Terminals 1 and 2 and delivering them to the Yorkdale or York Mills subway stations. The fare is only C$3.65 (US$2.60) but be warned—GO buses do not have under-floor luggage compartments. If you're traveling with only a carry-on bag, this bus can be a great option.

The cheapest way to go is by **bus and subway,** which takes about an hour. From Terminal 2, take the no. 58 bus to Lawrence West station, the no. 192 "Airport Rocket" bus to Kipling station, or the no. 307 bus to Eglinton West station. Only the no. 192 bus serves Terminal 3; there are no public buses from Terminal 1 (though there is a shuttle that will drop you off at Terminal 2 or 3). The fare of C$2.25 (US$1.80) includes free transfer to the subway. It doesn't matter which bus you use; they all take roughly the same amount of time. (The Airport Rocket reaches the subway fastest, but the subway ride to downtown is twice as long as from the other stations.) For more information, call the **Toronto Transit Commission,** or TTC (© 416/393-4636).

BY TRAIN

Trains arrive at Union Station on Front Street, 1 block west of Yonge Street, opposite the Fairmont Royal York hotel. The station has direct access to the subway, so you can easily reach any Toronto destination.

VISITOR INFORMATION

For hotel, dining, and other tourist information, head to (or write to) **Tourism Toronto,** 207 Queens Quay W., Suite 590, Toronto, ON M5J 1A7 (© **800/ 363-1990** or 416/203-2600; www.torontotourism.com). It's in the Queen's Quay Terminal at Harbourfront, and is open Monday to Friday from 9am to 5pm. Take the LRT (light rapid transit system) from Union Station to the York Street stop. The website has up-to-the-minute city calendar and events information.

More convenient is the drop-in **Ontario Visitor Information Centre** (© 416/314-5901), in the Eaton Centre, on Yonge Street at Dundas Street. It's on Level 1 (one floor below street level) and is open Monday to Friday from 10am to 9pm, Saturday from 9:30am to 6pm, and Sunday from noon to 5pm. Information is also available online at www.travelinx.com.

PUBLICATIONS & WEBSITES

Toronto has four daily newspapers: the *Globe and Mail,* the *National Post,* the *Toronto Star,* and the *Toronto Sun.* All have some local listings, but the best are in the *Star,* which lists events, concerts, theater performances, first-run films, and the like.

Even better bets are the free weeklies *Now* and *Eye,* both published on Thursday and available in news boxes and at cafes and shops around town. *Xtra!* is another weekly freebie; it lists events, seminars, and performances, particularly those of interest to the gay and lesbian community. A free annual directory called *The Pink Pages* targets Torontonians, but out-of-towners will find the information about gay- and lesbian-friendly restaurants, bars, and other businesses quite useful. It's available at shops, restaurants, and bars along Church Street.

Where Toronto is a glossy monthly magazine that lists events, attractions, restaurants, and shops; it's available free at most hotels in the city and at some restaurants in the Theater District. *Toronto Life* is an award-winning lifestyle

Underground Toronto

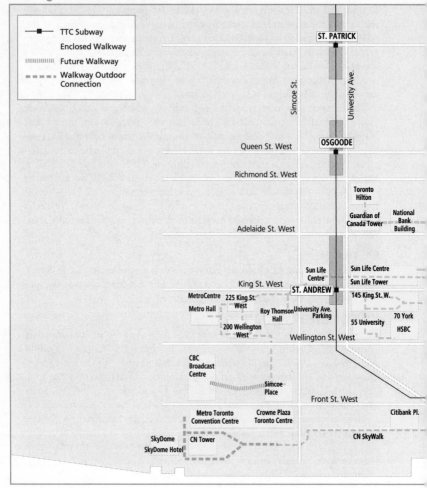

magazine that has excellent listings of kids' events, theater, speeches, and art exhibitions; the April issue contains a dining guide. *Fashion* magazine (formerly *Toronto Life Fashion*) will be of interest to serious shoppers.

Toronto.com (www.toronto.com), operated by the *Toronto Star,* offers extensive restaurant reviews, events listings, and feature articles. *Toronto Life*'s website (www.torontolife.com) is another popular choice, particularly for its restaurant reviews and contests. It includes events, shopping, and services listings.

CITY LAYOUT

Toronto is laid out in a grid . . . with a few interesting exceptions. **Yonge Street** (pronounced *Young*) is the main north-south street, stretching from Lake Ontario in the south well beyond Highway 401 in the north. Yonge Street divides western cross streets from eastern cross streets. The main east-west artery is **Bloor Street,** which cuts through the heart of downtown.

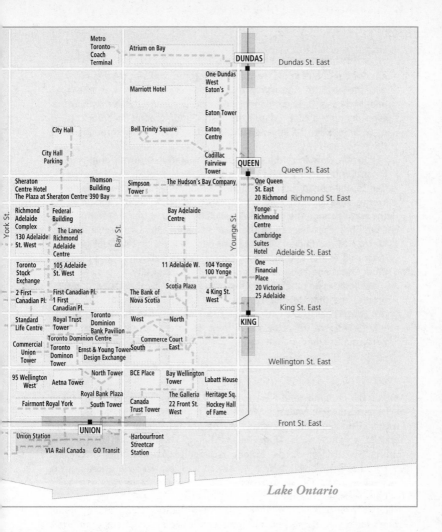

"Downtown" usually refers to the area from Eglinton Avenue south to the lake, between Spadina Avenue in the west and Jarvis Street in the east. Because this is such a large area, I have divided it into five sections. **Downtown West** runs from the lake north to College Street; the eastern boundary is Yonge Street. **Downtown East** goes from the lake north to Carlton Street (once College St. reaches Yonge, it becomes Carlton St.); the western boundary is Yonge Street. **Midtown West** extends from College Street north to Davenport Road; the eastern boundary is Yonge Street. **Midtown East/The East End** runs from Carlton Street north to Davenport and farther east along Danforth Avenue; the western boundary is Yonge Street. **Uptown** is the area north of Davenport Road.

In Downtown West, you'll find many of the lakeshore attractions—Harbourfront, Ontario Place, Fort York, Exhibition Place, and the Toronto Islands. It also boasts the CN Tower, City Hall, SkyDome, Chinatown, the Art Gallery of Ontario, and the Eaton Centre. Downtown East includes the St. Lawrence

Underground Toronto

It is not enough to know the streets of Toronto; you also need to navigate the labyrinth of walkways beneath the pavement. If the weather's bad, you can eat, sleep, dance, shop, and go to the theater without even donning a coat. Consult our map, "Underground Toronto," on p. 42, or look for the large, clear underground PATH maps throughout the concourse.

You can walk from the Dundas subway station south through the Eaton Centre until you hit Queen Street, turn west to the Sheraton Centre, then head south. You'll pass through the Richmond-Adelaide Centre, First Canadian Place, and Toronto Dominion Centre, and go all the way (through the dramatic Royal Bank Plaza) to Union Station. En route, branches lead off to the stock exchange, Sun Life Centre, and Metro Hall. Additional walkways link Simcoe Plaza to 200 Wellington West and to the CBC Broadcast Centre. Other walkways run around Bloor Street and Yonge Street and elsewhere in the city.

While its wide-ranging network makes this an excellent way to get around the downtown core when the weather is grim, the underground city has its own attractions, too. First Canadian Place in particular is known for free lunch-hour lectures, opera and dance performances, and art exhibits.

Market, the Hummingbird Centre, the St. Lawrence Centre for the Arts, and St. James Cathedral. Midtown West contains the Royal Ontario Museum, the Gardiner Museum, the University of Toronto, Markham Village, and chic Yorkville, a prime area for shopping and dining. Midtown East/The East End features Riverdale Farm, the historic Necropolis cemetery, and Greektown. Uptown has traditionally been a residential area, but it's now a fast-growing entertainment area, too. Its attractions include the Sunnybrook park system and the Ontario Science Centre.

North Toronto is another burgeoning area, with theaters, such as the Toronto Centre for the Arts, galleries, and some excellent dining. It's not yet a prime tourist destination, but it gets a few mentions throughout this guide.

Toronto sprawls so widely that quite a few of its primary attractions lie outside the downtown core. They include the Toronto Zoo, Paramount Canada's Wonderland, and the McMichael Canadian Art Collection. To reach these destinations, be prepared for some journeying.

FINDING AN ADDRESS   This isn't as easy as it should be. Your best bet is to call ahead and ask for directions, including landmarks and subway stations. Even the locals need to do this.

THE NEIGHBORHOODS IN BRIEF

Downtown West

The Toronto Islands These three islands in Lake Ontario—Ward's, Algonquin, and Centre—are home to a handful of residents and no cars. They're a spring and summer haven where Torontonians go to in-line skate, bicycle, boat, and picnic.

Centre Island, the most visited, holds the children's theme park Centreville. Catch the ferry at the foot of Bay Street by Queens Quay.

Harbourfront/Lakefront The landfill where the railroad yards and dock facilities once stood is now a glorious playground opening onto the lake. This is home to the Harbourfront Centre, one of the most important literary, artistic, and cultural venues in Canada.

Financial District Toronto's major banks and insurance companies have their headquarters here, from Front Street north to Queen Street, between Yonge and York streets. Toronto's first skyscrapers rose here; fortunately, some of the older structures have been preserved. Ultramodern BCE Place incorporated the facade of a historic bank building into its design.

Theater District An area of dense cultural development, this neighborhood stretches from Front Street north to Queen Street, and from Bay Street west to Bathurst Street. King Street West is home to most of the important sights, including the Royal Alexandra Theatre, the Princess of Wales Theatre, Roy Thomson Hall, and Metro Hall. Farther south are the Convention Centre and the CN Tower.

Chinatown Dundas Street West from University Avenue to Spadina Avenue and north to College Street are the boundaries of Chinatown. As the Chinese community has grown, it has extended along Dundas Street and north along Spadina Avenue. Here you'll see a fascinating mixture of old and new. Hole-in-the-wall restaurants share the sidewalks with glitzy shopping centers built with Hong Kong money.

Queen Street West This stretch from University Avenue to Bathurst Street offers an eclectic mix—

popular mainstream shops, funky boutiques, secondhand bookshops, and vintage-clothing emporiums. It's also home to Toronto's gourmet ghetto, with bistro after trattoria after cafe lining the street. There's excellent food along this strip, but it's too frequently served with heaps of attitude. Despite the intrusion of mega-retailers, many independently owned boutiques flourish.

West Queen West In the past, Queen Street West was considered edgy. Now, that appellation is applied to West Queen West, which starts at Bathurst Avenue and runs west past Ossington Avenue. The neighborhood is now known as one of the coolest places in the city. It's full of interesting boutiques for clothing, housewares, and antiques, excellent small art galleries, and up-and-coming restaurants.

Little Italy This thriving, lively area, filled with open-air cafes, trattorias, and shops, serves the Italian community along College Street between Euclid and Shaw. The trendies can't seem to stay away, which has driven up prices in this once-inexpensive neighborhood.

Downtown East

Old Town/St. Lawrence Market During the 19th century, this area, east of Yonge Street between the Esplanade and Adelaide Street, was the focal point of the community. Today the market's still going strong, and attractions like the glorious St. James Cathedral draw visitors.

The Beaches Communal, youthful, safe, and comfortable—these adjectives best describe the Beaches, just 15 minutes from downtown at the end of the Queen Street East streetcar line. It was a summer resort in the mid-1800s, and its boardwalk and beach continue to make it a casual, family-oriented neighborhood.

Midtown West

Queen's Park and the University Home to the Ontario Legislature and many of the colleges and buildings that make up the University of Toronto, this neighborhood extends from College Street to Bloor Street between Spadina Avenue and Bay Street.

Yorkville Originally a village outside the city, this area north and west of Bloor and Yonge streets became Toronto's Haight-Ashbury in the 1960s. Now, it's a haute district filled with designer boutiques, galleries, cafes, and restaurants.

The Annex This area fell into neglect for many years, but since the early 1980s much of it has been lovingly restored. It stretches from Bedford Road to Bathurst Street, and from Harbord Street to Dupont Avenue. Many of the tremendous turn-of-the-20th-century homes are still single-family dwellings, though as you walk west it segues into the U of T student ghetto. Revered urban-planning guru Jane Jacobs has long called this area home.

Koreatown The bustling blocks along Bloor Street West between Bathurst and Christie streets are filled with Korean restaurants, alternative-medicine practitioners such as herbalists and acupuncturists, and shops filled with made-in-Korea merchandise. One of the first Korean settlements in Toronto, it is now primarily a business district.

Midtown East/The East End

Rosedale Meandering tree-lined streets with elegant homes and manicured lawns are the hallmarks of this residential community, from Yonge and Bloor streets northeast to Castle Frank and the Moore Park Ravine. Named after Sheriff Jarvis's residence, its name is synonymous with Toronto's wealthy elite.

Church Street Between Gerrard Street and Bloor Street East along Church Street lies the heart of Toronto's gay and lesbian community. Restaurants, cafes, and bars fill this relaxed, casual neighborhood. Church Street is where 19th-century Toronto's grandest cathedrals stood.

Cabbagetown Once described by writer Hugh Garner as the largest Anglo-Saxon slum in North America, this gentrified neighborhood of Victorian and Edwardian homes stretches east of Parliament Street to the Don Valley between Gerrard Street and Bloor Street. The sought-after residential district got its name because the front lawns of the homes, occupied by Irish immigrants (who settled here in the late 1800s), were, it is said, covered with row upon row of cabbages. Riverdale, Toronto's only inner-city farm, is at the southeastern end of this district.

Greektown Across the Don Valley Viaduct, Bloor Street becomes the Danforth, which marks the beginning of Greektown. It's lined with old-style Greek tavernas and hip Mediterranean bars and restaurants that are crowded from early evening until early morning. The densest wining-and-dining area starts at Broadview Avenue and runs 6 blocks east.

Uptown

Forest Hill Second to Rosedale as the city's prime residential area, Forest Hill is home to Upper Canada College and Bishop Strachan School for girls. It stretches west of Avenue Road between St. Clair Avenue and Eglinton Avenue.

Eglinton Avenue The neighborhood surrounding the intersection of Yonge Street and Eglinton Avenue is jokingly known as "Young and Eligible." It's a bustling area filled with restaurants— (600-acre) Sunnybrook park system including some of the town's top- and with the Ontario Science rated—and nightclubs. To the east, Centre. it intersects with the 243-hectare

2 Getting Around

BY PUBLIC TRANSPORTATION

The **Toronto Transit Commission,** or TTC (℃ **416/393-4636** for 24-hr. information; recordings available in 18 languages; www.city.toronto.on.ca/ttc), operates the subway, bus, streetcar, and light rapid transit (LRT) system.

Fares, including transfers to buses or streetcars, are C$2.25 (US$1.60) or 10 tickets for C$19 (US$13.30) for adults. Students under 20 and seniors pay C$1.50 (US$1.05) or 10 tickets for C$13 (US$9.10), and children under 12 pay C50¢ (US35¢) or 10 tickets for C$4.25 (US$3). You can buy a special day pass for C$7.75 (US$5.40) that's good for unlimited travel for one person after 9:30am on weekdays, and all day on weekends. There's also a group pass for C$7.75 (US$5.40) that's good for up to six people (a maximum of two adults) anytime on Sunday and statutory holidays only. There are no multiple-day deals.

For surface transportation, you need a ticket, a token, or exact change. You can buy tickets and tokens at subway entrances and at authorized stores that display the sign TTC TICKETS MAY BE PURCHASED HERE. Bus drivers do not sell tickets, nor will they make change. Always obtain a free transfer *where you board the train or bus,* in case you need it. In the subways, use the push-button machine just inside the entrance. On streetcars and buses, ask the driver for a transfer.

THE SUBWAY It's fast (especially when compared to snarled surface traffic), clean, and very simple to use. There are two major lines—Bloor-Danforth and Yonge-University-Spadina—and one smaller line, Sheppard, in the northern part of the city. The Bloor Street east-west line runs from Kipling Avenue in the west to Kennedy Road in the east (where it connects with Scarborough Rapid Transit to Scarborough Centre and McCowan Rd.). The Yonge Street north-south line runs from Finch Avenue in the north to Union Station (Front St.) in the south. From there, it loops north along University Avenue and connects with the Bloor line at the St. George station. A Spadina extension runs north from St. George to Downsview station at Sheppard Avenue. The Sheppard line connects only with the Yonge line at Sheppard Station, and runs east through north Toronto for just 6km (4 miles).

The LRT system connects downtown to Harbourfront. The fare is one ticket or token. It runs from Union Station along Queens Quay to Spadina, with stops at Queens Quay ferry docks, York Street, Simcoe Street, and Rees Street, then continues up Spadina to the Spadina subway station. The transfer from the subway to the LRT (and vice versa) at Union Station is free.

The subway operates Monday to Saturday from 6am to 1:30am, and Sunday from 9am to 1:30am. From 1am to 5:30am, the Blue Night Network operates on basic surface routes. It runs about every 30 minutes. For route information, pick up a "Ride Guide" at subway entrances or call ℃ **416/393-4636.** Multilingual information is available. You can also use the automated information service at ℃ **416/393-8663.**

Smart commuters park their cars at subway terminal stations at Kipling, Islington, Finch, Wilson, Warden, Kennedy, York Mills, Victoria Park, and

Keele. Certain conditions apply. Call ✆ **416/393-8663** for details. You'll have to get there very early.

BUSES & STREETCARS Where the subway leaves off, buses and streetcars take over. They run east-west and north-south along the city's arteries. When you pay your fare (on bus, streetcar, or subway), always pick up a transfer so that you won't have to pay again if you want to transfer to another mode of transportation. For complete TTC information, call ✆ **416/393-4636.**

BY TAXI

As usual, this is an expensive mode of transportation. It's C$2.75 (US$1.90) the minute you step in, and C$1.32 (US90¢) for each additional kilometer. Fares can quickly mount up. You can hail a cab on the street, find one in line in front of a big hotel, or call one of the major companies—**Diamond** (✆ **416/ 366-6868**), **Royal** (✆ **416/777-9222**), or **Metro** (✆ **416/504-8294**). If you experience problems with cab service, call the **Metro Licensing Commission** (✆ **416/392-3082**).

BY CAR

Toronto is a rambling city, but that doesn't mean that a car is the best way to get around. Toronto has the dubious distinction of being recognized as the worst city in Canada in which to drive. It has gotten so bad that the government has started monitoring certain intersections with cameras, some especially designed to catch cars running red lights, which have been sarcastically dubbed "red light districts."

Humor aside, driving can be a frustrating experience because of the high volume of traffic, drivers' disregard for red lights, and meager but pricey parking options. This is particularly true downtown, where traffic inches along and parking lots are scarce. I strongly recommend that you avoid driving in the city.

RENTAL CARS If you decide to rent a car, try to make arrangements in advance. Companies with outlets at Pearson International Airport include **Thrifty** (✆ 800/367-2277), **Budget** (✆ 800/527-0700), **Avis** (✆ 800/ 331-1084), **Hertz** (✆ 800/654-3001), **National** (✆ 800/227-7368), and **Enterprise** (✆ 800/736-8222). Keep in mind that there's usually a steep fee when you rent a vehicle in one city and drop it off in another. The rental fee depends on the type of car you want, but the starting point is around C$50 (US$35) a day—not including the 15% in sales taxes. This also does not include insurance; if you pay with a particular credit card, you might get automatic coverage (check with your credit card issuer before you go). Be sure to read the fine print of the rental agreement—some companies add conditions that will boost your bill if you don't fulfill certain obligations, like filling the gas tank before returning the car. *Note:* If you're under 25, check with the company—many will rent on a cash-only basis, some only with a credit card, and others will not rent to you at all.

Car-rental insurance probably does not cover liability if you cause an accident. Check your own auto insurance policy, the rental company policy, and your credit card coverage for the extent of coverage: Is your destination covered? Are other drivers covered? How much liability is covered if a passenger is injured? (If you rely on your credit card for coverage, you may want to bring a second credit card with you, as damages may be charged to your card and you may find yourself stranded with no money.)

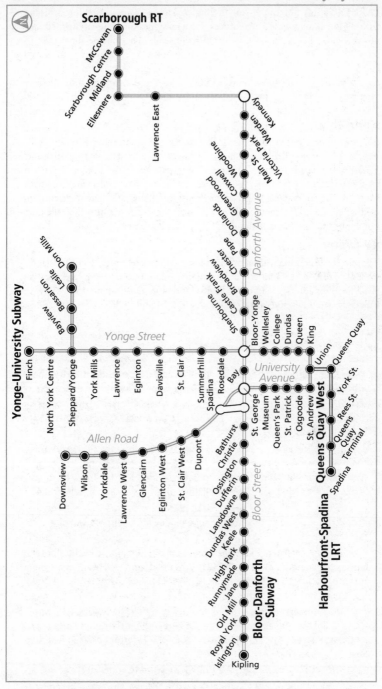

Scarborough RT

McCowan
Scarborough Centre
Midland
Ellesmere
Lawrence East
Kennedy
Warden
Victoria Park
Main St.
Woodbine
Coxwell
Greenwood
Donlands
Pape
Chester
Broadview
Castle Frank
Sherbourne

Danforth Avenue

Bloor-Yonge
Wellesley
College
Dundas
Queen
King
Union
Queens Quay

University Avenue

St. George
Museum
Queen's Park
St. Patrick
Osgoode
St. Andrew

Queens Quay West

York St.
Rees St.
Queens
Quay
Terminal
Spadina

Harbourfront-Spadina LRT

Yonge-University Subway

Don Mills
Leslie
Bessarion
Bayview

Finch
North York Centre
Sheppard/Yonge
York Mills
Lawrence
Eglinton
Davisville
St. Clair
Summerhill
Rosedale
Spadina
Bay

Yonge Street

Allen Road

Downsview
Wilson
Yorkdale
Lawrence West
Glencairn
Eglinton West
St. Clair West
Dupont
Bathurst
Christie
Ossington
Dufferin
Lansdowne
Dundas West
Keele
High Park
Runnymede
Jane
Old Mill
Royal York
Islington
Kipling

Bloor Street

Bloor-Danforth Subway

PARKING   It's not much fun finding parking in downtown Toronto, and parking lots have a wide range of fees. Generally speaking, the city-owned lots, marked with a big green "P," are the most affordable. They charge about C$1.75 to C$2.50 (US$1.20–US$1.75) per half-hour, with a C$15 to C$20 (US$10.50–US$14) maximum between 7am and 6pm. After 6pm and on Sunday, rates drop to around C$8 (US$5.60). Observe the parking restrictions— otherwise the city will tow your car away, and it'll cost more than C$100 (US$70) to get it back.

DRIVING RULES   A right turn at a red light is permitted after coming to a full stop, unless posted otherwise. The driver and front-seat passengers must wear seat belts; if you're caught not wearing one, you'll incur a substantial fine. The speed limit in the city is 50kmph (31 mph). You must stop at pedestrian crosswalks. If you are following a streetcar and it stops, you must stop well back from the rear doors so passengers can exit easily and safely. (Where there are concrete safety islands in the middle of the street for streetcar stops, this rule does not apply, but exercise care nonetheless.) Radar detectors are illegal.

BY FERRY

Toronto Parks and Recreation operates ferries that travel to the Toronto Islands. Call ✆ **416/392-8193** for schedules and information. Round-trip fares are C$6 (US$4.20) for adults, C$3.50 (US$2.45) for seniors and students 15 to 19 (with valid ID), and C$2.50 (US$1.75) for children 14 and under.

FAST FACTS: **Toronto**

Area Code   Toronto's area codes are **416** and **647**; outside the city, the code is **905** or **289**. You must dial all 10 digits for all local phone numbers.

Babysitting   Hotel concierges can suggest reliable sitters if there aren't child-care facilities on site. In a pinch, call **Care-on-Call** (✆ **416/975-1313**), a 24-hour service.

Business Hours   Banks are generally open Monday through Thursday from 10am to 3pm, Friday 10am to 6pm. Most stores are open Monday through Wednesday from 10am to 6pm and Saturday and Sunday from 10am to 5pm, with extended hours (until 8–9:30pm) on Thursday and usually Friday.

Currency Exchange   Generally, the best place to exchange your currency is at an ATM or bank. You can also change money at the airport, but at a less favorable rate.

Dentists   For emergency services from 8am till midnight, call the **Dental Emergency Service** (✆ **416/485-7121**). After midnight, your best bet is the **Toronto Hospital**, 200 Elizabeth St. (✆ **416/340-3948**). Otherwise, ask the front-desk staff or concierge at your hotel.

Doctors   The staff or concierge at your hotel should be able to help you locate a doctor. You can also call the **College of Physicians and Surgeons,** 80 College St. (✆ **416/967-2600**, ext. 626), for a referral between 9am to 5pm. See also "Emergencies," below.

Electricity   It's the same as in the United States—110 volts, 50 cycles, AC.

Embassies & Consulates   All embassies are in Ottawa, the national capital. They include the **Australian High Commission,** 50 O'Connor St., Suite 710,

Ottawa, ON K1P 6L2 (℃ 613/236-0841); the **British High Commission,** 80 Elgin St., Ottawa, ON K1P 5K7 (℃ 613/237-1530); the **Irish Embassy,** 130 Albert St., Ottawa, ON K1P 5G4 (℃ 613/233-6281); the **New Zealand High Commission,** 727–99 Bank St., Ottawa, ON K1P 6G3 (℃ 613/ 238-5991); the **South African High Commission,** 15 Sussex Dr., Ottawa, ON K1M 1M8 (℃ 613/744-0330); and the **U.S. Embassy,** 100 Wellington St., Ottawa, ON K1P 5T1 (℃ 613/238-4470). Consulates in Toronto include **Australian Consulate-General,** 175 Bloor St. E., Suite 314, at Church Street (℃ 416/323-1155); **British Consulate-General,** 777 Bay St., Suite 2800, at College (℃ 416/593-1290); and the **U.S. Consulate,** 360 University Ave. (℃ 416/595-1700).

Emergencies Call ℃ **911** for fire, police, or ambulance. The **Toronto General Hospital,** 200 Elizabeth St., provides 24-hour emergency service (℃ **416/340-3946** for emergency or 416/340-4611 for information). Also see "Hospitals," below.

Hospitals In the downtown core, go to **Toronto General,** 200 Elizabeth St. (℃ **416/340-4611,** or 416/340-3946 for emergency); **St. Michael's,** 30 Bond St. (℃ **416/360-4000,** or 416/864-5094 for emergency); or **Mount Sinai,** 600 University Ave. (℃ **416/596-4200,** or 416/586-5054 for emergency). Also downtown is the **Hospital for Sick Children,** 555 University Ave. (℃ **416/813-1500**). Uptown, there's **Sunnybrook Hospital,** 2075 Bayview Ave., north of Eglinton (℃ **416/480-6100,** or 416/480-4207 for emergency). In the eastern part of the city, go to **Toronto East General Hospital,** 825 Coxwell Ave. (℃ **416/461-8272,** or 416/469-6435 for emergency).

Hot Lines **Poison Information Centre** (℃ 416/813-5900); **Distress Centre** suicide prevention line (℃ 416/598-1121); **Rape Crisis Line** (℃ 416/ 597-8808); **Assaulted Women's Help Line** (℃ 416/863-0511); **AIDS & Sexual Health InfoLine** (℃ 800/668-2437); **Toronto Prayer Line** (℃ 416/ 929-1500). For kids or teens in distress, there's **Kids Help Phone** (℃ 800/ 668-6868).

Internet Access As in most other North American cities, the Web is a social magnet in Toronto. **Insomnia,** 563 Bloor St. W. (℃ **416/588-3907**), is more social than your average Net cafe—maybe it's the sign over the door that reads THE INTERNET IS A STRANGE PLACE. DON'T SURF ALONE. There are several curtained computer terminals (C$10/US$7 per hour), as well as comfortable couches and a big-screen TV. The pizza and panini are usually pretty good. Open daily from noon to 1am.

If you just want to surf fast and not hang out, look for a Kinko's. There are several in the city, but one sure bet is the location at 505 University Ave., at Dundas (℃ **416/970-8447**).

Laundry & Dry Cleaning **Bloor Laundromat,** 598 Bloor St. W., at Bathurst Street (℃ **416/588-6600**), is conveniently located. At the **Laundry Lounge,** 531 Yonge St., at Wellesley Street (℃ **416/975-4747**), you can do your wash while sipping a cappuccino and watching TV in the lounge. It's open daily from 7am to 11pm. **Careful Hand Laundry & Dry Cleaners Ltd.** has outlets at 195 Davenport Rd. (℃ **416/923-1200**), 1415 Bathurst St. (℃ **416/ 530-1116**), and 1844 Avenue Rd. (℃ **416/787-6006**); for pickup and delivery, call ℃ **416/787-6006.**

Liquor Laws The minimum drinking age is 19. Drinking hours are daily from 11am to 2am. The government is the only retail vendor. **Liquor Control Board of Ontario (LCBO)** stores sell liquor, wine, and some beers. They're open Monday through Saturday. Most are open from 10am to 6pm; some stay open evenings, and a few are open Sunday from noon to 5pm. One of the very best is at the **Manulife Centre,** 55 Bloor St. W. (© 416/925-5266), which has longer hours than most, opening at 9:30am and closing at 9pm Monday through Saturday, and noon to 5pm on Sunday.

The **Wine Rack** has several locations, including 77 Wellesley St. E., at Church (© 416/923-9393), and sells only Ontario wines. Most branches of the **Beer Store** (also part of the LCBO) are open Monday through Saturday from 10am to 8pm; there's a downtown location at 614 Queen St. W. (© 416/504-4665), near Bathurst.

Lost Property If you leave something on a bus, a streetcar, or the subway, call the **TTC Lost Articles Office** (© 416/393-4100) at the Bay Street subway station. It's open Monday through Friday from 8am to 5pm.

Luggage Storage & Lockers Lockers are available at Union Station and at the Eaton Centre.

Mail Postage for letter mail (up to 30 grams/about 1 ounce) to the United States costs C80¢ (US56¢); overseas, C$1.40 (US98¢). Mailing letters within Canada costs C49¢ (US34¢). Note that there is no discounted rate for mailing postcards.

Postal services are available at convenience and drug stores. Almost all sell stamps, and many have a separate counter where you can ship packages from 8:30am to 5pm. Look for the sign in the window indicating such services. There are also post office windows in **Atrium on Bay** (© 416/506-0911), in **Commerce Court** (© 416/956-7452), and at the **TD Centre** (© 416/360-7105).

Maps Free maps of Toronto are available in every terminal at **Pearson International Airport** (look for the Transport Canada Information Centre signs), the Metropolitan Toronto Convention & Visitors Association at **Harbourfront,** and the Visitor Information Centre in the **Eaton Centre.** Convenience stores and bookstores sell a greater variety of maps. Or try **Canada Map Company,** 63 Adelaide E., between Yonge and Church streets (© 416/362-9297), or **Open Air Books and Maps,** 25 Toronto St., near Yonge and Adelaide streets (© 416/363-0719).

Newspapers & Magazines The four daily newspapers are the *Globe and Mail,* the *National Post,* the *Toronto Star,* and the *Toronto Sun. Eye* and *Now* are free arts-and-entertainment weeklies. *Xtra!* is a free weekly targeted at the gay and lesbian community. In addition, many English-language ethnic newspapers serve Toronto's Portuguese, Hungarian, Italian, East Indian, Korean, Chinese, and Caribbean communities. *Toronto Life* is the major monthly city magazine; its sister publication is *Toronto Life Fashion. Where Toronto* is usually free at hotels and some Theater District restaurants.

Pharmacies One big chain is **Pharma Plus,** which has a store at 63 Wellesley St., at Church Street (© 416/924-7760). It's open daily from 8am to midnight. Other Pharma Plus branches are in College Park, Manulife Centre, Commerce Court, and First Canadian Place. The only 24-hour drugstore near downtown is **Shopper's Drug Mart** at 700 Bay St., at Gerrard Street West (🕻 **416/979-2424**).

Police   In a life-threatening emergency, call 🕻 **911.** For all other matters, contact the **Metro police,** 40 College St. ((🕻 **416/808-2222**).

Post Office   See "Mail," above.

Radio   The Canadian Broadcasting Corporation offers a great mix of intelligent discussion and commentary as well as drama and music. In Toronto, the **CBC** broadcasts on 99.1FM and 94.1FM. **CHIN** (1540AM and 100.7FM) will get you in touch with the ethnic and multicultural scene in the city; it broadcasts in more than 30 languages.

Restrooms   Finding a public restroom is usually not difficult. Most tourist attractions have them, as do hotels, department stores, and public buildings. There are restrooms at major subway stations such as Yonge/Bloor, but they are best avoided.

Safety   As large cities go, Toronto is generally safe, but be alert and use common sense, particularly at night. The Yonge/Bloor, Dundas, and Union subway stations are favorites with pickpockets. In the downtown area, Moss Park is considered one of the toughest areas to police. Avoid Allan Gardens and other parks at night.

Taxes   The provincial retail sales tax is 8%; on accommodations it's 5%. There is an additional 7% national goods-and-services tax (GST).

In general, nonresidents may apply for a tax refund. They can recover the accommodations tax, the sales tax, and the GST for nondisposable merchandise that will be exported for use, provided it is removed from Canada within 60 days of purchase. The following do not qualify for rebate: meals and restaurant charges, alcohol, tobacco, gas, car rentals, and such services as dry cleaning and shoe repair.

The quickest and easiest way to secure the refund is to stop at a duty-free shop at the border. You must have proper receipts with GST registration numbers. Or you can apply through the mail, but it will take about 4 weeks to receive your refund. For information, you can contact the **Visitor Rebate Program** Enquiries Line at 🕻 **800/668-4748**. You can also get information and an application form online at www.cra-arc.gc.ca/visitors. The forms are also available at tourism kiosks around town and in some shops.

Taxis   See "Getting Around," earlier in this chapter.

Telephone   A local call from a telephone booth costs C25¢ (US18¢). Watch out for hotel surcharges on local and long-distance calls; often a local call will cost at least C$1 (US70¢) from a hotel room. The United States and Canada are on the same long-distance system. To make a long-distance call between the United States and Canada, use the area codes as you would at home. Canada's international prefix is **1.**

Time   Toronto is on Eastern Standard Time. Daylight saving time is in effect from April to October.

Tipping   Basically it's the same as in major U.S. cities: 15% in restaurants (up to 20% in the finer spots), 10% to 15% for taxis, C$1 (US70¢) per bag for porters, C$1 to C$2 (US70¢–US$1.40) per day for hotel housekeepers (more if you're traveling with messy kids and/or pets).

Transit Information For information on the subway, bus, streetcar, and light rapid transit (LRT) system, call the TTC at © **416/393-4636** or check www.city.toronto.on.ca/ttc.

Weather Call the **talking yellow pages** (© **416/292-1010**) for a current weather report and lots of other information. Or check the *Toronto Star*'s website, **www.thestar.com**.

Where to Stay

Whether you're seeking a historic hotel with old-world elegance or looking for all the conveniences of the office in your "home" away from home, you'll find a perfect place to stay in Toronto. The city's accommodations run the gamut of everything from the intimacy of boutique inns to the large-scale comfort of convention hotels.

Wherever you stay, make sure to get the best deal you can. Proximity to major attractions, such as the Harbourfront Centre, SkyDome, and the Eaton Centre, can cost a bundle. Even budget hotels may charge more than C$100 (US$70) a night in the high season, which runs from April to October. And remember to factor the 5% accommodations tax and the 7% GST into what you spend (note that if you're not a Canadian resident, you can get a tax refund on the GST; see "Fast Facts: Toronto" in chapter 3 for details).

There are some guidelines to keep in mind when booking your accommodations. First, always ask for a discount when you make a reservation. Even the most expensive luxury hotel will reduce its rates during the low season and on weekends, and sometimes simply because the hotel isn't full. This discount can be anywhere from 20% to 50%—after all, having a guest pay a reduced rate is preferable to having an empty room that generates no revenue.

Don't be shy—always ask for a deal. Remember, if you belong to a group (such as the military, seniors, students, or an auto club) you'll often qualify for an automatic discount as long as you have appropriate ID. Members of frequent-flyer clubs may qualify for discounts, room upgrades, or other perks—if they ask for them. A hotel may offer special packages, which might include theater tickets, meals, or museum passes with the cost of your accommodations. At the risk of sounding like a broken record, I'll say it again: Always ask for a deal!

Before you make a reservation, it's important to have some sense of what you'd like to see and do in town. Toronto is a sprawling metropolis, with attractions, dining districts, and ethnic communities scattered throughout. Keep in mind that you want to be as close as possible to the sights that interest you most.

I have grouped accommodations by price and location. Most are in the neighborhoods defined in chapter 3 as Downtown West, Downtown East, Midtown West, Uptown, and Midtown East/The East End. I've also included a few hotels to the east of the city and close to Pearson International Airport.

TWO IMPORTANT NOTES ON PRICES The prices quoted in this chapter are rack rates; discounts can knock the price down as much as 50%. The 5% accommodations tax and the 7% GST are refunded to nonresidents upon application (see "Taxes" under "Fast Facts: Toronto," in chapter 3).

A NOTE TO NONSMOKERS Hotels that reserve floors for nonsmokers are now commonplace, so we don't single them out in this guide.

However, people who want a smoke-free room should make that clear when making a reservation. Rooms for smokers are concentrated on particular floors, and the rooms and even the hallways in those areas tend to smell strongly of tobacco, even in the cleanest hotels. Never assume that you'll get a smoke-free room if you don't specifically request one.

BED & BREAKFASTS   A B&B can be an excellent—and relatively inexpensive—alternative to standard hotel accommodations. **Toronto Bed & Breakfast,** 253 College St., P.O. Box 269, Toronto, ON M5T 1R5 (© **877/ 922-6522** or 416/588-8800; www. torontobandb.com), has a short but wide-ranging list of accommodations in the city. Doubles cost roughly C$75 to C$125 (US$53–US$88). The organization will make your reservation and send you a confirmation. The **Downtown Association of Bed-and-Breakfast Guest Houses,** P.O. Box 190, Station B, Toronto, ON M5T 2W1 (© **416/368-1420;** www. bnbinfo.com), lists only nonsmoking B&Bs. Doubles range from C$70 to C$130 (US$49–US$91). **Bed and Breakfast Canada,** P.O. Box 46093, College Park Post Office, 44 Yonge St., Toronto, ON M5B 2L8 (© **416/ 363-6362;** www.bbcanada.com), has a very long list of independent B&B operators. Doubles run from about C$65 to C$130 (US$46–US$91).

ACCOMMODATIONS SERVICES If you're having trouble finding a hotel, call **Tourism Toronto** (© **800/ 363-1990** or 416/203-2600), or visit the website at www.torontotourism. com for advice and special deals.

FOR TRAVELERS IN NEED   If you run into trouble in Toronto and you need a place to stay, call the **Travellers Aid Society of Toronto** (© **416/ 366-7788**). The organization provides shelter for people in crisis situations.

1 Downtown West

VERY EXPENSIVE

Hilton Toronto ★★   The Hilton Toronto isn't what it used to be—and that's a good thing. A few years ago the company splurged on a C$25-million (US$18-million) facelift, and suddenly the Hilton was one of the most attractive large hotels in the city. On the western edge of the Financial District, the 32-story Hilton boasts generously sized rooms decorated with streamlined luxury in mind. Because of the hotel's excellent location overlooking the wide boulevard of University Avenue, many rooms (and the glass elevators) have superb vistas. Because of its proximity to the Financial District, the Hilton is a favorite among business travelers. Executive rooms include perks such as an ultraplush terry bathrobe, a trouser press, and access to a private lounge that serves complimentary breakfast and evening snacks.

The Hilton is more cutting-edge than you'd expect from a business hotel, making it a sophisticated choice. The design of the grand foyer is dramatic, with an illuminated canopy, floor lights and backlights, and copious use of glass. There are photographic art exhibits on the public floors. Last but not least, as part of its renovation, the Hilton unveiled the magnificent Tundra, which serves top-notch Canadian cuisine (review on p. 88).

145 Richmond St. W., Toronto, ON M5H 2L2. © **800/445-8667** or 416/869-3456. Fax 416/869-1478. www.toronto.hilton.com. 601 units. C$269–C$449 (US$188–US$314) double. Extra person C$22 (US$15). Children 18 and under stay free in parent's room. Weekend packages available. AE, DC, MC, V. Parking C$22 (US$15). Subway: Osgoode. **Amenities:** 3 restaurants; bar; indoor and outdoor lap pools; health club; Jacuzzi; sauna; children's programs; concierge; business center; 24-hr. room service; massage; babysitting; same-day laundry service/dry cleaning. *In room:* A/C, TV, dataport, minibar, coffeemaker, hair dryer, iron.

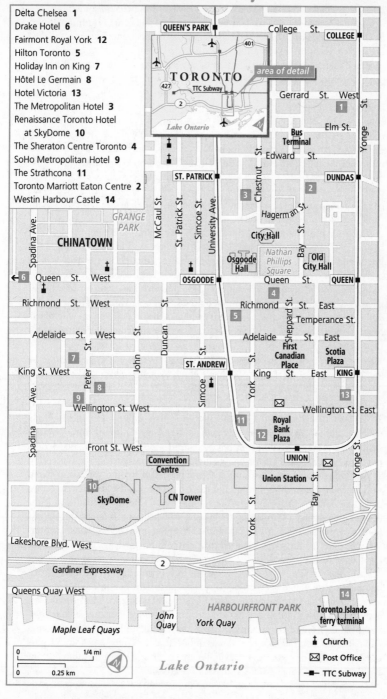

Delta Chelsea **1**
Drake Hotel **6**
Fairmont Royal York **12**
Hilton Toronto **5**
Holiday Inn on King **7**
Hôtel Le Germain **8**
Hotel Victoria **13**
The Metropolitan Hotel **3**
Renaissance Toronto Hotel
  at SkyDome **10**
The Sheraton Centre Toronto **4**
SoHo Metropolitan Hotel **9**
The Strathcona **11**
Toronto Marriott Eaton Centre **2**
Westin Harbour Castle **14**

TORONTO

TTC Subway

Lake Ontario

area of detail

QUEEN'S PARK

COLLEGE

College St.

Gerrard St. West

Elm St.

Bus Terminal

Edward St.

ST. PATRICK

DUNDAS

Chestnut St.

Hagerman St.

GRANGE PARK

McCaul St.

St. Patrick St.

Simcoe St.

University Ave.

City Hall

CHINATOWN

Spadina Ave.

Osgoode Hall

Nathan Phillips Square

Old City Hall

Queen St. West

OSGOODE

Queen St.

QUEEN

Richmond St. West

Richmond St. East

Sheppard St.

Temperance St.

Adelaide St. West

Duncan St.

Adelaide St. East

First Canadian Place

Scotia Plaza

King St. West

Peter St.

John St.

ST. ANDREW

Simcoe St.

King St. East

KING

Wellington St. West

York St.

Wellington St. East

Spadina Ave.

Front St. West

Royal Bank Plaza

UNION

Convention Centre

Union Station

Bay St.

SkyDome

CN Tower

York St.

Yonge St.

Lakeshore Blvd. West

Gardiner Expressway

Queens Quay West

HARBOURFRONT PARK

Toronto Islands ferry terminal

John Quay

York Quay

Maple Leaf Quays

Church
Post Office
TTC Subway

0   1/4 mi
0   0.25 km

Lake Ontario

Yonge St.

Hôtel Le Germain ★★ The Groupe Germain has become something of a legend in Québec for its excellent boutique hotels. Their first Toronto venture has been eagerly anticipated, and in spring 2003 it opened to instant accolades. Located in Toronto's Entertainment District, the Hôtel Le Germain has an elegant but slightly offbeat sensibility. Its design is edgier than what you'll find in other Toronto hotels. The public spaces are magnificent: The vast lobby manages the amazing trick of being at once intimate and grand. The library lounge area boasts a fireplace, an espresso maker, a wall of objets d'art, and cozy white couches. The breakfast "room" on the second floor is like an expansive landing (there's a staircase that leads down from here to the lobby), and the tables are all communal. Attention is paid to the smallest details, which explains why the elevators are "wrapped" in words of English and French poetry, and why the corridors are so broad (the Groupe Germain built this hotel from scratch, so they could do exactly as they pleased). Luce, the hotel's restaurant (pronounced "lu-chay"—Italian for light) is operated by the same people as the hip eatery Rain (p. 91), which is across the street.

The guest rooms are beautifully designed: The ceilings are high, the desk can be moved around to your liking (it's attached to the wall on one side), and the linens and robes are by Frette. My favorite feature, though, is the glass wall in every bathroom, which allows light in from the main room and makes everything feel more spacious (there are blinds for those who want their privacy). All guests have access to the exercise room on the 11th floor, which has floor-to-ceiling windows and an open-air terrace. The hotel will also pair you up with a personal trainer or arrange for an in-room massage for you (there are extra fees for these services).

30 Mercer St., Toronto, ON M5V 1H3. ℂ **866/345-9501** or 416/345-9500. Fax 416/345-9501. www.germain toronto.com. 122 units. From C$225 (US$158) double. AE, DC, MC, V. Parking C$25 (US$18). Subway: St. Andrew. **Amenities:** Restaurant; bar; health club; concierge; business center; 24-hr. room service; laundry service; dry cleaning. *In room:* A/C, TV, dataport, minibar, coffeemaker, hair dryer, iron, safe.

SoHo Metropolitan Hotel ★★★ I'm a huge fan of The Metropolitan Hotel (below), and so I've been anxiously awaiting the latest Toronto venture by this small hotel group. This gorgeous boutique hotel—opened in April 2003—does not disappoint. This is grown-up elegance at its most refined.

The guest rooms are beautiful: A serene palette of neutral tones and blond wood make for a soothing setting. But more importantly, the SoHo Met's rooms make the best use of technology I've found in any Toronto hotel. It's as if the designers compiled a list of all of the most frustrating aspects about staying in a hotel room and resolved to fix them. Hate hopping into bed and then discovering you have to jump out again to turn out a light? Switches adjacent to the headboard can control all of the lights in the room. Hate opening and closing curtains and drapes? All it takes here is the flick of another switch. Even better, another control will lower a privacy screen that lets light in but shields you from view. The marble bathroom floor heats up at your command. The in-room safe is big enough for a laptop and has an outlet inside so you can charge your computer battery. There are no tatty DO NOT DISTURB signs; instead, another control panel lets you indicate your desire to be left alone or request housekeeping as need be. And of course the telephones are cordless (it's a small thing but one I wish that other hotels would understand is important).

The SoHo Met is also home to one of Toronto's best restaurants, Senses (p. 91). It's appropriately named, because all of your senses will be charmed by this property. This is an excellent choice for both business and leisure travelers;

the only people I wouldn't recommend this property for are those with kids in tow, as it's a very glamorous spot for grown-ups.

318 Wellington St. W., Toronto, ON M5V 3T4. © **800/668-6600** or 416/599-8800. Fax 416/599-8801. www.metropolitan.com/soho. 86 units. From C$295 (US$207) double. AE, DC, MC, V. Valet parking C$15 (US$11), self-parking C$10 (US$7). Subway: St. Andrew. **Amenities:** Restaurant; bar; health club; concierge; business center; 24-hr. room service; laundry service; dry cleaning. *In room:* A/C, TV, dataport, minibar, coffeemaker, hair dryer, iron, safe.

EXPENSIVE

Fairmont Royal York ★★   Looming across from Union Station, Toronto's hub for rail travel, is the Fairmont Royal York, a historic hotel built by the Canadian-Pacific Railroad in 1929. Fairmont hotels across the country tend to the gigantic, and this one is no exception, with 1,365 guest rooms and suites, and 35 meeting and banquet rooms.

The old-fashioned lobby is magnificent, and just sitting on a plush couch and watching the crowd is an event. Still, you have to decide whether you want to stay under the same roof with more than 1,000 others—business travelers, shoppers, tour groups, and conventioneers. Service is remarkably efficient but necessarily impersonal; the downtown location, just steps from the Entertainment District and the Hummingbird Centre, is excellent.

The guest rooms are furnished with charming antique reproductions. Some are reasonably airy, but there's generally not much spare space. If you're willing to spring for a Fairmont Gold room (the extra cost is well worth it, in my opinion), you'll stay on a private floor with superior, spacious rooms, separate check-in and concierge, a private lounge, and complimentary breakfast.

If you're interested in pampering yourself, ask about special spa packages—the Elizabeth Milan Day Spa, in the shopping arcade, is one of the best in the city. Among the multitude of dining and drinking spots in the hotel, the don't-miss ones are Epic (p. 89) and the Library Bar, which serves the best martinis in the city.

Travelers who won't leave home without Fido, fear not: Fairmont has a VIP (Very Important Pets) program. For an extra C$30 (US$21) per night, guests and their furry friends can stay in a special "dog-friendly" room that comes with toys, treats, and other amenities. (Part of the extra fee is donated to the Toronto Humane Society.)

The hotel pays particular attention to accessibility, making adaptations to some guest rooms, so that they are specially designed for wheelchair users, the hearing impaired, and the visually impaired. And Fairmont completed renovations in 2003 that made every public area in the hotel wheelchair-accessible.

100 Front St. W., Toronto, ON M5J 1E3. © **800/441-1414.** Fax 416/368-9040. www.fairmont.com/royalyork. 1,365 units. C$175–C$370 (US$123–US$259) double. Packages available. AE, DC, DISC, MC, V. Parking C$26 (US$18). Subway: Union. Pets accepted. **Amenities:** 5 restaurants; 4 bars/lounges; skylit indoor pool; health club; spa (with special packages for guests); Jacuzzi; sauna; concierge; car-rental desk; business center; shopping arcade; salon; 24-hr. room service; babysitting; same-day laundry service/dry cleaning. *In room:* A/C, TV, dataport, minibar, coffeemaker, hair dryer, iron.

The Metropolitan Hotel ★★★   One of the few major hotels in Toronto that isn't part of a large chain, the Metropolitan prides itself on offering a boutique atmosphere (for the group's new and genuine boutique hotel, see the SoHo Met review above). The hotel caters to a business-oriented clientele, and it offers many of the same features and amenities as its competitors at a comparatively lower cost (which is not to say it's inexpensive, just very competitive). Just off Dundas Street West, the hotel is a 5-minute stroll north of the business district and about 2 minutes west of the Eaton Centre. But why walk when you can take advantage of the complimentary limo service to any downtown core address?

That perk is just one of the ways in which the Metropolitan attempts to compete with its pricier competitors. Rooms are spacious and furnished with comfort in mind. The luxury and executive suites boast Jacuzzis, Dolby Surround Sound televisions, and CD players. Many rooms also feature two-line cordless phones.

The two restaurants are huge draws. Lai Wah Heen (p. 90), which serves classic Cantonese cuisine, is a top choice for business entertaining with natives as well as visitors. The modern-style ground-floor Hemispheres restaurant offers a Continental menu. Also, the Metropolitan has a partnership with the Toronto Symphony Orchestra, which offers guests special packages.

108 Chestnut St., Toronto, ON M5G 1R3. 𝒞 416/977-5000. Fax 416/977-9513. www.metropolitan.com. 426 units. C$280–C$310 (US$196–US$217) double. Children 17 and under stay free in parent's room. AE, DC, DISC, MC, V. Valet parking C$24 (US$17), self-parking C$19 (US$13). Subway: St. Patrick. **Amenities:** 2 restaurants; bar; indoor pool; health club; Jacuzzi; sauna; concierge; courtesy limo; 24-hr. business center (w/PCs and Macs); limited room service; massage; babysitting; same-day laundry service/dry cleaning. *In room:* A/C, TV, dataport, minibar, coffeemaker, hair dryer, iron, safe.

Renaissance Toronto Hotel at SkyDome
A while ago, I was traveling and met a woman who had just visited Toronto. I asked where she'd stayed, and she told me that it was at "that hotel where they filmed people having sex and put it on a big screen." This is *that* hotel. It's a dream come true for diehard baseball fans—70 rooms overlook the diamond's verdant Astroturf. Unfortunately, those who enjoy the view should remember that it goes both ways: Just after it opened, the hotel became notorious when the amorous antics of a pair of guests ended up on the JumboTron (the giant screen that's supposed to be showing the on-field action). The incident is now a minor local legend. The lesson: All rooms have shades—remember to use them.

The guest rooms are pretty much all a good size, but there's a definite pecking order: Rooms that face the city are the least expensive, with uninspiring views. Still, this is a strong contender as a tourist hotel—it's in a great location for theater, dining, and sights.

1 Blue Jays Way, Toronto, ON M5V 1J4. 𝒞 **800/237-1512** or 416/341-7100. Fax 416/341-5091. www. renaissancehotels.com/yyzbr. 348 units. City view from C$200 (US$140) double; field side from C$305 (US$214) double. AE, DC, DISC, MC, V. Parking C$25 (US$18). Subway: Union. **Amenities:** Restaurant; bar; indoor pool; squash courts; health club; sauna; concierge; business center; 24-hr. room service; same-day laundry service/dry cleaning. *In room:* A/C, TV, dataport, coffeemaker, hair dryer, iron.

The Sheraton Centre Toronto ⋆⋆ *Kids*
A convention favorite, the Sheraton is across the street from New City Hall, a block from the Eaton Centre, and a short stroll from the trendy restaurant and boutique area of Queen Street West. It's entirely possible to stay here and never venture outside—the Sheraton complex includes restaurants, bars, and a cinema, and the building connects to Toronto's fabled underground city. If you long for a patch of green, the hotel provides that, too: The south side of the lobby contains a manicured garden with a waterfall. Am I making the place sound like a monolith? Well, it is. But it's an excellent home base for families because of its location and extensive list of child-friendly features, including a children's center and huge pool.

Most of the guest rooms in this skyscraper-heavy neighborhood lack a serious view, though as you near the top of the 46-story complex, the sights are inspiring indeed. Designed for business travelers, the Club Level rooms contain mini business centers with a fax/printer/copier and two-line speakerphone.

123 Queen St. W., Toronto, ON M5H 2M9. ℂ **800/325-3535** or 416/361-1000. Fax 416/947-4854. www.sheratoncentretoronto.com. 1,377 units. C$260–C$295 (US$182–US$207) double. Extra person C$20 (US$14). 2 children 17 and under stay free in parent's room. Packages available. AE, DC, MC, V. Parking C$33 (US$23). Subway: Osgoode. **Amenities:** 2 restaurants; bar; gigantic heated indoor/outdoor pool; health club; spa; Jacuzzi; sauna; children's center; concierge; activities desk; business center; shopping arcade; 24-hr. room service; babysitting; laundry service; dry cleaning. *In room:* A/C, TV, dataport, coffeemaker, hair dryer, iron.

Toronto Marriott Eaton Centre   Attention, shoppers: Those who want proximity to Toronto's central shrine to commerce should seriously consider checking in here. Connected to the Eaton Centre, the Marriott is just a few minutes' walk from the financial and theater districts, Chinatown, and SkyDome. This hotel caters to the tourist crowd: While a good concierge at any hotel can point you in the direction of, say, a hot restaurant, the Marriott has desks set up to facilitate day-trip planning and other activities. Because of its location, this is a fine choice for determined sightseers. One caveat is that the area immediately surrounding the Eaton Centre is pickpocket heaven. On the positive side, it's always busy in this neighborhood.

Most of the Marriott's guest rooms are well sized, which is all the better to store your loot. The views from many of the rooms aren't the best, because you'll find office towers in all directions. A pleasant surprise is the view of the beautiful 19th-century Holy Trinity Church from the Parkside restaurant.

525 Bay St. (at Dundas St.), Toronto, ON M5G 2L2. ℂ **800/905-0667** or 416/597-9200. Fax 416/597-9211. www.marriotteatoncentre.com. 459 units. C$189–C$239 (US$132–US$167) double. AE, DC, DISC, MC, V. Parking C$19 (US$13). Subway: Dundas. **Amenities:** 3 restaurants; bar; indoor rooftop pool; health club; Jacuzzi; sauna; concierge; activities desk; car-rental desk; business center; 24-hr. room service; massage; same-day laundry service/dry cleaning. *In room:* A/C, TV, dataport, coffeemaker, hair dryer, iron.

Westin Harbour Castle ⭐   A popular spot for conventions, the Westin is on the lakefront, just across from the Toronto Islands ferry docks and down the road from the Harbourfront Centre and Queens Quay. Not surprisingly, the views are among the best in the city. The trade-off is that this hotel is somewhat out of the way. It's a 5-minute walk to Union Station, but to get there you have to cross under the Gardiner Expressway, one of the ugliest and most desolate patches of the city. The hotel tries to get around this difficulty with shuttle bus service; there's also a public-transit stop and a queue of cabs at the hotel. But it's unlikely you'll want to go for an evening stroll around the neighborhood. On the other hand, you will get a good night's sleep here—all guest rooms boast Westin's trademarked Heavenly Beds, which really are divine.

Recognizing the lack of things to do in the vicinity, management has wisely populated the hotel with attractions. The dining options are extremely fine: The excellent restaurant, Toula, attracts Toronto residents as well as visitors in droves. There are also terrific sports facilities, giving this monolithic hotel the feel of a resort. Who needs to go outside anyway?

1 Harbour Sq., Toronto, ON M5J 1A6. ℂ **800/WESTIN-1** or 416/869-1600. Fax 416/361-7448. www.westin.com/harbourcastle. 977 units. C$180–C$360 (US$126–US$252) double; from C$335 (US$235) suite. Extra person C$30 (US$21). Children stay free in parent's room. Weekend packages available. AE, DC, MC, V. Parking C$25 (US$18). Subway: Union, then LRT to Queens Quay. **Amenities:** 2 restaurants; 2 bars; indoor pool; 2 tennis courts; 2 squash courts; excellent health club; spa; Jacuzzi; sauna; children's center; concierge; business center; salon; 24-hr. room service; laundry service; dry cleaning. *In room:* A/C, TV, dataport, minibar, coffeemaker, hair dryer, iron.

MODERATE

Delta Chelsea ⭐⭐ *Kids* *Value*   While not a budget hotel, the Delta Chelsea offers bang for the buck. Its downtown location draws heaps of tour groups and a smattering of business travelers, its family-friendly facilities lure those with tykes, and its weekend packages capture the cost-conscious. It's impossible for a hotel to be all things to all people, but the Delta Chelsea comes pretty close. Luxury seekers should look elsewhere, and backpackers won't be able to afford it, but the Delta Chelsea is talented at meeting the needs of many of those in between. This is a particularly good bet for young families.

This year the Delta Chelsea, which claims to be Canada's largest hotel, celebrates its 30th anniversary, and it certainly makes the most of its generous space, with features like the Corkscrew, a 4-story indoor waterslide. What 8-year-old could resist? The hotel has got some grown-up amenities too, such as the Bb33 Bistro and Brasserie, a two-in-one restaurant with a formal dining room and a fuss-free buffet room. There's also Deck 27, a lounge with a fantastic panoramic view of Toronto (it's only open to those who are of drinking age—that's 19 in Ontario).

The guest rooms are bright and cheery; a few have kitchenettes, which is always a plus for family travel. On the Signature Club floor for business travelers, rooms have cordless speakerphones, faxes, well-stocked desks, and ergonomic chairs.

One special feature of the Delta Chelsea is its entertainment department. The hotel has partnerships with CanStage, Soupepper Theatre, the CN Tower, and Paramount Canada's Wonderland, to mention a few. Guests enjoy access to tickets for everything from blockbuster shows to special events.

33 Gerrard St. W., Toronto, ON M5G 1Z4. ℂ 800/243-5732 or 416/595-1975. Fax 416/585-4362. www.delta hotels.com. 1,590 units. C$129–C$340 (US$90–US$238) double; C$149–C$360 (US$104–US$252) deluxe double; C$195–C$380 (US$137–US$266) Signature Club double (business floor); from C$475 (US$333) suite. Extra person C$20 (US$14). Children 17 and under stay free in parent's room. Weekend packages available. AE, DC, DISC, MC, V. Valet parking C$29 (US$20), self-parking C$22 (US$15). Subway: College. **Amenities:** 3 restaurants; 3 bars; 2 pools (1 for adults only); health club; Jacuzzi; sauna; children's center; billiards room; concierge; activities desk; business center; salon; babysitting; laundry service; dry cleaning. *In room:* A/C, TV, coffeemaker, hair dryer, iron.

Holiday Inn on King   The blinding-white facade of this building suggests that some architect mistook Toronto for the tropics. No matter—its location is hot, with the Theater District, gourmet ghetto, Chinatown, and SkyDome nearby. It's also close to the Financial District, which explains the mix of business travelers and vacationers. Half the floors are office space; guest rooms start at the 9th floor and go up to the 20th. The good-size, pastel-colored rooms are vintage Holiday Inn.

The hotel has a special program for female corporate travelers called STAYassured, which includes features such as room placement (close to elevators), an escort to the underground parking garage, and a discount on in-room spa services. Two percent of STAYassured room revenues are donated to the Rotman School of Business at the University of Toronto—they're earmarked for scholarships for female students.

370 King St. W. (at Peter St.), Toronto, ON M5V 1J9. ℂ 800/263-6364 or 416/599-4000. Fax 416/599-7394. www.hiok.com. 431 units. C$179–C$319 (US$125–US$223) double. Extra person C$15 (US$11). AE, DISC, MC, V. Parking C$18 (US$13). Subway: St. Andrew. Pets accepted. **Amenities:** Restaurant; bar; small outdoor pool; health club; Jacuzzi; sauna; limited room service; massage. *In room:* A/C, TV, coffeemaker, hair dryer.

INEXPENSIVE

The Drake Hotel ★★ *Finds*   The Drake only opened in February 2004, but it has already earned a following that includes some famous faces (musical group the Black Eyed Peas and actress Heather Graham have stayed here). Part of the appeal is the hotel's rags-to-riches pedigree: Formerly a flophouse in a run-down Toronto neighborhood called Parkdale, the Drake was rescued by owner Jeff Stober, who injected C$6 million into creating a boutique hotel. The renovation is gorgeous, and Stober's timing was excellent—when he bought the property in 2001, the steady march of gentrification had already begun on Queen Street West. Even though the Drake is on its western fringe, Parkdale is less shabby and more chic, and there are some terrific restaurants, galleries, and shops within walking distance.

The 19 guest rooms are tiny—they range from 14 to 28 sq. m (150–300 sq. ft.)—but they are cleverly designed and have good amenities (CD/DVD players and lovely linens, for example). But the Drake's strength is in its public spaces, and for a property this small, it has an awful lot. There's a restaurant and bar, a rooftop lounge, and a cafe; an exercise studio for yoga classes and a massage room; and a performance venue, the Underground, that features live music. There are also works of art throughout the hotel. The Drake has been warmly welcomed by Toronto's arts community, and this is the one hotel in town where you're far more likely to meet city residents than visitors. Still, there's no getting away from the fact that this hotel is far from the downtown core, and that access to public transit is limited to the Queen Street streetcar.

1150 Queen St. W., Toronto, ON M6J 1J3. ☎ **416/531-5042**. Fax 416/531-9493. www.thedrakehotel.ca. 19 units. C$99–C$129 (US$69–US$90) double. AE, MC, V. Subway: Osgoode, then streetcar west to Beaconsfield. **Amenities:** 2 restaurants; cafe; 2 bars; yoga studio; massage room. *In room:* A/C, TV, dataport, hair dryer, iron.

Hotel Victoria ⊛ (*Value*)   In a landmark downtown building near the Hummingbird Centre and the Hockey Hall of Fame, the Victoria boasts the glamorous touches of an earlier age, such as crown moldings and marble columns in the lobby. It's Toronto's second-oldest hotel (built in 1909), but all of the guest rooms underwent a complete renovation in 2000, and the facilities are upgraded annually. Because of its small size, the 56-room hotel offers an unusually high level of personal service and attention, which you normally wouldn't expect in budget accommodations; the staff is fluent in several languages. Standard rooms are on the small side but are nicely put together; deluxe rooms are larger and have coffeemakers and minifridges.

56 Yonge St. (at Wellington St.), Toronto, ON M5E 1G5. ☎ **800/363-8228** or 416/363-1666. Fax 416/363-7327. www.hotelvictoria-toronto.com. 56 units. C$105–C$159 (US$74–US$111) double. Extra person C$15 (US$11). Rates include continental breakfast. AE, DC, MC, V. Parking nearby from C$20 (US$14). Subway: King. **Amenities:** Restaurant; access to nearby health club; babysitting; laundry service; dry cleaning. *In room:* A/C, TV, dataport, hair dryer, iron.

The Strathcona ⊛   The Strathcona has a unique status: It's pretty much the only budget hotel that's right in the Financial District, and for years it has been one of the best buys in the city. It sits in the shadow of the Royal York, making this hotel a short walk from all major downtown attractions. If you want to be in this neighborhood but don't want to pay a bundle, this is your best option. The trade-offs aren't as extensive as you might think. The Strathcona's rooms may be on the small side, but they are designed with efficiency in mind. The hotel doesn't have a health club, but guests have access to the nearby Wellington Club for a C$10 (US$7) fee.

60 York St., Toronto, ON M5J 1S8. ☎ **800/268-8304** or 416/363-3321. Fax 416/363-4679. www.thestrathcona hotel.com. 194 units. May–Oct C$129–C$179 (US$90–US$125) double; Nov–Apr C$109–C$139 (US$76–US$97) double. AE, DC, MC, V. Parking nearby from C$20 (US$14). Subway: Union. **Amenities:** Cafe; bar; access to nearby health club; bike rental; children's center; concierge; tour desk; car-rental desk; limited room service; babysitting; laundry service; dry cleaning. *In room:* A/C, TV, hair dryer, iron.

2 Downtown East

VERY EXPENSIVE

Le Royal Meridien King Edward ★★ At one time, the King Eddy was the only place in Toronto that Hollywood royalty like Liz Taylor and Richard Burton would consider staying. In the 1980s, after many years of neglect, a group of local investors spent C$40 million (US$28 million) to rescue it. The result recalls its former glory, with rosy marble columns and a glass-domed rotunda dominating the lobby. The sense of grandeur carries into the accommodations. The guest rooms aren't what I'd call spacious—28 to 33 sq. m (300–350 sq. ft.) is standard—but their uniformly high ceilings give them a sweeping grandeur that is rare. The rooms are also charmingly appointed; unlike those at many competitors, where you'd be hard-pressed to tell the difference between one room and the next, these guest rooms have been decorated with a personal touch. The bathrooms are particularly nice, with generously proportioned marble tubs.

The formal dining room, Café Victoria, wins solid reviews for its cooking. This is one of the most glamorous settings in the city, and its astonishing Edwardian beauty is the reason the hotel wasn't torn down in the 1970s. Just off the lobby is a mirrored lounge that serves a traditional English afternoon tea; I highly recommend partaking in this delicious pastime whether or not you're a guest in the hotel (if you do, try the Lady Grey tea—it's irresistible). The wood-paneled Consort Bar is wonderfully clubby, and its 2.5m-high (8-ft.) windows afford fun people-watching while you sip a champagne cocktail. It's got a surprising long menu, which includes everything from crispy calamari to thin-crust pizzas.

37 King St. E., Toronto, ON M5C 2E9. ✆ 800/543-4300 or 416/863-3131. Fax 416/367-5515. www.toronto. lemeridien.com. 294 units. C$375–C$450 (US$263–US$315) double; from C$800 (US$560) suite. One child 12 or under stays free in parent's room (no more than 3 people are allowed in a room). AE, DC, MC, V. Parking C$30 (US$21). Subway: King. Pets accepted. **Amenities:** 2 restaurants; bar; health club; Jacuzzi; sauna; concierge; 24-hr. room service; babysitting; laundry service; dry cleaning. *In room:* A/C, TV, fax, dataport, minibar, hair dryer, iron.

EXPENSIVE

Cambridge Suites Hotel ★★ This hotel has three main selling points: location, location, and location. Sitting on the edge of the Financial District, it caters to a corporate crowd that never wants to be more than a few steps from the office. Of course there are other drawing cards, such as the fact that all units are suites. The emphasis is on luxury, and the Cambridge succeeds in making its point.

The suites start at a generous 51 sq. m (550 sq. ft.) and move up to deluxe duplexes. (In fact, the Jacuzzi-outfitted penthouse suites have come to the attention of celebrities tired of Toronto's tried-and-true star-catering hotels; the views are breathtaking.) The amenities for business travelers are solid. If you can drag yourself away from the comfy desk area, which has two two-line telephones and a fax, you can enjoy some of the comforts of home: refrigerator, microwave, and dining ware, plus coffee, tea, and snacks. And if you hand over your shopping list, the staff will stock the fridge, too.

15 Richmond St. E. (near Yonge St.), Toronto, ON M5C 1N2. ✆ 800/463-1990 or 416/368-1990. Fax 416/601-3751. www.cambridgesuiteshotel.com. 229 units. From C$179 (US$125). Rates include continental breakfast. AE, DC, DISC, MC, V. Parking C$16 (US$11). Subway: Queen. **Amenities:** Restaurant; bar; small health club (and access to much larger health club nearby); spa; Jacuzzi; sauna; concierge; business center; limited room service; babysitting; laundry service; dry cleaning. *In room:* A/C, TV, fax, dataport, minibar, fridge, coffeemaker, hair dryer, iron.

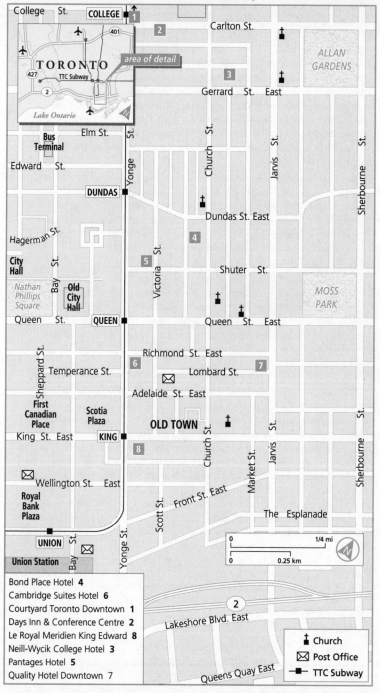

College St.

COLLEGE 1

2

Carlton St.

ALLAN GARDENS

3

Gerrard St. East

Elm St.

Bus Terminal

Edward St.

DUNDAS

Church St.

Jarvis St.

Sherbourne St.

Yonge St.

Dundas St. East

4

Hagerman St.

City Hall

Bay St.

Old City Hall

Nathan Phillips Square

5

Victoria St.

Shuter St.

MOSS PARK

QUEEN

Queen St.

Queen St. East

Richmond St. East

Sheppard St.

Temperance St.

6

Lombard St.

7

Adelaide St. East

First Canadian Place

Scotia Plaza

OLD TOWN

King St. East

KING

8

Church St.

Market St.

Jarvis St.

Sherbourne St.

Wellington St. East

Royal Bank Plaza

Scott St.

Front St. East

The Esplanade

UNION

Bay St.

Yonge St.

Union Station

0   1/4 mi

0   0.25 km

2

Lakeshore Blvd. East

Queens Quay East

Bond Place Hotel **4**
Cambridge Suites Hotel **6**
Courtyard Toronto Downtown **1**
Days Inn & Conference Centre **2**
Le Royal Meridien King Edward **8**
Neill-Wycik College Hotel **3**
Pantages Hotel **5**
Quality Hotel Downtown **7**

✝ Church
✉ Post Office
■— TTC Subway

TORONTO

401

427

2

TTC Subway

area of detail

Lake Ontario

Kids Family-Friendly Hotels

Delta Chelsea (p. 61)   This is a perennial family favorite—with good cause. The hotel boasts a Family Fun Zone, a multiroom play area with live bunnies and fish, a video arcade, and the only indoor waterslide in downtown Toronto (it's open year-round, too). You can play together in the family pool here or drop off the tyke for babysitting. Kids will enjoy the in-room family movies, Super Nintendo, cookie jar (replenished daily), and nightly turndown gift. Further reducing the strain on the family purse, kids have a half-price menu at some of the Delta Chelsea's restaurants.

Four Seasons Hotel Toronto (p. 68)   A hop and a skip from the Royal Ontario Museum, this hotel has its own attractions. There are free bicycles and video games for borrowing, and an indoor-outdoor pool. Upon arrival, room service brings the kids complimentary cookies and milk. The concierge and housekeeping staff work magic, including conjuring up excellent babysitting services.

The Sheraton Centre Toronto (p. 60)   The endless attractions of this complex—including restaurants with special menus for tykes, and a cinema—mean there's a lot to keep the little ones entertained. There's a supervised play center as well as on-call babysitting services. Kids also enjoy in-room video games and a welcome gift. There are a limited number of Family Guest Rooms, which boast a toy chest, some kid-size furniture, a fridge, and a microwave.

Pantages Suites Hotel Spa   This exciting hotel has only recently opened, and though the location is terrific—it's just a block away from the Eaton Centre, but Victoria Street is so quiet you'd never guess it—as of press time its restaurant and spa have yet to open, and some amenities (such as room service) won't be available for some time more. However, the hotel is trying to lure visitors with plenty of discounted packages, and though the place feels unfinished, the guest rooms are nicely designed in a serene palette of neutrals—and many rooms have a Jacuzzi tub, which is a definite plus. The hotel also pays attention to security, with features such as room key to access the elevator. If you want a prime downtown location, the Pantages is certainly a contender; but if you want certain amenities, be sure to ask if they'll be available.

200 Victoria St. (at Shuter St.), Toronto, ON M5B 1V8. © **866/852-1777** or 416/362-1777. Fax 416/214-5618. www.pantageshotel.com. 157 units. From C$179 (US$125) double. Rates include continental breakfast. AE, DC, MC, V. Parking C$20 (US$14). Subway: Queen. **Amenities:** Restaurant; bar; spa; Jacuzzi; sauna; concierge; business center; 24-hr. room service; laundry service; dry cleaning. *In room:* A/C, TV, fax, dataport, minibar, coffeemaker, hair dryer, iron.

MODERATE

Bond Place Hotel   The location is right—a block from the Eaton Centre, around the corner from the Pantages and Elgin theaters—and so is the price. Perhaps that's why this hotel tends to be popular with tour groups. (The fact that the staff speaks several European and Asian languages doesn't hurt, either.) The rooms are on the small side, but all were freshened up in a 2002 renovation and refurbishment.

65 Dundas St. E., Toronto, ON M5B 2G8. © 800/268-9390 or 416/362-6061. Fax 416/360-6406. www.bond placehoteltoronto.com. 287 units. High season C$140 (US$98) single or double; low season C$79 (US$55) single or double. Extra person C$15 (US$11). Weekend packages available. AE, DC, DISC, MC, V. Parking C$12 (US$8.40). Subway: Dundas. **Amenities:** Restaurant; bar; concierge; tour desk; car-rental desk; limited room service; laundry service; dry cleaning. *In room:* A/C, TV, hair dryer, iron.

Courtyard Toronto Downtown ⭐   Anyone who knows the Marriott chain of hotels knows that their Courtyard hotels are usually out of the city center, not smack-dab in the middle of things. Here's one exception: Marriott has taken on an over-the-hill property near Yonge and College (the former Westbury Hotel), stripped it down to its skeleton, and built it back up as a bright and shiny Courtyard by Marriott in 1999. The result is exactly what this neighborhood needed. The location is equally convenient to the Financial District downtown and the chic cafes and shops of Midtown—a claim few other hotels in the city can make.

The lobby with its double-sided fireplace has a surprisingly intimate feel given the size of the hotel (truth be told, there's actually a separate reception area for tour groups, and that's why). The guest rooms don't tend to be big, but they do have a lot of comforts, including windows that open, high-speed Internet access ports, and a second sink outside of the bathroom. Like all Marriott hotels, there is an ongoing refurbishment program here, so the guest rooms tend to look fresh rather than lived-in. While Courtyards are generally regarded as business hotels, this one has family-friendly facilities such as a children's wading pool.

475 College St., Toronto, ON M4Y 1X7. © 800/847-5075 or 416/924-0611. Fax 416/924-8692. www.courtyard. com/yyzcy. 575 units. C$149 (US$104) double. AE, DC, MC, V. Valet parking C$20 (US$14), self-parking C$15 (US$11). Subway: College. **Amenities:** 2 restaurants; bar; health club; tour desk; business center; limited room service; laundry service; dry cleaning. *In room:* A/C, TV, dataport, minibar, coffeemaker, hair dryer, iron, safe.

Days Inn & Conference Centre Toronto Downtown   Now that Maple Leaf Gardens is semi-retired (hockey has moved to the Air Canada Centre, and at the time of this writing, there's talk of tearing it down to make way for a jumbo-size supermarket), the Days Inn's location isn't what it used to be. Still, this hotel isn't far from the downtown core, and its reasonable rates continue to draw business, particularly with those traveling for leisure (and on a budget). Also, extensive renovations have really spruced up both the public areas and the guest rooms.

30 Carlton St., Toronto, ON M5B 2E9. © 800/329-7466 or 416/977-6655. Fax 416/977-0502. www. dayshoteltoronto.ca. 538 units. C$99–C$169 (US$69–US$118) double. Extra person C$15 (US$11). Children 17 and under stay free in parent's room. Summer discounts available. AE, DISC, MC, V. Parking C$18 (US$13). Subway: College. **Amenities:** Restaurant; cafe; bar; indoor pool; sauna; concierge; tour desk; car-rental desk; laundry service; dry cleaning. *In room:* A/C, TV, dataport, fridge, coffeemaker, hair dryer, iron.

INEXPENSIVE

Neill-Wycik College Hotel   During the school year, this is a residence for nearby Ryerson Polytechnic University. Some students work here in the summer, when the Neill-Wycik morphs into a guesthouse. Travelers on tight budgets won't mind the minimalist approach—rooms have beds, chairs, desks, and phones, but no air-conditioning or TVs (although there is a TV lounge). Groups of five bedrooms share two bathrooms and one kitchen with a refrigerator and stove. The hotel has two roof decks, on the 5th and 23rd floors. It's less than a 5-minute walk to the Eaton Centre. The neighborhood is not as appealing as that around Victoria University at the University of Toronto, which offers a similar arrangement (p. 72).

96 Gerrard St. E. (between Church and Jarvis sts.), Toronto, ON M5B 1G7. © 800/268-4358 or 416/977-2320. Fax 416/977-2809. www.neill-wycik.com. 300 units, none with private bathroom. C$61 (US$43) double; C$70 (US$49) family (2 adults plus children). MC, V. Parking nearby from C$15 (US$11). Closed Sept to early May. Subway: College. **Amenities:** Cafe; sauna; 24-hr. coin-op laundry.

Quality Hotel Downtown   Close to the Financial District and the Eaton Centre, this hotel always seems to be running a special promotion, so be sure to ask for a deal. Rooms tend to be small, though they do have all the standard amenities. This is basically a no-frills hotel whose main selling point is its location.

111 Lombard St. (between Adelaide and Richmond sts.), Toronto, ON M5C 2T9. ℂ **800/4-CHOICE** or 416/367-5555. Fax 416/367-3470. www.choicehotels.ca/cn311. 196 units. C$109–C$209 (US$76–US$146) double. Rates include continental breakfast buffet. Children 18 and under stay free in parent's room. AE, DC, DISC, MC, V. Parking C$18 (US$13). Subway: King or Queen. **Amenities:** Health club; laundry service; dry cleaning. *In room:* A/C, TV, coffeemaker, hair dryer, iron.

3 Midtown West
VERY EXPENSIVE

Four Seasons Hotel Toronto ⭐⭐ *Kids*   The Four Seasons is famous as the favored haunt of many visiting celebrities. The Rolling Stones call it home in Toronto, and during the Toronto International Film Festival every September you can't get in here for love or money. The hotel, in the ritzy Yorkville district, has earned a reputation for offering fine service and complete comfort. While not even close to being the largest hotel in the city, the building—with its myriad ballrooms, meeting rooms, and restaurants—is Byzantine. It's easy to get lost inside (I've done it myself).

Even if you do get lost, it's an interesting place. The public areas are decorated like a French parlor, with marble floors and dramatic floral arrangements. Once you make it to your room, you'll find that while it may tend to be on the small side (a standard model is only about 30 sq. m/325 sq. ft.), it's well designed and easy on the eye. Corner rooms have charming balconies—all the better to appreciate street scenes. The formal dining room, Truffles, is a Toronto institution (p. 102). The second-floor Studio Cafe is a favorite with the business crowd; its menu features many health-conscious, low-fat dishes. The Avenue bar is a perfect perch for people-watching—it overlooks Yorkville Avenue.

21 Avenue Rd., Toronto, ON M5R 2G1. ℂ **800/268-6282** or 416/964-0411. Fax 416/964-2301. www.fourseasons.com/toronto. 380 units. C$305–C$440 (US$214–US$308) double; from C$485 (US$340) suite. Weekend discounts and packages available. AE, DC, DISC, MC, V. Valet parking C$30 (US$21), self-parking C$24 (US$17). Subway: Bay. **Amenities:** 2 restaurants; 2 bars/lounges; indoor/outdoor pool; health club; Jacuzzi; bike rental; concierge; weekday courtesy limo to downtown; business center; 24-hr. room service; in-room massage; babysitting; same-day laundry service/dry cleaning. *In room:* A/C, TV, dataport, minibar, hair dryer, iron, safe.

Park Hyatt Toronto ⭐⭐⭐   With its ongoing C$60-million (US$42-million) renovations, the Park Hyatt has cemented its reputation for being the last word in luxe. It is, in my opinion, the very best hotel in Toronto at the moment, and it's where I'd choose to stay if price were no object (though both of the new boutique accommodations—the Hôtel Le Germain and the SoHo Metropolitan— are very tempting, too).

The location of the Park Hyatt is prime: It's in the posh Yorkville district, steps from the Royal Ontario Museum and the Bata Shoe Museum. Chicago-based Hyatt has renovated nearly every corner of the 71-year-old Art Deco building. The biggest change was the building of the North Tower, which is entirely new but designed to match the original structure (which is now known as the South Tower). The guest rooms in the North Tower are among the most generously proportioned in town—the *smallest* is 46 sq. m (500 sq. ft.). An extensive renovation and refurbishment of the South Tower was completed in 2003; here, the guest rooms are smaller, but they are more individual—there are

90 rooms and 40 different room layouts. All rooms in both towers have free high-speed Internet access.

A glamorous lobby dotted with Eastern-inspired objets d'art links the North and South towers. The ground-floor restaurant Annona (p. 102) is a treat for gourmets. While the Park Hyatt's neighbor, the Four Seasons, has for years been luring the glitterati, the Park Hyatt prides itself on luring the literati. The 18th-floor Roof Lounge is famous for attracting writers (Mordecai Richler famously called the lounge the only civilized place in Toronto). In winter you will appreciate the couches in front of the fireplace, but in any other season, the lounge's open-air terrace is the place to be for a perfect view of the city (and an impressive daiquiri).

Another major development for the hotel was the introduction of the Stillwater Spa, which is unique in both its design and some of its treatments. One signature therapy is a "watsu"-style massage, in which you float in a water-filled room while a therapist applies shiatsu moves—it's very soothing. My personal favorite is the Couples Sanctuary, which features a whirlpool tub, fireplace, and side-by-side massage tables. It's perfect for inseparable romantics. See "Spas & the City" on p. 152 for a complete review.

4 Avenue Rd., Toronto, ON M5R 2E8. ✆ 800/233-1234 or 416/925-1234. Fax 416/924-6693. www.park toronto.hyatt.com. 346 units. C$225–C$499 (US$158–US$349) double; from C$299 (US$209) suite. Weekend packages available. AE, DC, DISC, MC, V. Parking C$30 (US$21). Subway: Museum or Bay. Pets accepted. **Amenities:** Restaurant; 2 bars; health club; spa; Jacuzzi; sauna; concierge; business center; 24-hr. room service; babysitting; laundry service; dry cleaning. *In room:* A/C, TV, fax, dataport, minibar, coffeemaker, hair dryer, iron, safe.

EXPENSIVE

The Sutton Place Hotel ★★   Although it towers over the intersection of Bay and Wellesley, The Sutton Place boasts the advantages of a small hotel—particularly detail-oriented, personalized service. In addition to hosting a galaxy of stars and celebrities, the hotel draws sophisticated business and leisure travelers in search of serious pampering. The emphasis is on sophistication—famous guests expect to be left alone, and management protects their privacy. In other words, no autograph seekers.

The hotel aims for European panache, littering the public spaces with antiques and tapestries. The spacious guest rooms are decorated in a similar, though scaled-down, style. A few suites have full kitchens. Not that you'd want to cook while you're here—the lovely ground-floor Accents restaurant serves Continental fare, and across the street the star-studded Bistro 990 produces perfect French cuisine. One downside is that The Sutton Place stands alone in its neighborhood. It's about a 10- to 15-minute walk to attractions such as the Royal Ontario Museum and the Yorkville shopping district.

955 Bay St., Toronto, ON M5S 2A2. ✆ 800/268-3790 or 416/924-9221. Fax 416/924-1778. www.sutton place.com. 294 units. C$235–C$325 (US$165–US$228) double; from C$400 (US$280) suite. Extra person C$20 (US$14). Children 17 and under stay free in parent's room. Weekend discounts available. AE, DC, MC, V. Valet parking C$28 (US$20), self-parking C$20 (US$14). Subway: Wellesley. Pets accepted. **Amenities:** Restaurant; bar; indoor pool; health club; sauna; concierge; business center; salon; 24-hr. room service; massage; babysitting; laundry service; dry cleaning. *In room:* A/C, TV, dataport, minibar, coffeemaker, hair dryer, iron, safe.

MODERATE

Clarion Hotel & Suites Selby ★ *Finds*   This hotel is one of Toronto's better-kept secrets. Ornate chandeliers, stucco moldings, and high ceilings make the 1890s Victorian building an absolute stunner. In a predominantly gay neighborhood, the Selby attracts gay and straight couples, as well as seniors (the latter

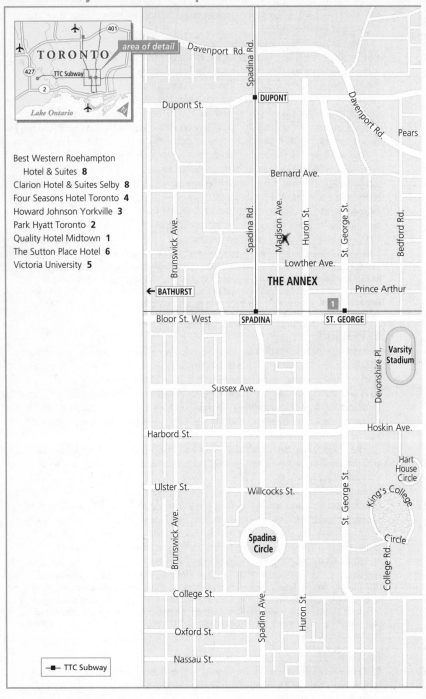

Best Western Roehampton
  Hotel & Suites **8**
Clarion Hotel & Suites Selby **8**
Four Seasons Hotel Toronto **4**
Howard Johnson Yorkville **3**
Park Hyatt Toronto **2**
Quality Hotel Midtown **1**
The Sutton Place Hotel **6**
Victoria University **5**

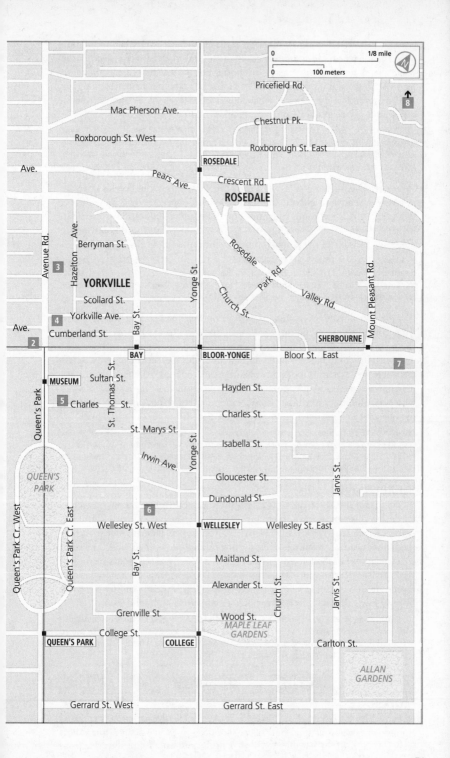

group gets special discounts). All of the rooms now have private bathrooms, but only a few have an old-fashioned claw-foot tub. The staff is very friendly, and while there's no concierge, there's no shortage of advice and recommendations for what to see and do. History buffs will love the fact that Ernest Hemingway lived here for a couple of years while he was on staff at the *Toronto Star* newspaper (and yes, there's a Hemingway suite).

592 Sherbourne St., Toronto, ON M4X 1L4. © 800/387-4788 or 416/921-3142. Fax 416/923-3177. www. choicehotels.ca. 82 units. C$120–C$210 (US$84–US$147) double; C$125–C$165 (US$88–US$116) suite. Rates include continental breakfast. AE, DISC, MC, V. Parking C$10 (US$7). Subway: Sherbourne. **Amenities:** Access to nearby health club; laundry room. *In room:* A/C, TV, dataport, coffeemaker, hair dryer, iron.

Howard Johnson Yorkville   Formerly the Venture Inn, this hotel is a bargain in a very expensive neighborhood. It's a little more expensive than it used to be, but it also has a few more amenities now. The Yorkville location is excellent, which is the trade-off for small rooms. As with many value-priced hotels, you're not going to want to spend much time in your room.

89 Avenue Rd., Toronto, ON M5R 2G3. © 800/446-4656 or 416/964-1220. Fax 416/964-8692. www.hojo-canada.com. 69 units. C$119–C$229 (US$83–US$160) double. Rates include continental breakfast. AE, DC, MC, V. Parking C$10 (US$7). Subway: Bay or Museum. Pets accepted. **Amenities:** Concierge; laundry service; dry cleaning. *In room:* A/C, TV, dataport, hair dryer, iron.

Quality Hotel Midtown *(Value*   Considering this hotel's tony location—steps from Yorkville and several museums, including the Royal Ontario Museum— the price is hard to beat. The rooms are small but comfortable, and outfitted with well-lit worktables. Choice Club members have access to in-house secretarial services; executive rooms have fax-modem hookups. However, there aren't many other amenities or services. This is a good home base for a leisure traveler who prizes location over other considerations. If you're not planning on hanging out a lot in your hotel room, it's a small trade-off to make for the price.

280 Bloor St. W. (at St. George St.), Toronto, ON M5S 1V8. © 416/968-0010. www.choicehotels.ca. 210 units. C$139–C$209 (US$97–US$146) double. Weekend and other packages available. AE, DC, DISC, MC, V. Parking C$12 (US$8.40). Subway: St. George. **Amenities:** Restaurant; coffee shop; access to nearby health club; limited room service; laundry service; dry cleaning. *In room:* A/C, TV, coffeemaker, hair dryer, iron.

INEXPENSIVE

Victoria University ★ *(Value*   This is a summer steal: You could not find a better deal in this part of town. From early May to late August, Victoria University (which is federated with the University of Toronto) makes its student accommodations available to travelers. Furnishings are simple—a bed, desk, and chair are standard—but the surroundings are splendid. Many of the rooms are in Burwash Hall, a 19th-century building that overlooks a peaceful, leafy quad. All rooms are down the street from the Royal Ontario Museum and up the street from Queen's Park. Guests are provided with linens, towels, and soap.

140 Charles St. W., Toronto, ON M5S 1K9. © 416/585-4524. Fax 416/585-4530. www.vicu.utoronto.ca. 700 units, none with private bathroom. C$67 (US$47) double. Rates include breakfast. MC, V. Nearby parking C$15 (US$11). Closed Sept to early May. Subway: Museum. **Amenities:** Access to health club with Olympic-size pool; tennis courts; laundry room. *In room:* No phone.

4 Uptown

MODERATE

Best Western Roehampton Hotel & Suites   The Roehampton is removed from downtown attractions, but still well located—for some people. It is a short walk from one of the best dining districts in the city, and a short bus ride from the Ontario Science Centre and 243 hectares (600 acres) of parkland (including hiking and cross-country skiing trails, and the Sunnybrook stables). The large, nicely furnished rooms boast big windows and peaceful views. With the wealth of hotels downtown, there's no reason to come this far north unless you need to—but if you do, this is a nice, relatively inexpensive place to stay.

808 Mount Pleasant Rd., Toronto, ON M4P 2L2. ⓒ 800/387-8899 or 416/487-5101. Fax 416/487-5390. www.bestwestern.com. 109 units. C$145–C$175 (US$102–US$123) double. Packages available. Children 17 and under stay free in parent's room. AE, DC, DISC, MC, V. Parking C$12 (US$8.40). Subway: Eglinton. **Amenities:** Restaurant; outdoor rooftop pool; health club; concierge; limited room service; babysitting; laundry service; dry cleaning. *In room:* A/C, TV, dataport, minibar, coffeemaker, hair dryer, iron.

5 The East End

Although it's not close to the downtown attractions, this area has many sights that are worth noting. They include the Ontario Science Centre, the Toronto Zoo, the Scarborough Bluffs (which homesick English settlers compared to the white cliffs of Dover), and the Scarborough Town Centre, a vast shopping complex.

There are some moderately priced chain hotels in this area. They include **Crowne Plaza,** 1250 Eglinton Ave. E., Don Mills, ON M3C 1J3 (ⓒ 888/ 303-1746); **Delta,** 2035 Kennedy Rd., Scarborough, ON M1T 3G2 (ⓒ 877/ 814-7706); and **Ramada,** 185 Yorkland Blvd., Don Mills, ON M2J 4R2 (ⓒ 800/2-RAMADA).

EXPENSIVE

Westin Prince Hotel ⭐   This hotel is less than half an hour from downtown, but its location and 6 hectares (15 acres) of parkland make it feel like a secluded resort. The generously proportioned rooms are designed for comfort. Many have a bay window or balcony, and the view makes Toronto look like one big forest. Standard features include a refrigerator, two phones, and a marble bathroom.

900 York Mills Rd., Don Mills, ON M3B 3H2. ⓒ 800/WESTIN-1 or 416/444-2511. Fax 416/444-9597. www.westin.com. 384 units. C$150–C$320 (US$105–US$224) double. Extra person C$20 (US$14). Children 17 and under stay free in parent's room. Weekend packages available. AE, DC, MC, V. Free parking. Subway: York Mills. **Amenities:** 3 restaurants; bar; outdoor heated pool; 9-hole putting green; tennis courts; health club; sauna; children's center; concierge; business center; 24-hr. room service; laundry service; dry cleaning. *In room:* A/C, TV, fridge, coffeemaker, hair dryer, iron.

INEXPENSIVE

University of Toronto at Scarborough   Like the downtown U of T campus, this student residence opens to travelers from mid-May to late August. The greenery-surrounded student village consists of town houses that sleep a maximum of six. Each has a complete kitchen, but none has air-conditioning, a telephone, or a TV.

Student Village. Scarborough Campus, University of Toronto, 1265 Military Trail, Scarborough, ON M1C 1A4. ⓒ 416/287-7356. Fax 416/287-7323. www.utsc.utoronto.ca. 81 units. C$180 (US$126) double with 2-night minimum; each additional night C$90 (US$63). Family rates available. MC. V. Free parking. Closed Sept to mid-May. Subway: Kennedy, then Scarborough Rapid Transit to Ellesmere, then bus no. 95 or 95B to college entrance. By car: Take exit 387 north from Hwy. 401. **Amenities:** Cafeteria; pub; access to health club with squash and tennis courts. *In room:* No phone.

6 At the Airport

Don't be fooled by anyone who tells you that the airport isn't far from the city. It's at least a 30-minute drive to downtown, depending on traffic. A taxi downtown costs roughly C$36 (US$25); the cheap public-transit options from the airport take an hour. Many of the hotels along the airport strip cater to business travelers. Others may wish to stay in this area if they're planning to divide their time between Toronto and its outlying areas, such as the Niagara region. Serious golfers come here for the area's many golf courses, including the 18-hole championship layout at the Royal Woodbine Golf Club.

EXPENSIVE

Hilton Toronto Airport ⭐ I'm not enthusiastic about staying out by Pearson International Airport, but one of the luxuries of doing so is that you can expect a spacious room. The Hilton certainly makes good on this opportunity. In fact, one of its main attractions is its 152 minisuites—all of which have a king-size bed in the bedroom, a sofa bed in the living room, a color TV in both rooms, and three phones. Another lure is the chain's well-regarded array of business-oriented amenities.

5875 Airport Rd., Mississauga, ON L4V 1N1. ℂ **800/567-9999** or 905/677-9900. Fax 905/677-7782. www.hilton.com. 413 units. From C$219 (US$153) double; from C$244 (US$171) minisuite. Extra person C$25 (US$18). Children stay free in parent's room. Weekend packages available. AE, DC, DISC, MC, V. Parking C$12 (US$8.40). **Amenities:** Restaurant; bar; indoor pool; nearby golf course; health club; spa; sauna; children's center; concierge; car-rental desk; business center; 24-hr. room service; same-day laundry service/dry cleaning. *In room:* A/C, TV, fax, dataport, minibar, coffeemaker, hair dryer, iron.

Sheraton Gateway Hotel in Toronto International Airport ⭐ Talk about convenience: You don't even need to go outdoors to get here—just take the skywalk from Terminal 3 (or a free shuttle from the other terminals). If you're planning a very short trip that requires flying out of the city almost as soon as you fly in, this hotel makes an awful lot of sense. Rooms are comfortable, spacious, and, more to the point, fully soundproof (remember, you're still at the airport!). Club rooms have extra inducements, such as ergonomic chairs, a fax/printer/copier, and access to a private lounge that serves complimentary breakfast and snacks.

Toronto AMF, Box 3000, Toronto, ON L5P 1C4. ℂ **800/325-3535** or 905/672-7000. Fax 905/672-7100. www.sheraton.com. 474 units. C$190–C$280 (US$133–US$196) double. AE, DC, DISC, MC, V. Parking C$19 (US$13). Pets accepted. **Amenities:** Restaurant; bar; indoor pool; health club; Jacuzzi; sauna; concierge; business center; 24-hr. room service; in-room massage; babysitting; laundry service; dry cleaning. *In room:* A/C, TV, dataport, minibar, coffeemaker, hair dryer, iron, safe.

Wyndham Bristol Place ⭐⭐ For a hotel by the airport, the Wyndham has a lot to offer. I'd never recommend staying near the airport unless you absolutely have to, but if you do, the Wyndham is an excellent choice. This is undoubtedly the most glamorous hotel for miles around—and the only one with a waterfall in its lobby. The decor throughout the building is sophisticated, but the hotel's real claim to fame is its personalized service. (You'll need to register for the Wyndham by Request program, which you can do online at www.wyndham.com; it's free, and filling out the questionnaire about everything from your dining to bedding preferences will improve your stay immeasurably.)

Guest rooms are well lit and spacious. Because it's a 30-minute journey to downtown Toronto, the good news is that the Wyndham boasts lots of amenities to keep you in the vicinity. The main dining room, Zachary's, aims high, with a seasonal menu and glamorously appointed dining room.

950 Dixon Rd., Toronto, ON M9W 5N4. ℂ **800/WYNDHAM** or 416/675-9444. Fax 416/675-4426. www. wyndham.com. 287 units. C$175–C$295 (US$123–US$207) double; from C$400 (US$280) suite. Extra person C$20 (US$14). Children 17 and under stay free in parent's room. Packages available. AE, DC, DISC, MC, V. Parking C$12 (US$8.40). **Amenities:** 2 restaurants; bar; large skylit indoor pool; health club; sauna;

concierge; business center; 24-hr. room service; babysitting; laundry service; dry cleaning. *In room:* A/C, TV, dataport, minibar, coffeemaker, hair dryer, iron.

MODERATE

Delta Meadowvale Resort & Conference Centre   Set on 9 hectares (22 acres) of greenery, the Delta has all the attributes of a restful resort. There are hiking and biking trails, tennis and squash courts, and indoor and outdoor swimming pools. The cozy rooms have modern wooden furniture, and each boasts a small balcony, a refrigerator, and two phones. The Regatta Bar & Grille serves a variety of dishes throughout the day; there are also two lounges for evening drinks (one only in summer, as it's out of doors).

6750 Mississauga Rd. (at Hwy. 401), Mississauga, ON L5N 2L3. © **800/422-8238** or 905/821-1981. Fax 905/542-4036. www.deltahotels.com. 374 units. C$169–C$240 (US$118–US$168) double. Weekend discounts available. AE, DC, DISC, MC, V. Free parking. Downtown shuttle C$11 (US$7.70) one-way. **Amenities:** 2 restaurants; 2 bars; children's center; business center; salon; 24-hr. room service; babysitting; laundry service; dry cleaning. *In room:* A/C, TV, coffeemaker, hair dryer.

Toronto Airport Marriott Hotel   One of the newest airport hotels, the Marriott is popular with business travelers. Of course, everything out here is really for business travelers. However, the Marriott is trying to attract leisure travelers, too, so expect a weekend discount of up to 50%. Rooms are comfortable and spacious. The amenities are in keeping with the Marriott name—no surprises here. There are two restaurants off the lobby: Take note of the Mikado, a Japanese restaurant where your meal can be cooked right at your table (think food as performance art).

901 Dixon Rd, Toronto, ON M9W 1J5. © **800/905-2811** or 416/674-9400. Fax 416/674-8292. www.marriott. com. 424 units. C$120–C$245 (US$84–US$172) double. Extra person C$15 (US$11). Weekend packages available. AE, DC, DISC, MC, V. Parking C$12 (US$8.40). **Amenities:** 2 restaurants; cafe; bar; skylit indoor pool; nearby golf course; health club; Jacuzzi; sauna; concierge; car-rental desk; business center; 24-hr. room service; babysitting; same-day laundry service/dry cleaning. *In room:* A/C, TV, dataport, minibar, coffeemaker, hair dryer, iron.

INEXPENSIVE

Days Hotel—Toronto Airport   For the price, this is a very good bet on the airport strip; the facilities are similar to those at pricier hotels. The guest rooms are bright and cheery; 20 of them are Corporate Plus rooms geared towards business travelers. Upgraded units have bathrobes (unusual at a hotel in this price range), irons and ironing boards, and fax-modem hookups. The Garden Café Restaurant is open all day.

6257 Airport Rd., Mississauga, ON L4V 1N1. © **800/387-6891** or 905/678-1400. Fax 905/678-9130. www.daysinn.com. 201 units. C$90–C$169 (US$63–US$118) double. Extra person C$10 (US$7). Children 16 and under stay free in parent's room. Weekend packages available. AE, DC, DISC, MC, V. Parking C$8 (US$5.60) per day. **Amenities:** Restaurant; outdoor pool; exercise room; sauna; limited room service; coin-op laundry. *In room:* A/C, TV, coffeemaker, hair dryer.

Where to Dine

Dining out is nothing short of a passion in Toronto. It's not that residents are too lazy to cook, but we are spoiled by the embarrassment of edible riches in all parts of the city. Many restaurants are just as busy on a Wednesday as they are on a weekend, because dining out is a hallmark of the local culture.

The city is a restaurant-goer's nirvana for a wealth of reasons. For starters, there are more than 5,000 eateries. They represent cooking styles from any country or nationality you can name, making Toronto's culinary scene both eclectic and palate teasing. Eating out is also remarkably affordable: While the most expensive restaurants have some entrees priced above C$40 (US$28), many more boast top-notch cooking for bargain-basement prices—it's a very competitive market. (Keep in mind, too, that for American visitors, even the most expensive Toronto restaurants aren't so pricey given the weak Canadian dollar.)

Mediterranean and Asian cuisines dominate the scene—and often appear on the same plate. Fusion cooking caught on big here and has never lost its steam. Many restaurants that started out as, say, Italian, have incorporated ingredients and cooking styles from Southeast Asia and North Africa, among other *haute* spots. Each wave of immigration has carried new ideas and flavors.

While restaurants of all descriptions are found across the city, certain neighborhoods are renowned for their specialties: Little Italy for its trattorias, Chinatown for its Chinese and Vietnamese eateries, and the Danforth for its Greek tavernas. King Street West has unexpectedly become a new hot spot for in-the-know gourmets, offering a bevy of bistros and boîtes.

DINING NOTES Dining out does not have to be an expensive venture, but the tax level is high. Meals are subject to the 8% provincial sales tax and to the 7% GST. In other words, tax and tip together can add 30% to your bill. Restaurants normally leave tipping to the diners' discretion, unless there are six or more people at the table. The usual amount for good service is 15%, jumping to 20% at the pricier establishments. The price of a bottle of wine is generally quite high because of the tax on imports; get around it by ordering an Ontario vintage—local wines enjoy a rising international reputation. Remember that there is a 10% tax on alcohol, whatever you're sipping.

NOTES ON THE REVIEWS Restaurants are grouped by neighborhood and listed alphabetically under the following main-course price ranges (not counting tax and tip): very expensive, C$30 (US$21) and up; expensive, C$20 to C$29 (US$14–US$20); and moderate, C$10 to C$19 (US$7–US$13). At inexpensive restaurants, it's possible to eat an entire meal for C$15 (US$11) or less. Many restaurants' offerings veer into higher and lower categories, so the ranges are general guidelines. Keep in mind that many restaurants change their menus and policies at a

> **Tips** A Note on Smoking
>
> Almost all Toronto restaurants are nonsmoking, the result of an anti-smoking bylaw that went into effect on June 1, 2001. Exceptions are made for patios and separately ventilated dining rooms. Some restaurants chose to designate themselves as bars to get around the restriction, but as of June 1, 2004, that loophole closed when Toronto banned smoking in bars, too. Restaurateurs vowed to fight the regulation, which subjects both patrons and establishments to fines of C$200 to C$5,000 (US$140–US$3,500) for infractions, but it doesn't look like anything is going to change soon. When making a reservation, ask about the restaurant's smoking policy.

moment's notice. If a listing says a restaurant doesn't accept reservations, but you have your heart set on eating there, it doesn't hurt to call and ask if a reservation (or an exception) could be made.

1 Restaurants by Cuisine

AMERICAN

Far Niente ★★ (Downtown West, $$$, p. 89)

Jump Cafe & Bar ★★ (Downtown West, $$$, p. 90)

Oliver & Bonacini Café & Grill ★★ (Uptown, $$$, p. 113)

ASIAN

Fortune Cookie ★ (Downtown West, $$, p. 93)

Monsoon ★ (Downtown West, $$$$, p. 87)

Queen Mother Cafe (Downtown West, $, p. 97)

Rain ★ (Downtown West, $$$, p. 91)

SpringRolls (Midtown West, $, p. 107)

BELGIAN

Café Brussel (The East End, $$$, p. 108)

BISTRO

Biff's ★★ (Downtown East, $$$, p. 97)

Brassaii ★★★ (Downtown West, $$, p. 92)

Cities (Downtown West, $$, p. 92)

Crush ★ (Downtown West, $$, p. 93)

Lakes ★ (Uptown, $$$, p. 112)

La Palette ★ (Downtown West, $$, p. 93)

Le Sélect Bistro (Downtown West, $$, p. 93)

Lolo ★★ (Uptown, $$, p. 114)

Pony (Downtown West, $$, p. 95)

Stork on the Roof ★ (Uptown, $$, p. 115)

Torch (Downtown East, $$$, p. 98)

Wish ★ (Downtown East, $$, p. 100)

CAJUN

Southern Accent (Midtown West, $$, p. 105)

CANADIAN

Canoe Restaurant & Bar ★ (Downtown West, $$$$, p. 86)

Splendido Bar and Grill (Midtown West, $$$, p. 103)

Tundra ★★ (Downtown West, $$$$, p. 88)

Key to Abbreviations: $$$$ = Very Expensive $$$ = Expensive $$ = Moderate $ = Inexpensive

Where to Dine in Downtown

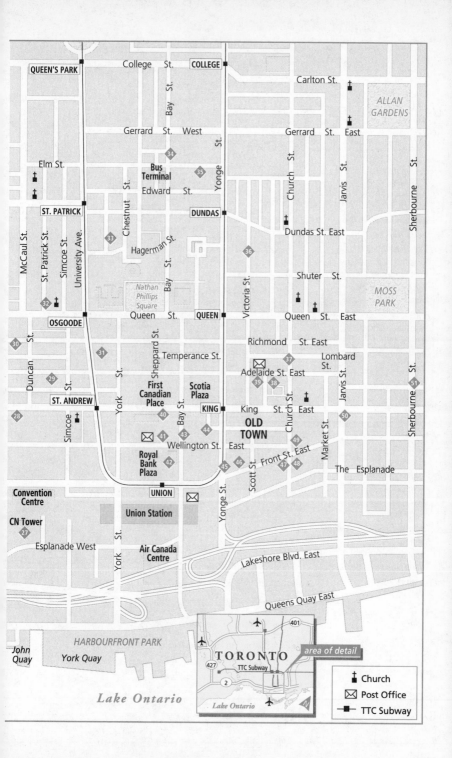

Where to Dine in Midtown West & Uptown

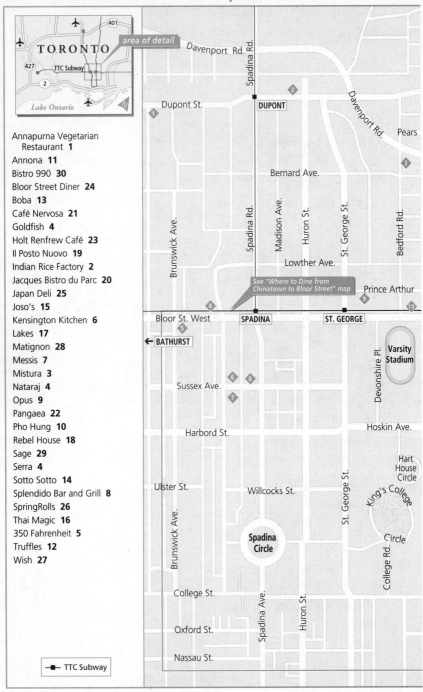

Annapurna Vegetarian
  Restaurant **1**
Annona **11**
Bistro 990 **30**
Bloor Street Diner **24**
Boba **13**
Café Nervosa **21**
Goldfish **4**
Holt Renfrew Café **23**
Il Posto Nuovo **19**
Indian Rice Factory **2**
Jacques Bistro du Parc **20**
Japan Deli **25**
Joso's **15**
Kensington Kitchen **6**
Lakes **17**
Matignon **28**
Messis **7**
Mistura **3**
Nataraj **4**
Opus **9**
Pangaea **22**
Pho Hung **10**
Rebel House **18**
Sage **29**
Serra **4**
Sotto Sotto **14**
Splendido Bar and Grill **8**
SpringRolls **26**
Thai Magic **16**
350 Fahrenheit **5**
Truffles **12**
Wish **27**

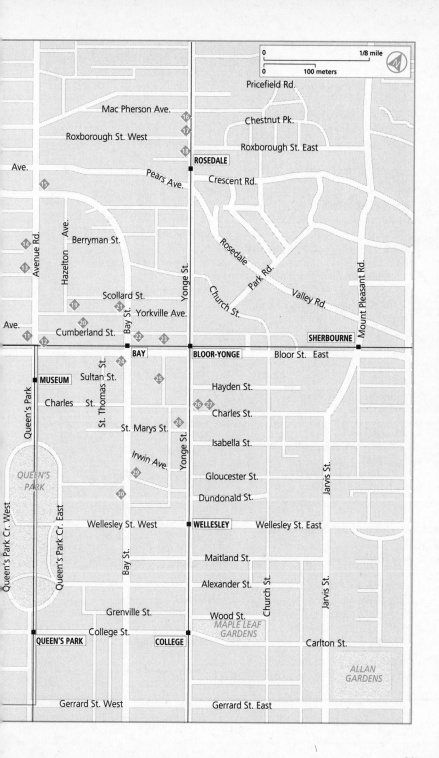

Pricefield Rd.

Mac Pherson Ave.

Roxborough St. West

Chestnut Pk.

Roxborough St. East

Ave.

ROSEDALE

Pears Ave.

Crescent Rd.

Berryman St.

Hazelton Ave.

Avenue Rd.

Scollard St.

Yorkville Ave.

Yonge St.

Rosedale

Church St.

Park Rd.

Valley Rd.

Mount Pleasant Rd.

Cumberland St.

Bay St.

SHERBOURNE

Ave.

BAY

BLOOR-YONGE

Bloor St. East

MUSEUM

Sultan St.

St. Thomas St.

Charles St.

Hayden St.

Charles St.

Queen's Park

St. Marys St.

Isabella St.

Yonge St.

Irwin Ave.

Gloucester St.

Dundonald St.

Jarvis St.

QUEEN'S
PARK

Wellesley St. West

WELLESLEY

Wellesley St. East

Queen's Park Cr. West

Queen's Park Cr. East

Bay St.

Maitland St.

Alexander St.

Church St.

Jarvis St.

Grenville St.

Wood St.

MAPLE LEAF
GARDENS

QUEEN'S PARK

College St.

COLLEGE

Carlton St.

ALLAN
GARDENS

Gerrard St. West

Gerrard St. East

CHINESE

Grand Yatt ✸ (North of the City, $$, p. 117)

Happy Seven (Downtown West, $, p. 96)

Lai Wah Heen ✸✸✸ (Downtown West, $$$, p. 90)

Lee Garden (Downtown West, $, p. 96)

Sang Ho ✸ (Downtown West, $$, p. 95)

CONTINENTAL

Centro ✸✸ (Uptown, $$$$, p. 111)

HotHouse Cafe (Downtown East, $$, p. 99)

Opus (Midtown West, $$$$, p. 101)

Oro (Downtown West, $$$, p. 90)

360 Revolving Restaurant (Downtown West, $$$$, p. 87)

Truffles ✸ (Midtown West, $$$$, p. 102)

DELI

Shopsy's (Downtown East, $, p. 101)

ECLECTIC

Avalon ✸✸ (Downtown West, $$$$, p. 85)

Citron (Downtown West, $$, p. 93)

The Fifth ✸ (Downtown West, $$$$, p. 87)

Goldfish ✸✸ (Midtown West, $$, p. 104)

Messis ✸ (Midtown West, $$, p. 105)

Mildred Pierce ✸✸ (Downtown West, $$, p. 94)

Swan (Downtown West, $$, p. 95)

Taro Grill ✸ (Downtown West, $$, p. 95)

ETHIOPIAN

Lalibela (Midtown West, $, p. 106)

FRENCH

Auberge du Pommier ✸ (Uptown, $$$$, p. 111)

Bistro 990 ✸✸✸ (Midtown West, $$$$, p. 101)

Bodega (Downtown West, $$, p. 92)

Jacques Bistro du Parc (Midtown West, $$, p. 104)

Matignon (Midtown West, $$, p. 105)

Quartier ✸ (Uptown, $$$, p. 113)

FUSION

Boba ✸ (Midtown West, $$$, p. 102)

Eau (Downtown West, $$$$, p. 86)

Pangaea ✸ (Midtown West, $$$, p. 103)

The Rivoli ✸✸ (Downtown West, $, p. 97)

Susur ✸✸✸ (Downtown West, $$$$, p. 87)

Veni Vidi Vici ✸✸ (Downtown West, $$, p. 96)

GREEK

Astoria (The East End, $, p. 109)

Avli ✸ (The East End, $, p. 109)

Christina's (The East End, $$, p. 109)

Mezes (The East End, $, p. 110)

Myth ✸✸ (The East End, $$, p. 109)

Ouzeri (The East End, $, p. 110)

Pan on the Danforth ✸ (The East End, $$, p. 109)

Penelope (Downtown West, $, p. 96)

INDIAN

Indian Rice Factory (Midtown West, $, p. 106)

Nataraj ✸ (Midtown West, $, p. 107)

Xacutti ✸✸ (Downtown West, $$$, p. 91)

Where to Dine from Chinatown to Bloor Street

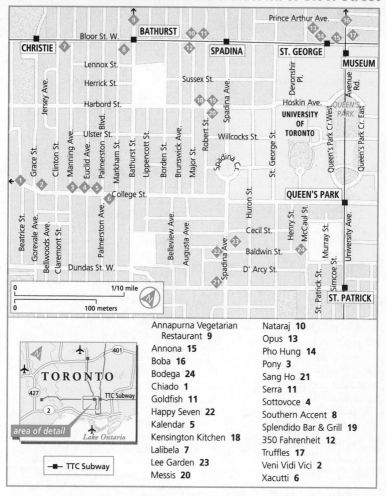

Annapurna Vegetarian
  Restaurant **9**
Annona **15**
Boba **16**
Bodega **24**
Chiado **1**
Goldfish **11**
Happy Seven **22**
Kalendar **5**
Kensington Kitchen **18**
Lalibela **7**
Lee Garden **23**
Messis **20**

Nataraj **10**
Opus **13**
Pho Hung **14**
Pony **3**
Sang Ho **21**
Serra **11**
Sottovoce **4**
Southern Accent **8**
Splendido Bar & Grill **19**
350 Fahrenheit **12**
Truffles **17**
Veni Vidi Vici **2**
Xacutti **6**

INTERNATIONAL

Annona ✦ (Midtown West, $$$,
  p. 102)
Brassaii ✦✦✦ (Downtown West,
  $$, p. 92)
Bymark (Downtown West, $$$$,
  p. 86)
Courthouse Market Grille (Down-
  town East, $$$, p. 98)
Epic ✦✦ (Downtown West, $$$,
  p. 89)
Jamie Kennedy Wine Bar ✦✦✦
  (Downtown East, $$, p. 99)

North 44 ✦✦✦ (Uptown, $$$$,
  p. 111)
Rosewater Supper Club ✦ (Down-
  town East, $$$, p. 98)
Scaramouche ✦ (Uptown, $$$$,
  p. 112)
Senses ✦✦✦ (Downtown West,
  $$$, p. 91)
Terra ✦✦ (North of the City, $$$,
  p. 116)
YYZ ✦✦ (Downtown West, $$$$,
  p. 88)

ITALIAN

Amore Trattoria ✸✸ (Uptown, $$, p. 113)

Café Nervosa (Midtown West, $$, p. 103)

Dante's ✸✸ (North of the City, $, p. 117)

Grano ✸ (Uptown, $$, p. 113)

Il Posto Nuovo (Midtown West, $$$, p. 102)

La Bruschetta ✸ (Uptown, $$$, p. 112)

Mistura ✸ (Midtown West, $$$, p. 103)

Serra ✸✸ (Midtown West, $, p. 107)

Sotto Sotto ✸✸ (Midtown West, $$, p. 105)

Terroni (Downtown East, $$, p. 100)

Veni Vidi Vici ✸✸ (Downtown West, $$, p. 96)

JAPANESE/SUSHI

Blowfish Restaurant & Sake Bar ✸✸ (Downtown West, $$$, p. 89)

Hiro Sushi ✸ (Downtown East, $$$, p. 98)

Japan Deli (Midtown West, $, p. 106)

LAOTIAN

Vanipha Lanna ✸✸ (Uptown, $$, p. 116)

LIGHT FARE

Bloor Street Diner (Midtown West, $, p. 106)

Hannah's Kitchen (Uptown, $, p. 116)

Hello Toast (Downtown East, $, p. 100)

Holt Renfrew Café ✸ (Midtown West, $$, p. 104)

HotHouse Cafe (Downtown East, $$, p. 99)

Jamie Kennedy Wine Bar ✸✸✸ (Downtown East, $$, p. 99)

Kalendar ✸✸ (Downtown West, $, p. 96)

Peter Pan (Downtown West, $$, p. 94)

Rebel House (Uptown, $, p. 116)

Sottovoce (Downtown West, $, p. 97)

Terroni (Downtown East, $$, p. 100)

350 Fahrenheit (Midtown West, $, p. 107)

MEDITERRANEAN

Agora ✸ (Downtown West, $$$, p. 88)

Kensington Kitchen ✸✸ (Midtown West, $, p. 106)

Millie's Bistro ✸✸ (Uptown, $$$, p. 112)

Myth ✸✸ (The East End, $$, p. 109)

Sage (Midtown West, $$, p. 105)

MIDDLE EASTERN

Mezzetta (Uptown, $$, p. 115)

PORTUGUESE

Chiado (Downtown West, $$$, p. 89)

QUEBECOIS

Le Papillon (Downtown East, $, p. 100)

Montréal Bistro & Jazz Club (Downtown East, $$, p. 100)

SEAFOOD

Joso's (Midtown West, $$, p. 104)

Rodney's Oyster House (Downtown West, $$, p. 95)

Sang Ho ✸ (Downtown West, $$, p. 95)

STEAK

Barberian's ✸ (Downtown West, $$$$, p. 85)

TEX-MEX

Tortilla Flats (Downtown West, $, p. 97)

THAI

Thai Magic ✦ (Uptown, $$$, p. 113)

Vanipha Lanna ✦✦ (Uptown, $$, p. 116)

Young Thailand ✦✦ (Downtown East, $, p. 101)

VEGETARIAN

Annapurna Vegetarian Restaurant (Midtown West, $, p. 114)

Fressen (Downtown West, $$, p. 114)

Juice for Life (Downtown West, $, p. 114)

350 Fahrenheit (Midtown West, $, p. 107)

VIETNAMESE

Pho Hung (Midtown West, $, p. 107)

2 Downtown West

This is where you will find Toronto's greatest concentration of great restaurants. **Little Italy,** which runs along **College Street,** and **Chinatown,** which radiates from **Spadina Avenue,** has more restaurants than any other parts of the city.

You'll see a lot of high-price, low-quality eateries in the area, too. There also tends to be more attitude from waitstaffs, particularly along the gourmet ghetto of **Queen Street West.** I'm a firm believer that even the best food can't make up for shoddy service, so the restaurants I've selected generally get high marks in both categories. Because service is so important to me, you won't find reviews of restaurants where it's totally substandard. A case in point is Little Italy's **Trattoria Giancarlo,** which has gained renown for its very good cooking and its celeb sightings. Unfortunately, you pretty much have to be a star to get even a glass of water brought to your table. Personally, no matter how charming a meal is, I find that lousy service leaves a bad taste in my mouth.

VERY EXPENSIVE

Avalon ✦✦ ECLECTIC   Follow the slim marble staircase into the elegant, compact dining room. Careful attention to detail is clear, whether in the spray of fresh flowers on each table or the daily chef's menu. (The regular menu changes with the seasons.) Avalon has one of the most inventive kitchens in the city, and it demonstrates its creativity through pairings of flavors rather than a showy multiplicity of ingredients. Main courses favor fish and fowl, such as steamed Boston fluke and Alaskan king crab with a sweet-pea sauce, or lightly smoked Moulard duck breast with pommes Anna and a black currant coulis. Desserts include treats like pear-and-elderflower sorbet and a wide selection of cheeses. The globetrotting wine list represents New World and Old.

270 Adelaide St. W. (at John St.). ✆ **416/979-9918.** www.avalonrestaurant.ca. Reservations required. Main courses C$29–C$40 (US$20–US$28). AE, DC, MC, V. Thurs noon–2pm; Mon–Sat 5:30–10pm. Subway: St. Andrew.

Barberian's ✦ STEAK   Not getting enough protein? Get thee to Harry Barberian's upscale steakhouse, which has been going strong since 1959 (his son, Arron, has since taken over). The room is cozy in a clubby way, with dark woods, framed newspapers, and pre-Confederation doodads. The menu rarely changes, but you won't hear any grousing—the crowd is too busy slurping martinis. The highlights are the eight steaks, from 9-ounce sirloin to 23-ounce porterhouse, all served with rice and spuds. The less traditional can partake of dishes like cheese or beef fondue for two, which is on the late-night menu (10pm–midnight). For all intents and purposes, there is only one dessert: Grand Marnier soufflé for two. The wine list is about 1,000 strong, so bring your reading specs. Celebrity sightings aren't uncommon, but autograph seeking is frowned upon.

7 Elm St. ✆ **416/597-0335.** www.barberians.com. Reservations required. Main courses C$22–C$37 (US$15–US$26). AE, DC, MC, V. Mon–Fri noon–2:30pm; daily 5pm–midnight. Subway: Dundas.

Bymark *(Overrated* INTERNATIONAL   I feel terrible: For years I've hoped that Mark McEwan, the excellent chef behind North 44—one of my favorite restaurants in any city (p. 111)—would open a restaurant in downtown Toronto. Now that he has, I can hardly believe my disappointment. While the food here is very good and the design is subtly beautiful, the service is lacking and the atmosphere is abominable. If you don't mind your very expensive meal being disrupted repeatedly by drunken louts in suits at the neighboring tables, you've found your restaurant! This is one of the hot see-and-be-seen spots of the moment, and, if you're determined to stop in, take my advice and bypass Bymark's dining room for its bar.

66 Wellington St. W. ✆ **416/777-1144.** www.bymark.ca. Reservations required. Main courses C$30–C$48 (US$21–US$34). AE, DC, MC, V. Mon–Fri 11:30am–2:30pm; Mon–Sat 5–10pm. Subway: King.

Canoe Restaurant & Bar ✪ CANADIAN   The inspiring view makes this the place to see Toronto lit up at night. The interior isn't so shabby, either, with polished wooden floors and furnishings. Corporate types predominate, not only because Canoe is in the Financial District, but also because the prices best suit expense accounts. The meat-heavy menu showcases modern Canadian cuisine. Grilled veal tenderloin served with acorn squash and warm sage-infused goat cheese vies for attention with Maritime sea scallops served with a tartlet of caramelized potatoes and double-smoked bacon. A few "spa inspired" dishes are lower in fat. The wine list only scratches the surface—roughly two-thirds of the bottles in stock aren't included—so if you're craving a certain vintage, be sure to ask.

54th floor, Toronto Dominion Tower, 66 Wellington St. W. ✆ **416/364-0054.** www.canoerestaurant.com. Reservations required. Main courses C$24–C$40 (US$17–US$28). AE, DC, MC, V. Mon–Fri 11:45am–2:30pm and 5–10:30pm. Subway: King.

Eau FUSION   There's a certain segment of the Toronto population that likes to think that their city is the New York of the North. That type would surely gravitate to Eau, one of the restaurants that is enlivening the formerly sedate King Street West area. It's cool, it's stylish, and it's way overpriced. The cocktail menu is funny without meaning to be: With martinis like the "bubble-eau-seven" (peach and pineapple juices with vodka) and "the-big-eau" (vodka, champagne and ice wine) costing C$13 to C$18 (US$9.10–US$13) apiece, there must be some kind of joke afoot. But there is good news here: The kitchen does a fine job with appetizers like blue-crab-and-avocado salad and entrees like roasted duck breast drizzled with a glaze of sour cherry and bourbon. Furthermore, while the gorgeous staff do pose a bit, they are actually very sweet and helpful.

609 King St. W. ✆ **416/203-9399.** Reservations strongly recommended. Main courses C$27–C$39 (US$19–US$27). AE, DC, MC, V. Wed–Sat 5:30–10:30pm. Subway: St Andrew.

The Fifth ✹ ECLECTIC   *Je pense que Le Cinquième n'est pas comme des autres.*
Ah, *pardon,* was I just speaking French? I must have been confused by the menu
at The Fifth, which insists on listing all its plates *en français* and *en anglais.*
Crème Arlequin is translated as—get ready for this—crème Arlequin (no, I'm not
joking). *Ça va?* In fairness, though, the kitchen does serve stellar fare, like tur-
bot and Digby sea scallop with a maple-infused olive-pecan tapenade. Now if
they could just fire the translator . . . (**One caveat:** Reservations are an absolute
must at The Fifth, and they have to be confirmed with a credit card. And yes,
the restaurant is serious about charging C$50/US$35 per person for no-shows.)

225 Richmond St. W. ⓒ **416/979-3005.** www.easyandthefifth.com. Reservations required. 3-course prix-fixe
menu C$85 (US$60). Thurs–Sat 6pm–midnight. Subway: Osgoode.

Monsoon ✹ ASIAN   Monsoon is more famous for its award-winning interior
design than for its food. That's a pity, because, while the brown-on-black Zen-
like setting and the fabulously flattering lighting are easy on the eye, the cooking
is subtly sensual. Sophisticated palates are familiar with Thai, Chinese, Japanese,
and Indian flavors, but it's unusual to find them so seductively intertwined with
North American staples—take for example the exquisite beef tenderloin in a
Cabernet-teriyaki reduction that is teamed up with wasabi mashed potatoes. The
wine list runs the gamut from French bordeaux to Australian shiraz.

100 Simcoe St. ⓒ **416/979-7172.** www.monsoonrestaurant.ca. Reservations required. Main courses
C$21–C$37 (US$15–US$26). AE, DC, MC, V. Mon–Fri noon–2:30pm; Mon–Sat 5pm–midnight. Subway: St.
Andrew.

Susur ✹✹✹ FUSION   If you visited Toronto a few years ago, you might have
had the good fortune to dine at an exquisite restaurant called Lotus. The eatery's
chef and owner, Susur Lee, broke the hearts of the city's foodies when he decided
to close it and travel abroad. After some stints in foreign kitchens—he got as far
away as Singapore—Lee is back and better than ever. Susur is a delight. For such
a high-end establishment, its decor is refreshingly low-key, with stark white walls
and oyster-pale upholstery warmed with colored lights. There is no pretension
here, in either the ambience or the fine service.

But the biggest draw is what's on the plate. Lee serves stellar cuisine in the
true fusion spirit, blending Asian and Western ingredients, cooking methods,
and presentation. The menu changes frequently, with bold, savory offerings like
rare venison loin with Gorgonzola-hawberry–red-wine sauce. The cooking is
complex, and the wine list, while pricey, has been put together with extreme
care. When in doubt, ask the well-informed serving staff for recommendations.

601 King St. W. ⓒ **416/603-2205.** www.susur.com. Reservations required. Main courses C$29–C$43
(US$20–US$30). AE, MC, V. Mon–Sat 6–10pm. Subway: St. Andrew, then streetcar west to Bathurst St. and
walk 1 block west to Portland St.

360 Revolving Restaurant *Overrated* CONTINENTAL   Let's be frank: Most
people do not come here for the food. The view's the thing, a breathtaking, awe-
inspiring panorama that will make you see the city in a new light. Unfortunately,
the kitchen doesn't keep pace—it offers uninspiring fare like cold crab and
shrimp salad on Bibb lettuce. The highlight of the dessert list is a chocolate ren-
dition of the CN Tower. The wine list makes for interesting viewing, with its collection of three-figure vintages, though there are a few choices by the glass.

CN Tower, 301 Front St. W. © **416/362-5411.** www.cntower.ca. Reservations required. Main courses C$25–C$40 (US$18–US$28). AE, DC, MC, V. May–Sept daily 10:30am–2:30pm; year-round daily 4:30–10:30pm. Subway: Union.

Tundra ★★ CANADIAN   A key element of the Hilton's C$25-million (US$18-million) renovation was the creation of this luxurious restaurant just off its foyer. Sophisticated and opulent, the restaurant is designed to evoke elements of the Canadian landscape. How does one suggest the majesty of, say, a giant redwood? With columns wrapped in semitransparent fabric and lit from within, of course! (The stunning result is like a gargantuan Naguchi lamp.) Every detail, from the one-armed wing chairs to the Frette linens, is beautifully executed.

The sense of theater doesn't stop with the design—the cuisine is just as artful. Arctic char (a fish that's often called a hybrid of salmon and trout) is paired with Malapeque oysters and fried leeks; Nova Scotia lobster mates with tomato-avocado-bean salad and Yukon Gold potatoes. The results are elegantly complex. While the wine list is exhaustive, don't hesitate to ask for recommendations—service is well informed and helpful.

Hilton Toronto, 145 Richmond St. W. © **416/860-6800.** www.toronto.hilton.com. Reservations strongly recommended. Main courses C$28–C$40 (US$20–US$28). AE, DC, MC, V. Daily 6:30–11:30am and 5:30–10pm; Mon–Fri 11:30am–2pm. Subway: Osgoode.

YYZ ★★ INTERNATIONAL   If you visited Toronto in 2001 or earlier, you were perhaps fortunate enough to experience the Mercer Street Grill. While that restaurant is no more, its owner, Simon Bower, has created a striking spot in YYZ. Named after the call letters of Toronto's airport, the setting brings to mind a futuristic lounge—all chrome, steel, and glass. While the palette veers to the cool (unlike the city's other modernist spaces, there's not so much as a hint of greenery to temper its android appeal), this is now home to some of the hottest cooking in town. For starters, rare duck breast is paired with both spicy ginger and sweet pineapple. The substantial mains, like the rack of lamb with a celery-root-and-potato mash and mint purée, are artfully done. Do try to save space for dessert: The warm pumpkin tart is a great way to finish.

345 Adelaide St. W. © **416/599-3399.** www.yyzrestaurant.com. Reservations required. Main courses C$26–C$34 (US$18–US$24). AE, MC, V. Mon–Sat 5–10:30pm. Subway: Osgoode.

EXPENSIVE

Agora ★ MEDITERRANEAN   I'm biased—restaurants attached to larger institutions usually scare me off. Agora at the Art Gallery of Ontario is an exception. Located in the beautiful Tannenbaum sculpture gallery, and open only for lunch and brunch, Agora serves food that's inventive without being artsy. It's worth a trip even if you're not visiting the gallery. The menu does have its precious moments, like "Still life with aubergine," but the food is uniformly delightful. Some dishes play it straight with a Continental flair, like grilled niçoise-style tuna with French green beans. The weekend brunch glams up scrambled eggs with fresh truffle shavings and chives; the cinnamon crepes with an almond-ricotta filling and apricot coulis are a treat.

At the Art Gallery of Ontario, 317 Dundas St. W. © **416/977-0414.** www.ago.net. Reservations recommended for lunch. Main courses C$12–C$20 (US$8.40–US$14). AE, DC, MC, V. Tues–Fri noon–2:30pm; Sat–Sun 11am–3pm. Subway: St. Patrick.

Blowfish Restaurant & Sake Bar ★★ JAPANESE/SUSHI Taking its name from a high-risk Japanese delicacy, this great spot only adds to the glamour of King Street West. Tucked inside a former bank building whose soaring ceilings lend the room true grandeur, this restaurant is a rare pleasure—just like the blowfish. Eateries in trendy areas come and go, but Blowfish's impressive attention to detail makes me hope that this one will be around for a while.

The menu features the expected sushi and sashimi, and the quality and presentation is uniformly excellent. But there are lots of other options, from the starters (barbecued salmon skin and green salad make a stellar pair in peppery dressing) to the mains (sea bass or black cod in a sweet miso marinade). Even the free bowls of warm and salty edamame are delicious, and the service is friendly and helpful. My one caveat to diners is to dine here on the early side, since the restaurant transforms into a lounge at 11pm.

668 King St. W. ✆ 416/860-0606. www.blowfishrestaurant.com. Reservations strongly recommended. Main courses C$14–C$24 (US$9.80–US$17). AE, MC, V. Mon–Sat 5pm–2am. Subway: St Andrew, then street-car west to Bathurst.

Chiado PORTUGUESE Alone in this Mediterranean-obsessed part of town, Chiado serves modern Portuguese cuisine. Designed to evoke opulence, with marble floors, oil paintings, and fresh orchids, it draws a sophisticated crowd. Servers are models of Euro professionalism, attentive without hovering. The menu favors seafood, from starters—such as grilled squid with roasted peppers—to entrees, such as poached or grilled salted cod. Fresh fish is flown in daily. The fowl and game dishes include a choice of braised rabbit or capon. Don't skimp on the lovingly prepared sweets. The wine list is a treat. It includes many unfamiliar but rich and complex wines, most priced in the bargain range.

484 College St. (at Concorde Ave.). ✆ 416/538-1910. Reservations required. Main courses C$17–C$30 (US$12–US$21). AE, DC, MC, V. Mon–Sat noon–3pm; Mon–Thurs 5–10pm; Fri–Sat 5pm–midnight. Subway: Queen's Park, then any streetcar west to Bathurst St.

Epic ★★ INTERNATIONAL Not that I would ever counsel a visitor to stay within the confines of his or her hotel, but this stunning restaurant at the Fairmont Royal York is definitely worth a visit. The scene here is one of unabashed luxury, with velvety banquettes and Murano glass chandeliers. The attentive service is in keeping with the elegant atmosphere—don't come here if you don't want to be pampered.

The menu holds up its end of the deal, with luxurious ingredients that are cleverly matched up. The starters set the tone—think Dungeness crab salad with Segruva caviar, or a seafood tower that is built with the freshest lobster, scallops, and oysters. Mains are equally well turned out, varying from truffle-and-polenta-stuffed pheasant with asparagus and shallots, to the morel-crusted venison loin with seared Québec foie gras. One of my favorite dishes—the tempura-fried halibut and hand-cut fries (an upscale version of fish and chips)—is available only at lunch.

Fairmont Royal York, 100 Front St. W. ✆ 416/860-6949. www.fairmont.com/royalyork. Reservations recommended. Main courses C$22–C$34 (US$15–US$24). AE, DC, MC, V. Mon–Fri 7–10am, noon–2pm, and 5:30–10pm (till 11pm on Fri); Sat 7–11am and 5:30–11pm; Sun 7am–2pm and 5:30–10pm. Subway: Union.

Far Niente ★★ AMERICAN A hangout favored by the suited set, this restaurant offers fine cuisine in a casual setting. The room recalls California, with an earthy palette, mounds of greenery, wine racks, and simple wooden tables and chairs. The kitchen uses garden-fresh ingredients and a light touch. The menu designates many staples—including tuna steak, grilled salmon, and even a Caesar salad—as "living well" dishes, which have reduced fat, cholesterol, and calories. You might try Sonoma spinach salad with cherry tomatoes, button mushrooms, and bean sprouts; the pumpkin ravioli with cranberries and pecans in apple cider butter sauce; or the skillet-seared sea bass in a saffron-vanilla sauce with ginger-scented veggies and mashed Yukon Gold potatoes. Steaks are a specialty, with filet mignon and New York strip loin available in 6- to 14-ounce cuts.

Downstairs is **Soul of the Vine,** a wine bar that has its own menu, mainly appetizers and pasta. The room can get loud and smoky, so serious eaters should stay upstairs.

187 Bay St. (at Wellington St.). ℂ **416/214-9922.** www.farnientegrill.com. Reservations recommended. Main courses C$18–C$36 (US$13–US$25). AE, DC, MC, V. Mon–Fri 11:30am–11pm; Sat–Sun 5–11pm. Subway: King.

Jump Cafe & Bar ★★ AMERICAN   Jump is, appropriately enough, always hopping. A sprawling space in Commerce Court, it can be tricky to find. Just follow the buzz—as the decibel level rises (above romantic, but not uncomfortable), you'll know you're on the right track. Power brokers drop by for lunch or after-work drinks. The dinner scene is a mix of celebratory couples and suits in deal-making mode. The restaurant is such a see-and-be-seen spot that you might suspect it's all show and no substance. Actually, the food is anything but an afterthought. To start, consider steamed mussels in ginger-and-coconut-milk broth, or grilled tiger shrimps on Thai mango-peanut salad. The menu features "suitable" dishes such as grilled 10-ounce New York Black Angus steak with Yukon Gold fries, salsa, and mushroom gravy. The more adventurous have other choices, such as roasted sea bass with fragrant coconut basmati rice and green curry, or *osso buco* with spinach-and-lemon risotto. The wine list favors the New World, and there are a fair number of selections by the glass. Luxe desserts will set your diet back by about a month. Service is smooth, and the only complaint I could possibly make is that Jump never seems to settle down.

1 Wellington St. W. ℂ **416/363-3400.** www.jumpcafe.com. Reservations required. Main courses C$19–C$32 (US$13–US$22). AE, DC, MC, V. Mon–Fri 11:45am–11:30pm; Sat 5pm–11:30pm. Subway: King.

Lai Wah Heen ★★★ CHINESE   This is one hotel dining room where you'll find more locals than visitors. The interior is vintage Art Deco; spare pictograms dominate the walls of the two-level space. A suited-up crowd dominates at lunch; at dinner, a few dolled-up couples manage to sneak in. The massive menu is mainly Cantonese, with some Szechuan specialties. It offers more than a dozen shark's fin soups, from thick broth with bamboo fungi to Alaska king crab bisque. Abalone gets similar attention, shredded and stir-fried with bean sprouts or braised with fresh vegetables and oyster sauce. Those with tamer tastes (or restricted budgets) can choose from meat or noodle dishes; the dim sum list alone goes on for several pages. There are several lunch and dinner prix-fixe specials, which offer five or six dishes for C$38 (US$27) and up.

In the Metropolitan Hotel, 110 Chestnut St. ℂ **416/977-9899.** www.metropolitan.com/lwh. Reservations recommended. Main courses C$16–C$30 (US$11–US$21). AE, DC, MC, V. Daily 11:30am–3pm; Sun–Thurs 5:30–10:30pm; Fri–Sat 5:30–11pm. Subway: St. Patrick.

Oro CONTINENTAL   The trappings of modern luxury set the scene, with blond wood, a tile floor, and a substantial fireplace that warms that room (figuratively if not always literally). In its Eaton Centre neighborhood, Oro is uniquely sophisticated. Softly lit tables sit far apart—this is the perfect spot for a romantic rendezvous. The menu ventures further and further from its Italianate roots, with showstoppers like West-meets-East hoisin-tamarind glazed pork tenderloin accompanied by cumin-scented red onion purée. Desserts like the white chocolate cheesecake bombe are equally delightful. The lengthy wine list leans toward Italy and America, with only a select few by the glass. The oft-praised service is relaxed but attentive.

45 Elm St. © 416/597-0155. www.ororestaurant.com. Reservations recommended. Main courses C$18–C$40 (US$13–US$28). AE, DC, MC, V. Mon–Fri noon–2:30pm; Mon–Sat 5:30–10:30pm. Subway: Dundas.

Rain ⭐ ASIAN   One of Toronto's trendiest spots, Rain has gained a certain notoriety for employing a bouncer at the door; word has it that the bouncer determines who's chic enough to make it into this den of cool, reservations be damned. The *Toronto Star*'s restaurant critic was turned away, despite having a reservation; most famously, pop star Nelly Furtado was refused entry to her own private party (the restaurant's owners refuse to discuss the incident). You either love it or you hate it—Rain evokes strong emotions. Everyone agrees that the decor is a seductive hit, with its waterfall walls, backlit frosted-glass bars and screens, and sophisticated low black banquettes. The menu is equally sleek, albeit a tad confusing: Instead of dividing appetizers from entrees, it jumbles dishes together, with only their price tags indicating their relative size. The cooking is lovely, with some standouts like five-spice Peking duck roll, and miso black cod atop tatsoi greens. While the service is adequate, it's a little clunky for such a swank place.

19 Mercer St. © 416/599-7246. Reservations required. Main courses C$10–C$30 (US$7–US$21). AE, MC, V. Tues–Sat 5:30–11pm. Subway: St. Andrew.

Senses ⭐⭐⭐ INTERNATIONAL   Harry Wu, who already has two excellent restaurants—Lai Wah Heen (p. 90) and Hemispheres—at the Metropolitan Hotel, is the man behind this venture, which is located at his SoHo Metropolitan Hotel (p. 58). The Senses brand now encompasses a bakery, cafes, and a gourmet food emporium (see p. 190 in chapter 8), but this is the granddaddy of them all. Dining here is an experience for—what else?—all the senses. The serene sandy tones are serious eye candy, the background music soothes, and velvety banquettes rub you the right way. The whole setting is opulent and luxurious and sets you up for the delights you'll find on the plate. Smell and taste get revved up for starters like the salad of seared tuna, cucumber, nashi pear, and avocado, or the lobster and scallops layered with osetra caviar and spicy mayonnaise. The main-dish triple-seared beef tenderloin with stilton and miso tart and foie gras sauce is beautifully executed. Make an effort to leave some room for dessert—the apple crumble with cardamom ice cream is a fantastic finish. Service is extremely well informed and professional.

At the SoHo Metropolitan, 318 Wellington St. W. © 416/961-0055. www.senses.ca. Reservations strongly recommended. Main courses C$19–C$46 (US$13–US$32). AE, DC, MC, V. Wed–Sun 6pm–10pm; bar and bistro daily 4pm–1am. Subway: St. Andrew.

Xacutti ⭐⭐ INDIAN   There are a lot of reasons to love Xacutti (pronounced sha-koo-tee). One is that it brings a new and exotic flavor to the well-traveled Little Italy restaurant strip. Another is that the Indian-inspired cuisine is just so beautifully executed. Starters include galangal prawns in a lime-mint curry or baby greens in a kumquat vinaigrette; mains range from cardamom-smoked lamb with mango chutney and ginger frites to pan-fried cod with new potatoes, spinach, and coconut-tomato curry. The weekend brunch menu is just as excellent, though it veers away from Indian food, serving up treats like blueberry pancakes with maple syrup and Devonshire cream or a wild-mushroom-and-goat-cheese omelet. The thoughtful service matches the cuisine.

503 College St. © **416/323-3957**. www.xacutti.com. Reservations strongly recommended. Main courses C$17–C$34 (US$12–US$24). AE, DC, MC, V. Mon–Sat 6:30pm–midnight; Sat 10:30am–3pm; Sun 10:30am–4pm. Subway: Queen's Park, then streetcar west to Palmerston.

MODERATE

Bodega FRENCH   This is a quiet spot infused with Gallic charm. In a turn-of-the-20th-century town house, Bodega is a short walk from the Art Gallery of Ontario. The two dining rooms have fireplaces, picturesque tapestries, and gilt-framed mirrors lining the walls. The menu is traditional French, with a focus on meats. Grilled beef tenderloin soaks up cognac sauce, and duck breast mixes well with wild blueberries. The wine list boasts some Bordeaux grandes dames, and there's a nice mix of Ontario vintages, too.

30 Baldwin St. © **416/977-1287**. www.bodegarestaurant.com. Reservations recommended. Main courses C$15–C$27 (US$11–US$19). AE, DC, MC, V. Daily 11:30am–2:30pm and 5–11pm. Subway: St. Patrick.

Brassaii ★★★ 〔Value〕 BISTRO/INTERNATIONAL   This is one of my favorite Toronto restaurants. Named for a 1920s French photographer—his black-and-white prints adorn the walls—Brassaii offers a picture-perfect setting. The long, cavernous dining room is decorated in dusky grey and black, and tall vases stand in the windows, each holding a single long-stemmed calla lily. The effect feels much like being inside a photograph, and the flattering lighting from the halogen spotlights that hang from the ceiling only enhance this image. Still, on King Street West these days, everyone looks cool (Eau, Blowfish, and others). But Brassaii still manages to stand out by offering both excellent cooking and brilliant service—and doing so for prices that are lower than most of its competition in the area. The kitchen really knows its stuff. While the menu frequently changes, it might include entrees such as braised duck atop lentils and spinach, or shoulder of lamb with chickpeas and tomato. The desserts are not to be missed, particularly the elegant apple crumble with berries and caramel ice cream. The wine list is substantial, and there are some very good vintages available by the glass. Still, my favorite drink here is the Brassaii martini, which blends a couple of types of fruit juice with 7-Up and vodka. I know it sounds bizarre, but it's a deliciously sweet drink.

One more thing: Also unlike its competition, Brassaii is open for breakfast, lunch, and dinner on weekdays. Bon appétit, indeed.

461 King St. W. © **416/598-4730**. www.brassaii.com. Reservations recommended. Main courses C$14–C$22 (US$9.80–US$15). AE, MC, V. Mon–Fri 7am–midnight; Sat 5:30pm–midnight. Subway: St. Andrew, then streetcar west to Spadina Ave.

Cities BISTRO   This charming bistro, where a rococo Elvis presides over the bar, personifies the pleasures and problems of metropolitan life. It's overcrowded—19 tables for two cram the narrow room, forcing neighbors to rub elbows. The food, however, makes it all worthwhile. The menu is deliberately short, allowing the kitchen to focus hothouse-flower care on its featured selections: rack of lamb, Atlantic salmon, veal tenderloin. Starters, like three-mushroom salad, get equal attention.

859 Queen St. W. © **416/599-7720**. Main courses C$12–C$20 (US$8.40–US$14). AE, MC, V. Daily noon–2:30pm and 5–10:30pm. Subway: Osgoode, then any streetcar west to Bathurst St.

Citron ECLECTIC   At once chic and attitude-free, Citron draws casual but hip 20-somethings. The menu borrows heavily from every corner of the globe, favoring seafood and vegetarian offerings. North African couscous stew, Tex-Mex lasagna, and Thai-spiced salmon compete for attention. For dessert, my sweet-tooth side recommends the divine white chocolate cheesecake.

813 Queen St. W. *C* **416/504-2647.** Reservations not accepted. Main courses C$12–C$20 (US$8.40–US$14). AE, MC, V. Mon–Thurs 5–10:30pm; Fri–Sat 5–11pm. Subway: Osgoode, then any streetcar west to Bathurst St.

Crush ✪ BISTRO   This lively spot is another reason that King Street West is now a major foodie destination. Crush is part bistro and part wine bar, and its atmosphere is appropriately convivial. The high-ceilinged, warehouse-like space has a huge open kitchen, so you can be entertained by the goings-on that are usually kept behind the scenes. Better still, you can be impressed by the results: The goat-cheese-and-tomato napoleon or the mussels on the half-shell topped with escargot butter make great opening acts. The juicy pork chop in Madeira sauce is a star is its own right. The wine list is diverse, with many varieties available by the glass (you can even choose whether to have a 3-oz. or 5-oz. serving, a boon for oenophiles who want to try new things). Service is smooth and obliging, making this a great place to go if you're planning on catching a show at one of the nearby theaters. The only potential problem with Crush is the decibel level: This is a lively spot, and warehouse spaces aren't known for great acoustics.

455 King St. W. *C* **416/977-1234.** Reservations recommended. Main courses C$14–C$25 (US$9.80–US$18). AE, MC, V. Mon–Fri noon–10:30pm; Sat 5–10:30pm; Sun 5–10pm. Subway: St. Andrew, then streetcar west to Spadina Ave.

Fortune Cookie ✪ *Kids* ASIAN   Gourmet it isn't, but I really do like Fortune Cookie. Why? For starters, it's one of the best deals in the Entertainment District: For C$23 (US$16) per person (or C$10/US$7 for children 9 and under), you can order whatever you want from a 39-item tasting menu. You can also order as much as you like, so while the portions do tend to be small, you can get more of the General Tao chicken or the deep-fried spring rolls if you want. It's also a great way of getting around the problem of trying new things: If you always get the orange beef, here's your chance to try it *and* a slew of other dishes, too. The waitstaff are friendly and helpful, even when you keep sending them back for more . . . and more . . . and more . . .

291 King St. W. *C* **416/599-9995.** Reservations recommended. Tasting menu C$23 (US$16) per person (C$10/US$7 for children 9 and under). AE, DC, MC, V. Sun–Thurs 11:30am–10pm; Fri 11:30am–11pm; Sat noon–11pm. Subway: St. Andrew.

La Palette ✪ BISTRO   This is a terrific, offbeat addition to the Kensington Market neighborhood. It's so good, in fact, that you almost wonder why no one else ever thought of locating a classic French bistro on the edge of Chinatown. A quartet of Gallic flags announces its presence; inside, the 30-seat dining room is cozy and informal, with considerate, low-key service. The menu is classic, from ballantine of chicken stuffed with peppers and rice to lamb chops with a crusty coating of mustard and rosemary. If you're as much as a dessert fiend as I am, save room for irresistible citron tart and dark chocolate cake.

256 Augusta Ave. *C* **416/929-4900.** Reservations recommended. Main courses C$10–C$18 (US$7–US$13). AE, MC, V. Sun–Thurs 5:30–11pm; Fri–Sat noon–midnight. Subway: St. Patrick, then streetcar west to Augusta Ave.

Le Sélect Bistro BISTRO   What says Paris bistro to you? Le Sélect sets the tone with posters, decorative objects straight from *grand-mère*'s attic, and sultry jazz in the background. Breadbaskets hang from the ceiling above each table, and require gentle coaxing to reach the diners. The menu emphasizes traditional rib-sticking fare such as steak frites and cassoulet, all nicely done. The service can be a trifle slow, but the casually dressed professionals don't seem to mind.

328 Queen St. W. ✆ 416/596-6405. www.leselect.com. Reservations recommended. Main courses C$13–C$33 (US$9.10–US$23). AE, DC, MC, V. Sun–Wed 11:30am–11pm; Thurs 11:30am–11:30pm; Fri–Sat 11:30am–midnight. Subway: Osgoode.

Mildred Pierce ★★ ECLECTIC Named after a Joan Crawford film, this restaurant is appropriately theatrical. Murals of a Roman feast cover the walls (a local in-joke, they depict characters including the restaurant's owner). The menu fits right in, rich in inspiration and dramatic flourishes borrowed from different countries. Grilled salmon accompanies saffron risotto and a ragout of fennel, baby beets, and bok choy, while a Thai hot pot boasts tiger shrimp, scallops, mussels, and clams brewing in a coconut-lime-cilantro sauce. The short wine list includes options from Italy, Spain, South Africa, and California. Lush desserts include maple crème brûlée, and a rustic cranberry and walnut tart.

99 Sudbury St. ✆ 416/588-5695. www.mildredpierce.com. Reservations recommended; not accepted for Sun brunch. Main courses C$17–C$26 (US$12–US$18). AE, DC, MC, V. Mon–Fri noon–2pm; Sun 10am–3pm; Sun–Thurs 5:30–10pm; Fri–Sat 5:30–11pm. Subway: Osgoode, then any streetcar west to Dovercourt; walk south on Dovercourt and turn right at Sudbury.

Peter Pan LIGHT FARE When I was in high school, Peter Pan was the classy restaurant you went to for pre-prom dinner or a big date. The crowd at this fun, relaxed place is forever young, easily impressed by the old-fashioned bar, ever-changing art exhibits, and friendly service. The menu is awash in Eurasian food-speak; simpler dishes are best. The Peter Pan burger is always a top choice. Desserts are strictly for sweet tooths.

⟨Kids Family-Friendly Restaurants

Fortune Cookie (p. 93) The food offerings in the Entertainment District grow ever more sophisticated—a great thing, unless you're looking for a place to take the small fry. The all-you-can-order 39-item tasting menu is a mere C$9.95 (US$7) for children 9 and under.

Grano (p. 113) Don't worry that a noisy babe-in-arms might disrupt diners—this lively, slightly chaotic eatery welcomes families. The owners have four kids, and they love to fuss over the *bambini*.

Kensington Kitchen (p. 106) Whimsically decorated, with colorful toys and model airplanes. It seems to be easier to get kids to eat their greens when veggies are tucked into pita sandwiches, like the ones here.

Millie's Bistro (p. 112) This is a perennially popular spot with families. There's a special menu for tykes, and most of the Mediterranean food can be eaten without cutlery.

Shopsy's (p. 101) When the kids are sick of eating out and craving comfort food, this is where to take them. Home-style chili and macaroni and cheese hit the spot, and ice cream dominates a whole section of the menu.

373 Queen St. W. Ⓒ 416/593-0917. Reservations recommended. Main courses C$10–C$18 (US$7–US$13). AE, MC, V. Mon–Wed noon–midnight; Thurs–Sat noon–1am; Sun noon–11pm. Subway: Osgoode.

Pony BISTRO   On the periphery of hyper-trendy Little Italy, Pony is nevertheless the kind of place where you can relax. The candlelit dining room is charming, the upholstered chairs are comfy, and the service is smooth. The menu sticks mainly to bistro classics, such as roasted chicken stuffed with prosciutto, smoked mozzarella, and apple slices. The Caesar salad has the creamiest dressing in town—even a devoted calorie-counter won't be able to resist.

488 College St. Ⓒ 416/923-7665. Reservations recommended. Main courses C$16–C$25 (US$11–US$18). AE, MC, V. Mon–Sat 5–11pm. Subway: Queen's Park, then any streetcar west to Bathurst.

Rodney's Oyster House SEAFOOD   A favorite with the Financial District set, Rodney's is rowdy at all times of day. The setting is as unpretentious as you could find: Think lobster traps dangling from the ceiling and fishing nets hanging across the walls. The main draw is the incredibly fresh oysters, and the lobster and salmon dishes are worth more than a look.

469 King St. W. Ⓒ 416-363-8105. www.rodneysoysterhouse.com. Reservations recommended. Main courses C$16–C$40 (US$11–US$28). AE, DC, MC, V. Mon–Sat 11:30am–midnight. Subway: St. Andrew.

Sang Ho ⭑ CHINESE/SEAFOOD   There's no end of eateries in the eastern end of Chinatown, but Sang Ho will be the one with the longest queue out front. The restaurant boasts not only a top-notch kitchen, but also a lovely dining room filled with several teeming aquariums. The regular menu of 100-plus dishes never changes; wall-mounted boards list many specials of the day. Seafood—shrimp, clams, or red snapper—is the obvious choice. Service is speedy and responsive. Try to go on a weeknight, when there's no more than a short wait for a table.

536 Dundas St. W. Ⓒ 416/596-1685. Reservations not accepted. Main courses C$8–C$18 (US$5.60–US$13). MC, V. Sun–Thurs noon–10pm; Fri–Sat noon–11pm. Subway: St. Patrick.

Swan ECLECTIC   The room brings to mind a retro soda fountain, with a counter and swirly stools on one side, and booths with Formica tables on the other. Just don't expect to find a strawberry-banana float on the menu. The youngish hipsters who congregate here slurp up martinis and oysters. Happily, the menu avoids the trendy trap, managing both roasted capon with bourbon gravy and corn fritters, and braised beef short ribs marinated in beer and marmalade. There's a nice selection of wines, almost all available by the glass. The popular weekend brunch features the usual eggy plates as well as some surprises: spicy Moroccan olives or smoked arctic char salad, anyone?

892 Queen St. W. Ⓒ 416/532-0452. Reservations recommended. Main courses C$15–C$20 (US$11–US$14). AE, DC, MC, V. Mon–Fri noon–4:30pm; Sat–Sun 11:30am–2:30pm; Sun–Fri 5–10:30pm; Sat 5–11pm. Subway: Osgoode, then any streetcar west to Euclid Ave.

Taro Grill ⭑ ECLECTIC   Pass through the curtain hanging at the door, and enter a hip new world. Actually, it's not that new, but the Taro Grill has something that most hot spots of the moment can't claim—staying power. Its secret? A mix of clever cooking, helpful service, and a glamorous high-ceilinged space. The menu refuses to be easily characterized. Just when you think you've pegged the Cal-Ital pizza-pasta-salad triad, out of the blue comes tempura veggies or Asian-influenced New Zealand lamb. Affordable bottles, mainly from Australia and South Africa, fill the wine list.

492 Queen St. W. Ⓒ **416/504-1320.** Reservations recommended. Main courses C$13–C$20 (US$9.10–US$14). AE, MC, V. Daily noon–4pm and 6–10pm. Subway: Osgoode, then any streetcar west to Bathurst St.

Veni Vidi Vici ★★ ITALIAN/FUSION   This is a Little Italy gem that serves delicious food in a swanky setting—but, unlike many of its neighborhood cousins, it does so without attitude. I like it even better than established neighborhood favorite Ecco La. There's no sign outside, just a gilt-covered fresco of a mustachioed deity looming over the doorway. Inside, the staff is quick to usher diners to high-backed velvet banquettes.

The menu can be divided into two parts. On the Italian side, there are pasta dishes such as linguine with mixed seafood, or risotto with portobello, cremini, and porcini mushrooms. But the Asian-inspired fusion plates are the showstoppers: Think cashew-studded sea bass with fennel, or phyllo-wrapped salmon with basmati rice. Desserts return to the classics, like crème brûlée with fresh berries. The wine list is particularly strong in Italian reds.

650 College St. (at Grace St.). Ⓒ **416/536-8550.** Reservations recommended. Main courses C$13–C$25 (US$9.10–US$18). AE, MC, V. Tues–Sun 11am–3pm and 5pm–midnight. Subway: Queen's Park, then streetcar west to Grace St.

INEXPENSIVE

Happy Seven CHINESE   This eatery boasts kitschy touches like plastic Buddhas and a tank full of fish and crawly critters. They may not be everybody's cup of (green) tea, but the kitchen is widely acknowledged as one of the best in Chinatown. The menu is classic Cantonese, with a few Szechuan choices. Seafood dishes are a favorite, though there are many plates for vegetarians; portions are extremely generous.

358 Spadina Ave. Ⓒ **416/971-9820.** Reservations not accepted. Main courses C$7–C$15 (US$4.90–US$11). MC, V. Daily 4pm–5am. Subway: Spadina, then LRT south to Baldwin St.

Kalendar ★★ LIGHT FARE   This has been a gem for years, and it shows no signs of slowing down. The food inspires satisfied sighs. There are sandwiches stuffed with portobello mushrooms, havarti, and roasted red peppers, and five "scrolls"—phyllo pastries filled with delights like artichoke hearts, eggplant, and hummus. The "nannettes" (pizzas) are baked nan breads topped with ingredients like smoked salmon, capers, and red onions. The ambience recalls a French bistro. In summer the sidewalk patio is just the place to sit and watch the world.

546 College St. (just west of Bathurst St.). Ⓒ **416/923-4138.** www.kalendar.com. Main courses C$10–C$13 (US$7–US$9.10). MC, V. Mon–Fri 11am–midnight; Sat-Sun 11am-3pm. Subway: Queen's Park, then any streetcar west to Bathurst St.

Lee Garden CHINESE   If lines are a measure of the success of a restaurant, then Lee Garden is, deservedly, the hands-down Toronto champ. The draw is a Cantonese menu weighted heavily toward seafood. Although there's no shark fin, there's no shortage of shrimp, lobster, and cod. The signature dish is fork-tender grandfather smoked chicken with honey and sesame seeds, and the kitchen works wonders with tofu, too.

331 Spadina Ave. Ⓒ **416/593-9524.** Reservations not accepted. Main courses C$10–C$22 (US$7–US$15). AE, MC, V. Daily 4pm–midnight. Subway: Spadina, then LRT south to Baldwin St.

Penelope GREEK   If you're in a rush to see a show at the Royal Alex or Roy Thomson Hall, this is one of your best bets. Give the friendly staff an hour or less, and they will stuff you with spanakopita, moussaka, or souvlakia. This is the home of hearty food in a hurry.

225 King St. W. ✆ **416/351-9393.** Reservations recommended for pre-theater dinner. Main courses C$13–C$22 (US$9.10–US$15). AE, DC, MC, V. Mon–Wed 11:30am–10pm; Thurs–Fri 11:30am–11:30pm; Sat 4:30–11:30pm. Subway: St. Andrew.

Queen Mother Cafe ASIAN   Fussy dowager this is not. Beloved by vegetarians, trend-hoppers, and reformed hippies, the Queen Mum is a Queen Street West institution with old-fashioned wooden furnishings and an underlit interior. The menu's lengthy descriptions are required reading. "Ping Gai" turns out to be chicken breast marinated in garlic, coriander, and peppercorns, served with lime sauce atop steamed rice. "Salmon Sottha" is served with hotter-than-hot Cambodian chile sauce and black rice. The menu is anything but pricey, so the wine list is a surprise, with few bargains in sight.

208 Queen St. W. ✆ **416/598-4719.** Reservations accepted only for groups of 6 or more. Main courses C$11–C$18 (US$7.70–US$13). AE, MC, V. Daily noon–1am. Subway: Osgoode.

The Rivoli ★★ FUSION   The Riv is better known as a club than as a restaurant—the 125-seat back room plays host to live music, stand-up comics, and poetry readings. What most people don't know is that the kitchen is just as creative. Chicken marinated in jerk spices comes with sautéed spinach and plantain chips; mussels are steamed in green curry jazzed up with coconut and lime. The less adventurous can partake of the spinach-and-pear salad or the house burger (beef on a challah bun with caramelized onions). The low prices draw a mixed crowd of starving artists, budget-conscious boomers, and Gen-Xers. *One caveat:* If you're planning to talk over dinner, get there before the back room starts filling up.

332 Queen St. W. ✆ **416/597-0794.** www.rivoli.ca. Reservations accepted only for groups of 6 or more. Main courses C$9–C$19 (US$6.30–US$13). AE, MC, V. Daily noon–2am. Subway: Osgoode.

Sottovoce LIGHT FARE   The name of this tiny eatery is more than a little misleading. *Sotto* (soft) it isn't. Forget trying to have a conversation and instead try to score one of the window seats, which afford a full view of College Street. The youngish crowd that mills in after 7pm enjoys the pumped-up music that refuses to stay in the background. In the middle of this frenetic scene you will find the most lovingly prepared, and least expensive, salads and focaccia sandwiches in town. There are daily pasta specials, and many wines by the glass.

595 College St. ✆ **416/536-4564.** Reservations not accepted. Main courses C$6–C$12 (US$4.20–US$8.40). AE, MC, V. Mon–Sat 5:30–11pm. Subway: Queen's Park, then any streetcar west to Clinton St.

Tortilla Flats TEX-MEX   Park your fear of sour cream and oil at the door, because it will spoil the fun. The dining room is all riotous color and Southwestern knickknacks; think Georgia O'Keeffe meets Salvador Dalí. The crowd is mainly 20- to 30-somethings, and a number of boomers come for the weekend brunch and the best frozen margaritas in town. The menu never changes, though there are some daily specials. Potato skins piled high with bacon and sharp cheddar are at the top of my list; the enchilada and chimichurri platters, which include rice, salad, and refried beans, are pretty satisfying, too.

429 Queen St. W. ✆ **416/593-9870.** Reservations accepted only for groups of 5 or more. Main courses C$8–C$20 (US$5.60–US$14). MC, V. Sun–Wed noon–10pm; Thurs–Sat noon–11pm. Subway: Osgoode, then any streetcar west to Spadina Ave.

3 Downtown East

EXPENSIVE

Biff's ★★ BISTRO   The same team that created a trio of excellent eateries with Jump, Canoe, and Auberge du Pommier have been hard at work again. The intent this time was to create a classic bistro, with dishes priced somewhat lower than at the other establishments (in keeping with true bistro tradition, *naturellement*). The setting hits all the right notes, with wood paneling and potted palms among the cozy-but-chic touches. The menu is equally fine, with pan-fried halibut covered with a second skin of thinly sliced potatoes, and traditional roast leg of lamb. The prime downtown location is a boon for Financial District types at lunch and theatergoers in the evening (the St. Lawrence and the Hummingbird centers are a stone's throw away).

4 Front St. E. (at Yonge St.). © 416/860-0086. www.biffsrestaurant.com. Reservations strongly recommended. Main courses C$18–C$28 (US$13–US$20). AE, DC, MC, V. Mon–Fri 11:30am–2:30pm; Mon–Sat 5:30–11pm. Subway: Union or King.

Courthouse Market Grille INTERNATIONAL This hangout for the suited set boasts gargantuan fluted columns, sky-high ceilings, swinging chandeliers, and miles of marble—which is not bad for an 1850 building that used to be a jail. Financial District types lap it up, along with generous martinis. The menu features grilled and rotisserie meats of excellent quality, though timid seasoning will not please daring palates. Appetizers are uniformly fine, with simple but well-executed numbers like steamed Prince Edward Island mussels in creamy white-wine sauce. The wine list includes some impressive vintages—and prices.

57 Adelaide St. E. © 416/214-9379. Reservations required. Main courses C$15–C$32 (US$11–US$22). AE, DC, MC, V. Mon–Wed 11:30am–10pm; Thurs–Fri 11:30am–midnight; Sat 5:30pm–midnight. Subway: King.

Hiro Sushi ❀ JAPANESE/SUSHI Widely regarded as the best sushi chef in the city, Hiro Yoshida draws a horde of Financial District types at lunch and mainly couples at dinner. The monochromatic setting is comfortably minimalist, and diners are encouraged to relax and leave their meal in Hiro's capable hands. The sushi varieties range from the expected to the inventive; you can also choose sashimi, tempura, and bento box combinations. Service can be rather slow. Forget the few wines listed in favor of sake or beer.

171 King St. E. © 416/304-0550. Reservations recommended. Main courses C$20–C$30 (US$14–US$21). AE, DC, MC, V. Mon–Fri noon–2:30pm; Mon–Sat 6–10:30pm. Subway: King.

Rosewater Supper Club ❀ INTERNATIONAL This triple-decked pleasure dome is packed almost every night with dressed-up diners who pass the time checking each other out. Personally, I'm still caught on the scenery: Marble, moldings, and a waterfall make quite the impression. So does the menu, which casually tours the globe. First up are delectables like carpaccio of seared caribou with a citrus-gin relish. Main courses include roast sirloin of lamb with parsnip gratin and hazelnut sauce, and coq au vin with butternut squash. The can't-miss desserts include rhubarb apple crisp with a vanilla-plum sorbet. The serious wine list focuses mainly on France and California, with some excellent Ontario vintages.

19 Toronto St. (at Adelaide). © 416/214-5888. Reservations required. Main courses C$20–C$32 (US$14–US$22). AE, DC, MC, V. Mon–Fri 11:30am–2:30pm and 5:30–10:30pm; Sat 5:30–11:30pm. Subway: King.

Torch BISTRO The Senator Restaurant brought back the days when red meat, rich food, and cigar smoking weren't considered a threat to one's health. It closed in 2000 to make way for Torch, a paean to the classic French bistro. The decor is much the same, with etched-glass doors and heavy wood paneling, but the menu is entirely different: Dishes include smoked duck breast with shiitake mushroom risotto, or grilled provimi calves' liver with braised red cabbage and crispy pancetta. Upstairs, things haven't changed at all: There's live jazz at the glamorous Top O' the Senator (p. 213).

Tips Savory Surfing

Trying to decide between two equally tantalizing restaurants? Why not sneak a peek at their menus online? The websites listed here will give you different perspectives on the city's eateries.

Martini Boys (www.martiniboys.com): The Boys are well known in Toronto for their bar and lounge reviews, but their restaurant reviews are terrific too. They're highly opinionated and witty, and they're often the first to review newly opened spots.

Toronto.com (www.toronto.com): This site boasts a lot of features, but its restaurant reviews are the biggest draw for me. A photo or two usually accompanies the reviews, to give you a sense of what that space is like.

Toronto Life Online (www.torontolife.com): Look to this magazine's "Best of T.O." section to learn where to find the city's best bets for gelato, falafel, or panini. The site also offers a section filled with reviews of just about every restaurant around town.

---

249 Victoria St. ① **416/364-7517**. Reservations required. Main courses C$16–C$36 (US$11–US$25). AE, DC, MC, V. Tues–Sun 5–11pm. Subway: Dundas.

MODERATE

HotHouse Cafe CONTINENTAL/LIGHT FARE   When restaurants make the claim of having "something for everyone," I usually run the other way. But the HotHouse Cafe is an exception. The exhaustive menu ranges from salads to pizzas, omelets to pastas, and burgers to vegetarian mains, and they do a nice job with it all. (Don't expect complicated fare here—the HotHouse keeps things simple, which is a very wise move when offering so much.) The restaurant is famous for its Sunday buffet brunch, which at C$16 (US$11) per person is a good value if you're in the mood to indulge: there are made-to-order omelet stations, lots of options, and live jazz music.

35 Church St. ① **416/366-7800**. www.hothousecafe.com. Reservations strongly recommended, particularly for Sunday brunch. Main courses C$10–C$20 (US$7–US$14). AE, DC, MC, V. Mon–Tues 11am–10:30pm; Wed–Thurs 11am–midnight. Subway: King or Union.

Jamie Kennedy Wine Bar ★★★ *Value* INTERNATIONAL/LIGHT FARE One casualty of the otherwise fantastic expansion plans for the Royal Ontario Museum (see chapter 6), was its stellar terrace bistro, Jamie Kennedy at the Museum. Well, Kennedy is back with an even more interesting venture. This cubbyhole-size wine bar is one of the hottest spots in town, and for good reason. Their innovative take on bistro cuisine is reminiscent of a tapas bar – all of the plates are small (with prices to match), but the cooking is delectably memorable. The dishes range from lamb poutine with crisp frites to tender *osso buco*. The staff is very helpful and knowledgeable; ask about the difference between a glass of Ontario riesling and a French sauvignon blanc, and you're likely to get taste of each as well as an explanation.

My one quibble with this otherwise divine eatery is in its reservations policy. They simply won't take reservations for dinner, which means you must arrive here by 5:30pm if you want to have any hope of scoring a seat. In all honesty, it's worth it.

9 Church St. ⓒ **416/362-1957.** Reservations required for lunch but not accepted for dinner. Small courses C$5–C$11 (US$3.50–US$7.70). AE, MC, V. Tues–Sat 11:30am–11pm. Subway: King or Union.

Montréal Bistro & Jazz Club QUEBECOIS   Ontario and Québec share a border, but it's no mean feat to find top-notch *tourtière* (traditional beef, veal, and pork pie) in Toronto. Anyone who craves Québecois staples like pea soup and smoked-meat sandwiches can return their train ticket to Montréal and stop at this bistro. Besides being a restaurant, this is one of the city's premier jazz clubs, so you can *écouter* while you *manger*.

65 Sherbourne St. (at Adelaide). ⓒ **416/363-0179.** www.montrealbistro.com. Reservations recommended. Main courses C$10–C$22 (US$7–US$15). AE, DC, MC, V. Mon–Fri 11:30am–3pm; Mon–Thurs 6–11pm; Fri–Sat 6pm–midnight. Subway: King, then any streetcar east to Sherbourne St.

Terroni ITALIAN/LIGHT FARE   From its humble beginnings on Queen Street West, Terroni has grown into a local minichain with three locations. The setting is informal, with kitchen-style tables and chairs and a wall-mounted chalkboard that heralds the daily specials. The antipasti, salads, and pizzas, essentially the same at all three locations, are uniformly delightful. They range from the simplest margherita pizza (tomato, mozzarella, basil) to a gourmet salad of cooked oyster mushrooms drizzled with balsamic vinegar and served atop a bed of arugula. The two other locations are at 720 Queen St. W. and 1 Balmoral Ave.

106 Victoria St. ⓒ **416/955-0258.** Main courses C$10–C$18 (US$7–US$13). MC, V. Mon–Sat 9am–10pm. Subway: Queen.

Wish ⭐ *(Finds)* BISTRO   This is a dream come true: Hidden behind a simple whitewashed facade, Wish is a charmer that offers cozy ambience, excellent cooking, and friendly service (a rare combination in this neighborhood). In summer, the vibrant patio might draw you to it, but during the rest of the year you have to wait till you're through the front door before you're seduced by the setting, which is dominated by white-slipcovered couches, plush cushions, and baroque details—very shabby chic. The menu is just as elegant, with starters such as Pernod-glazed calamari. Mains run the gamut from meat and fish to pasta and risotto. Note that the dessert selection is very limited, as is the wine list.

3 Charles St. E. ⓒ **416/935-0240.** Reservations recommended. Main courses C$14–C$25 (US$9.80–US$18). AE, MC, V. Daily 11am–2am. Subway: Yonge/Bloor.

INEXPENSIVE

Hello Toast LIGHT FARE   Humorist Fran Lebowitz once asked why there were places called Bonjour Croissant but not Hello Toast. Well, now there is. Gleaming toasters and retro furniture bedeck the kitschy dining room. The menu is a mix of pizza and pasta specials, with a few salads, soups, and rich desserts mixed in. If you're springing for toast, choose the inspired challah.

993 Queen St. E. ⓒ **416/778-7299.** Main courses C$7–C$15 (US$4.90–US$11). MC, V. Tues–Sun noon–10pm. Subway: Queen, then any streetcar east to Pape Ave.

Le Papillon QUEBECOIS   If you thought crepes were simply for breakfast, stop by Le Papillon for re-education. While there are many fruit-filled numbers, the best are savory crepes, which combine, for example, bacon, apples, and cheddar. Created from a mixture of white and buckwheat flour, the crepes make a satisfying lunch. For dinner, add some onion soup and a green salad, or go for *tourtière*, a traditional Québecois pie that includes beef, veal, *and* pork.

16 Church St. (between Front St. E. and Esplanade). © 416/363-0838. www.lepapillon.ca. Reservations recommended. Crepes C$6–C$10 (US$4.20–US$7). AE, DC, MC, V. Tues–Fri noon–2:30pm; Tues–Wed 5–10pm; Thurs 5–11pm; Fri 5pm–midnight; Sat 11am–midnight; Sun 11am–10pm. Subway: Union.

Shopsy's *Kids* DELI This Toronto institution has been in business for more than three-quarters of a century. Its large patio, festooned with giant yellow umbrellas, draws crowds for breakfast, lunch, dinner, and in between. This is where you go for heaping corned beef or smoked-meat sandwiches served on fresh rye. There is also a slew of comfort foods, like macaroni and cheese and chicken potpie. Shopsy's also boasts one of the largest walk-in humidors in the city (which is not subject to the smoking crackdown).

33 Yonge St. © 416/365-3333. Reservations accepted only for groups of 6 or more. Main courses C$7–C$14 (US$4.90–US$9.80). AE, MC, V. Mon–Wed 6:30am–11pm; Thurs–Fri 6:30am–midnight; Sat 8am–midnight; Sun 8am–10pm. Subway: Union or King.

Young Thailand ★★ THAI Wandee Young was one of the first chefs to awake Toronto's taste buds to the joys of Thai cuisine. That was more than 2 decades ago, and Young Thailand is still going strong, with several locations around the city. The large dining room contains a few Southeast Asian decorative elements, but it's the low-priced, high-quality cuisine that attracts the hip-but-broke and boomers alike. The bargain buffet at lunch is always a mob scene. The dinner menu is a la carte, with popular picks like spiced chicken and bamboo shoots in coconut milk, satays with fiery peanut sauce, and the ever-present pad Thai. Soups tend to be sinus-clearing, and mango salads offer a sweet antidote.

81 Church St. (south of Lombard St.). © 416/368-1368. www.youngthailand.com. Reservations recommended. Lunch buffet C$9.95 (US$7); main courses C$8–C$16 (US$5.60–US$11). AE, DC, MC, V. Mon–Thurs 11:30am–10pm; Fri 11:30am–11pm; Sat 4:30–11pm; Sun 4:30–10pm. Subway: Queen or King.

4 Midtown West

VERY EXPENSIVE

Bistro 990 ★★★ FRENCH Because Hollywood types frequent Toronto, it's no surprise to see the stars out for a night on the town. Bistro 990 is just across the street from the tony Sutton Place Hotel, so it drags in more than its fair share of big names. (One friend has had a couple of Whoopi Goldberg sightings here. Why do these things never happen when I'm around?) In any case, the Gallic dining room is charming, and the service is all-around attentive. The menu offers updated hors d'oeuvres, such as octopus and veggies in citrus marinade. Main dishes stick to *grand-mère's* recipes, like the satisfying roasted half chicken with garlicky mashed potatoes, and calves' liver in white-wine sauce. Sweets, such as the pineapple tarte tatin with kiwi coulis and blueberry ice cream, are made daily. The three-course prix-fixe menus are an excellent value, at C$20 (US$14) for lunch and C$25 (US$18) for dinner.

990 Bay St. (at St. Joseph). © 416/921-9990. Reservations required. Main courses C$19–C$40 (US$13–US$28). AE, DC, MC, V. Mon–Fri noon–3pm; Mon–Sat 5–11pm. Subway: Wellesley.

Opus CONTINENTAL Popular with the price-is-no-object set, Opus is nonetheless low-key. Smooth, personable servers make you feel at home in the elegant renovated town house, which contains several small dining areas. The look is casually chic, and there's no shortage of suits. The menu changes every other month, and always features classic French as well as lightened-up dishes. Tuna tartare meets its match with black sesame seeds and lotus chips, and beef tenderloin with dauphinoise potatoes and rosemary-shallot *jus* is memorable. Desserts are easy on the eye and the palate. The wine list runs to volumes, with highlights of New and Old worlds; the knowledgeable staff can set you straight.

37 Prince Arthur Ave. ℂ 416/921-3105. www.opusrestaurant.com. Reservations recommended. Main courses C$25–C$39 (US$18–US$27). AE, DC, MC, V. Daily 5:30–11:30pm; bar until 2am. Subway: St. George.

Truffles ⭐ CONTINENTAL   On the second floor of the Four Seasons Hotel, this formal dining room is a study in elegance. Every last detail has been attended to, from the exotic sculptures to the stunning parquetry floor. The clientele is a mix of hotel guests and local businesspeople—it's a bit of an older crowd. Appetizers boast exquisite ingredients, with results such as pan-seared foie gras atop pineapple and mango chutney. Main courses, such as bacon-wrapped veal tenderloin served side-by-side with morel mushroom ravioli, are more down-to-earth. Desserts like peach napoleon and lemon soufflé are uniformly delightful. The mile-long wine list frequently veers into the stratosphere.

In the Four Seasons Hotel, 21 Avenue Rd. ℂ 416/928-7331. www.fourseasons.com/toronto. Reservations required. Main courses C$34–C$46 (US$24–US$32). AE, DC, MC, V. Mon–Fri 6–10pm; Sat 5:30–10pm. Subway: Bay.

EXPENSIVE

Annona ⭐ INTERNATIONAL   Why are so many of the city's fascinating restaurants in hotels? Annona, at the Park Hyatt, is the latest case in point. This street-level dining room is an exercise in elegance, with dusky blue draperies and banquettes, gold accents, and floor-to-ceiling windows (all the better to people-watch, my dears). It draws a business crowd, Yorkville shoppers, and hotel guests, serving scrambled eggs with smoked salmon and capers for breakfast, seafood risotto with morel mushrooms and asparagus at lunch, and pan-seared Black Angus medallions in red-wine sauce for dinner. The desserts are to die for, especially the caramelized pineapple tart with rum ice cream.

Park Hyatt Toronto, 4 Avenue Rd. ℂ 416/924-5471. www.parktoronto.hyatt.com. Reservations recommended for dinner. Main courses C$16–C$30 (US$11–US$21). AE, DC, MC, V. Mon–Fri 6:30am–11pm; Sat–Sun 7am–11pm. Subway: Museum or Bay.

Boba ⭐ FUSION   There is no shortage of stunning turn-of-the-20th-century houses in this part of town, and Boba happens to be in one of the most charming. Set back from the street, it has a front patio for summer dining. Inside, the pastel-hued walls and tasseled lampshades exude warmth, Provençal style. Boba is a scene every night, with a mix of dressed-up and dressed-down professionals table-hopping with abandon. What draws them is the inventive cuisine, which has turned co-chefs Barbara Gordon and Bob Bermann into local celebrities. One highlight is Gordon's wonderful Muscovy duck two ways, with the breast cooked rare and the leg braised. Grilled salmon is also just so, nicely mated with curried vegetable risotto. Desserts are overwhelming, particularly the Valrhona chocolate triangle with crème fraîche ice cream, raspberries, and berry coulis.

90 Avenue Rd. ℂ 416/961-2622. Reservations recommended. Main courses C$20–C$34 (US$14–US$24). AE, DC, MC, V. Mon–Sat 5:45–10pm. Subway: Bay.

Il Posto Nuovo ITALIAN   All of those ladies who lunch can't be wrong. White-linened tables sit cheek-by-jowl, making this an eavesdropper's Eden. The service is among the best in the city, considerate, efficient, and well versed in the intricacies of the menu. And what a menu it is, rich with classic dishes like bresaola salad (thinly sliced air-cured beef and Asiago cheese atop a bed of arugula), and ravioli stuffed with veal and spinach. The wine cellar favors Italy, France, and California; it's constantly updated, so do ask for recommendations.

148 Yorkville Ave. (at Avenue Rd.). ⓒ 416/968-0469. Reservations required. Main courses C$14–C$25 (US$9.80–US$18). AE, DC, MC, V. Mon–Sat noon–2:30pm and 6–11pm. Subway: Bay or Museum.

Mistura ⭐ ITALIAN   While the curvy bar up front is a favorite place to meet, the modern Italian menu is the real draw for the well-dressed 20- and 30-somethings who dine at Mistura. The food is satisfying without being overly heavy—think spinach and ricotta gnocchi with light but creamy Gorgonzola sauce and toasted walnuts. The meaty entrees might include a tender veal chop with rosemary roasted potatoes and portobello mushrooms, or sweetbreads with chickpea polenta and caramelized root veggies. The well-organized wine list is heavy with Italian and California vintages.

265 Davenport Rd. ⓒ 416/515-0009. Reservations recommended. Main courses C$20–C$28 (US$14–US$20). AE, DC, MC, V. Mon–Sat 5–11pm. Subway: Bay.

Pangaea ⭐ FUSION   I used to think this location was cursed. For years, I watched restaurants open with a bang and fold with a whimper. Well, Pangaea seems to have broken that losing streak—and deservedly so. The massive dining room is as dramatic as ever, complete with an undulating aluminum ceiling and coral walls. Perhaps to compete with the surroundings, the chic crowd likes to dress up. The menu changes every month. Appetizers such as white asparagus soup with roasted shallots and morel mushrooms are classically French. Main dishes strike boldly in different directions: glazed salmon with bok choy, water chestnuts, and ginger, for example, or rack of lamb roasted in sunflower seeds and honey and served with whiskey sauce. The professional staff knows its way around the wide-ranging wine list, which favors the Western Hemisphere.

1221 Bay St. ⓒ 416/920-2323. Reservations recommended. Main courses C$22–C$28 (US$15–US$20). AE, DC, MC, V. Mon–Sat 11:30am–11:30pm. Subway: Bay.

Splendido Bar and Grill CANADIAN   The dining room pairs brown with beige (much more attractive than it sounds), dark wood, and leather chairs. The result is intimate, and very like a private club. Mains run the gamut from a seared B.C. halibut filet in leek-and-champagne vinaigrette to Ontario butternut-squash ravioli. For dessert, the lemon pudding cake with caramelized mango is hard to beat. The international wine list is pricey, but some nice vintages are available by the glass.

88 Harbord St. ⓒ 416/929-7788. Reservations required. Main courses C$20–C$30 (US$14–US$21). AE, DC, MC, V. Mon–Sat 5–11pm. Subway: Spadina, then LRT south to Harbord St.

MODERATE

Café Nervosa ITALIAN   There are reed-thin models playing with their food at the next table, leopard skin decking the room, and limos parked out front. Where are you? One possible answer is Café Nervosa, a casually hip Yorkville hangout. The name is borrowed from the coffee shop on TV's *Frasier,* with a wacky ambience all its own. The menu boasts nicely constructed panini, pizzas, and salads, and the portions tend to be generous (curious, given the you-can-never-be-too-rich-or-too-thin crowd).

75 Yorkville Ave. ⓒ 416/961-4642. www.cafenervosa.ca. Reservations only for groups of 6 or more. Main courses C$10–C$25 (US$7–US$18). AE, DC, MC, V. Mon–Wed 11am–11pm; Thurs–Sat 11am–midnight; Sun 10:30am–3pm. Subway: Bay.

Goldfish ★★ *Value* ECLECTIC   Behind the floor-to-ceiling front window, dining here is rather like being in a fishbowl. The cool, crisp lines of Scandinavian design mix with miniature Japanese plants for an upscale Zen ambience. While the look may be trendier-than-thou, the staff's attitude is consistently considerate. The menu is far less austere than the surroundings. Main dishes run the gamut from ostrich tenderloin with lobster orzo and cranberry coulis to orange-poppy-seed-crusted salmon in an apple cider reduction. Even the simplest green salad benefits from dollops of pumpkin seeds and a light dressing that contains a hint of lavender emulsion. The short dessert list includes some inventive pairings, such as delicious apple tart with rosemary ice cream. The wine list is short but contains 10 selections by the glass.

372 Bloor St. W. ℭ 416/513-0077. Reservations strongly recommended. Main courses C$13–C$27 (US$9.10–US$19). AE, DISC, MC, V. Wed–Fri 11:30am–3:30pm; Sat–Sun 10am–3pm; daily 5:30–10:30pm. Subway: Spadina.

Holt Renfrew Café ★ *Finds* LIGHT FARE   Tucked into Holt Renfrew's renovated third floor, this small restaurant is a perfect place to grab breakfast or lunch in midtown. Given the very expensive clothing just a few yards away, you might expect the prices here to be stratospheric, but they're surprisingly affordable. True, C$15 is steep for an open-faced sandwich, but let me explain: Given that the bread is flown in fresh from the Poilane bakery in Paris three times a week, the toppings run along the lines of seared Ahi tuna with wasabi mayonnaise, and the sandwiches are accompanied by a delicious green salad, the price seems fair. The airy space is also a good bet for cocktails.

At Holt Renfrew, 50 Bloor St. W., 3rd floor ℭ 416/922-2223. Reservations not accepted. Main courses C$8–C$18 (US$5.60–US$13). AE, DC, MC, V. Mon–Wed 10am–6pm; Thurs–Fri 10am–8pm; Sat 10am–6pm; Sun noon–6pm. Subway: Yonge/Bloor.

Jacques Bistro du Parc FRENCH   There are about three ladies who lunch for every lad who happens by Jacques Bistro du Parc around noontime. In the evening, the ratio evens out. The menu is that of a genuine French brasserie, with omelets, quiches, and niçoise salads galore. There are meatier main courses, too, like green peppercorn steak and Dijon-coated rack of lamb. Many wines are available by the glass, and bottles tend to be reasonably priced. Service can be considered relaxed or slow, depending on your mood.

126A Cumberland St. ℭ 416/961-1893. Reservations recommended on weekends. Main courses C$12–C$30 (US$8.40–US$21). AE, MC, V. Mon–Sat 11:30am–3pm and 5–10:30pm. Subway: Bay.

Joso's SEAFOOD   This Annex mainstay keeps packing 'em in, drawing a crowd of regulars and a sprinkling of celebrities. The Spralja family has a show-biz history (chef Joso was half of the folk-singing duo of Malka and Joso, who appeared on *The Tonight Show*), which may explain the theatricality of the surroundings. The two-story house is crammed with art depicting the female form in all its naked glory. Tables are inches apart, foiling intimate conversation but letting you get to know your neighbors. Fresh seafood is carted to your table for inspection, then returned to the kitchen for cooking. There is also a selection of pastas, such as delightful spaghettini al Leonardo, which combines shrimp, octopus, and capers. Desserts range from jam-filled crepes to sorbets.

202 Davenport Rd. (just east of Avenue Rd.). ℭ 416/925-1903. Reservations recommended. Main courses C$14–C$44 (US$9.80–US$31); pasta dishes C$10–C$16 (US$7–US$11). AE, MC, V. Mon–Fri 11:30am–2:30pm; Mon–Sat 5:30–11pm. Subway: Bay.

Matignon *(Finds* FRENCH   A bit off the beaten track, this small restaurant offers the thrill of discovery. Spread over two floors, the intimate rooms are festooned with all things French. The crowd includes many regulars, and the ambience is that of a low-key bistro. The short menu is filled with classics from the old country, including Angus steak rolled in crushed pepper and flambéed with cognac, and rack of lamb with mustard and herbs of Provence. Desserts, like vanilla ice cream under hot chocolate sauce, stay on the same track.

51 St. Nicholas St. ⓒ **416/921-9226.** Reservations recommended. Main courses C$14–C$18 (US$9.80–US$13). AE, MC, V. Mon–Fri 11:30am–2:30pm; Mon–Thurs 5–10pm; Fri–Sat 5–11pm. Subway: Wellesley.

Messis ⭐ *(Value* ECLECTIC   This is one of Toronto's prime training grounds for up-and-coming young chefs. The food is for gourmets, though the prices are comparatively low. That explains the presence of earnest artsy types and casual boomers in the small, saffron-walled dining room. The menu changes frequently, keeping as its mainstays Italian pastas and Mediterranean meat dishes, and ranging into Asia, too. For a starter, the herbed goat cheese and cumin phyllo pastry is a delicious choice. Main courses include oven-roasted Atlantic salmon with jasmine rice and sun-dried fruit. Service is well intentioned though occasionally clunky. The California-dominated wine list is as reasonably priced as the food.

97 Harbord St. ⓒ **416/920-2186.** Main courses C$11–C$21 (US$7.70–US$15). AE, MC, V. Sun–Thurs 5:30–10pm; Fri–Sat 5:30–11pm. Subway: Spadina, then LRT south to Harbord St.

Sage MEDITERRANEAN   Sage injects some creative cookery—and a pleasantly relaxed vibe—into an area that could benefit from cutting loose a little. Main courses run the gamut from gnocchi with caramelized sweet onions and roasted garlic to grilled chicken breast marinated in Moroccan spices. Side plates, including the delicious sautéed buttered mushrooms, are ordered separately. Portions are on the generous side, but do try to save space for the light but luscious Pavlova.

1033 Bay St. ⓒ **416/923-8159.** www.sagerestaurant.ca. Reservations recommended. Main courses C$16–C$25 (US$11–US$18). AE, MC, V. Mon–Fri 11am–3pm; Mon–Sat 5pm–midnight. Subway: Wellesley.

Sotto Sotto ⭐⭐ ITALIAN   Imagine the Bat Cave decorated by a Florentine, with aged frescoes, wall-mounted stonework, and wax-dripping candelabra. A few steps down from street level, this restaurant transports diners a world away. Tables are cheek-by-jowl, but the jovial suits and couples don't seem to mind. Efficient service lacks warmth, though the kitchen makes up for it. The menu leans to the lightweight, with a few irresistible creamy-sauced pastas. Main courses of meat or fish, like Cornish hen and swordfish, are nicely grilled. The risotto is fine—though, annoyingly, at least two people at the table must order it. There's a nice wine list, with many selections available by the glass.

116A Avenue Rd. (north of Bloor St.). ⓒ **416/962-0011.** Reservations required. Main courses C$14–C$24 (US$9.80–US$17). AE, DC, MC, V. Daily 5:30pm–midnight. Subway: Bay or Museum.

Southern Accent CAJUN   Cajun food isn't Toronto's claim to fame, so this down-home Annex eatery is a find. Background blues and zydeco set the tone, and the menu attracts casual neighborhood boomers. Anyone who has admired the work of New Orleans celebrity chef Paul Prudhomme will cotton to the blackened entrees—chicken, steak, lamb, and fish all get the treatment. Gumbo and crawfish make occasional appearances, too. *Warning:* The corn bread is a mite addictive.

595 Markham St. ✆ 416/536-3211. Reservations recommended on weekends. Main courses C$13–C$26 (US$9.10–US$18). AE, DC, DISC, MC, V. Tues–Sun 5:30pm–1am. Subway: Bathurst.

INEXPENSIVE

Bloor Street Diner LIGHT FARE   If you've shopped until you've dropped along Bloor Street West, this is just the place to grab a bite to eat and let your feet and your credit card recover. It's two restaurants in one: Le Café/Terrasse is an informal bistro that serves decent soups, salads, and sandwiches all day; La Rotisserie is a slightly more upscale dining room with heartier Provençal-style fare. The basics are what they do best. Try to snag a seat on the umbrella-covered patio overlooking Bay Street (all the better for people-watching).

In the Manulife Centre, 55 Bloor St. W. ✆ 416/928-3105. Main courses C$10–C$18 (US$7–US$13). AE, DC, MC, V. Daily 7am–1am. Subway: Bay or Yonge/Bloor.

Indian Rice Factory INDIAN   Since it opened in the late 1970s, the Indian Rice Factory has become a Toronto institution. The corduroy banquettes and macramé wall hangings still draw boomers who started coming here back when the place first opened. The Punjabi-influenced menu features heaping helpings of beef *dhansak* (braised with lentil-eggplant-tomato curry) and chicken *khashabad,* stuffed with almonds, cashews, and raisins in coconut-milk cream. There are many beers from local microbreweries, and a small but well-chosen wine list.

414 Dupont St. ✆ 416/961-3472. www.indianricefactory.com. Reservations recommended. Main courses C$8–C$18 (US$5.60–US$13). AE, MC, V. Daily 5–10:30pm. Subway: Dupont.

Japan Deli JAPANESE/SUSHI   Tucked into a cubbyhole on a side street just off Bloor Street West, Japan Deli succeeds at bringing tempura and teriyaki to the masses. Fine Japanese cuisine takes hours to prepare, but this is more like what time-pressed Tokyo residents are used to—a friend who used to live in Japan swears that this is as close as you can get to the experience without boarding a plane. Complete dinners include miso soup, salad, a meat dish, side vegetables, and fresh fruit for dessert—all nicely prepared, and all for under C$10 (US$7).

11 Balmuto St. ✆ 416/920-2051. Reservations not accepted. Main courses C$7–C$9 (US$4.90–US$6.30). MC, V. Mon–Sat noon–9pm. Subway: Yonge/Bloor.

Kensington Kitchen ★★ (Kids) MEDITERRANEAN   Drawing a crowd of regulars—students and profs—from the nearby University of Toronto, Kensington Kitchen is a perennial gem. The decor hasn't changed in years, with Oriental carpets covering the walls, a painted wood floor, and decorative objects scattered about. The tradition of big portions at small cost stays constant, too. The menu ventures between the ports of the Mediterranean. There's angel-hair pasta with heaps of shrimp, scallops, and mussels in tomato-coriander sauce; saffron paella with chicken and sausage; and Turkish-style braised lamb stuffed with raisins, eggplant, apricots, and figs. In clement weather, head to the rooftop patio, in the shade of a mighty Manitoba maple.

124 Harbord St. ✆ 416/961-3404. Reservations recommended. Main courses C$10–C$14 (US$7–US$9.80). AE, DC, MC, V. Mon–Sat 11:30am–11pm; Sun 11:30am–10pm. Subway: Spadina, then LRT south to Harbord St.

Lalibela ETHIOPIAN   Perhaps it's the fact that you don't need cutlery to dine in Ethiopian style that makes it so much fun. A flatbread called *injera* takes the place of flatware as you scoop up spicy hot meats and thick lentil stews. Lalibela has numerous choices for vegetarians and meat-lovers, and the helpful staff will arrange mixed plates with three different dishes for tasting.

869 Bloor St. W. ℂ **416/535-6615**. Main courses C$5–C$9 (US$3.50–US$6.30). MC, V. Mon–Thurs 6–10pm; Fri–Sat 6–11pm. Subway: Christie.

Nataraj ★INDIAN   There's usually a bit of a wait for a table—Nataraj's upscale cuisine is popular with Annex residents, and its downscale prices are affordable to U of T students. But the service is swift, so tables do open up rather quickly. The cooking is from the northern part of the subcontinent, so there are lots of fish and seafood dishes. A number of plates will appeal to vegetarians. The tandoor-baked breads are simply sublime.

394 Bloor St. W. ℂ **416/928-2925**. Reservations not accepted. Main courses C$7–C$12 (US$4.90–US$8.40). MC, V. Mon–Sat 5:30–10:30pm. Subway: Spadina.

Pho Hung VIETNAMESE   Pho usually translates as "soup," but that's a bit of a misnomer—it's more like a meal in a bowl. There's 15 good choices here, and the lemon grass– or coriander-scented broths are chock-full of meat, noodles, and vegetables. There's also a range of chicken, pork, and seafood dishes, and a tangy beef fondue. The clientele includes both suits and students, and the wine list is longer and better than you might expect.

200 Bloor St. W. ℂ **416/963-5080**. Reservations recommended for groups of 4 or more. Main courses C$7–C$15 (US$4.90–US$11). V. Mon–Sat 11am–10pm. Subway: St. George or Museum.

Serra ★★ *Finds* ITALIAN   I've been dining at Serra since my student days at the University of Toronto. Back then, I loved it for its excellent food, friendly service, and reasonable prices. Guess what? It hasn't changed. This is an upscale-looking spot: The diners are casually chic, and Serra's look is sleek, with a wood-paneled bar in one corner and mahogany tables for two. The trattoria-worthy fare includes thin-crust pizza topped with olives, prosciutto, and goat cheese; light-sauced pasta dishes teeming with shrimp; and grilled focaccia sandwiches.

378 Bloor St. W. ℂ **416/922-6999**. www.serrarestaurant.com. Main courses C$10–C$18 (US$7–US$13). AE, DC, MC, V. Daily noon–11pm (no lunch on summer weekends). Subway: Spadina.

SpringRolls ASIAN   What to have for dinner tonight: Chinese, Vietnamese, Thai, Singaporean? If you can't decide, your best bet is SpringRolls. The name may make you think its offerings are meager, but the multi-page menu will set you straight. Tenderly executed barbecued pork and fried shrimp dishes abound. Vegetarians don't have as many choices as you might expect, though there are a few top-notch vermicelli-and-veggie plates.

693 Yonge St. ℂ **416/972-7655**. Reservations recommended. Main courses C$6–C$15 (US$4.20–US$11). MC, V. Sun–Thurs 11am–11pm; Fri–Sat 11am–midnight. Subway: Yonge/Bloor.

350 Fahrenheit LIGHT FARE/VEGETARIAN   This new restaurant has a great concept, but it's a mix of hits and misses. The menu is built around the premise that just about everyone is on a diet these days; instead of dining alone at home, dieters should be able to nosh in public and know exactly what they're eating. So the menu at 350 Fahrenheit caters to those on a range of programs (Atkins, South Beach, Suzanne Sommers, Bernstein, and Eat Right for Your Blood Type), as well as vegetarians and vegans. Every dish is identified with the appropriate diet(s), along with complete details of the grams of protein, carbs, fat, and fiber per serving. Brilliant! However, the dishes themselves aren't consistently appetizing (some are nicely spiced, but others are bland as, um, diet food). A bigger problem is the service, which is completely inept.

467 Bloor St. W. ℂ **416/929-2080**. www.350fahrenheit.com. Reservations recommended. Main courses C$12–C$18 (US$8.40–US$13). AE, MC, V. Daily 6–11pm. Subway: Spadina.

Great Greasy Spoons

While I'm enchanted by Toronto's top-notch dining spots, I just can't resist the lure of the greasy spoon. You know the kind of place I mean: fluorescent lighting, a bottle of ketchup on every Formica tabletop, vinyl-upholstered booths, and aromas of strong coffee and frying bacon. Some suggestions:

Perhaps Toronto's best-known greasy spoon, **Mars,** 432 College St. at Bathurst Street (© 416/921-6332), sports a neon sign that claims the diner is "Just out of this world." In addition to the all-day breakfast menu, it boasts cheese blintzes, grilled burgers, and a great turkey club. There's another location at 2363 Yonge St., just north of Eglinton Avenue (© 416/322-7111), but its kitschy mock-diner decor doesn't hold a candle to the real McCoy.

Avenue Diner, 222 Davenport Rd. at Avenue Road (© 416/924-5191), is just up the street from the Park Hyatt and the Four Seasons hotels, which explains the frequent celebrity sightings (signed and framed photos stand as a permanent record of stars' visits). In business since 1946, the Avenue serves a steady supply of omelets, French toast, and hamburgers.

The Goof, 2379 Queen St. E. (© 416/694-3605), is officially named the Garden Gate Restaurant. But certain letters burned out of the neon "Good Food" sign, giving this Beaches neighborhood mainstay its name. In addition to the usual diner grub, this spot has star power, as evidenced by Jennifer Lopez sightings.

Finally, there's **Fran's,** at the Pantages Hotel, 200 Victoria St. If you visited Toronto 3 or more years ago, you might remember a diner called Fran's. There used to be branches on College, St. Clair, and Eglinton avenues, and it was something of a Toronto institution. Now the Pantages is reopening Fran's as their in-house restaurant. I can't quite picture it (the hotel is upscale, and the diner certainly wasn't) but I'm looking forward to seeing it.

5 The East End

Just about everything *will* be Greek to you in the East End along Danforth Avenue. Known appropriately enough as Greektown, this is where to come for low-cost, delicious dining—though some of the restaurants have become quite trendy in recent years.

EXPENSIVE

Café Brussel BELGIAN   Perhaps this was to be a challenge to the supremacy of Greek food in this neighborhood. The Café Brussel is defiantly . . . Belgian? The only such eatery in the city, it draws a neighborhood crowd. The menu could pass for French in most regards, with staples like onion soup and duck confit. This is food you could get drunk on—try *carbonnades flamandes* (beef simmered in dark ale), or *moules au bourbon* (seafood with shots of hard stuff). There's also a great selection of European lagers and wines.

124 Danforth Ave. ℭ **416/465-7363**. Reservations recommended. Main courses C$15–C$28 (US$11–US$20). AE, MC, V. Tues–Sat 5–11pm; Sun 5–10pm. Subway: Broadview.

MODERATE

Christina's GREEK   The walls are plastered with photographs of celebrities caught in the act of dining here. (There's one infamous old snapshot of *Friends* star Matt LeBlanc dining with Alanis Morissette.) The menu offers reliable souvlakia and eggplant pies, but it veers into pasta and burger territory, too. The hearty all-day breakfast of feta-spiked omelets and herbed taters is a popular choice.

492 Danforth Ave. ℭ **416/463-4418**. Reservations recommended. Main courses C$10–C$24 (US$7–US$17). AE, DC, MC, V. Daily 11am–4am. Subway: Chester.

Myth 🌟🌟 GREEK/MEDITERRANEAN   Part trendy bar, part restaurant, this generous space is large enough to encompass both. The ambience is classical Greece meets MTV. Ornate oversize shields share space with a series of TVs running an endless loop of mythic movies. Who can pay attention to what's on the plate with so much going on? Fortunately, the food calls attention to itself. Starters, ranging from traditional spanakopita to tuna tartare with beet and taro-root chips, are impossible to ignore. Main courses, such as rabbit braised in port and cinnamon, or pizza topped with spiced lamb, zucchini, and onion purée, are just as demanding. As the night goes on, the crowd gathers at the bar, where a DJ starts spinning music at 11pm.

417 Danforth Ave. (between Logan and Chester). ℭ **416/461-8383**. Reservations recommended. Main courses C$14–C$26 (US$9.80–US$18). AE, MC, V. Mon–Wed 5–11pm; Thurs–Sun noon–11pm; bar open till 2am nightly. Subway: Chester.

Pan on the Danforth 🌟 GREEK   To the best of my knowledge, Pan was a god of music, not of food. I must have mixed it up, because if he is the inspiration for this restaurant, he certainly knows his way around a kitchen. This long-established eatery updates classic Greek dishes with panache. Salmon is stuffed with mushrooms and spinach and wrapped in phyllo pastry, and a smoked baked pork chop comes with feta-scalloped potatoes and zucchini relish. The well-chosen wine list favors the New World. The crowd is fairly sophisticated, which may explain the cryptic message over the bar: YOU'VE DONE IT ALREADY.

516 Danforth Ave. ℭ **416/466-8158**. www.panonthedanforth.com. Reservations accepted only for parties of 3 or more. Main courses C$13–C$19 (US$9.10–US$13). AE, MC, V. Sun–Thurs 5–11pm; Fri–Sat 5pm–midnight. Subway: Chester or Pape.

INEXPENSIVE

Astoria GREEK   The restaurant subtitles itself a shish-kebab house, but its offerings are much broader. And it's more upscale than the name would suggest, with a patio fountain and colorful decor. Whatever the protein, it seems to respond well to broiling—beef, lamb, chicken, and seafood all get similar treatment. There are several choices for vegetarians, including souvlakia and moussaka. Expect a wait if you arrive after 8:30pm or so on weekends.

390 Danforth Ave. ℭ **416/463-2838**. Reservations recommended; accepted on weekdays only. Main courses C$9–C$15 (US$6.30–US$11). AE, MC, V. Mon–Wed and Fri–Sat 11am–1am; Thurs and Sun 11am–midnight. Subway: Chester.

Avli 🌟 GREEK   A white stucco archway contributes to the cave-like feel of the narrow street-level room, though the recent expansion to the second floor has created an airier place to dine. Always noisy, occasionally raucous, this taverna serves up some of the best food on the Danforth—nongreasy, thoughtfully

Sleepless in Toronto: What to Do When the Midnight Munchies Attack

There are cities that never sleep. Well, Toronto isn't one of them. The city starts to doze off around 11:30pm, even on weekends. Sure, there are 24-hour doughnut shops, but if you're looking for something more substantial, try one of the following late-night options:

- **Happy Seven** (p. 96) serves reliable Chinese food in a kitschy setting until 5am.

- **7 West Café,** 7 Charles St. W. (© **416/928-9041**), is open 24 hours a day. Delish sandwiches and pasta platters hit the spot. Those with severe sugar cravings can indulge in cakes and pies from several of the city's best bakers. Subway: Yonge/Bloor.

- If you're on the Danforth, you're in luck: Many of the terrific Greek tavernas and restaurants there, like **Myth** (p. 109) and **Christina's** (p. 109), stay open until the wee hours even on weeknights.

prepared, and carefully seasoned. Meze starters are standard: *kopanisti* (spicy feta with peppers) and hummus for those who want cold food, grilled octopus and steamed mussels for those who like it hot. Main courses are standouts. The half chicken stuffed with cashews, dates, apples, and rice is exquisite, and the meat moussaka is the best around.

401 Danforth Ave. © 416/461-9577. www.avlirestaurant.com. Reservations recommended. Main courses C$9–C$19 (US$6.30–US$13). AE, DC, MC, V. Daily noon–midnight. Subway: Chester.

Mezes GREEK   This sophisticated space doles out exactly what it promises. *Mezes* are the Greek equivalent of tapas—light snacks meant to keep you going until you have a real dinner in front of you. Still, it's worth spoiling your appetite to indulge in these appetizers. Choices range from grilled calamari and octopus to spicy eggplant dip and leek pie. Do try to save room for the honey-sweet baklava.

456 Danforth Ave. © 416/778-5150. Reservations not accepted. Appetizers C$4–C$10 (US$2.80–US$7). AE, MC, V. Mon–Thurs 11am–midnight; Fri–Sat 11am–1am; Sun noon–midnight. Subway: Chester.

Ouzeri GREEK   One of the longtime stars of the neighborhood, Ouzeri has been packing in the crowds for years and shows no sign of slowing down. Just inside the foyer, TV sets make it look like a sports bar. Farther inside, colorful ceramic tiles and wrought iron surround terrazzo tables and wicker chairs. Charming as the interior is, if you're lucky you'll be outside on the small patio. Portions of main dishes, such as lamb pies and pork kebabs, tend to be quite generous. As the evening goes on, the convivial atmosphere evolves into festival-like celebration; on Tuesday nights, there's live Greek music.

500A Danforth Ave. © 416/778-0500. Reservations recommended. Main courses C$8–C$18 (US$5.60–US$13). AE, DISC, MC, V. Sun–Mon and Wed–Thurs 11am–midnight; Tues and Fri–Sat 11am–2am. Subway: Chester.

6 Uptown

This area is too large to be considered a neighborhood, stretching as it does from north of Davenport Road to Steeles Avenue. While it doesn't have the concentration of restaurants that the downtown area enjoys, a number of stellar options make the trip north worthwhile.

VERY EXPENSIVE

Auberge du Pommier ★ FRENCH   Don't have time to drop by your French country house this weekend? To the rescue comes Auberge du Pommier, a cozy château that exudes Provençal-style charm. Diners outfitted in business casual relax in the care of expert servers. The menu doesn't offer many surprises, but, what it does, it does well. Appetizers set a high standard, with dishes like creamy lobster and white-bean soup, and baked artichokes stuffed with French goat cheese. Entrees, like pan-seared scallops with braised oxtail in a Cabernet *jus,* keep up the pace.

4150 Yonge St. ℰ **416/222-2220.** Reservations recommended. Main courses C$33–C$38 (US$23–US$27). AE, DC, DISC, MC, V. Mon–Fri 11:30am–2:30pm; Mon–Sat 5–10pm. Subway: York Mills.

Centro ★★ CONTINENTAL   The palace-grand main room, with its oxblood walls, is always bustling. The dressed-up all-ages crowd often starts out schmoozing at the wine bar downstairs, moves up to the main floor for dinner, then migrates back downstairs for R&B music and a nightcap (the wine bar stays open until 2am). The seasonal menu pays tribute to the restaurant's Northern Italian origins, with pasta dishes like homemade egg tagliolini with smoked chicken in a truffle emulsion. Many choices lean to contemporary Canadiana, like the grain-fed Québec capon paired with a foie gras mousse and sun-dried cherries, or French modern, like the rack of lamb in a Provençal honey-mustard crust. Delicious desserts run the gamut from traditional tiramisu to warm banana-bread pudding. The stellar wine list is sure to thrill oenophiles.

2472 Yonge St. ℰ **416/483-2211.** www.centro.ca. Reservations required. Main courses C$28–C$42 (US$20–US$29). AE, DC, MC, V. Mon–Sat 5–11:30pm. Subway: Eglinton.

North 44 ★★★ INTERNATIONAL   This is the one restaurant that even people who've never set foot in Toronto have heard about. It's profiled extensively in food and travel magazines, but can it possibly live up to its reputation? In a word, yes. The spare Art Deco decor recently got a face-lift, and the results are stunning. The soft lighting and strategically situated mirrors wrap the dining room—and its occupants—in a gorgeous glow. The menu, which changes with the seasons, borrows from Mediterranean, American, and Asian sources. The results are inspiring to the palate and the eye. On the list of main courses you might find grilled veal tenderloin with orange peppercorns, toasted barley, and root veggies, or roasted Muscovy duck breast with orange-soy marinade and foie gras. There are always a few pasta and pizza choices, such as caramelized squash ravioli with black truffle essence. It's impossible to come here without being seduced into a three-course meal. The desserts, like lemon meringue millefeuille, are among the best in the city, and there's a wide selection of accompanying ice wines. The wine list is comprehensive, though most of the prices veer off into the stratosphere. What really sets North 44 apart is its seamless service. Those who don't like to be pampered should stay away.

2537 Yonge St. ℰ **416/487-4897.** Reservations required. Main courses C$27–C$45 (US$19–US$32). AE, DC, MC, V. Mon–Sat 5–11pm. Subway: Eglinton.

Scaramouche ✿ INTERNATIONAL   This is a contender for those who don't mind spending top dollar on splendid food. Tucked into an upscale apartment building, it isn't easy to find. That enhances its snob appeal—and the crowd here is more old money than the patrons at either of its uptown competitors, Centro and North 44. Scaramouche is blessed with one of the most romantic settings in the city. Floor-to-ceiling windows afford a panoramic view of the downtown skyline. (Securing a window seat is no mean feat, but fortunately most tables have decent sightlines.) The unobtrusive servers pay attention to the details. The menu is laden with caviar, foie gras, truffles, and oysters; main dishes include the likes of venison loin wrapped in smoked bacon in a red-wine glaze. The wine list has a broad reach, and there's a nice selection of cognacs.

1 Benvenuto Place (off Avenue Rd.). ✆ 416/961-8011. Reservations required. Main courses C$25–C$40 (US$18–US$28); pasta dishes C$16–C$25 (US$11–US$18). AE, DC, MC, V. Dining room Mon–Sat 5:30–10pm; pasta bar Mon–Fri 5:30–10:30pm, Sat 5:30–11pm. Subway: St. Clair, then streetcar west to Avenue Rd., walk 4 blocks south to Edmund Ave.; Benvenuto is the first street on the left.

EXPENSIVE

La Bruschetta ✿ ITALIAN   Star sightings are common in Toronto, but at La Bruschetta they're almost an everyday event. The entryway is covered from floor to ceiling with plates decorated by celebs such as Kelsey Grammer and Bette Midler. It's a surprise, then, to find the homey, kitchen-like dining room. Owner Benito Piantoni, who charms patrons with tales of Italy and Hollywood gossip, provides local color. The menu lists a dozen pastas, with cream sauces ranging from brandy to Gorgonzola. Mouthwatering main courses include veal medallions simply presented in white-wine sauce with garlic and mushrooms. After a rich meal, you'll welcome the delicate lemon ice for dessert.

1317 St. Clair Ave. W. ✆ 416/656-8422. Reservations recommended. Main courses C$14–C$26 (US$9.80–US$18). AE, DC, MC, V. Mon–Sat 5:30–11:30pm. Subway: St. Clair West, then any streetcar west to Dufferin St.

Lakes ✿ BISTRO   Plush banquettes and close-set tables heighten the sense of intimacy in the narrow dining room. A casually well-dressed crowd drops by during the week; on Saturday, couples spend candlelit quality time. The menu changes every few months, with jazzed-up bistro classics such as duck confit with cranberry-shallot glaze and garlic mashed potatoes, grilled provimi veal liver, and Gruyère-and-Emmenthal fondue for two making frequent appearances. The banana crème brûlée is a perennial favorite dessert.

1112 Yonge St. ✆ 416/966-0185. Reservations strongly recommended. Main courses C$14–C$26 (US$9.80–US$18). AE, DC, MC, V. Mon–Fri noon–3pm and 5:30–11pm; Sat 6–11pm. Subway: Rosedale.

Millie's Bistro ✿✿ *Kids* MEDITERRANEAN   Subtle as its signage is, Millie's is hard to miss. The sole gastronomic draw in this neighborhood, it lures even jaded downtown dwellers. It attracts an unusual mix of young-to-middle-age courting couples, families with tiny tykes, and groups gearing up for a night on the town. The sprawling menu includes dishes from Spain, southern France, Italy, Turkey, and Morocco. There is a kids' menu, too. Start with tapas—perhaps Catalan-style goat cheese with basil and olive oil; Turkish flatbread with a topping of lamb, yogurt, and mint; or a *b'stilla* (aromatic chicken wrapped in herbed semolina). Better still, sample them all—the cheery staff will arrange them on ceramic platters for sharing. Main dishes include paella with saffron, shrimp, clams, quail, and chorizo sausage. Sweets are seductive, though generous portions make saving room for dessert almost impossible. On the wide-ranging wine list, Spanish selections are a particularly good value.

1980 Avenue Rd. (south of York Mills). ℂ **416/481-1247**. Reservations recommended. Main courses C$10–C$27 (US$7–US$19). AE, DC, MC, V. Daily 11:30am–11pm. Subway: York Mills, then walk (10–15 min.) west or take a taxi (about C$5/US$3.50).

Oliver & Bonacini Café & Grill ⭐⭐ AMERICAN   The new Sheppard subway line has spurred growth in the neighborhoods it serves. My favorite development so far is the Oliver & Bonacini Café & Grill. Located at the upscale Bayview Village mall, this restaurant has quickly become a local wonder. The menu isn't exotic—mains include grilled Atlantic salmon atop a spinach salad, and roasted rack of lamb with a potato-chèvre gratin—but the food is excellent. For dessert, the molten lemon cake with stewed blueberries is irresistible. Service is impeccably friendly and swift.

At Bayview Village, 2901 Bayview Ave. (at Sheppard Ave.) ℂ **416/590-1300**. Reservations only for groups of 6 or more. Main courses C$12–C$25 (US$8.40–US$18). AE, MC, V. Mon 11:30am–9pm; Tues–Thurs 11:30am–10pm; Fri–Sat 11:30am–10:30pm; Sun 11am–9pm. Subway: Bayview.

Quartier ⭐ FRENCH   The old-world elegance is palpable as you step into this refined bistro. Is it the languid sound of Edith Piaf's voice? Perhaps the baroque mirrors and look-again prints on the walls? No matter. The French-born proprietor, Marcel Rethore, has created a romance-tinged atmosphere for a casually chic crowd. The menu boasts classic dishes such as duck confit with sautéed potatoes and garlic-dressed endive, and Breton bouillabaisse. Desserts, for those who have room, include a tender lemon-cream mille-feuille and a delicate crème brûlée. The short wine list is particularly well chosen—it's hard to go wrong.

2112 Yonge St. ℂ **416/545-0505**. Reservations recommended. Main courses C$17–C$27 (US$12–US$19). AE, MC, V. Mon–Fri 11:30am–2:30pm; Mon–Sat 5:30–10:30pm. Subway: Eglinton.

Thai Magic ⭐ THAI   Arrangements of orchids, cascading vines, and Thai statuary grace the enchanting entry. The serene staff handles frenetic crowds with ease; this spot is filled with locals, especially on Thursday and Friday nights. The meal is served Western-style, rather than in the Thai fashion of bringing all courses to the table at once. Delicate appetizers like chicken-filled golden baskets vie for attention with not-too-spicy soups. Entrees range from chicken with cashews and whole dried chiles to a coriander-infused lobster in the shell.

1118 Yonge St. ℂ **416/968-7366**. Reservations recommended. Main courses C$12–C$20 (US$8.40–US$14). AE, MC, V. Mon–Sat 5–11pm. Subway: Summerhill.

MODERATE

Amore Trattoria ⭐⭐ ITALIAN   This double-decker restaurant is a neighborhood favorite with groups and families alike. Pandemonium reigns on the first floor; upstairs, the cognoscenti can gaze over a balcony at the tumult below. The cheerful staff takes it all in stride. Reading the menu takes much too long: With 22 pastas, 21 pizzas, 6 meat dishes, and daily specials, it can be an intimidating experience for the indecisive. Fortunately, the kitchen consistently produces top-notch dishes, from simple salads of mesclun and goat cheese to spaghetti in brandy-tomato sauce with sweet Bermuda onion. Wine is served in tumblers in classic rustic-Italian style.

2425 Yonge St. ℂ **416/322-6184**. Reservations accepted only for groups of 6 or more. Main courses C$10–C$18 (US$7–US$13). AE, MC, V. Daily noon–3pm and 5:30–10:30pm. Subway: Eglinton.

Grano ⭐ *Kids* ITALIAN   While Toronto has no shortage of Italian eateries, few spots have as much ambience as Grano. The old-fashioned trattoria contains several dining areas, with wooden furnishings, distressed stucco, and piles of

Vegetarian Delights

It used to be that vegetarian dining in Toronto was often more of an exercise in virtue than in good taste. Crunchy granola might be healthful for the body, but it's hell on the palate. But now a new wave of vegetarian eateries are making meat-free meals a gourmet's delight. Several of the city's finest restaurants are also offering special vegetarian tasting menus. Here are some of the best bets. (Contact the Toronto Vegetarian Association at ℂ **416/544-9800** or www.veg.ca for more information.)

- **Annapurna Vegetarian Restaurant,** 1085 Bathurst St. (ℂ **416/537-8513;** subway: Bathurst). Annapurna has been around for more than 20 years, and it's still serving Indian vegetable dishes, hearty tofu burgers, and a variety of fruit and vegetable juices to a crowd of students and boomers. In keeping with the aura of health, Annapurna hosts free meditation classes every week. Main courses C$8–C$12 (US$5.60–US$8.40); MC, V; Mon–Tues and Thurs–Sat 11:30am–9pm, Wed 11:30am–6:30pm.

- **Fressen,** 478 Queen St. W. (ℂ **416/504-5127;** subway: Osgoode). This is a vegetarian oasis for sophisticates. From the freshly baked beet-infused buns to tender tofu with both hot-tomato and sweet-teriyaki sauces, this hot spot makes every mouthful a gourmet delight. It's a hit with vegetarians *and* their carnivorous friends. Main courses C$12–C$14 (US$8.40–US$9.80); MC, V; Mon–Thurs 5:30–10pm, Fri 5:30–11pm, Sat 10:30am–3:30pm and 5:30–11pm, Sun 10:30am–3:30pm and 5:30–10pm.

- **Juice for Life,** 336 Queen St. W. (ℂ **416/599-4442;** subway: Osgoode). If there's such a thing as an elixir of life, one of the bartenders at this

greenery. The small courtyard at the back is heaven on sunny days. This is a high-energy spot that attracts celebratory groups (one clever friend of mine had her wedding-rehearsal dinner here); it's also welcoming to families accompanied by *bambini*. The cooking is hearty, from tender *osso buco* to ricotta gnocchi paired with shrimp in white-wine sauce. The desserts are a serious draw—I insist that everyone try the divine white chocolate and raspberry tart at least once.

2035 Yonge St. ℂ **416/440-1986.** Reservations recommended. Main courses C$11–C$20 (US$7.70–US$14). AE, DC, MC, V. Mon–Fri 9:30am–11pm; Sat 9am–11pm. Subway: Davisville or Eglinton.

Lolo ★★ *Finds* BISTRO   Tiny and intimate, Lolo is a perfect little bistro. Its romantic ambience is heightened by the fact that it has barely 40 seats neatly fitted between its deep-red walls. The mirrors and gold-painted crown molding around the room add a special touch, as does the warm and unrushed service. But for all of its charming airs, the menu—and the prices—are refreshingly down-to-earth. The mains are bistro classics, from the roasted supreme of chicken stuffed with spinach and mushrooms, to the grilled rib-eye steak with green-peppercorn sauce and crispy frites. In addition to the a la carte menu,

Annex favorite is sure to find it one day. They've already developed a Bionic Brain Tonic (peach, strawberry, and orange juices with gotu kola and ginseng) and about 40 other blends intended to boost your immune system, sex drive, or mood. The noodle and rice dishes have equally esoteric names (Buddha, Green Goddess), though their contents are down-to-earth. The high-protein almond grain burgers and hemp-seed bread get top marks. Main courses C$8–C$12 (US$5.60–US$8.40); Mon–Fri 8:30am–6:30pm, Sat 9am–6:30pm, Sun 10am–6pm.

- **Kalendar** (p. 96) may be a small bistro, but its list of vegetarian offerings is substantial.
- **Mezzetta** (see below) offers a collection of Middle Eastern appetizers, few of which contain meat; ordering a selection of three of four makes for a substantial meal.
- **Millie's Bistro** (p. 112) has vegetarian lasagna with portobello mushrooms, sweet roasted peppers, and leeks that will make you wonder why anyone would want to add beef. The Mediterranean menu has many meat-free plates.
- **350 Fahrenheit** (p. 107) offers healthy food complete with nutritional information, with plenty of choices for vegetarians and vegans.
- **Truffles** (p. 102) is a top-notch restaurant with a vegetarian tasting menu. Called the Menu Terroir, it might feature the likes of white-bean-and-truffle soup, or a salad of frisee with Roquefort, walnuts, and apples; C$65 (US$46) for five courses.

there's a prix-fixe option that lets you have three courses for a mere C$23 (US$16). All of the desserts—including the divine lemon tart—are made on the premises.

619 Mount Pleasant Rd. ℂ **416/483-8933.** Reservations recommended. Main courses C$13–C$21 (US$9.10–US$15). AE, DC, MC, V. Daily 5–11pm. Subway: Eglinton, then bus east to Mount Pleasant Rd.

Mezzetta MIDDLE EASTERN   Tapas bars are a dime a dozen in Madrid, but in Toronto they're few and far between. Mezzetta is one such gem. Everything on the menu is served in appetizer-size portions, from cold salads of feta, olives, and tomatoes to steamy *kofta*, an Egyptian dish of beef, lamb, and potato in a spicy sauce. There are also pita sandwiches and barbecued items. Much of the menu will appeal to vegetarians. The wine list is short but priced for value, and there's a lengthy list of brews, too.

681 St. Clair Ave. W. ℂ **416/658-5687.** Reservations recommended on weekends. Appetizers C$3 (US$2.10). MC, V. Tues–Fri noon–2:30pm; Tues–Sun 5–10:30pm. Subway: St. Clair.

Stork on the Roof ⭐ BISTRO   The stork in question is a Dutch sign of good fortune. And luck it is to discover this charming bistro. The menu abounds with pan-European classics warmed by exotic elements, such as grilled pork tenderloin with lemon curry sauce. Asian inspirations are in evidence, particularly in seafood dishes, like sautéed squid served with satay-worthy peanut sauce and pickled vegetables. For dessert, Dutch spiced apple pie is the standout.

2009 Yonge St. ℰ 416/483-3747. Reservations required. Main courses C$15–C$17 (US$11–US$12). AE, MC, V. Wed–Fri noon–2pm; Tues–Sat 6–10pm. Subway: Davisville.

Vanipha Lanna ⋆⋆ LAOTIAN/THAI   There's no shortage of Thai eateries in Toronto, but only a few specialize in the cooking of Thailand's northwestern Lanna region. Many Laos natives have relocated to Lanna, and strong, spicy Laotian influences permeate the cooking. One of the house specialties is grilled chicken and garlic served with lime-chile sauce. The busy dining room attracts casually dressed diners of all ages, all of whom the thoughtful staff treats with care.

471 Eglinton Ave. W. ℰ 416/484-0895. Reservations recommended. Main courses C$8–C$15 (US$5.60–US$11). AE, MC, V. Mon and Wed noon–10pm; Tues and Thurs 5–10pm; Fri noon–10:30pm; Sat 1–10:30pm. Subway: Eglinton.

INEXPENSIVE

Hannah's Kitchen LIGHT FARE   National magazines and newspapers have published several of its recipes, but this cubbyhole-like eatery remains defiantly low-key. Diners seat themselves at wooden banquettes or tiny tables. The menu includes many pasta dishes, both cold (pesto radiatore salad with chicken and pine nuts is the top pick) and hot (penne arrabiata has the spiciest sauce in town), with three or four daily specials. Occasional forays into the exotic include a few Indonesian rice dishes and the ever-popular pad Thai. Desserts are a must, so check out the selection behind the counter on your way in.

2221 Yonge St. ℰ 416/481-0185. Reservations not accepted. Main courses C$7–C$12 (US$4.90–US$8.40). MC, V. Mon–Fri 10am–10pm. Subway: Eglinton.

Rebel House LIGHT FARE   This casual spot is beloved by locals. Is the draw the warm welcome, the better-than-average pub grub, or the impressive selection of microbrews? The crowd is mainly 20- to 30-somethings decked out in designer casual wear, more intent on socializing than eating. The specialty of the house is hearty, simple fare; grilled Atlantic salmon and seared Angus strip loin are top picks. Pastas and salads are worth a taste, too.

1068 Yonge St. ℰ 416/927-0704. Reservations not accepted. Main courses C$8–C$18 (US$5.60–US$13). AE, MC, V. Mon–Sat 11:30am–11pm; Sun 11:30am–10pm (bar open till 1am Mon–Sat and 11pm Sun). Subway: Rosedale.

7 North of the City

Toronto is a sprawling city, and as it has expanded, new and inspiring restaurants have cropped up in formerly out-of-the-way regions. The area north of Steeles Avenue is experiencing a remarkable boom. These restaurants are beyond the reach of the Toronto subway system. If you've rented a car to go to the McMichael Canadian Art Collection in Kleinburg or to the Canada's Wonderland theme park, you might want to stop on the way back downtown. (For driving directions, see chapter 6.)

EXPENSIVE

Terra ⋆⋆ INTERNATIONAL   This restaurant feels as if it was airlifted out of the downtown core. Sleek and sophisticated, it is the sibling of uptown's North 44, and the cooking at Terra is appropriately splendid. The kitchen favors seafood, from appetizers like butter-poached lobster with shallots and honey mushrooms to entrees like pan-fried sea bream with baby bok choy, candied beets, and fava beans. There are several steak plates, with everything from a 10-ounce filet of beef to a 16-ounce porterhouse. Believe it or not, there are also numerous vegetarian offerings. Desserts include classic crème brûlée and a more unusual pecan and blueberry cheesecake. The lengthy wine list hits all the international high notes, though most bottles are quite pricey.

8199 Yonge St. (just south of Hwy. 407), Thornhill. © 905/731-6161. www.terrarestaurant.ca. Reservations recommended. Main courses C$17–C$49 (US$12–US$34). AE, DC, MC, V. Tues–Sun 6–11pm.

MODERATE

Grand Yatt ⭐ CHINESE   There's a Grand Yatt restaurant at the Westin Harbour Castle hotel; this is the original. The large space is quite plain in comparison with its downtown offspring, but the cooking here is widely considered better. This is Cantonese cuisine at its finest. The seafood—black cod, geoduck (a large clam), or jumbo shrimp—is fresh as a daisy, and needs only light seasoning to bring out the intense natural flavors. Shark's fin soup is a perennial favorite. The swift servers are extremely helpful.

9019 Bayview Ave., Richmond Hill. © 905/882-9388. Main courses C$12–C$18 (US$8.40–US$13). AE, MC, V. Daily 9am–3pm and 6–10pm.

INEXPENSIVE

Dante's ⭐⭐ ITALIAN   Predating the current boom in the area, Dante's has been the favorite local spot for down-home cooking since 1976. It's not hard to figure out why. The menu has something for everyone, the food is consistently good, and the prices are reasonable. Don't expect to find exotic risottos—stick to heaping plates of pasta like rigatoni with black and green olives, or homemade cannelloni. One serving of chicken parmigiano can feed two adults.

267 Baythorn Dr. (just off Yonge St.), Thornhill. © 905/881-1070. Main courses C$7–C$14 (US$4.90–US$9.80). AE, MC, V. Mon–Thurs noon–10pm; Fri–Sat noon–midnight.

6

What to See & Do

First the good news: Toronto has amazing sights to see and places to be that appeal to travelers of all stripes. The bad news? No matter how long your stay, you won't be able to fit everything in. Toronto is a sprawling city, and while downtown and midtown boast a sizable collection of attractions, some wonderful sights are in less accessible areas. Travelers in 2005 should note that some of the city's great sites, such as the Royal Ontario Museum, the Art Gallery of Ontario, and the George R. Gardiner Museum of Ceramic Art, will be undergoing extensive renovations throughout the year, making substantial parts of their collections unavailable for viewing, or shutting down the venue completely.

Keep in mind that many Toronto attractions could take up a whole day. Ontario Place, Harbourfront, the Ontario Science Centre, and Paramount Canada's Wonderland all come to mind. That's not even mentioning the parks, the arts scene, or the shopping possibilities. My best advice is to relax and bring a good pair of walking shoes. There's no better way to appreciate Toronto than on foot.

SUGGESTED ITINERARIES
If You Have 1 Day

Start out early in the morning in **Kensington Market,** and pick up breakfast from one of the Middle Eastern, Asian, or North African cafes. Kensington adjoins Toronto's main **Chinatown;** stroll down Spadina Avenue and head east along Dundas Street to enjoy it. Along Dundas you'll find the **Art Gallery of Ontario;** spend at least a couple of hours there, and be sure to take in the collection of sculptures by British artist Henry Moore.

For lunch, you can head to the gallery's marvelous restaurant, Agora, or to nearby Baldwin Street for Chinese food. It's a short walk from here to **Queen's Park,** where the Ontario Legislature meets; the surrounding greenery affords a respite from the asphalt jungle. Head north past some of the **University of Toronto**'s gorgeous buildings to trendy **Yorkville,** with its small galleries, boutiques, and cafes. If you have kids in tow, you might want to check out the dinosaur displays at the **Royal Ontario Museum** (much of the ROM is under renovation, but the Egyptian, Greek, and Roman galleries will be open, as are the insect and reptile exhibits, the Maiasaur Project section, and the interactive Hands-On Biodiversity Gallery).

Before dinner, try to buy same-day tickets to a show in the adjoining **Theater District.** Then dine out at one of the fine restaurants along **King Street West** (see chapter 5 for suggestions).

If You Have 2 Days

On the first day, follow the itinerary for 1 day. On day 2, start by wandering the grounds of **Exhibition**

Place, and arrive at the gates of Ontario Place at 10am sharp; allow about half a day for Ontario Place. If it's a clear sunny day, you may wish to go up to the top of the CN Tower (if it's an overcast day, I wouldn't bother). Glance over at SkyDome as you pass by. Head up to the architectural wonder that is City Hall at Nathan Phillips Square, then continue east to the Eaton Centre.

After you've shopped until you drop, ride a streetcar to Little Italy, along College Street. There's no end of dining options—try to score a patio seat if the weather's fine. This is another prime neighborhood for nightlife, so unless you've scored tickets to a game at the Air Canada Centre, you can hang out here.

If You Have 3 Days

This is when I'd recommend going a little farther afield. (You could also just allot more time to the previously mentioned sights.) Start your day at the highly interactive Ontario Science Centre. If the weather's good, you could spend the rest of the day reveling in the 240 hectares (600 acres) of Sunnybrook Park. If the weather isn't so favorable, this could be your afternoon to explore Casa Loma or the Hockey Hall of Fame. If another

museum isn't your thing, head to the Harbourfront Centre, which offers restaurants, live music, activities for kids, and varied events. At night, go to Greektown along the Danforth, where the many tavernas stay open late.

If You Have 4 Days or More

Now you can really start to explore Toronto. If you've followed the itinerary for the first 3 days, you might want to return to some sights. Otherwise, you could head north of Toronto to see the McMichael Canadian Art Collection in Kleinburg or, if the kids outvote you, to spend the day at Paramount Canada's Wonderland. There's no better way to spend a day than picnicking on the lush Toronto Islands, where you can rent bicycles, take the kids to Centreville amusement park, and get a whole new view of the city. A less traveled site is scenic Cabbagetown, with its Edwardian and Queen Anne–style architecture, Riverdale Farm, and Gothic Necropolis. With 4 days or more, you should also be able to sample the city's lively arts scene, taking in a theater or dance performance. Try to hit a comedy club while you're at it, and check out one of Toronto's sports teams, too.

1 The Top Attractions

ON THE LAKEFRONT

Harbourfront Centre ★★★ (Kids   Back in 1972, the federal government took over a 38-hectare (96-acre) strip of waterfront land to preserve the vista. It wasn't exactly prime real estate at the time, but that has changed in the decades since. The abandoned warehouses and crumbling factories have yielded to a stunning urban playground that now stretches over the old piers. Today, Harbourfront is one of the most popular destinations for locals and visitors alike: a great place to spend a day strolling, picnicking, gallery-hopping, biking, shopping, and sailing.

Queens Quay, at the foot of York Street, is the first stop you'll encounter on the LRT line from Union Station (you can also get there in 5 min. on foot walking south from Front St., but that requires walking under the Gardiner Expwy., which I personally hate). From here, boats depart for harbor tours, and ferries

What to See & Do in Downtown

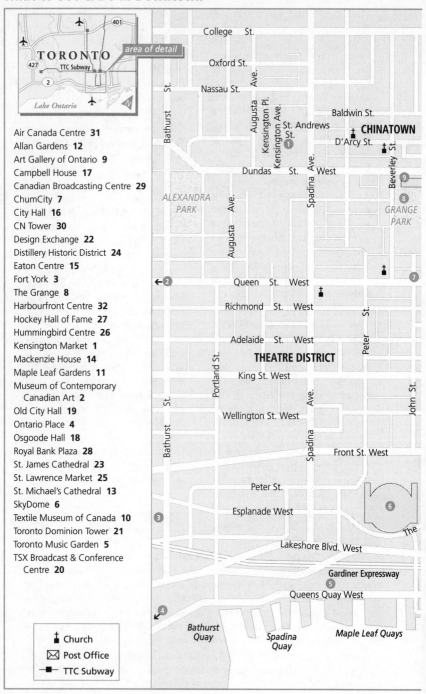

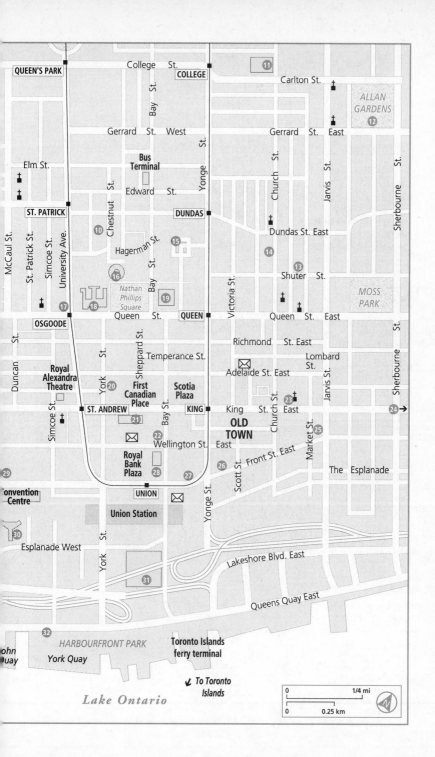

What to See & Do in Midtown

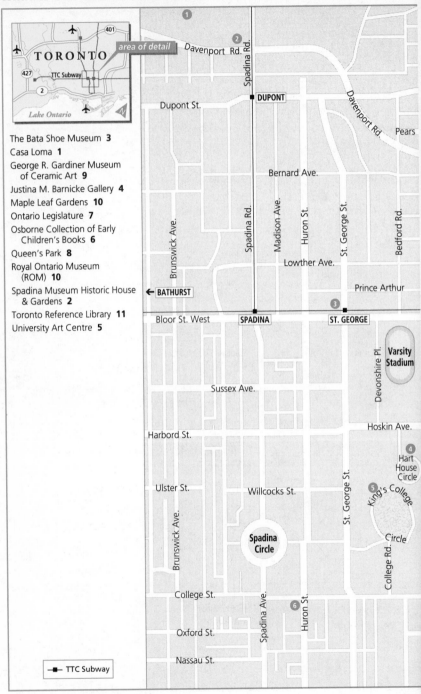

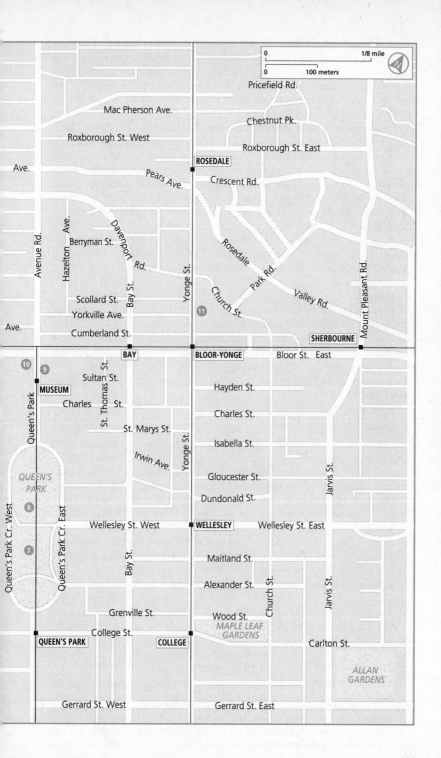

leave for the Toronto Islands. In this renovated warehouse you'll find the Premiere Dance Theatre and two floors of shops. To get something to eat, you can stay at Queens Quay for the casual Boathouse Grill or walk west to **York Quay** for its new Lakeside Terrace restaurant. York Quay also boasts an art gallery and ever-changing art installations, and an information booth where you can pick up information on Harbourfront events.

Harbourfront has several venues devoted to the arts. There's the **Power Plant,** a contemporary art gallery, and behind it, the **Du Maurier Theatre Centre.** At the **Craft Studio** you can watch artisans blow glass, throw pots, and make silk-screen prints, and if you're inspired you can buy their works at **Bounty Contemporary Canadian Craft Shop.** There are the **Artists' Gardens,** which currently include 23 diverse outdoor gardens created by landscape architects, designers, and other artists. In summer, one don't-miss experience is a visit to the **Toronto Music Garden,** which was created by cellist Yo-Yo Ma and landscape designer Julie Moir Messervy to invoke Bach's First Suite for Unaccompanied Cello. Does it succeed? That's a matter of opinion, but in mine the series of free musical performances that run from late June to early September make this a heavenly place to visit.

More than 4,000 events take place annually at Harbourfront, including the **Harbourfront Reading Series** in June and the **International Festival of Authors** in October (see "Toronto Calendar of Events" in chapter 2). Other happenings include films, dance, theater, music, children's events, multicultural festivals, and marine events. Harbourfront is at its best in the summer, but it is a great destination for the whole family year-round.

235 Queens Quay W. ℭ **416/973-4000.** www.harbourfrontcentre.com. Subway: Union, then LRT to Queens Quay or York Quay.

Ontario Place ★ *Kids*   When this massive recreation complex on the shores of Lake Ontario opened in 1971, it seemed futuristic. Thirty-three years later, it still does. (The major face-lift in 1989 no doubt helped.) From a distance, you'll see five steel-and-glass pods suspended on columns 32m (105 ft.) above the lake, three artificial islands, and a huge geodesic dome. The five pods contain a multimedia theater, a children's theater, a high-technology exhibit, and displays that tell the story of Ontario in vivid kaleidoscopic detail. The dome houses Cinesphere, where an 18-by-24m (60-by-80-ft.) screen shows specially made IMAX movies year-round.

Ontario Place has introduced several new attractions targeted at kids in the past couple of years. These include the **H2O Generation Station,** a gigantic "soft play" structure with twisting slides, towers, and walkways. There's also the new **Atom Blaster,** which claims to be Canada's largest foam-ball free-for-all—this is fun for the whole family. For the small fry, there's the new **MicroKids** play area with its ball pit, climbing platforms, and other tot-appropriate draws.

At night, the **Molson Amphitheatre** can accommodate 16,000 concert-goers: 9,000 can fit in the reserved seating area under the canopy, and 7,000 more can find seating on the surrounding grass. For concert information, call ℭ **416/260-5600;** for tickets, call **Ticketmaster** (ℭ **416/870-8000**).

955 Lakeshore Blvd. W. ℭ **416/314-9811,** or 416/314-9900 for recorded info. www.ontarioplace.com. Admission to grounds and Children's Village only is C$13 (US$9.10) for ages 4 and over, free for children 3 and under; separate fees for rides and events. Play All Day pass C$29 (US$20) adults and children 6 and over, C$17 (US$12) seniors, C$15 (US$11) children 4–5, free for children 3 and under (at press time, you can get discounted admission by ordering tickets online in advance). IMAX movies C$10 (US$7) adults, C$8 (US$5.60) seniors and children 13 and under. Mid-May to Labour Day, daily 10am–dusk; evening events end and dining

---

Value A Real Deal

You can save a lot of money on visiting Toronto's attractions by purchasing a **Toronto CityPass**. See the Royal Ontario Museum, the Art Gallery of Ontario, the Ontario Science Centre, the CN Tower, Casa Loma, and the Toronto Zoo for C$46 (US$32) for adults, and C$29 (US$20) for kids from 4 to 12. Each booklet of tickets is valid for 9 days from when the first one is used. CityPass deals have been available in several U.S. cities for a while, but went on sale in Toronto for the first time in 2004. You can buy the package at any of the six attractions listed above, or online at www.citypass.com.

---

spots close later. Closed (except Cinesphere) early Sept to early May. Subway: Bathurst or Dufferin, then Bathurst streetcar south.

The Toronto Islands 🌟 *Kids*   In only 7 minutes, an 800-passenger ferry takes you to 245 hectares (605 acres) of island parkland crisscrossed by shaded paths and quiet waterways—a glorious spot to walk, play tennis, bike, feed the ducks, putter around in boats, picnic, or lap up the sun. Of the 14 islands, the two major ones are **Centre Island** and **Ward's Island.** The first is the most popular with tourists; Ward's is more residential (about 600 people live in modest cottages on the islands). Originally, the land was a peninsula, but in the mid-1800s a series of storms shattered the finger of land into islands.

On Centre Island, families enjoy **Centreville** (© **416/203-0405**), an old-fashioned amusement park that's been in business since 1966. You won't see the usual neon signs, shrill hawkers, and greasy hot-dog stands. Instead you'll find a turn-of-the-20th-century village complete with a Main Street, tiny shops, a firehouse, and the Far Enough Farm, where the kids can pet lambs, chicks, and other barnyard animals. The kids will also love trying out the antique cars, fire engines, old-fashioned train, authentic 1890s carousel, flume ride, and aerial cars. An all-day ride pass costs C$17 (US$12) for those less than 124cm (49 in.) tall, C$23 (US$16) for those over 1.3m (4 ft.). Centreville is open from 10:30am to 6pm, daily from mid-May to Labour Day, and weekends in early May and September.

Lake Ontario. © 416/392-8193 for ferry schedules. Round-trip fare C$6 (US$4.20) adults, C$3.50 (US$2.45) seniors and children 15–19, C$2.50 (US$1.75) children 3–14, free for children 2 and under. Ferries leave from docks at the bottom of Bay St. Subway: Union Station, then LRT to Queens Quay.

DOWNTOWN

Art Gallery of Ontario 🌟 *Kids*   The European collections are fine, but the Canadian galleries are the real treat at the AGO. The paintings by the Group of Seven—which includes Tom Thomson, F. H. Varley, and Lawren Harris—are extraordinary. In addition, other galleries show the genesis of Canadian art from earlier to more modern artists. And don't miss the extensive collection of Inuit art. At press time, the AGO was still unveiling details about its extensive renovation plans. The gallery is being reinvented by Toronto son Frank Gehry, and his design is spectacular (as well as practical—it will increase viewing space by 40%). However, details regarding how the overhaul will interfere with viewing the current collections are sketchy. The renovations will begin in spring 2005 and are scheduled for completion in fall 2007.

In terms of the current collections, the AGO's offerings are already impressive. The **Henry Moore Sculpture Centre,** with more than 800 pieces (original plasters, bronzes, maquettes, woodcuts, lithographs, etchings, and drawings), is the largest public collection of his works. The artist gave them to Toronto because he was so moved by the citizens' enthusiasm for his work—public donations bought his sculpture *The Archer* to decorate Nathan Phillips Square at City Hall after politicians refused to free up money for it. In one room, under a glass ceiling, 20 or so of his large works stand like silent prehistoric rock formations. Along the walls flanking a ramp are color photographs showing Moore's major sculptures in their natural locations, which reveal their magnificent dimensions.

The European collection ranges from the 14th century to the French Impressionists and beyond. Works by Pissarro, Monet, Boudin, Sisley, and Renoir fill an octagonal room. De Kooning's *Two Women on a Wharf* and Karel Appel's *Black Landscape* are just two of the modern pieces. There are several works of particular interest to admirers of the pre-Raphaelite painters, including one by Waterhouse. Among the sculptures, you'll find two beauties—Picasso's *Poupée* and Brancusi's *First Cry.*

Behind the gallery, connected by an arcade, stands **the Grange.** Dating back to 1817, it's Toronto's oldest surviving brick house, and it was the gallery's first permanent space. Originally the home of the Boulton family, it was a gathering place for many of the city's social and political leaders and for such eminent guests as Matthew Arnold, Prince Kropotkin, and Winston Churchill. Meticulously restored and furnished to reflect the 1830s, it is a living museum of mid-19th-century Toronto life. Entrance is free with admission to the art gallery.

The gallery has an attractive restaurant, Agora (p. 88), which is open for lunch, as well as a cafeteria and a gallery shop. There's also a full program of films, concerts, and lectures.

317 Dundas St. W. (between McCaul and Beverley sts.). Ⓒ **416/977-0414.** www.ago.net. Admission C$12 (US$8.40) adults, C$9 (US$6.30) seniors and students, C$6 (US$4.20) children 6–15, free for children 5 and under. Free admission Wed 6–8:30pm. Tues and Thurs–Fri 11am–6pm; Wed 11am–8:30pm; Sat–Sun 10am–5:30pm. Grange House Tues–Sun noon–4pm; Wed noon–9pm. Closed Jan 1, Dec 25. Subway: St. Patrick.

CN Tower *Kids* As you approach the city, whether by plane, train, or automobile, the first thing you notice is this slender structure. Glass-walled elevators glide up the 553m (1,815-ft.) tower, the tallest freestanding structure in the world. The elevators stop first at the 346m-high (1,136-ft.) Look Out level. (It takes just 58 seconds, so prepare for popping ears.) You can walk down one level to experience the Glass Floor, my favorite spot at the tower: Through it you can see all the way down to street level (even as your heart drops into your shoes). As a bonus, if you wait long enough, you'll undoubtedly see some alpha males daring each other to jump on the glass. (They do, and no, it doesn't break—the glass can withstand the weight of 14 adult hippos. Now *that's* a sight I'd like to see . . . .)

⌐ *Fun Fact* **Tough Enough**

The CN Tower is built of sturdy stuff to resist the elements—contoured reinforced concrete covered with thick glass-reinforced plastic—and designed to keep ice accumulation to a minimum. The structure can withstand high winds, snow, ice, lightning, and earth tremors.

The tower attractions are often revamped. Some perennial draws are the IMAX theater and two flight simulators (one gentle and calm, the other a rugged ride through caves and over mountains). A series of interactive displays showcase the CN Tower along with such forerunners as the Eiffel Tower and the Empire State Building. The Look Out also contains broadcasting facilities, a nightclub, and the underwhelming **360 Revolving Restaurant** (p. 87).

Above the Look Out is the world's highest public observation gallery, the Skypod, 447m (1,466 ft.) above the ground (C$7/US$4.90 additional charge). From here, on a clear day you can't quite see forever, but the sweeping vista stretches to Niagara Falls, 161km (100 miles) south, and to Lake Simcoe,

---

Moments **Great Toronto Vistas**

While I know I should be impressed by the view from the CN Tower, I find it uninspiring. Don't get me wrong, it's great to see Niagara Falls on a clear day—but what I like is the view of Toronto itself, which looks more like a map and less like a metropolis from these dizzying heights. Here are some of my favorite viewing spots, where you'll get an altogether different picture of Toronto.

Bloor Street Viaduct   The viaduct over the Don Valley connects Bloor Street in midtown Toronto with the East End (where Bloor becomes the Danforth). The pedestrian walkway will afford you what is possibly the most enchanting view of the city there is to be had. From here, Toronto doesn't even look like a city—it seems like a lush forest. There are trees as far as the eye can see, with skyscrapers and towers jutting out here and there. If you don't see it for yourself, you won't believe it. Subway: Castle Frank, and walk east along Bloor to the viaduct.

Canoe Restaurant   Yes, there's glorious food to be had here but the view's the thing. Located on the 54th floor of the imposing Toronto Dominion Tower, Canoe boasts an amazing view of the castles of commerce in the Financial District, and the city beyond. If you don't want to shell out for an expensive dinner here (see review on p. 86), stop by for a drink. Toronto Dominion Tower, 66 Wellington St. W. ✆ 416/364-0054. Subway: King.

Casa Loma   Toronto's castle on a hill is one of the best perches from which to savor the city's beauty. Casa Loma has two towers, each with its own charms. The enclosed Scottish tower on its east side offers the highest viewing point, but the open-air Norman tower on the west side has my favorite vista. 1 Austin Terrace. ✆ 416/923-1171. Subway: Dupont, then walk 2 blocks north.

The Roof Lounge at the Park Hyatt   It's only 18 stories up in Midtown, and yet this classic watering hole has one of the best views in town. If the weather's even halfway decent, you might try score a table on the south-facing balcony. From here you can appreciate the sweeping grandeur of Queen's Park and of the historic University of Toronto grounds. Park Hyatt Toronto, 4 Avenue Rd. ✆ 416/924-5471. Subway: Bay or Museum.

193km (120 miles) north. Unless you're really taken with the tower, I wouldn't recommend it—the view from the Glass Floor is majestic enough for me (for other great—and less expensive—ways to view Toronto, see "Great Toronto Vistas," below). Atop the tower sits a 102m (335-ft.) antenna mast erected over 31 weeks with the aid of a giant Sikorsky helicopter. It took 55 lifts (and no hippos) to complete the operation.

301 Front St. W. (✆) **416/868-6937**. www.cntower.ca. Basic admission (Look Out and Glass Floor) C$19 (US$13) adults, C$17 (US$12) seniors, C$14 (US$9.80) children 4–12; Observation Experience (Look Out, Glass Floor, and Skypod) C$24 (US$17) adults, C$22 (US$15) seniors, C$19 (US$13) children 4–12; Total Tower Experience (includes Look Out, Glass Floor, Skypod, film, and 2 rides) C$32 (US$22) all ages. Motion simulator rides C$8 (US$5.60). Daily 9am–11pm. Closed Dec 25. Subway: Union, then walk west on Front St.

MIDTOWN

George R. Gardiner Museum of Ceramic Art   Across the street from the ROM, North America's only specialized ceramics museum houses a great collection of 15th- to 18th-century European pieces. Unfortunately, the Gardiner will be closed for most of 2005; the good news is that when it reopens it will be grander than ever. Like its neighbor across the street, the museum will undergo a massive renovation. The C$15-million (US$11-million) All Fired Up plan will increase the Gardiner's floor space from 1,765 sq. m (19,000 sq. ft.) to 2,694 sq. m (29,000 sq. ft.), and will allow far more of the vast—and growing—collection to be on display.

In case you manage to get to the Gardiner before the work begins, here's a taste of what you'll see. The pre-Columbian gallery contains fantastic Olmec and Maya figures and objects from Ecuador, Colombia, and Peru. The majolica gallery displays spectacular 16th- and 17th-century salvers and other pieces from Florence, Faenza, and Venice, and a Delftware collection that includes fine 17th-century chargers. Upstairs, the galleries contain 18th-century Continental and English porcelain—Meissen, Sèvres, Worcester, Chelsea, Derby, and other great names. All are spectacular. Among the highlights are objects from the Swan Service—a 2,200-piece set that took four years (1737–41) to make—and an extraordinary collection of commedia dell'arte figures.

111 Queen's Park. (✆) **416/586-8080**. www.gardinermuseum.on.ca. Admission C$10 (US$7) adults, C$6 (US$4.20) seniors and students with ID. Free admission on the first Tues of every month. Mon, Wed, Fri 10am–6pm; Tues, Thurs 10am–8pm; Sat–Sun 10am–5pm. Closed Jan 1, Dec 25. Subway: Museum.

Royal Ontario Museum ★ *Kids*   This is one of my favorite museums anywhere. The ROM (rhymes with "tom"), as it's affectionately called, is Canada's largest museum, with more than 6 million objects in its collections. Unfortunately, in 2005, many of those pieces won't be on display because of the museum's ambitious renovation plan. Called Renaissance ROM, this C$200-million (US$140-million) project will add six new galleries overlooking Bloor Street West. The galleries will be encased inside an über-modern palace of jutting crystal prisms designed by Daniel Libeskind. Personally, it brings to mind Superman's crystal palace at the North Pole, but I have to admit that the designs look spectacular (check out the ROM's website at www.rom.on.ca for details and a webcam that shows the work-in-progress).

While the results promise to be grand and will allow the ROM to display far more of its impressive collections, in the here and now the renovation makes the museum a less appealing place to visit. The breathtaking terrace galleries, which housed the world-renowned T. T. Tsui Galleries of Chinese Art, are one casualty of the makeover, and the ROM has also lost its stellar restaurant, Jamie Kennedy

(Finds   Serenity Now

While I'm all for progress, my one complaint about the ROM's extensive renovation plan is that it has temporarily shut down the **Bishop White Gallery,** which used to house a group of serene Southeast Asian Buddhas. The Bishop White Gallery is worth remembering because it's supposed to be put back in place when the renovation runs its course. In the meantime, serenity-seekers should head upstairs to the third-floor **History of Style** wing of the **Samuel European Galleries.** While the kids are busy with the dinosaurs one floor down, adults can rest in the roomy window seat–style nooks that dot the exhibit. Each one has an audio presentation that's well worth listening to; my favorite is the one about lighting, which includes several passages from *Madame Bovary.* Who knew that light at night used to be considered the ultimate luxury?

at the Museum, which was one of the best in the city. (Fortunately, Mr. Kennedy has a new venture; see p. 99 for a review.) The temporary closures at press time affect some of its best displays, such as the **Gallery of Korean Art,** the largest exhibit of its kind in North America (it holds more than 200 works from the Bronze Age through modern times), the **Christopher Ondaatje South Asian Gallery** (in case you're curious, Christopher is the brother of Michael Ondaatje, author of *The English Patient*), and the **Inco Limited Gallery of Earth** with its kid-friendly interactive exhibits.

However, the ROM still deserves the one star it gets this year, because many of the exhibits that kids love best are still here. Some of the big draws are the **Ancient Egypt Gallery,** which features several mummies; the Maiasaur Project, which re-creates the life and times of a dinosaur; the Hands-On Biodiversity Gallery, which has a hardwood forest, a cave, and multiple microscopes; and the **Roman Gallery,** the most extensive collection of its kind in Canada.

100 Queen's Park. © 416/586-8000. www.rom.on.ca. Admission C$10 (US$7) adults, C$7 (US$4.90) seniors and students with valid ID, C$6 (US$4.20) children 5–14, free for children 4 and under. Pay what you can Fri 4:30–9:30pm. Mon–Thurs 10am–6pm; Fri 10am–9:30pm; Sat 10am–6pm; Sun 11am–6pm. Closed Jan 1, Dec 25. Subway: Museum.

ON THE OUTSKIRTS

The McMichael Canadian Art Collection   In Kleinburg, 40km (25 miles) north of the city, the McMichael is worth a visit for the setting as well as the art. The collection occupies a log-and-stone gallery that sits amid quiet stands of trees on 40 hectares (99 acres) of conservation land. Specially designed for the landscape paintings it houses, the gallery is a work of art. The lobby has a pitched roof that soars 8m (26 ft.) on massive rafters of Douglas fir; throughout the gallery, panoramic windows look south over white pine, cedar, ash, and birch.

The collection includes the work of Canada's famous circle of landscape painters, the Group of Seven, as well as David Milne, Emily Carr, and their contemporaries. An impressive collection of Inuit and contemporary Native Canadian art and sculpture is also on display. In addition, four galleries contain changing exhibitions of works by contemporary artists.

Founded by Robert and Signe McMichael, the gallery began in 1965 when they donated their property, home, and collection to the province of Ontario. The collection has expanded to include more than 6,000 works. The museum has a good book and gift store, filled with reproductions as well as one-of-a-kind crafts, carvings, and wall hangings by Canadian artisans.

10365 Islington Ave., Kleinburg. (☎) **888/213-1121** or 905/893-1121. www.mcmichael.com. Admission C$15 (US$11) adults, C$12 (US$8.40) seniors and students with ID, free for children 5 and under. May 1–Oct 31 daily 10am–5pm; Nov 1–Apr 30 daily 10am–4pm. Closed Dec 25. Parking C$5 (US$3.50). By car: From downtown, take Gardiner Expwy. to Hwy. 427 north, follow it to Hwy. 7, and turn east. Turn left (north) at first light onto Hwy. 27. Turn right (east) at Major Mackenzie Dr. and left (north) at first set of lights to Islington Ave. and the village of Kleinburg. Or take Hwy. 401 to Hwy. 400 north. At Major Mackenzie Dr., go west to Islington Ave. and turn right. By bus: From Islington station, take bus no. 37 to Steeles Ave., then take the York Region bus no. 13 to the museum driveway (it's about a 10-min. walk up the driveway from the bus stop); note that separate fares are required for the 2 buses.

Ontario Science Centre ★★ (Kids) Described as everything from the world's most technical fun fair to a hands-on museum for the 21st century, the Science Centre holds a series of wonders for children—800 interactive exhibits in 10 cavernous exhibit halls. More than a million people visit every year, so it's best to arrive promptly at 10am to see everything.

Wherever you look, there are things to touch, push, pull, or crank. Test your reflexes, balance, heart rate, and grip strength; surf the Internet; watch frozen-solid liquid nitrogen shatter into thousands of icy shards; study slides of butterfly wings, bedbugs, fish scales, or feathers under a microscope; tease your brain with a variety of optical illusions; land a spaceship on the moon; watch bees making honey; see how many lights you can light or how high you can elevate a balloon with your own pedal power. The fun goes on and on through the 10 exhibit halls.

Throughout, small theaters show film and slide shows, and you can see regular 20-minute demonstrations of lasers, metal casting, and high-voltage electricity (which will literally make your hair stand on end). Another draw is the Omnimax Theatre, with a 24m (79-ft.) domed screen that creates spectacular effects. There are two eateries on-site: Galileo's Bistro, a buffet-style restaurant that serves alcohol, and Valley Marketplace, a cafeteria. The Mastermind shop has a vast collection of educational toys and games.

While most of the Ontario Science Centre's offerings are fun for the small fry, one area that adults will appreciate is the re-creation of a rainforest environment. On the bottom level of the building, it's large enough that you can wander a bit and forget the noise and blinking lights of the science arcade just beyond. ***One caveat:*** Roam in here for long and you'll feel as if you've hit a sauna.

770 Don Mills Rd. (at Eglinton Ave. E.). (☎) **416/696-3127,** or 416/696-1000 for Omnimax tickets. www.ontariosciencecentre.ca. Admission C$14 (US$9.80) adults, C$10 (US$7) seniors and children 13–17, C$8 (US$5.60) children 5–12, free for children 4 and under. Omnimax admission C$11 (US$7.70) adults, C$8 (US$5.60) seniors and children 13–17, C$7 (US$4.90) children 5–12, free for children 4 and under. Combination discounts available. July 1–Sept 4 daily 10am–6pm; Sept 5–June 30 daily 10am–5pm. Closed Dec 25. Parking C$8 (US$5.60). Subway: Yonge St. line to Eglinton, then no. 34 Eglinton bus east to Don Mills Rd. By car: From downtown, take Don Valley Pkwy. to Don Mills Rd. exit and follow signs.

Paramount Canada's Wonderland ★ (Kids) Thirty minutes north of Toronto lies Canada's answer to Disney World. The 120-hectare (300-acre) park features more than 140 attractions, including 60 rides, a water park, a play area for tiny tots (KidZville), and live shows.

Adults and kids alike come for the thriller rides. Because the park relies on the local audience, it introduces new rides every year. In 2003, it opened Tomb Raider, which it calls Canada's only "flying roller coaster" (you're supposed to feel as if you're flying on its many twists and turns). Other top attractions include the Fly, a roller coaster designed to make every seat feel as if it's in the

---

(**Finds** **Retro Thrills**

With the fanfare given to the new rides Paramount Canada's Wonderland introduces each summer, many park-goers overlook the older attractions. The Wilde Beaste is one of the original roller coasters, and it's still one of the best. The first few times you hurtle along the track you'll be convinced that the whole rickety structure is about to fall down at any moment. Guess what—it was designed to feel that way! (Wonderland's safety standards are top-notch, so have no worries on that front.) Other tried-and-true favorites include the Minebuster and the Dragon Fire. A bonus: shorter queues!

---

front car (the faint of heart can't hide at the back of this one!); Sledge Hammer, a "menacing mechanical giant" that stands 24m (80 ft.) tall and hurls riders through accelerated jumps and free-falls; Drop Zone, in which riders free-fall 70m (230 ft.) in an open cockpit; Cliffhanger, a "super swing" that executes 360-degree turns and makes riders feel immune to gravity; and the Xtreme Skyflyer, a hang-gliding and skydiving hybrid that plunges riders 46m (151 ft.) in a free-fall. The roller coasters range from the looping, inverted Top Gun, to the track-free suspended Vortex.

The Splash Works water park offers a huge wave pool and 16 water rides, from speed slides and tube rides to special scaled-down slides and a kids' play area. You'll also find Hanna-Barbera characters, including Scooby-Doo, strolling around the park (and ready to get their picture taken with the kids). Additional attractions include Wonder Mountain and its high divers (they take the 20m/66-ft. plunge down Victoria Falls to the mountain's base), restaurants, and shops. The Kingswood Theatre books top-name entertainers.

9580 Jane St., Vaughan. (**C**) **905/832-7000** or 905/832-8131. www.canadas-wonderland.com. Pay-One-Price Passport (includes unlimited rides and shows but not parking, special attractions, or Kingswood Music Theater) C$38 (US$27) adults and children 7 and over, C$28 (US$20) seniors and children 3–6, free for children 2 and under. Admission only (no rides) C$25 (US$18). June 1–25 Mon–Fri 10am–8pm, Fri–Sat 10am–10pm; June 26 to Labour Day daily 10am–10pm; late May and early Sept to early Oct Sat–Sun 10am–8pm. Closed mid-Oct to mid-May. Parking C$7.50 (US$5.25). Subway: Yorkdale or York Mills, then GO Express Bus to Wonderland. By car: From downtown, take Yonge St. north to Hwy. 401 and go west to Hwy. 400. Go north on Hwy. 400 to Rutherford Rd. exit and follow signs. By car from the north, exit at Major Mackenzie.

The Toronto Zoo *(Kids)*   Covering 284 hectares (701 acres) of parkland, this unique zoological garden contains some 5,000 animals, plus an extensive botanical collection. Pavilions—including Africa, Indo-Malaya, Australasia, and the Americas—and outdoor paddocks house the plants and animals.

One popular zoo attraction is at the **African Savanna** project. It re-creates a market bazaar and safari through Kesho (Swahili for "tomorrow") National Park, past such special features as a bush camp, rhino midden, elephant highway, and several watering holes. It also includes the **Gorilla Rainforest,** one of the most popular sights at the zoo—little wonder, as this is the largest indoor gorilla exhibit in North America. Another hit is Splash Island, a kids-only water park that includes a replica of a Canadian Coast Guard ship.

Ten kilometers (6 miles) of walkways offer access to all areas of the zoo. During the warmer months, the Zoomobile takes visitors around the major walkways to view the animals in the outdoor paddocks. The zoo has restaurants, a gift shop, first aid, and a family center. Visitors can rent strollers and wagons,

Where to Eat When You're Going to . . .

In my experience, one of the most difficult things about travel is coordinating where you want to go with where you want to eat. All too often you find yourself at a great museum, only to realize that the great restaurant you wanted to try out is on the other side of town. To make your planning easier, here are some of Toronto's top attractions, and the excellent restaurants that are nearby (note that all restaurants mentioned here are reviewed in chapter 5).

- **Art Gallery of Ontario:** The AGO has an excellent restaurant, **Agora,** but it's only open for lunch. Instead, head over to Chinatown for **Sang Ho** (536 Dundas St. W.), **Happy Seven** (358 Spadina Ave.), or **Lee Garden** (331 Spadina Ave.). Or, if you're in the mood for French cuisine, the best nearby is at **Bodega** (30 Baldwin St.).

- **CN Tower** and **SkyDome:** The tower's main dining room, **360,** is popular with tourists, and while I can certainly recommend the view I'm less enthusiastic about the food. But it's a very short walk to **Senses** (at the SoHo Metropolitan Hotel, 318 Wellington St. W.), **Brassaii** (461 King St. W.), and **Fortune Cookie** (291 King St. W.).

- **Hummingbird Centre** and **Hockey Hall of Fame:** You're in luck here, because the stellar **Biff's** (4 Front St. E.) is just across the street. You're also right by **Le Papillon** (16 Church St.), **Jamie Kennedy Wine Bar** (9 Church St.), and **Young Thailand** (81 Church St.)—three well-priced places that serve impressive food.

- **Ontario Science Centre:** While people who work at the OSC love to point out that it's in the geographic center of Toronto, it's Nowheresville as far as food is concerned. But if you head west to Yonge Street you'll be spoiled for choice. If you went to the OSC, presumably you have kids in tow, so **Grano** (2035 Yonge St.) would be an excellent choice. Other good bets include **Hannah's Kitchen** (2221 Yonge St.), which is open only on weekdays, or **Amore Trattoria** (2425 Yonge St.), which is open 7 days a week.

- **Royal Ontario Museum:** The ROM has lost its stellar restaurant to its ongoing renovations, but fortunately the elegant **Annona** (in the Park Hyatt, 4 Avenue Rd.) is just across the street. Nearby Yorkville is full of great spots, including **Jacques Bistro du Parc** (126A Cumberland St.). Head just a few blocks west past Spadina and you'll find a wide selection of moderately priced spots such as **Serra** (378 Bloor St. W.) and **Nataraj** (394 Bloor St. W.).

and borrow wheelchairs. The African pavilion has an elevator for strollers and wheelchairs. There's ample parking and plenty of picnic areas with tables.

Meadowvale Rd. (north of Hwy. 401 and Sheppard Ave.), Scarborough. © **416/392-5900.** www.toronto zoo.com. Admission C$18 (US$13) adults, C$12 (US$8.40) seniors, C$10 (US$7) children 4–12, free for children 3 and under. Summer daily 9am–7:30pm; spring and fall daily 9am–6pm; winter daily 9:30am–4:30pm. Last admission 1 hr. before closing. Closed Dec 25. Parking C$8 (US$5.60). Subway: Bloor–Danforth line to Kennedy, then bus no. 86A north. By car: From downtown, take Don Valley Pkwy. to Hwy. 401 east, exit on Meadowvale Rd., and follow signs.

2 More Museums

Bata Shoe Museum ★★   Imelda Marcos—or anyone else obsessed with shoes—will love this museum, which houses the Bata family's 10,000-item collection. The building, designed by Raymond Moriyama, is spectacular. The main gallery, "All About Shoes," traces the history of footwear. It begins with a plaster cast of some of the earliest known human footprints (discovered in Africa by anthropologist Mary Leakey), which date to 4 million B.C.

You'll come across such specialty shoes as spiked clogs used to crush chestnuts in 17th-century France, Elton John's 12-inch-plus platforms, and Prime Minister Pierre Trudeau's well-worn sandals. One display focuses on Canadian footwear fashioned by the Inuit, while another highlights 19th-century ladies' footwear. The second-story galleries house changing exhibits.

327 Bloor St. W. (at St. George St.). © 416/979-7799. www.batashoemuseum.ca. Admission C$6 (US$4.20) adults, C$4 (US$2.80) seniors and students with ID, C$2 (US$1.40) children 5–14, C$12 (US$8.40) family (2 adults, 2 children). Free to all first Tues of the month. Tues–Wed and Fri–Sat 10am–5pm; Thurs 10am–8pm; Sun noon–5pm. Subway: St. George.

Black Creek Pioneer Village *Kids*   Life here moves at the gentle pace of rural Ontario as it was more than a century ago. The original pioneers on this land were Daniel and Elizabeth Strong, a newlywed couple in 1816 who cleared 40 hectares (100 acres) of wilderness for farming and built a log house in their spare time. Eventually a village developed around this site, and many of the existing buildings date from the 1860s. You can watch the authentically dressed villagers going about their chores—spinning, sewing, rail splitting, sheep shearing, and threshing. Visitors can enjoy the villagers' cooking, wander through the cozily furnished homesteads, visit the working mill, shop at the general store, or rumble past the farm animals in a horse-drawn wagon. The beautifully landscaped village has more than 30 restored buildings to explore. Special events take place throughout the year, from a great Easter egg hunt to Christmas by lamplight.

The restaurant is open from 11am to 3pm and features a special children's menu. Light snacks and refreshments are on sale all day at the visitor centre.

Finds   Pssst . . . Want in on a Secret?

Toronto has a unique museum that is one of the city's best-kept secrets. It's the **History of Contraception Museum,** at the Janssen-Ortho building, 19 Green Belt Dr. (© **416/449-9444**). The collection occupies an airy atrium and contains more than 600 items, some of which will make your jaw drop. (Ever wonder what mule earwax, weasel testicles, and crocodile dung have in common? This is your chance to find out.) The museum is extremely well curated, and many of the prophylactics have fascinating stories behind them.

The only downside to the museum is that it's far off the beaten track—though the Ontario Science Centre is just a 5-minute drive away. If you've already made it that far, hop on a southbound Don Mills Road bus; there's a stop at Green Belt Drive, and the Janssen-Ortho building is a 2-minute walk up the street. It's open Monday through Friday from 9am to 5pm, and admission is free.

1000 Murray Ross Pkwy. (at Steeles Ave. and Jane St.), Downsview. ✆ 416/736-1733. www.blackcreek.ca. Admission C$11 (US$7.70) adults, C$10 (US$7) seniors, C$7 (US$4.90) children 5–14, free for children 4 and under. May–June Mon–Fri 9:30am–4:30pm, Sat–Sun and holidays 10am–5pm; July–Sept daily 10am–5pm; Oct–Dec Mon–Fri 9:30am–4pm, Sat–Sun and holidays 10am–4:30pm. Closed Jan–Apr, Dec 25. Parking C$6 (US$4.20). Subway: Finch, then bus no. 60 west to Murray Ross Parkway.

Design Exchange Located in the old Stock Exchange Building, the Design Exchange—or DX, as it prefers to be known—has become an important Canadian design museum. It showcases professionals' work, but its main purpose is to nurture designers of all types—graphic, industrial, interior, landscape, and urban. It also serves as a clearinghouse and resource center for the design community. One of its most popular programs is CONNECT, DX's national student-design competition, which is intended to foster and promote young design talent. Note that Kubo DX, the on-site restaurant, is well worth a stop.

234 Bay St. ✆ 416/363-6121. www.dx.org. Admission C$8 (US$5.60) adults, C$5 (US$3.50) seniors and students with ID, free for children 13 and under. Mon–Fri 10am–6pm; Sat–Sun noon–5pm. Closed Jan 1, Dec 25. Subway: King.

Justina M. Barnicke Gallery at Hart House ★ *Finds* Hart House is, well, the heart of the University of Toronto community, and the Justina M. Barnicke Gallery is one of its treasures. But don't be taken in by the gallery's small size: its extensive collection of Group of Seven paintings and other Canadian artworks, both historical and contemporary, are scattered throughout the hallways and rooms of Hart House (it's a public building so feel free to wander and explore; just remember that the small plaques naming the work and its artist are hidden on the lower-right side of each frame or canvas). The Barnicke is a two-room gallery that features an ever-changing series of monthly exhibits. Occasionally it will show historical works, but its primary focus is on works by contemporary artists working with various media. Some of the shows may shock: *Martyrs Murder*, by Manitoba artist Diana Thorneycroft, was one that got to me. Thorneycroft created dioramas depicting the martyrdom of several Christian saints using children's plastic dolls and photographed the results. It was one of the most memorable exhibits I've ever seen.

At Hart House, 7 Hart House Circle. ✆ 416/978-8398. www.utoronto.ca/gallery. Free admission. Sept–June Mon–Fri 11am–7pm, Sat–Sun 1pm–4pm; July–Aug Mon–Fri 11am–6pm, Sat 1pm–4pm. Closed for all statutory holidays. Subway: St. George or Museum.

Museum of Contemporary Canadian Art MOCCA, as this museum is known, will have a new lease on life by 2005. It's moving away from its uptown roots and heading for new digs right in the very hot West Queen West neighborhood. Currently, it Canadian collection includes works by Stephen Andrews, Genevieve Cadieux, Ivan Eyre, Betty Goodwin, Micah Lexier, Arnaud Maggs, and Roland Poulin, among many others. MOCCA's mandate has been widening in recent years, and that has made this gallery increasingly interesting. Some of the temporary exhibits have been real eye-openers, in particular one about tattoo art entitled "Art for the Human Canvas."

952 Queen St. W., Toronto. Phone, admission, and hours not available at press time. www.moccas moving.com. Subway: Osgoode, then streetcar west to Shaw St.

Textile Museum of Canada ★ This fascinating museum is internationally recognized for its collection of more than 8,000 historic and ethnographic textiles and related artifacts. You'll find fine Oriental rugs, and cloth and tapestries from all over the world. One gallery presents the work of contemporary artists.

The museum is small, so only a tiny portion of the collection is on display, but you'll always find a vibrant, interesting show.

55 Centre Ave. ☎ 416/599-5321. www.museumfortextiles.on.ca. Admission C$8 (US$5.60) adults, C$6 (US$4.20) seniors, students, and children 5 and over, free for children 4 and under. Pay what you can Wed 5–8pm. Tues and Thurs–Fri 11am–5pm; Wed 11am–8pm; Sat–Sun noon–5pm. Closed Jan 1, Dec 25. Subway: St. Patrick.

University of Toronto Art Centre ★★ *Finds* This is an incredible find—and unfortunately it's one that very few people outside of the Toronto university community know about. (That may change by the time you read this as the Art Centre is set to stage a high-profile Picasso ceramics show in the fall of 2004 and early winter 2005.) You can enter the center from the University College quad, an Oxford-style cloistered garden that is a work of art itself. Inside you'll find a gallery housing the Malcove Collection, which consists mainly of Byzantine art dating from the 14th to the 18th centuries. There are early stone reliefs and numerous icons from different periods. One of the Malcove's gems was painted by a German master in 1538: Lucas Cranach the Elder's *Adam and Eve.* The rest of the Art Center is devoted to temporary exhibitions, which may display University College's large collection of Canadian art, or special exhibits such as the aforementioned Picasso.

15 King's College Circle. ☎ 416/978-1838. www.utoronto.ca/artcentre. Free admission (charge for some special exhibits). Tues–Fri noon–5pm; Sat noon–4pm. Closed for all statutory holidays. Subway: St. George or Museum.

3 Exploring the Neighborhoods

Toronto is a patchwork of neighborhoods, and the best way to discover its soul and flavor is to meander along its streets. On foot you can best appreciate the sights, sounds, and smells—those elements that lend a particular area its unique character. Following are some of the most interesting neighborhoods.

DOWNTOWN WEST

CHINATOWN ★ Stretching along Dundas Street west from Bay Street to Spadina Avenue and north and south along Spadina Avenue, Chinatown is home to some of Toronto's 350,000 Chinese-Canadian residents. Packed with fascinating shops and restaurants, it even has bilingual street signs.

In **Dragon City,** a large shopping mall at Spadina and Dundas, you'll find all kinds of stores. Some sell Chinese preserves (like cuttlefish, lemon ginger, whole mango, ginseng, and antler), and others specialize in Asian books, tapes, records, fashion, and food. Downstairs, a fast-food court features Korean, Indonesian, Chinese, and Japanese cuisine.

As you stroll through Chinatown, stop in at some of the shops and teahouses. A couple of my favorites are **Tap Phong** (p. 160) and **B&J Trading** (p. 190). A walk through Chinatown at night is especially exciting—the sidewalks fill with people, and neon lights shimmer everywhere. You'll pass gleaming noodle houses, windows where ducks hang, record stores selling the Top 10 in Chinese, and trading companies filled with Asian produce.

To get to Chinatown, take the subway to St. Patrick and walk west. For more details, see "Walking Tour 1: Chinatown & Kensington Market," in chapter 7.

LITTLE ITALY Along College Street between Euclid and Shaw, Little Italy competes with West Queen West for the hottest spot in the city. The area hums at night, as people crowd the coffee bars, pool lounges, nightclubs, and trattorias.

Notable restaurants in the area include **Sottovoce** (p. 97), **Chiado** (p. 89), and **Veni Vidi Vici** (p. 96). There are also some great boutiques in the area, such as **Sim & Jones** (p. 187), which features chic, smart casual clothing for women, and **Mink** (p. 193), a glittering oasis of faux gemstones. To get there, ride any College Street streetcar west to Euclid Avenue.

QUEEN STREET WEST This street has over the years been known as the heart of Toronto's avant-garde scene. That would be a serious stretch today. Sure, it's home to several clubs—such as the **Rivoli** (p. 97)—where major Canadian artists and singers have launched their careers (see chapter 9), but it's also where you'll find mainstream shops such as Club Monaco, Gap, and Le Chateau. Edgy? Queen Street West would love to be, but it just isn't anymore. (See "West Queen West," below, if you want a walk on the—somewhat—wilder side.)

Queen Street West officially starts at Yonge Street, but it doesn't really pick up, style-wise, till you cross University Avenue; it ends at Bathurst Street. There are lots of great bistros in this neighborhood, such as **Le Sélect** (p. 93) and the **Taro Grill** (p. 95). This is also prime shopping territory, with one-of-a-kind clothing boutiques such as **Price Roman** (p. 189) and **Peach Berserk** (p. 189). You'll also find a number of fine antiquarian bookstores, antiques and/or junk shops, nostalgic record emporiums, kitchen supply stores, and discount fabric houses.

To start exploring, take the subway to Osgoode and walk west along Queen Street West.

WEST QUEEN WEST Queen Street West beyond Bathurst Street used to be a no-man's land—not because it was dangerous, but because little of importance was believed to be that far from the downtown core. How times have changed: West Queen West, as the neighborhood is now known, is one of the liveliest 'hoods in the city (one magazine dubbed it the coolest in the country—not that a typically modest Torontonian would tell you that!). In 2004 it became home to the new **Drake Hotel** (p. 62) and the **Museum of Contemporary Canadian Art** (p. 134), and the area is continuing to thrive.

West Queen West is all funky fun. It's got great shops for housewares and antiques, such as **Quasi-Modo** (p. 192), and excellent small art galleries, such as the **Stephen Bulger** (p. 180). The clothing boutiques are exceptionally fine: Stop by the bodacious **Boudoir** (p. 198) for vintage, **Girl Friday** (p. 188) for original designs, and **Delphic** (p. 187) for men's clothes. It's also got some fine-but-affordable dining, at spots like **Swan** (p. 95) and **Cities** (p. 92). To start exploring, take the subway to Osgoode and the streetcar over to Bathurst, and start walking west from there.

DOWNTOWN EAST

THE BEACHES This is one of the neighborhoods that makes Toronto a unique city. Here, near the terminus of the Queen Street East streetcar line, you can stroll or cycle along the lakefront boardwalk. Because of its natural assets, it has become a popular residential neighborhood for young boomers and their families, and there are plenty of browseable stores along Queen Street, such as **Zig Zag** (p. 176) and **Book City** (p. 181). There are also some nice spots to stop and grab a bite, such as **Hello Toast** (p. 100). Just beyond Waverley Road, you can turn down through Kew Gardens to the boardwalk and walk all the way past the Olympic Pool to Ashbridge's Bay Park. To get to the Beaches, take any Queen Street East streetcar to Woodbine Avenue.

MIDTOWN WEST

YORKVILLE This area stretches north of Bloor Street West, between Avenue Road and Bay Street. Since its founding in 1853 as a village outside the city proper, Yorkville has experienced many transformations. In the 1960s, it was Toronto's answer to Haight-Ashbury. In the 1980s, it became the hunting ground of the chic, who spent liberally at **Hermès, Chanel,** and **Cartier,** and at the neighborhood's many fine-art galleries, such as **Kinsman Robinson** (p. 179), and **Feheley Fine Arts** (p. 178). In the early 1990s, the recession left its mark—but today the energy is back. **Hazelton Lanes** and Bloor Street continue to attract high-style stores, including a branch of **Tiffany's.**

Stroll around and browse, because this is still a shopper's paradise. **Jeanne Lottie** (p. 188), **Pusateri's** (p. 189), and **Teatro Verde** (p. 192) might bring out my spendthrift side, but they won't break the bank. People-watching is also a popular pastime here; pick a perch at a cafe on Yorkville or Cumberland, and watch the parade go by. If you really want to indulge, visit the **Stillwater Spa** (p. 152) at the Park Hyatt hotel, or the **Estée Lauder Spa** (p. 153), at Holt Renfrew. (Massage is my favorite remedy for jetlag, for stress . . . for just about everything, actually!)

While you're in the neighborhood (especially if you're an architecture buff), take a look at the red-brick building on Bloor Street at the end of Yorkville Avenue that houses the **Toronto Reference Library.** Step inside and you'll find one of Toronto's most serene spots. To reach Yorkville, take the subway to Bay.

MIRVISH VILLAGE One of the city's most illustrious characters is Honest Ed Mirvish, who started his career in the 1950s with a no-frills department store at the corner of Markham and Bloor streets (1 block west of Bathurst). Even from blocks away, neon signs race and advertisements touting bargains hit you from every direction. Among his other accomplishments, Mirvish saved the Royal Alexandra Theatre on King Street from demolition, established a row of adjacent restaurants for theater patrons, and developed this block-long area with art galleries, restaurants, and bookstores. He was responsible for saving and renovating London's Old Vic, too.

Stop by and browse, and don't forget to step into **Honest Ed's** (see "The Best Bargains" on p. 184). To start your visit, take the subway to Bathurst.

THE EAST END

THE DANFORTH/GREEKTOWN This eclectic area along Danforth Street east of the Don River is hot, hot, hot. It swings until the early hours, when the restaurants and bars are still crowded and frenetic. During the day, visitors can browse the traditional Greek stores—like **Akropol,** a Greek bakery at no. 458 (© **416/465-1232**) that displays stunning multitiered wedding cakes in the window. The neighborhood is becoming more ethnically diverse, and its new character is reflected by stores like **Blue Moon,** no. 375 (© **416/778-6991**), which sells beautiful crafts from the developing world (the store supports only producers that provide healthy working conditions and fair pay), and **El Pipil,** no. 267 (© **416/465-9625**), which has colorful clothing, knapsacks, and jewelry. To get to the Danforth, ride the subway to Broadview and walk east.

4 Architectural Highlights

Toronto is a beautiful city in spite of itself—or rather, in spite of some of the city planners and developers who have torn down valuable parts of the city's architectural legacy in the name of progress. Toronto grew by leaps and bounds in the Victorian and Edwardian eras, which is why there are so many stunning buildings from those times (take a walk around the **University of Toronto campus** for a quick introduction to the different styles; also, the **Ontario Legislature** and the **old City Hall** stand out as particularly striking examples). However, much of the 20th century wasn't as kind: Clumsy planners plonked the Gardiner Expressway near the waterfront—making what should have been prime territory into a wasteland—and roughly 28,000 buildings were demolished between 1955 and 1975. A few of the buildings that went up during that era were stunners, such as Ludwig Mies van der Rohe's black-glass **Toronto-Dominion Centre** and Viljo Rewell's **new City Hall.** Still, there are a lot of forgettable buildings in town, but enough Gothic-inspired ones survived that Toronto makes a convincing stand-in for New York on-screen. If you're interested in exploring Toronto's architectural history, the Royal Ontario Museum's **ROMwalks** programs are an excellent way to go (see "Organized Tours" later in this chapter).

Casa Loma ★★★ *Kids*   Every city has its folly, and Toronto has an unusually charming one. It's complete with Elizabethan-style chimneys, Rhineland turrets, secret passageways, an underground tunnel, and a mellifluous name: Casa Loma.

Sir Henry Pellatt, who built it between 1911 and 1914, had a lifelong fascination with castles. He studied medieval palaces and gathered materials and furnishings from around the world, bringing marble, glass, and paneling from Europe, teak from Asia, and oak and walnut from North America. He imported Scottish stonemasons to build the massive walls that surround the 2.5-hectare (6-acre) site.

It's a fascinating place to explore. Wander through the majestic Great Hall, with its 18m-high (60-ft.) hammer-beam ceiling; the Oak Room, where three artisans took 3 years to fashion the paneling; and the Conservatory, with its elegant bronze doors, stained-glass dome, and pink-and-green marble. The castle encompasses battlements and a tower; Peacock Alley, designed after Windsor Castle; and a 1,800-bottle wine cellar. A 244m (800-ft.) tunnel runs to the stables, where the luxury of Spanish tile and mahogany surrounded the horses.

I find it amusing to compare the Pellatts's private suites. Lady Mary's is overwhelmingly extravagant—you could house a family of four in her bathroom, never mind the bedroom, sitting area, sunroom, and so on. Sir Henry's suite is surprisingly modest: It's relatively tiny, with the greatest extravagance being the 18-inch-diameter showerhead in the bathroom. It does make you wonder which of them was the *real* driving force behind the building of the castle.

Finds **Walk This Way**

Several doors on the first story of Casa Loma open to a grand terrace that overlooks the gardens; most visitors step out, look at the gorgeous fountain and flowers below, and then proceed with the castle tour, which is truly a mistake. From the terrace, it's almost impossible to see the entrances to several winding paths that lead around the extensive grounds and command amazing views. Follow the grand staircase down and enjoy a leisurely ramble.

The tour is self-guided; pick up an audiocassette, available in eight languages, upon arrival. From May to October, the gardens are open, too. There's also a Druxy's deli (part of a local chain) on-site, which is good to know, as there aren't many dining options nearby. Casa Loma hosts special events every March, July, and December.

1 Austin Terrace. ✆ **416/923-1171.** www.casaloma.org. Admission C$12 (US$8.40) adults, C$7.50 (US$5.25) seniors and children 14–17, C$6.75 (US$4.70) children 4–13, free for children 3 and under. Daily 9:30am–5pm (last entry at 4pm). Parking C$2.30 (US$1.60) per hour. Closed Jan 1, Dec 25. Subway: Dupont, then walk 2 blocks north.

City Hall ✮   An architectural spectacle, City Hall houses the mayor's office and the city's administrative offices. Daringly designed in the late 1950s by Finnish architect Viljo Revell, it consists of a low podium topped by the flying-saucer-shaped Council Chamber, enfolded between two curved towers. Its interior is as dramatic as its exterior. A free brochure detailing a self-guided tour of City Hall is available from its information desk.

In front stretches **Nathan Phillips Square** (named after the mayor who initiated the project). In summer you can sit and contemplate the flower gardens, fountains, and reflecting pool (which doubles as a skating rink in winter), as well as listen to concerts. Here you'll find Henry Moore's *The Archer* (formally, *Three-Way Piece No. 2*), purchased through a public subscription fund, and the Peace Garden, which commemorates Toronto's sesquicentennial in 1984. In contrast, to the east stands the **Old City Hall,** a green-copper-roofed Victorian Romanesque–style building.

100 Queen St. W. ✆ **416/338-0338.** www.city.toronto.on.ca/city_hall_tour/nps.htm. Free admission. Self-guided tours Mon–Fri 8:30am–4:30pm. Subway: Queen, then walk west to Bay.

The Distillery Historic District ✮✮   The district started to be built up in 1832, but it wasn't until 2003 that this 45-building complex was reinvented as a historic district (before that, the glorious buildings were best known for appearing in many period-piece movies). This was once the home of the Good-erham-Worts Distillery, which was Canada's largest distilling company in the 19th century. The first building on the site, a windmill that was intended to power a grain mill, was built by a miller named James Worts, who had emigrated from Scotland in 1831 (the millstone he brought with him is still on display). His brother-in-law, William Gooderham, soon joined him in the business. In 1834, Worts's wife died in childbirth and, in despair, Worts drowned himself in the mill's well. Gooderham took over the business and adopted Worts's son, who eventually joined the business.

The complex is an outstanding example of industrial design from the 19th century. Much of the construction here was done with that Victorian favorite, red brick, and you'll see it in everything from the buildings to the streets themselves. One exception is the mill building, which was built out of stone and thus managed to survive an 1869 fire. See chapter 9 for the performing arts venues and troupes based in the district.

55 Mill St. ✆ **416/367-1800.** www.thedistillerydistrict.com. Free admission. Subway: King, then streetcar east to Parliament St.

Eaton Centre   Buttressed at both ends by 30-story skyscrapers, this high-tech center, which cost over C$250 million (US$175 million) to build, stretches from Dundas Street south along Yonge Street to Queen Street, an area that encompasses 557,418 sq. m (6,000,000 sq. ft.). A **Sears** department store

---

Finds A Place in the Sun

While it's easy to get carried away in the shops of Eaton Centre, don't overlook Trinity Square, on the west side of the building near the Sears department store. The complex surrounds two of Toronto's oldest landmarks: **Trinity Church,** dating to 1847, and **Scadding House** (℡ **416/ 598-4521**), home of Trinity's rector. Concerned citizens demanded that the developers not block sunlight from reaching the buildings. They got their way—the sun continues to shine on the church's twin towers.

(which replaced the original Eaton's store) anchors the north sections, and more than 285 stores and restaurants and two garages fill the rest. Some 20 million people shop here annually.

Inside, the structure opens into the impressive **Galleria,** a 264m-long (866-ft.) glass-domed arcade dotted with benches, orchids, palm trees, and fountains; it's further adorned by Michael Snow's 60 soaring Canada geese, titled *Step Flight.* The birds are made from black-and-white photos mounted on cast fiberglass frames. Three tiers rise above, reached by escalator and glass elevators, which afford glorious views over this Crystal Palace and Milan–style masterpiece designed by Eb Zeidler (who also designed Ontario Place). Don't be surprised by the twittering of sparrows, some of which have decided that this environment is as pleasant as the outdoors.

Dundas and Yonge sts. ℡ **416/598-8700.** www.torontoeatoncentre.com. Mon–Fri 10am–9pm; Sat 9:30am–7pm; Sun noon–6pm. Subway: Dundas or Queen.

Ontario Legislature ⭐ At the northern end of University Avenue, with University of Toronto buildings to the east and west, lies Queen's Park. Embedded in its center is the rose-tinted sandstone-and-granite Ontario Legislature, with stately domes, arches, and porte cocheres. At any time of year other than summer, drop in around 2pm—when the legislature is in session—for some pithy comments during the question period, or take one of the regular tours. It's best to call ahead to check times.

111 Wellesley St. W. (at University Ave.). ℡ **416/325-7500.** www.ontla.on.ca. Free admission. Year-round Mon–Fri; Victoria Day to Labour Day Sat–Sun. Weekend tours every ½ hour 9–11:30am and 1–4pm; call ahead at other times. Subway: Queen's Park.

Royal Bank Plaza Shimmering in the sun, Royal Bank Plaza looks like a pillar of gold, and with good reason. During its construction, 2,500 ounces of gold went into the building's 14,000 windows as a coloring agent. More important, the structure is a masterpiece of architectural design. Two triangular towers of bronze mirror glass flank a 40m-high (130-ft.) glass-walled banking hall. The external walls of the towers are built in a serrated configuration so that they reflect a phenomenal mosaic of color from the skies and surrounding buildings.

In the banking hall, hundreds of aluminum cylinders hang from the ceiling, the work of Venezuelan sculptor Jesús Raphael Soto. Two levels below, there's a waterfall and pine-tree setting that's naturally illuminated from the hall above.

Front and Bay sts. Free admission. Subway: Union.

Toronto Reference Library Step inside—a pool and a waterfall gently screen out the street noise, and the space opens dramatically to the sky. Light and air flood every corner. This structure is another masterwork by Toronto architect Raymond Moriyama, who also designed the Bata Shoe Museum.

789 Yonge St. ℂ 416/395-5577. Free admission. Year-round Mon–Thurs 10am–8pm, Fri–Sat 10am–5pm; Thanksgiving–Apr also Sun 1:30–5pm. Subway: Bloor.

5 Historic Buildings

Campbell House   Just across from Osgoode Hall (see below) sits the 1822 mansion of Sir William Campbell, a Loyalist and sixth chief justice of Upper Canada. In 1829, he retired to this mansion, where he lived until his death in 1834. It was moved several blocks from its original location in 1972. The beautifully restored building features a collection of period furniture. Guided tours take about half an hour and provide insight into Toronto's early history.

160 Queen St. W. (at University Ave.). ℂ 416/597-0227. Admission C$4.50 (US$3.15) adults; C$2.50 (US$1.75) seniors, C$3 (US$2.10) students with ID, C$2 (US$1.40) children ages 5–12, C$10 (US$7) family (2 adults, 2 children). Year-round Mon–Fri 9:30am–4:30pm; May–Oct also Sat–Sun noon–4:30pm. Subway: Osgoode.

Colborne Lodge   This charming, English-style Regency cottage with a three-sided verandah was built in 1836 and 1837 to take advantage of the view of Lake Ontario and the Humber River. At the time, it was considered way out in the country, and a bother to travel to during the harsh winters. In 1873, the owner, a Toronto surveyor and architect named John Howard, donated the house and surrounding land to the city in return for an annual salary. That created High Park (see "Parks, Gardens & Cemeteries," below), a great recreational area.

High Park. ℂ 416/392-6916. Admission C$4 (US$2.80) adults, C$2.75 (US$1.90) seniors and children 13–18, C$2.50 (US$1.75) children 12 and under. Tues–Sun 10am–4pm. Call ahead; hours vary. Subway: High Park.

Fort York ★ *Kids*   This base was established by Lieutenant Governor John Graves Simcoe in 1793 to defend "little muddy York," as Toronto was then known. Americans sacked it in April 1813, but the British rebuilt that same summer. Fort York was used by the military until 1880, and it was also pressed into service during both World Wars.

You can tour the soldiers' and officers' quarters, clamber over the ramparts, and view demonstrations. The fort really comes to life in summer, with daily demonstrations of drill, music, and cooking. If you can, try to visit on Victoria Day, Canada Day, or Simcoe Day (see "Holidays," p. 18), when there are plenty of special events—including the ever-popular Kids' Drill. The fort is a few blocks west of the CN Tower and 2 blocks east of Exhibition Place.

100 Garrison Rd., off Fleet St., between Bathurst St. and Strachan Ave. ℂ 416/392-6907. www.fortyork.ca. Admission C$5 (US$3.50) adults, C$3.25 (US$2.30) seniors and children 13–18, C$3 (US$2.10) children 6–12, free for children 5 and under. Free parking. Mid-May to Labour Day daily 10am–5pm; Sept to mid-May Mon–Fri 10am–4pm, Sat–Sun 10am–5pm. Subway: Bathurst, then streetcar no. 911 south.

Mackenzie House   This Greek Revival brick row house dates from the mid–19th century. It was once the home of William Lyon Mackenzie, a fiery orator and newspaper editor who had a most unusual career. He became Toronto's first mayor in 1836 . . . and then in 1837 he led the Upper Canada rebellion against British rule. Mackenzie fled to the U.S. with a bounty on his head but returned to Toronto after influential friends arranged a pardon. Some of those same friends bought this house for him, and Mackenzie lived here from 1859 until his death in 1861. It's furnished in 1850s style, and in the back there's a print shop designed after Mackenzie's own. Mackenzie was born in Scotland, and celebrations for Hogmanay and Robbie Burns Day are always special here. The house is 2 blocks east of Yonge and south of Dundas.

82 Bond St. © 416/392-6915. Admission C$4 (US$2.80) adults, C$2.75 (US$1.90) seniors and children 13–18, C$2.50 (US$1.75) children 5–12, free for children 4 and under. May–Sept 1 Tues–Sun noon–5pm; Sept 2–Dec Tues–Sun noon–4pm; Jan–Apr Sat–Sun noon–5pm. Subway: Dundas.

Osgoode Hall West of City Hall, an impressive, elegant wrought-iron fence extends in front of an equally gracious public building, Osgoode Hall. Folklore has it that the fence was built to keep cows from trampling the flowerbeds. Tours of the interior reveal the splendor of the grand staircase, the rotunda, the Great Library, and the fine portrait and sculpture collection. Construction began in 1829, and troops were billeted here after the Rebellion of 1837. It's currently the home of the Law Society of Upper Canada, the headquarters of Ontario's legal profession. The Court of Appeal for Ontario has several magnificent courtrooms here. The courts are open to the public.

130 Queen St. W. © 416/947-3300. Free admission. Mon–Fri 9am–6pm. Free tours July–Aug Mon–Fri 1:15pm. Subway: Osgoode.

Spadina Museum Historic House & Garden ✪ How do you pronounce "Spadina"? In the case of the avenue, it's Spa-*dye*-na; for this lovely landmark, it's Spa-*dee*-na. Why? Who knows! But if you want to see how the leading lights of the city lived in days gone by, visit the historic home of financier James Austin. The exterior is beautiful, the interior even more impressive. Spadina House contains a remarkable collection of art, furniture, and decorative objects. The Austin family occupied the house from 1866 to 1980, and successive generations modified and added to the house and its decor.

Tours (the only way to see the house) start on the quarter-hour. Be warned that while the guides are excellent, the video that they force you to watch before the tour is laughable. (The narrator is the "spirit of the house," and his rambling comments—paired with a stagy Irish brogue—will make you wonder if the video is a joke. It isn't!) In summer, you can also tour the gorgeous gardens.

285 Spadina Rd. © 416/392-6910. Guided tour C$6 (US$4.20) adults, C$5 (US$3.50) seniors and children over 12, C$4 (US$2.80) children 12 and under. Tues–Fri noon–4pm; Sat–Sun noon–5pm. Subway: Dupont.

St. James Cathedral ✪ This stunning early English Gothic–style Anglican cathedral owes its existence at least in part to a group of American Loyalists. They joined with a group of British immigrants to found a congregation in 1797, and they were given a plot of land, which today is bounded by Church, King, Jarvis, and Adelaide streets. The congregation started building Toronto's first church on this site in 1803. The original frame building was enlarged in 1818 and replaced in 1831—and that burned down in 1839. The first cathedral replaced it, only to be destroyed in the great fire of 1849. The present building was begun in 1850 and completed in 1874. It boasts the tallest steeple in Canada. Inside, at the northern end of the east aisle, there's a Tiffany window in memory of William Jarvis, one of Toronto's founding fathers. All of the

---

(Finds **Park Yourself Here**

Spadina House is the next-door neighbor of Casa Loma (p. 138). Between the two is a small but lovely park that is almost hidden by the trees that shade it. Many visitors don't notice it, but locals love it. Grab a bench here if you want to take a breather.

stained glass windows are dazzling, but my favorite is the High Altar window—its lower panel bears a distinct resemblance to Leonardo da Vinci's painting of the Last Supper.

In addition to being a great work of architecture, St. James is a good place to stop and rest for a bit. Unless there's a service going on it doesn't draw much of a crowd, so it feels like a private oasis in the middle of downtown. St. James also hosts free concerts every Tuesday at 1pm from September through June.

65 Church St. ✆ 416/364-7865. Free admission. Sun–Fri 7:30am–5:30pm; Sat 9am–3pm. Subway: King.

St. Michael's Cathedral ⭐ The principal seat of the Catholic archdiocese of Toronto, St. Michael's is another 19th-century neo-Gothic structure. Built between 1845 and 1848, it originally had a plain interior design with clear glass windows and white walls. That changed in 1850, when Armand de Charbonnel became the second Bishop of Toronto. Charbonnel was a Frenchman who had lived in Montréal, and at first he was so opposed to his new position that he actually traveled to Rome to beg Pope Pius IX not to make him take it. The Pope had other ideas and used Charbonnel's visit to consecrate him in the Sistine Chapel. However when the new bishop finally arrived in Toronto in September 1850, he threw himself—body and soul—into beautifying St. Michael's. He sold lands that he owned in France and donated all of the proceeds to the cathedral. He bought dazzling stained-glass windows from France, built interior chapels, and commissioned paintings; he also imported the Stations of the Cross from France (that's why they're in French). While improvements and additions have been made since Charbonnel's time, no one did more to make St. Michael's the masterpiece it is.

St. Michael's is particularly venerated for its musical tradition. It has its own boys' choir—which has won awards internationally—and they sing four masses every week, including three on Sunday.

65 Bond St. ✆ 416/364-0234. Free admission. Mon–Sat 6am–6pm; Sun 6am–10pm. Subway: Queen or Dundas.

6 For Sports Fans

Air Canada Centre Toronto's newest sports and entertainment complex is home to the Maple Leafs (hockey) and the Raptors (basketball). Longtime fans were crushed when the Leafs moved here in 1999 from Maple Leaf Gardens—the arena that had housed the team since 1931—but the Air Canada Centre has quickly become a fan favorite. Seating 18,700 for hockey, 19,500 for basketball, and 20,000 for concerts, the center was designed with comfort in mind. Seating is on a steeper-than-usual grade so that even the "nosebleed" sections have decent sightlines, and the seats are wider . . . and upholstered. If you want to take the one-hour tour of the complex, it's imperative to call ahead—not because it's hard to get a ticket, but because tours are canceled because of events.

40 Bay St. (at Lakeshore Blvd.). ✆ 416/815-5500. www.theaircanadacentre.com. Tours C$12 (US$8.40) adults, C$10 (US$7) seniors and students with ID, C$8 (US$5.60) children 12 and under. Tours on the hour daily 11am–3pm. Call ahead; no tours during events. Subway: Union, then LRT to Queens Quay.

Canada's Sports Hall of Fame In the center of Exhibition Place, this three-floor space celebrates the country's greatest male and female athletes in all major sports. Complementing the displays are touch-screen computers that tell you everything you could want to know about particular sports personalities and Canada's athletic heritage.

Exhibition Place. © 416/260-6789. Free admission. Mon–Fri 10am–4:30pm. Subway: Bathurst, then street-car no. 511 south to end of line.

Hockey Hall of Fame ★ *Kids*   Ice hockey fans will be thrilled by the artifacts collected here. They include the original Stanley Cup (donated in 1893 by Lord Stanley of Preston), a replica of the Montréal Canadiens' locker room, Terry Sawchuck's goalie gear, Newsy Lalonde's skates, and the stick Max Bentley used. You'll also see photographs of the personalities and great moments in hockey history. Most fun are the shooting and goalkeeping interactive displays, where you can take a whack at targets with a puck or don goalie gear and face down flying video pucks or sponge pucks.

In BCE Place, 30 Yonge St. (at Front St.). © 416/360-7765. www.hhof.com. Admission C$12 (US$8.40) adults, C$8 (US$5.60) seniors and children 4–18, free for children 3 and under. Late June to Labour Day Mon–Sat 9:30am–6pm, Sun 10am–6pm; Sept to mid-June Mon–Fri 10am–5pm, Sat 9:30am–6pm, Sun 10:30am–5pm. Closed Jan 1, Dec 25. Subway: Union.

SkyDome   In 1989, the opening of 53,000-seat SkyDome, home to the Toronto Blue Jays baseball team and the Toronto Argonauts football team, was a gala event. In 1992, SkyDome became the first Canadian stadium to play host to the World Series, and the Blue Jays won the championship for the first of two consecutive years. The stadium represents an engineering feat, featuring the world's first fully retractable roof, which spans more than 3 hectares (7½ acres), and a gigantic video scoreboard. It is so large that a 31-story building would fit inside the complex when the roof is closed.

1 Blue Jays Way. © 416/341-2770. www.skydome.com. Tours C$13 (US$8.75) adults, C$8.50 (US$5.95) seniors and children 12–17, C$7 (US$4.90) children 4–11, free for children 3 and under. Tours on the hour daily 11am–3pm. Call ahead; no tours during events. Subway: Union.

7 Markets

Toronto's markets are an important part of its heritage—and not just because they bring regional produce into the city. The markets have traditionally been surrounded by neighborhoods that have absorbed wave after wave of immigrants into the city's fabric. Make like a local and dive into the fray.

Kensington Market ★★   This colorful, lively area should not be missed. You'll hear Caribbean, Portuguese, Italian, and other accents as merchants spread out their wares—squid and crabs in pails; chickens, pigeons, bread, cheese, apples, pears, peppers, ginger, and mangoes from the West Indies; salted fish from Portuguese dories; lace, fabrics, and other colorful remnants. There's no market on Sunday. Kensington Avenue itself is a treasure trove of vintage clothing stores. Admittedly there's a lot of junk here, but there are also amazing finds to be had at shops such as **Courage My Love** (14 Kensington Ave.; © 416/979-1992). Most of the shops display their wares out-of-doors in decent weather, adding to the color and charm of the area.

Finds **Say Cheese**

One Kensington Market spot I can't resist is the **Global Cheese Shoppe,** 76 Kensington Ave. (© 416/593-9251). It stocks excellent offerings from around the world, and the staff is happy to let you try anything. One irresistible choice is the made-in-Ontario goat cheese. Mmm . . .

Bounded by Dundas St., Spadina Ave., Baldwin St., and Augusta Ave. No central phone. Most stores open Mon–Sat. Subway: St. Patrick, then Dundas St. streetcar west to Kensington.

St. Lawrence Market   This handsome food market is in a vast building constructed around the facade of the second city hall, built in 1850. Vendors sell fresh meat, fish, fruit, vegetables, and dairy products as well as other foodstuffs. The best time to visit is early Saturday morning, shortly after the farmers arrive.

92 Front St. E. ✆ **416/392-7219.** Tues–Thurs 8am–6pm; Fri 8am–7pm; Sat 5am–5pm. Subway: Union.

8 Parks, Gardens & Cemeteries

DOWNTOWN

Allan Gardens   George William Allan gave the city these gardens. He was born in 1822 into a wealthy merchant-banking family, and went on to become an alderman, then mayor, and eventually a senator. He was also a philanthropist, and the 4 hectares (10 acres) he donated formed Toronto's first civic park. Originally called the Horticultural Gardens, the city renamed it after Allan died in 1901. The stunning glass-domed conservatory dates back to 1910 and contains six greenhouses that cover 1,486 sq. m (15,995 sq. ft.). They are filled with colorful flora from around the world. The outdoor park is rather seedy and should be avoided after sunset.

Between Jarvis, Sherbourne, Dundas, and Gerrard sts. ✆ **416/392-1111.** Free admission. Daily dawn–dusk. Subway: Dundas.

MIDTOWN

High Park   This 160-hectare (400-acre) park in the far west of Midtown was surveyor and architect John G. Howard's gift to the city. He lived in Colborne Lodge, which still stands in the park. The grounds contain a large lake called Grenadier Pond (great for ice-skating), a small zoo, a swimming pool, tennis courts, sports fields, bowling greens, and vast expanses of green for baseball, jogging, picnicking, bicycling, and more.

1873 Bloor St. W., stretching south to the Gardiner Expwy. No phone. Free admission. Daily dawn–dusk. Subway: High Park.

Necropolis   Located in Midtown East, this is one of the city's oldest cemeteries, dating to 1850. Many of the remains were originally buried in Potters Field, where Yorkville stands today.

Before strolling through the cemetery, pick up a History Tour at the office. You'll find the graves of William Lyon Mackenzie, leader of the 1837 rebellion, as well as those of his followers Samuel Lount and Peter Matthews, who were hanged for their part in the rebellion. Anderson Abbot, the first Canadian-born black surgeon; Joseph Tyrrell, who discovered dinosaurs in Alberta; world-champion oarsman Ned Hanlan; and many more notable Torontonians lie in the 6-hectare (15-acre) cemetery. Henry Langley, who is also buried here, designed the porte cochere and Gothic Revival chapel.

200 Winchester St. (at Sumach St.). ✆ **416/923-7911.** www.mountpleasantgroupofcemeteries.ca. Free admission. Daily 8am–dusk. Subway: Castle Frank, then bus no. 65 south on Parliament St. to Wellesley and walk 3 blocks east to Sumach.

UPTOWN

Edwards Gardens ⭐   This quiet, formal 14-hectare (35-acre) garden is part of a series of parks that stretch over 240 hectares (593 acres) along the Don Valley. Gracious bridges arch over a creek, rock gardens abound, and roses and other seasonal flowers add color and scent. The garden is famous for its rhododendrons. The Civic Garden Centre operates a gift shop and offers free walking tours on Tuesday and Thursday at 11am and 2pm. The Centre also boasts a fine horticultural library.

777 Lawrence Ave. E. (at Leslie St.). ℂ 416/397-8186. Free admission. Daily dawn–dusk. Subway: Eglinton, then no. 51 (Leslie) or no. 54 (Lawrence) bus.

Mount Pleasant Cemetery ★★ Home to one of the finest tree collections in North America, this cemetery is also the final resting place of many fascinating people. Of particular note are Glenn Gould, the celebrated classical pianist; Dr. Frederick Banting and Dr. Charles Best, the University of Toronto researchers who discovered insulin in 1922; golfer George Knudson; the Massey and Eaton families, whose mausoleums are impressive architectural monuments; Prime Minister William Lyon Mackenzie King; Canada's greatest war hero, Lieutenant Colonel William Barker; and writer and editor Jim Cormier.

375 Mount Pleasant Rd., north of St. Clair Ave. ℂ 416/485-9129. www.mountpleasantgroupofcemeteries. ca. Free admission. Daily 8am–dusk. Subway: St. Clair.

9 Especially for Kids

The city puts on a fabulous array of special events for children at **Harbourfront.** In March, the **Children's Film Festival** screens 40 entries from 15 countries. In April, **Spring Fever** celebrates the season with egg decorating, puppet shows, and more; on Saturday mornings in April, the 5-to-12 set enjoys **cushion concerts.** In May, the **Milk International Children's Festival** brings 100 international performers to the city for a week of great entertainment. For additional information, call ℂ **416/973-3000.**

For 30 years, the **Young Peoples Theatre,** 165 Front St. E., at Sherbourne Street (ℂ **416/862-2222** for box office, or 416/363-5131 for administration), has been entertaining youngsters. Its season runs from August to May.

Help! We've Got Kids is an all-in-one directory for attractions, events, shops and services appropriate for kids under 13 in the Greater Toronto area. It doesn't provide a lot of detail about most of the entries, but the listings make a great starting point. A print copy costs C$12 (US$8.40); info is free at **www.helpweve gotkids.com.**

Look in the sections above for the following Toronto-area attractions that have major appeal for kids of all ages. Tied for best venue (at least from a kid's point of view) are:

- **Harbourfront** (p. 119): Kaleidoscope is an ongoing program of creative crafts, active games, and special events on weekends and holidays. There's also a pond, winter ice-skating, and a crafts studio.
- **Ontario Place** (p. 124): The Children's Village, water slides, huge Cinesphere, futuristic pod, and other entertainment are the big hits at this recreational and cultural park. In the Children's Village, kids under 13 can scramble over rope bridges, bounce on an enormous trampoline, or drench one another in the water-play section.
- **Ontario Science Centre** (p. 130): Kids race to be the first at this paradise of hands-on games, experiments, and push-button demonstrations—800 of them.
- **Paramount Canada's Wonderland** (p. 130): The kids can't wait to get on the theme park's roller coasters and daredevil rides. And don't forget to budget for video games.

- **Toronto Zoo** (p. 131): One of the best in the world, modeled after San Diego's—the animals in this 284-hectare (710-acre) park really do live in a natural environment.

For more specialized interests:

- **Art Gallery of Ontario** (p. 125): For its hands-on kids' exhibit.
- **Black Creek Pioneer Village** (p. 133): For craft and other demonstrations.
- **Casa Loma** (p. 138): The stables, secret passageway, and fantasy rooms capture children's imaginations.
- **CN Tower** (p. 126): Especially for the interactive simulator games and the terror of the glass floor.
- **Fort York** (p. 141): For its reenactments of battle drills, musket and cannon firing, and musical marches with fife and drum.
- **Hockey Hall of Fame** (p. 144): Who wouldn't want the chance to tend goal against Mark Messier and Wayne Gretzky (with a sponge puck), and to practice with the fun and challenging video pucks?
- **Royal Ontario Museum** (p. 128): The top hits are the Ancient Egypt Gallery, the Hands-On Biodiversity Gallery, and the Maiasaur Project.
- **Toronto Islands–Centreville** (p. 125): Riding a ferry to this turn-of-the-20th-century amusement park is part of the fun.

Chudleigh's   A day here introduces kids to life on a farm. They'll enjoy hayrides, pony rides, and, in season, apple picking. There's a playground, a straw maze, and more. The store sells pies, cider, and other produce.

9528 Hwy. 25 (3km/1¾ miles north of Hwy. 401), Milton. © 905/826-1252. www.chudleighs.com. Orchard admission C$5 (US$3.50), free for children 3 and under, C$16 (US$11) for a family of 4. July–Oct daily 10am–5pm. By car: From downtown, take Hwy. 401 west to Hwy. 25 (exit 320); follow Hwy. 25 north for about 3km (1.8 miles).

Cullen Gardens & Miniature Village   The half-scale village has great appeal. The 11 hectares (27 acres) of gardens, playground (with two splash ponds), shopping, and live entertainment only add to the fun. There are special events year-round, including various flower festivals in summer, Halloween pumpkin carving in October, and fireworks at midnight on New Year's Eve.

Taunton Rd., Whitby. © 905/686-1600. www.cullengardens.com. Admission C$13 (US$8.75) adults, C$9 (US$6.30) seniors, C$5.50 (US$3.85) children 3–12, free for children 2 and under. Free parking. Summer daily 9am–8pm; spring and fall daily 10am–6pm. Closed early Jan to mid-Apr. By car: From downtown, take Hwy. 401 east to Hwy. 12 (exit 410); drive north on Hwy. 12 to Taunton Rd.; turn left (west) at Taunton Rd. and drive 1km (½ mile).

Finds   A Storybook Sanctuary

The **Osborne Collection of Early Children's Books** is a treasure trove for bibliophiles of all ages. Located at the Lillian H. Smith Branch of the Toronto Public Library (239 College St.; © 416/393-7753), the collection includes a 14th-century manuscript of Aesop's fables, Victorian and Edwardian adventure and fantasy tales, 16th-century schoolbooks, storybooks once owned by British royalty, an array of "penny dreadfuls" (cheap thrillers from the days when a paperback book cost a penny), and Florence Nightingale's childhood library. There are always special exhibits at the Osborne, often featuring whimsical subjects such as dragons. You can visit the library on weekdays between 10am and 6pm, or on Saturdays from 9am to 5pm.

Playdium   The Playdium is an interactive pleasure palace, with its 3,066-sq.-m (33,002-sq.-ft.) space filled with more than 200 games and simulators. It also has rock-climbing walls, a 1.2km (¾-mile) Go-Kart track, an IMAX theater, batting cages, minigolf, a lounge, and restaurant. Beyond the sliding steel door activated by an infrared sensor, you'll discover a surreal scene of huge TV screens, circuit boards, and neon and strobe-lit "alien squid mushrooms."

99 Rathburn Rd. W. ⓒ 905/273-9000. www.playdium.com. C$10 (US$7) for 40 credits; average game costs 3 credits. Mon–Thurs noon–midnight; Fri noon–2am; Sat 10am–2am; Sun 10am–midnight. By car: Take Hwy. 401 to Hwy. 10 (Hurontario St.), and go south to Rathburn Rd. W.

Riverdale Farm ⋆   Idyllically situated on the edge of the Don Valley Ravine, this working farm right in the city is a favorite with small tots. They enjoy watching the cows and pigs, and petting the other animals. There are farming demonstrations daily at 10:30am and 1:30pm.

201 Winchester St. (at Sumach St.). ⓒ 416/392-6794. Free admission. Daily 9am–6pm in spring and summer; daily 9am-4pm in fall and winter. Subway: Castle Frank, then bus no. 65 south on Parliament St. to Wellesley and walk 3 blocks east to Sumach.

Wild Water Kingdom   A huge water theme park, Wild Water Kingdom encompasses a 1,858-sq.-m (20,000-sq.-ft.) wave pool, tube slides, speed slides, giant hot tubs, and thrilling water rides (try the Midnight Express, which spirals through some very dark tunnels). There are bumper boats, pedal boats, canoes, batting cages, and minigolf, too. Note that the park may not be open in inclement weather, so call ahead if in doubt.

Finch Ave., 1.6km (1 mile) west of Hwy. 427, Brampton. ⓒ 416/369-0123 or 905/794-0565. www.wildwater kingdom.com. Admission C$26 (US$18) adults and children 10 and over, C$19 (US$13) seniors and children 4–9, free for children 3 and under, flat rate of C$15 (US$11) per person after 4pm. June daily 10am–6pm; July to mid-Aug daily 10am–8pm; late Aug to Sept 2 daily 10am–6pm. By car: Take Hwy. 401 to Hwy. 427 north; exit at Finch Ave. and drive 1.6km (1 mile) west. Or from downtown, take Queen Elizabeth Way (QEW) to Hwy. 427 north; exit at Finch Ave. and drive 1.6km (1 mile) west.

10 Organized Tours

For summer weekends, it's always a good idea to make tour reservations in advance. At slower times, you can usually call the same day or simply show up.

BUS TOURS

If you enjoy bus tours, try the **Hop-On Hop-Off City Tour** offered by **Gray Line,** 184 Front St. E. (ⓒ **416/594-3310;** www.grayline.ca). It goes to such major sights as the Eaton Centre, City Hall, Casa Loma, Chinatown, Harbourfront, SkyDome, and the CN Tower, and a ticket allows you to get on and off the bus over a 2-day period. These narrated tours, which operate daily starting at 10am, cost C$32 (US$22) for adults, C$28 (US$20) for seniors, and C$17 (US$12) for children 4 to 11; free for children 3 and under.

HARBOR & ISLAND TOURS

Mariposa Cruise Line (ⓒ **800/976-2442** or 416/203-0178; www.mariposa cruises.com) operates 1-hour narrated tours of the harborfront and the Toronto Islands from mid-May to September. There are five cruises a day, departing between 11am and 4pm, and the cost is C$17 (US$12) for adults, C$15 (US$11) for seniors and students, and C$12 (US$8.40) for children 4 to 11. Tours leave from the Queen's Quay Terminal at 207 Queens Quay W.

For a real thrill, board the *Kajama,* a three-masted, 50m (164-ft.) schooner, for a 90-minute cruise. The schedule varies, but through July and August there are three tours a day on weekdays and weekends. Prices for the cruise are C$20 (US$14) for adults, C$18 (US$13) for seniors and students, and C$11 (US$7.70) for children. For more information, call the **Great Lakes Schooner Company,** 249 Queens Quay W., Suite 111 (✆ **800/267-3866** or 416/260-6355; www.greatlakesschooner.com).

INDUSTRIAL TOURS

Canadian Broadcasting Centre ★★   The headquarters for the CBC's English-language networks (including television and radio), this building was designed by Bregman + Hamann/Scott Associates, with John Burgee and Philip Johnson as consultants. It's one of the largest and most modern broadcasting facilities in North America. The tour, which includes a visit to the rooftop studios, is well worth the money; one caveat is that the CBC doesn't recommend its tour for children under 6. However, the whole family can stop by to check out the **CBC Museum** (✆ **416/205-5574**). The museum has a series of interactive exhibits and film clips showcasing the CBC's broadcast history, and it also stages temporary exhibits that explore subjects such as radio sound effects. It's open weekdays from 9am to 5pm and Saturdays from noon to 4pm—and it's free!

250 Front St. W. ✆ 416/205-8605. www.cbc.radio-canada.ca or www.cbc.ca/museum. Tour C$7 (US$4.90) adults, C$5 (US$3.50) seniors, students, and children. Tour schedule changes monthly, so call ahead for information. Subway: Union.

ChumCity   This innovative television station contrasts dramatically with the CBC's formality. Housed in a beautifully restored early-20th-century building, it's a television factory where cameras are not hard-wired to studios or control rooms. Instead of formal shows confined to studios, programs can flow minute by minute from any working area in the building, including the hallways and rooftop. From this location, the cutting-edge company operates three channels: **Citytv,** a popular local news and "infotainment" station; **MuchMusic,** which is devoted to interviews with rock stars, videos, and live music; and **Bravo,** a 24-hour arts channel. ChumCity has 100 permanently fixed remote-control cameras, 25 mobile news cruisers, plus remote terminals at key locations such as City Hall, Metro Hall, the TTC, and police headquarters. The results air on "CityPulse" at noon, 6pm, and 11pm.

This futuristic, interactive TV station invites casual visitors to air their opinions and grievances. Simply enter **Speakers Corner,** a video booth at the corner of John and Queen streets, and bare your soul before the camera. If you're compelling or bizarre enough, you'll get your 15 seconds of fame on a weekly half-hour show, or in short blurbs on Citytv and MuchMusic.

299 Queen St. W. (at John St.). ✆ 416/591-7400, ext. 2770. www.citytv.com. Tours are free but are booked only for groups of 10 or more; you can also get a tour if you attend a taping of "CityLine" (call for information and free tickets, which must be booked in advance). Subway: Osgoode.

TSX Broadcast & Conference Centre   The Toronto Stock Exchange no longer has a trading floor—all of its transactions are electronic now—but this information center will be of interest to anyone who wants to learn more about buying low and selling high. Newly renovated and expanded in 2003, the Centre is a popular site for private corporate events, so it's essential to call ahead to make sure it's open to the public on any given weekday.

Exchange Tower, 130 King St. W. (at York St.). ✆ 800/729-5556 or 416/947-4676. www.tse.com. Free admission. Mon–Fri 10am–5pm. Call ahead to ensure site is open the day of your visit. Subway: St. Andrew.

WALKING & BIKING TOURS

Toronto is a city made for walking, and there's no shortage of options for those willing to pound the pavement. The **Royal Ontario Museum** has a **ROMwalks** program (© 416/586-5513) throughout the summer that offers guided tours of neighborhoods from the Entertainment District to the Danforth. Tours start at 6pm Wednesday and 2pm Sunday come rain or shine. Many of the walks are free, though a few cost C$10 (US$7) per person. Also during the summer, the **Toronto Historical Board** (© 416/392-6827) offers free walking tours of several neighborhoods, including Cabbagetown and Rosedale. Call ahead for details.

Year-round, **A Taste of the World Neighbourhood Bicycle Tours and Walks** ✦ (© 416/923-6813; www.torontowalksbikes.com) leads visitors through the nooks and crannies of places like Chinatown, Yorkville, and Rosedale. Walking tours cost C$15 (US$11) for adults, C$13 (US$9.10) for seniors and students, and C$9 (US$6.30) for children under 12. Bike tours cost C$45 (US$32), C$40 (US$28), and C$30 (US$21), respectively; the price includes bike and helmet rental.

11 Outdoor Activities

Toronto residents love the great outdoors, whatever the time of year. In summer, you'll see people cycling, boating, and hiking; in winter, there's skating, skiing, and snowboarding.

For additional information on facilities in the parks, golf courses, tennis courts, swimming pools, beaches, and picnic areas, call **Toronto Parks and Recreation** (© 416/392-8186; www.city.toronto.on.ca/parks). Also see "Parks, Gardens & Cemeteries," earlier in this chapter.

BEACHES

The Beaches is the neighborhood along Queen Street East from Coxwell Avenue to Victoria Park. It has a charming boardwalk that connects the beaches, starting at **Ashbridge's Bay Park,** which has a sizable marina. **Woodbine Beach** connects to **Kew Gardens Park** and is a favorite with sunbathers and volleyball players. Woodbine also boasts the **Donald D. Summerville Olympic Pool.** Snack bars and trinket sellers line the length of the boardwalk.

The **Toronto Islands** are where you'll find the city's favorite beaches. The ones on **Centre Island,** always the busiest, are favorites with families because of nearby attractions like **Centreville.** The beaches on **Wards Island** are much more secluded. They're connected by the loveliest boardwalk in the city, with masses of fragrant flowers and raspberry bushes along its edges. **Hanlan's Point,** also in the Islands, is Toronto's only nude beach.

Tips **Don't Drink the Water!**

Situated on Lake Ontario, Toronto boasts several beaches where you can lap up the sun. Just don't lap up the polluted H_2O, even though you'll see many Torontonians doing just that as they swim through the murky waters. Lake Ontario has high counts of *escherichia coli,* a very nasty bacteria that can cause ear, nose, and throat infections; skin rashes; and diarrhea—not exactly the kind of souvenir you were looking for.

CANOEING & KAYAKING

The **Harbourfront Canoe and Kayak School,** 283A Queens Quay W. (© **800/960-8886** or 416/203-2277; www.paddletoronto.com), rents canoes for C$40 (US$28) a day. Kayaks go for C$50 to C$65 (US$35–US$46). Private instruction is also available.

You can also rent canoes, rowboats, and pedal boats on the **Toronto Islands** just south of Centreville.

CROSS-COUNTRY SKIING

Just about every park in Toronto becomes potential cross-country skiing territory as soon as snow falls. Best bets are Sunnybrook Park and Ross Lord Park, both in North York. For more information, call **Toronto Parks and Recreation** (© **416/392-8186;** www.city.toronto.on.ca/parks). Serious skiers interested in day trips to excellent out-of-town sites like Horseshoe Valley can call **Trakkers Cross Country Ski Club** (© **416/763-0173;** www.trakkers.ca), which also rents equipment.

CYCLING

With biking trails through most of the city's parks and more than 29km (18 miles) of street bike routes, it's not surprising that Toronto has been acclaimed as one of the best cycling cities in North America. Favorite pathways include the **Martin Goodman Trail** (from the Beaches to the Humber River along the waterfront); the **Lower Don Valley** bike trail (from the east end of the city north to Riverdale Park); **High Park** (with winding trails over 160 hectares/395 acres); and the **Toronto Islands,** where bikers roam free without fear of cars. For advice, call the **Ontario Cycling Association** (© **416/426-7416**) or **Toronto Parks and Recreation** (© **416/392-8186**).

Bike lanes are marked on College/Carlton streets, the Bloor Street Viaduct leading to the Danforth, Beverly/St. George streets, and Davenport Road. The Convention and Visitors Association can supply more detailed information.

There's no shortage of bike-rental options. For an up-to-date list of rental shops, contact the **Toronto Bicycling Network** (© 416/766-1985) or see the website at www.tbn.ca. Renting usually runs about C$12 to C$27 (US$8.40–US$20) a day. One sure bet is **Wheel Excitement,** 249 Queens Quay West, unit 110 (© 416/260-9000; www.wheelexcitement.ca). If you're interested in cycling with a group, or want information about daily excursions and weekend trips, call the Toronto Bicycling Network.

FITNESS CENTERS

The **Metro Central YMCA,** 20 Grosvenor St. (© **416/975-9622;** www.ymca toronto.org), has excellent facilities, including a 25m (82-ft.) swimming pool, all

---

Finds **Walk/Jog/Cycle in Peace**

One of the best places to walk, jog, or cycle in the city is the sprawling **Mount Pleasant Cemetery** (p. 146). No, I'm not joking! The wide paths of the cemetery are like roads, and there's lots of space for everyone, from athletic types to parents pushing strollers. Locals love this park-like space, which abounds with trees and antique statuary, not just tombstones. It's a lively scene, and it's anything but depressing.

Moments Spas & the City

Maybe you have a kink in your neck you just can't work out. Maybe you've got a nasty case of jet lag that won't quit. Or perhaps you're just in the mood for some pampering. In Toronto, you won't have to look too far: This city is spa heaven as far as I'm concerned. The standards are top-notch, the treatments range from the tried-and-true to the innovative, and the prices tend to be quite reasonable. All of the spas listed here cater to both women and men—so boys, don't be shy about trying them out.

Elizabeth Milan Hotel Day Spa Located in the underground concourse beneath the Fairmont Royal York, this spa has 11 treatment rooms, including a luxuriously appointed bank vault that is now a VIP treatment room for those who *really* want privacy. This spa has a number of treatments designed for men, including the Balinese Coffee Scrub, a 60-minute treatment that exfoliates the skin and detoxes the body. For men and women, there's the Chocolate Body Indulgence, a 90-minute therapy that promises to soothe your body and mind. By the way, there really is an Elizabeth Milan, and you'll find her at work at her eponymous spa every day. Fairmont Royal York, 100 Front St. W. ℂ 416/350-7500. www.elizabethmilanspa.com. Subway: Union.

Estée Lauder Spa Located in one of Toronto's most luxurious stores is, appropriately enough, one of the city's most luxurious spas. Decorated in modern-chic blond wood and glass (and with a seemingly endless number of private treatment rooms), the spa provides a full range of services, from manicures to massage. One of the most interesting treatments is the Jet Lag facial, which rehydrates the skin; during the facial, "lymphatic leg therapy" reduces puffiness and swelling (the new Uplifting Facial has similar results). My personal favorite is the 90-minute Hot Lava Rock Body Massage, which will leave you soothed and happy after a 90-minute deep-tissue massage. Just say aaaaaahhh . . . That *really* hit the spot. Holt Renfrew, 50 Bloor St. W. ℂ 416/960-2909. www.holtrenfrew.com. Subway: Yonge/Bloor.

kinds of cardiovascular machines, Nautilus equipment, an indoor track, squash and racquetball courts, and aerobics classes. A day pass costs C$15 (US$11). The **University of Toronto Athletic Centre,** 55 Harbord St., at Spadina Avenue (ℂ 416/978-3436; www.utoronto.ca/physical), offers similar facilities for the same fee.

For yoga aficionados, there's no better place to stretch than the **Yoga Studio,** 344 Bloor St. W. (ℂ 416/923-9366; www.yogastudio.net). A single class costs C$15 (US$11), or you can attend five classes for C$70 (US$49); there's also a pay-what-you-can "Karma Yoga" class available. Incidentally, the studio has been known to draw visiting celebrities.

GOLF

Toronto is obsessed with golf, as evidenced by its more than 75 public courses within an hour's drive of downtown. Here's information on some of the best.

Stillwater Spa   This is as serene a setting as you'll find anywhere in the city. Water is the theme here, and it undulates in streams under transparent floor panels and courses down walls in miniwaterfalls. Before you even get to the treatment rooms, you'll be dazzled by the changing areas, which include the expected whirlpool and sauna, but also have private cabana-like nooks where you can recline which watching TV with a headset (come in for a spa treatment and you can spend all day here—seriously). Venture into the main lounge area and you'll find an aquarium, a fireplace, and a generous supply of biscotti. Many of the treatments are hydrocentric too, like the delicious-smelling Mandarin Honey Body Glow, which uses a Vichy shower (you lie on the table while warm water cascades over you). My favorite spot is the romantic Couples Sanctuary, which has a whirlpool tub, a fireplace, and two massage tables. Park Hyatt Toronto, 4 Avenue Rd. ✆ 416/924-5471. www.stillwaterspa.com. Subway: Bay or Museum.

Victoria Spa   I'm a longtime massage fan, and one of the best I've ever had was at the Victoria Spa, which is located on the third floor of the InterContinental Hotel. Decorated in an elaborate style that veers from the classical to the baroque, this spa is wrapped around an indoor pool and lounge. The woman behind the spa is Victoria Sutherland, and you'll find her daily at her pride and joy. The Victoria Spa is famous for its luxurious pedicures, which involve a hot milk or herbal foot bath, salt scrub, and massage—but in my opinion, all of the treatments, from facials to body therapies, meet the same standard of excellence. The new Rose Massage is a sensual treat: Smell the fragrance of roses in the air, lie down on a (massage) bed of velvety rose petals, and get massaged with rose-infused oil. By the time you stroll out it's impossible to look at the world without rose-colored glasses. Inter-Continental Hotel, 225 Front St. W. ✆ 416/413-9100. www.victoriaspa.com. Subway: St. Andrew or Union.

- **Don Valley,** 4200 Yonge St. south of Highway 401 (✆ **416/392-2465**). Designed by Howard Watson, this is a scenic par-71 course with some challenging elevated tees. The par-3 13th hole is nicknamed the Hallelujah Corner (it takes a miracle to make par). It's a good place to start your kids. Greens fees are C$45 (US$32) from Monday to Thursday, and C$49 (US$34) Friday through Sunday.
- **Humber Valley,** 40 Beattie Ave., at Albion Road (✆ **416/392-2488**). The relatively flat par-70 course is easy to walk, and gets lots of shade from towering trees. The three final holes require major concentration (the 16th and 17th are both par-5s). Greens fees are C$27 to C$42 (US$19–US$29).
- The **Tam O'Shanter,** at 2481 Birchmount Ave., north of Sheppard Avenue East (✆ **416/392-2547**). The par-70 course features links holes and water hazards among its challenges. Greens fees are C$27 to C$43 (US$19–US$30).

- The **Glen Abbey Golf Club,** 1333 Dorval Dr., Oakville (© **905/844-1800;** www.glenabbey.com). The championship course is one of the most famous in Canada. Designed by Jack Nicklaus, the par-73 layout traditionally plays host to the Canadian Open. Greens fees are C$130 (US$91) in early spring and fall, C$235 (US$165) in summer.

Other championship courses of note include the **Lionhead Golf Club** in Brampton (© **905/455-8400**). It has two 18-hole par-72 courses; greens fees are C$135 (US$95) for the tougher course, C$125 (US$88) for the easier course. In Markham, the **Angus Glen Golf Club** (© **905/887-5157**) has a Doug Carrick–designed par-72 course. The greens fees range from C$120 to C$175 (US$84–US$123).

Travelers who are really into golf might want to consider a side trip to **Muskoka** (see chapter 10). This area just 90 minutes north has some of the best golfing in the country at courses such as **Taboo** and the **Deerhurst Highlands.**

ICE-SKATING & IN-LINE SKATING

Nathan Phillips Square in front of City Hall becomes a free ice rink in winter, as does an area at Harbourfront Centre. Rentals are available on-site. More than 25 parks contain artificial rinks (also free), including Grenadier Pond in High Park—a romantic spot, with a bonfire and vendors selling roasted chestnuts. They're open from November to March.

In summer, in-line skaters pack Toronto's streets (and sidewalks). Go with the flow and rent some blades from **Wheel Excitement** (see "Cycling," above).

JOGGING

Downtown routes might include **Harbourfront** and along the lakefront, or through **Queen's Park** and the University. The **Martin Goodman Trail** runs 20km (12 miles) along the waterfront from the Beaches in the east to the Humber River in the west. It's ideal for jogging, walking, or cycling. It links to the **Tommy Thompson Trail,** which travels the parks from the lakefront along the Humber River. Near the Ontario Science Centre in the Central Don Valley, **Ernest Thompson Seton Park** is also good for jogging. Parking is available at the Thorncliffe Drive and Wilket Creek entrances.

These areas are generally quite safe, but you should take the same precautions you would in any large city.

PARACHUTING

The **Parachute School of Toronto** (© 800/361-5867; www.parachute school.com), is based at the Baldwin Airport, about 40 minutes north of Toronto. Going for a dive costs C$220 (US$154) during the summer (the prices drop to C$150/US$105 in winter). After morning instruction, you jump in the afternoon. Reservations aren't required, but it's essential to call ahead to make sure the school's plane is sky-bound that day. Geronimo!

Tips **Skate till You Drop?**

Let's say you'd like to go skating while your traveling companion wants to hit the shops. If you head to **Hazelton Lanes,** you can both get what you want. A central courtyard doubles as a skating rink. Better yet, the shopping center's **Customer Service Centre** (© 416/968-8600) offers complimentary skate rentals. It's hard to beat a deal like that.

ROCK-CLIMBING

Toronto has several climbing gyms, including **Joe Rockhead's,** 29 Fraser Ave. (© 416/538-7670), and the **Toronto Climbing Academy,** 100 Broadview Ave. (© 416/406-5900). You can pick up the finer points of knot tying and belaying. Both gyms also rent equipment.

SNOWBOARDING & SKIING

The snowboard craze shows no sign of abating, at least from January to March (or anytime there's enough snow on the ground). One popular site is the **Earl Bales Park,** Bathurst Street (just south of Sheppard Ave.), which offers rentals. The park also has an alpine ski center, which offers both equipment rentals and coaching. Call **Toronto Parks and Recreation** (© 416/392-8186) for more information.

SWIMMING

The municipal parks, including High and Rosedale parks, offer a dozen or so outdoor pools (open June–Sept). Several community recreation centers have indoor pools. For **pool information,** call © 416/392-7838.

Visitors may buy a day pass (C$15/US$11) and use the pools at the **YMCA,** 20 Grosvenor St. (© 416/975-9622), and the **University of Toronto Athletic Centre,** 55 Harbord St., at Spadina Avenue (© 416/978-4680).

TENNIS

More than 30 municipal parks have free tennis facilities. The most convenient are the courts in High, Rosedale, and Jonathan Ashridge parks. They are open in summer only. At Eglinton Flats Park, west of Keele Street at Eglinton Avenue, six of the courts can be used in winter. Call City Parks (© 416/392-8186) for additional information.

12 Spectator Sports

AUTO RACING The **Molson Indy** (© 416/872-4639; www.molsonindy. com) runs at the Exhibition Place Street circuit, usually on the third weekend in July.

BASEBALL **SkyDome,** 1 Blue Jays Way, on Front Street beside the CN Tower, is the home of the **Toronto Blue Jays.** For information, contact the Toronto Blue Jays, P.O. Box 7777, Adelaide St., Toronto, ON M5C 2K7 (© 416/341-1000; www.bluejays.ca). For tickets, which cost C$16 to C$60 (US$11–US$42), call © 416/341-1234.

BASKETBALL Toronto's basketball team, the **Raptors,** used to be the hottest ticket in town, but it's much easier to get one now. The team's home ground is the **Air Canada Centre,** 40 Bay St., at Lakeshore Boulevard. The NBA schedule runs from October to April. The arena seats 19,500 for basketball. For information, contact the **Raptors Basketball Club,** 40 Bay St. (© 416/815-5600; www.nba.com/raptors). For tickets, which cost C$25 to C$125 (US$18–US$88), call **Ticketmaster** (© 416/870-8000).

FOOTBALL Remember Kramer on *Seinfeld?* He would only watch Canadian football. Here's your chance to catch a game. **SkyDome,** 1 Blue Jays Way, is home to the **Argonauts** of the Canadian Football League. They play between June and November. For information, contact the club at SkyDome, Gate 3, Suite 1300, Toronto, ON M5V 1J3 (© 416/341-5151; www.argonauts.on.ca).

Argos tickets cost C$13 to C$48 (US$9.10–US$34); call **Ticketmaster** (© **416/870-8000**).

GOLF TOURNAMENTS Canada's national golf tournament, the **Bell Canadian Open,** usually takes place at the **Glen Abbey Golf Club** in Oakville, about 40 minutes from the city (© **905/844-1800**). Most years, it runs over the Labour Day weekend.

HOCKEY While basketball is still in its honeymoon phase in Toronto, hockey is a longtime love. The **Air Canada Centre,** 40 Bay St., at Lakeshore Boulevard, is the home of the **Toronto Maple Leafs** (www.torontomapleleafs. com). Though the arena seats 18,700 for hockey, tickets are not easy to come by, because many are sold by subscription. The rest are available through **Ticket-master** (© **416/870-8000**); prices are C$25 to C$100 (US$18–US$70).

HORSE RACING Thoroughbred racing takes place at **Woodbine Race-track,** Rexdale Boulevard and Highway 427, Etobicoke (© **416/675-6110** or 416/675-7223). It's famous for the Queen's Plate (usually contested on the third Sun in June); the Canadian International, a classic turf race (Sept or Oct); and the North America Cup (mid-June). Woodbine also hosts harness racing in spring and fall.

TENNIS TOURNAMENTS Canada's international tennis championships, the **AT&T Rogers Cup** (for women) and the **Montréal/Toronto Tennis Masters Series** (for men), are important stops on the pro tours. They attract stars like Jennifer Capriati, the Williams sisters, and Andre Agassi to the National Tennis Centre at York University in August. The men and women's championships alternate cities each year. In 2004, the women play in Montréal and the men in Toronto. For more information, call © **416/665-9777** or check www.tenniscanada.com.

7

City Strolls

Toronto is one of the best walking cities in the world. I know I'm boasting, but look at the evidence: the patchwork of dynamic, ethnic neighborhoods; the impressive architecture; and the many parks. Because the city is such a sprawling place, however, you'll need to pick your route carefully.

The walking tours in this chapter aren't designed to give you an overview. They offer a look at the most colorful, exciting neighborhoods in the city, as well as areas that are packed with sights on almost every corner.

WALKING TOUR 1 — CHINATOWN & KENSINGTON MARKET

Start:	Osgoode subway station.
Finish:	Queen's Park subway station.
Time:	At least 2 hours. Depending on how long you want to linger at the Art Gallery of Ontario and at various stops, perhaps as long as 8 hours.
Best Times:	Tuesday through Saturday during the day.
Worst Times:	Monday, when the Art Gallery is closed.

This walk takes you through the oldest of Toronto's several Chinatowns. The original Chinatown was on York Street between King and Queen streets, but skyscrapers replaced it long ago. Although today there are at least four Chinatowns and most Chinese live in the suburbs, the intersection of Dundas Street and Spadina Avenue is still a major shopping and dining area for the Asian community. As a new wave of immigrants has arrived from Southeast Asian countries—Thailand and Vietnam in particular—this old, original Chinatown has taken them in. Today, many businesses are Vietnamese or Thai.

Successive waves of immigration have also changed the face of the nearby Kensington Market. From the turn of the 20th century until the 1950s, it was the heart of the Jewish community. In the 1950s, Portuguese immigrants arrived to work in the food-processing and meatpacking industries and made it their home. In the '60s, a Caribbean presence arrived. Today, traces of all these communities remain in the vibrant life of the market.

From the St. Patrick subway station, exit on the northwest corner of Dundas Street and University Avenue, and walk west on Dundas Street. Turn right onto McCaul Street. At no. 131 you'll see:

❶ St. Patrick's Church
Built in 1861 for Toronto's Irish Catholic community (you could have guessed that from the name, couldn't you?), this church became the base of German-speaking Catholics from 1929 through the late 1960s. Inside you'll find some of the most beautiful stained glass in Toronto. The church is also a popular site for concerts.

Turn back towards Dundas Street; walking towards it you'll see:

❷ Sharp Centre for Design

This new building that looks as if it were inspired by a cartoon (it looks like a checkerboard box on stilts) is part of the **Ontario College of Art & Design.** The Sharp Centre won a Worldwide Award from the Royal Institute of British Architects in 2004; they described it as "courageous, bold and just a little insane." And so it is.

Cross Dundas Street, turn right and cross McCaul Street to head west again. On Dundas Street, you'll almost immediately encounter a Henry Moore sculpture, *Large Two Forms,* which describes precisely what it is. On your left is the entrance to the:

❸ Art Gallery of Ontario

Both the Canadian and international collections here are excellent, and they will be expanded by architect Frank Gehry's design for a renovated AGO. But if you're not in the mood for gallery-gazing, you can still browse the AGO's large shop without paying admission. The gallery's wonderful restaurant, **Agora** (p. 88), is open for lunch.

Cross to the north side of Dundas Street, opposite the Art Gallery. A worthwhile stop is:

❹ Bau-Xi

This gallery, at 340 Dundas St. W. (ⓒ **416/977-0600**), represents modern Canadian artists. From here, continue west along Dundas Street.

At the northwest corner of Dundas and Beverley is the:

❺ Consulate General of Italy

It doesn't look like a government building: The rambling late-19th-century mansion, with its sandy brick, quasi-Gothic windows, and wrought-iron decoration, is a beauty. Too bad it doesn't offer tours.

You're now walking into the heart of Chinatown, with its grocery stores, bakeries, bookstalls, and emporiums selling foods, handcrafts, and other items from Asia.

What follows are some of my favorite stops along the stretch of Dundas Street between Beverley Street and Spadina Avenue. On the south or left side as you go west is:

❻ Tai Sun Co.

At nos. 407–09, the supermarket carries dozens of different mushrooms, all clearly labeled in English, as well as fresh Chinese vegetables, meats, fish, and canned goods. **Melewa Bakery,** no. 433, has a wide selection of pastries, like mung-bean and lotus-paste buns. Outside **Kiu Shun Trading,** no. 441, dried fish are on display; inside you'll find numerous varieties of ginseng and such miracle remedies as "Stop Smoking Tea."

On the north side of the street is:

❼ J & S Arts and Crafts

This shop, at no. 430, is a good place to pick up souvenirs, including kimonos and happy coats, kung-fu suits, address books, cushion covers, and all-cotton Chinatown T-shirts. **Kim Moon,** no. 438, is an Asian bakery that features almond cookies, deep-fried taro pastries, and dim sum pork buns.

TAKE A BREAK
Ten Ren Tea at no. 454, sells all kinds of tea—black, oolong, green—stored in large canisters at the back of the store. Charming ceramic teapots and cups are on sale here, along with gnarled root ginseng. You can break here for tea—but even if you don't want to sit down, the staff will probably make you sample an unfamiliar variety in a tiny cup. Don't worry, it will taste surprisingly good.

At the northwest corner of Huron and Dundas streets, is:

❽ WY Trading Co.

At no. 456, **W Y Trading Co., Inc.,** has a great selection of records, CDs,

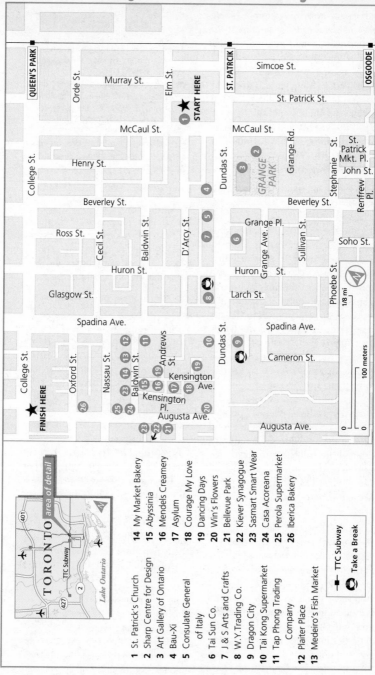

1 St. Patrick's Church
2 Sharp Centre for Design
3 Art Gallery of Ontario
4 Bau-Xi
5 Consulate General
   of Italy
6 Tai Sun Co.
7 J & S Arts and Crafts
8 W.Y. Trading Co.
9 Dragon City
10 Tai Kong Supermarket
11 Tap Phong Trading
    Company
12 Plaiter Place
13 Medeiro's Fish Market
14 My Market Bakery
15 Abyssinia
16 Mendels Creamery
17 Asylum
18 Courage My Love
19 Dancing Days
20 Win's Flowers
21 Bellevue Park
22 Klever Synagogue
23 Sasmart Smart Wear
24 Casa Acoreana
25 Perola Supermarket
26 Iberica Bakery

■◗ TTC Subway
◗ Take a Break

and tapes—everything from Chinese folk songs and cantatas to current hit albums from Hong Kong and Taiwan. Even if you don't go in you'll hear music blaring from inside. At no. 482A, **Po Chi Tong** is a fun store that sells exotic remedies, like deer-tail extract and liquid-gold ginseng or royal jelly. The best remedy of all time is the "slimming tea." Watch the staff weigh each item out and total the bill with a fast-clicking abacus.

At Spadina Avenue, cross over to the southwest corner to:

⑨ Dragon City

The three-level Asian shopping complex at 280 Spadina Ave. is complete with a food court. Here you'll find books, music, clothing, toys, and homeopathic remedies under one roof.

Spadina (pronounced spa-*dye*-na) Avenue is the widest street in the city because the wealthy Baldwin family had a 40m (132-ft.) swath cut through the forest from Queen Street to Bloor Street so that they could view the lake from their new home on top of Spadina Hill. Later, in the early 20th century, Spadina Avenue became Toronto's garment center and the focal point of the city's Jewish community. Although it's still the garment center, with wholesale and discount fashion houses, as well as the fur district (farther south around Adelaide), today it's more Asian than Jewish.

If you enjoy strolling through supermarkets filled with exotic Asian delights, including such fruits as durian in season, visit the:

⑩ Tai Kong Supermarket

Look at all the different provisions—chile and fish sauces, fresh meat and fish (including live tilapia in tanks), preserved plums, chrysanthemum tea and other infusions, moon cakes, and large sacks of rice.

TAKE A BREAK
For fine, reasonably priced food, a Chinatown favorite is **Happy Seven**, 358 Spadina Ave. (© 416/971-9820; see p. 96). If you don't mind lining up, head for the ever-popular **Lee Garden**, 331 Spadina Ave. (© 416/593-9524; see p. 96). For speedy service, check out **Co Yen**, 334 Spadina Ave. (© 416/597-1573), a Vietnamese takeout spot (there are no seats). Continuing north, cross St. Andrews Street.

⑪ Tap Phong Trading Company

This shop, at 360 Spadina Ave., stocks terrific wicker baskets of all shapes and sizes, as well as woks and ceramic cookware, attractive mortars and pestles, and other household items.

Cross Baldwin Street and you'll come to:

⑫ Plaiter Place

At 384 Spadina Ave., Plaiter Place has a huge selection of finely crafted wicker baskets, birdcages, woven blinds, bamboo steamers, hats, and other fun items. **Fortune Housewares,** no. 388, carries kitchen and household items—including brand names—for at least 20% off prices elsewhere in the city.

Now double back to Baldwin Street. You're heading into the heart of the **Kensington Market** area, which has always reflected the city's waves of immigration. Once it was primarily a Jewish market; later it became a Portuguese neighborhood. Today, it is largely Asian and Caribbean, but there are still many Jewish and Portuguese elements.

As you walk west, you'll find:

⑬ Medeiro's Fish Market, Seven Seas, and Coral Sea

At these and other fish stores on the north side of the street, folks buy their supplies of salt cod.

⑭ My Market Bakery

The merchandise at 172 Baldwin St. (𝄢 **416/593-6772**) will doubtless lure you in to buy some bread. Focaccia, sourdough—you name it, they have it.

When you reach Kensington Avenue, turn left and you'll find:

⑮ Abyssinia

Abyssinia specializes in African and West Indian products. You'll also find **Patty King,** which stocks Jamaican breads and other West Indian goods, including roti, bread pudding, and tamarind balls. Several **seafood stores** display a variety of fresh fish and salted cod piled in boxes on the sidewalk; and the **Royal Food Centre** sells a variety of Jamaican specialties, including goat.

⑯ Mendels Creamery

This shop, at no. 72, sells smoked fish, herring, cheeses, and fine dill pickles. Another door down, **Global Cheese,** no. 76, offers an enormous selection at good prices.

As you stroll south along Kensington Avenue and pass Andrews Street, you will find a series of secondhand and vintage clothing stores.

⑰ Asylum

At no. 42 Kensington Ave., on the west side of the street, the store has good jeans, leather jackets, and assorted accessories. I once found a silk Anne Klein scarf for C50¢ (US35¢) in one of the bargain bins here.

⑱ Courage My Love

The best spot for cheap but chic vintage clothing is at no. 14. It stocks retro gowns and wedding dresses, suits, and accessories, as well as new jewelry and beads for do-it-yourself projects.

⑲ Dancing Days

At no. 17 (on the east side of the street), you'll find party-ready glad rags that will make you look like an extra in *Grease!*

When you reach Dundas Street, turn right and walk 1 block to Augusta Avenue. Along the way you pass:

⑳ Win's Flowers

This shop has gorgeous greenery and blossoms. The jade plants in particular are extraordinarily beautiful.

Turn right on Augusta Avenue. As you walk north, in the center of Denison Square, you'll find:

㉑ Bellevue Park

The houses facing the south edge of the park have cherry trees in front of them; they are a colorful sight in season.

Stroll through the park; at the corner of Bellevue Avenue and Denison Square you'll find:

㉒ Kiever Synagogue

This building at 28 Denison Square was completed in 1927. Architect Benjamin Swartz designed it with Byzantine style in mind. The most striking features outside are the twin domes atop the building; inside, stained-glass windows, brass ornaments, and a gigantic Holy Ark dominate the space. (The Kiever Synagogue was the first specifically Jewish building designated a historic site by the province of Ontario.)

Turn back toward Augusta Avenue and you'll see:

㉓ Sasmart Smart Wear

This discount store has the strangest assortment of goods you'll find anywhere. OshKosh clothing for kids is on display near antique china; a little farther along is kitchen gear (new and used), luggage, and gadgets. It's a weird, cluttered space, but the prices are unbeatable.

Walk north on Augusta to:

㉔ Casa Acoreana

An old-fashioned store at no. 235, it stocks a full range of fresh coffees, as well as great pecans and filberts. Just up the block at no. 214 is the **Alvand Food Mart** (𝄢 **416/597-2252**), which specializes in Middle Eastern foods and stocks imported goods from the region.

Just up the street is:

㉕ Perola Supermarket

This store at 247 Augusta Ave. displays cassava and strings of peppers—ancho, arbol, pasilla—hung up to dry and sitting in bins, plus more exotic fruits and herbs.

TAKE A BREAK
If you're in the neighborhood after 5:30pm, a perfect place to stop is **La Palette,** 256 Augusta Ave. (✆ 416/929-4900; p. 93). Enjoy a meal of classic French bistro staples—or tuck into one of the many divine desserts.

Cross Nassau Street to get to:

㉖ Iberica Bakery

The bakery, where you can enjoy coffee and pastries at a handful of tables, is on the east side of the street at 279 Augusta Ave. It represents one of the few remaining traces of the Portuguese presence in the Kensington Market area. Other vestiges are the Portuguese church on Nassau Street and the Portuguese radio station around the corner on Oxford Street. Now just walk up to College Street and hop on the streetcar that runs east to the Queen's Park subway station. The southbound train will take you back downtown.

WALKING TOUR 2   HARBOURFRONT

Start:	Union Station.
Finish:	Toronto Music Garden.
Time:	At least 2 hours.
Best Times:	Weekdays in summer.
Worst Time:	Weekends in summer, when Harbourfront is packed from end-to-end. Weekends during the rest of the year are much better.

As you start your tour, pause to look at the Beaux Arts interior of **Union Station,** which opened in 1927. The hall has a cathedral-like ceiling and 22 pillars that weigh 70 tons each. From here, either take the LRT to York Quay or walk south along York Street (away from the Fairmont Royal York hotel) to Queens Quay West. On the way you'll pass the **Air Canada Centre,** home to the Toronto Maple Leafs hockey team and the Toronto Raptors basketball team. The Gardiner Expressway looms overhead, making this a noisy, dark spot.

When you reach the end of the street, you're at Queens Quay West. Look across to:

❶ Queen's Quay Terminal

This large complex houses more than 100 shops and restaurants. On the third floor is a theater designed for dance performances. Built in 1927 when lake and railroad trade flourished, this eight-story concrete warehouse has been attractively renovated. The light, airy two-story marketplace has garden courts, skylights, and waterfalls. Condos occupy the floors above.

Although you'll find few bargains here, there are some charming stores on the street level. They include **Oh Yes Toronto,** which specializes in souvenirs and Toronto-centric clothing.

On the upper level, options include the classic **Tilley Endurables,** founded by Torontonian Alex Tilley (who invented the world's most adaptable hat). **First Hand Canadian Crafts** represents more than 200 contemporary folk artists who make both decorative and functional pieces.

TAKE A BREAK
If you want to sit out and watch the lakefront traffic—boat and human—go for a light meal or a drink at the **Boathouse Cafe** (✆ 416/203-6300), on the ground floor of Queens Quay. **Pearl Harbourfront Chinese Cuisine** (✆ 416/203-1233) offers more formal dining. The Queens Quay complex also has a variety of cafes, and food vendors just outside.

From Queen's Quay Terminal, walk along the water to the:

❷ Power Plant Contemporary Art Gallery

This was indeed a power plant when it was built in 1927. Identifiable by its towering smokestack, the space has been converted to display modern art. The same building houses the Du Maurier Theatre Centre, which presents works in French.

Behind this building, adjacent to Queens Quay West, is the Tent in the Park, where events take place during the summer season.

Walk next door to the:

❸ York Quay Centre

A complex converted from a 1940 trucking warehouse, it contains a number of interesting restaurants and galleries. Spend some time in the Craft Studio watching the glassblowers, potters, jewelry makers, and other artisans at work, and browse in the store that sells their work.

On the waterfront side in front of York Quay, there's a pond where kids operate model boats in summer; in winter it turns into an ice-skating rink.

From York Quay, cross the Amsterdam Bridge above Marina 4, checking out the wealth that's bobbing down below. You'll arrive on:

❹ John Quay

The first building you'll come to contains four restaurants, beyond which are the towers of the:

❺ Radisson Plaza Hotel Admiral and Admiralty Point Condominiums

The complex sits across Queens Quay West from the HarbourPoint Condominiums. The ground level of the Admiralty Point Condos houses a few interesting stores. The **Nautical Mind** sells marine books, photographs, navigational charts, and boating videos; the **Dock Shoppe** overflows with all kinds of sailing gear and fashions.

TAKE A BREAK
Pop into the **Radisson Plaza Hotel Admiral** (✆ 416/203-3333), 249 Queens Quay W. It has a couple of dining options (the **Commodore's Dining Room** and the **Gallery Café**, which serves light fare), plus a pleasant terrace if it's a sunny day.

Continue west along Queens Quay West past:

❻ Maple Leaf Quay

You can stop at the Nautical Centre to sign up for sailing classes first. Continue west and you'll see the Maple Leaf Quay Apartments on your right and the Harbour Terrace Condominiums farther along on your left, on the waterfront.

Next door to the westernmost tower of the Maple Leaf Quay Apartments is the:

❼ Toronto Music Garden

A terrific destination for whiling away an afternoon, the Music Garden was designed by world-renowned cellist Yo-Yo Ma and landscape architect Julie Moir Messervy to invoke Bach's First Suite for Unaccompanied Cello. The venue is open 7 days a week and admission is free. Even better, there are special musical performances scheduled here throughout the summer, on both weekdays and weekends.

To return to downtown, board the LRT and head back to Union Station.

Walking Tour: Harbourfront

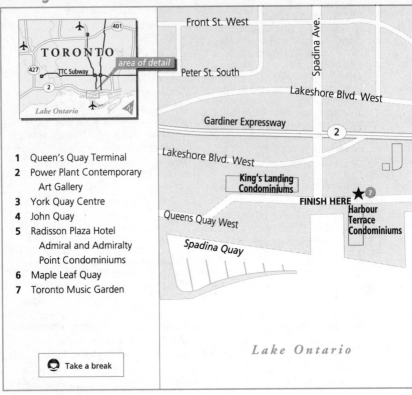

1 Queen's Quay Terminal
2 Power Plant Contemporary
   Art Gallery
3 York Quay Centre
4 John Quay
5 Radisson Plaza Hotel
   Admiral and Admiralty
   Point Condominiums
6 Maple Leaf Quay
7 Toronto Music Garden

Take a break

WALKING TOUR 3   **UNIVERSITY OF TORONTO**

Start:	Queen's Park subway station.
Finish:	The Roof bar at the Park Hyatt Toronto.
Time:	2 to 4 hours.
Best Time:	Weekdays during business hours, or Saturdays.
Worst Times:	Sundays, when many buildings are closed or reserved for weddings.

The St. George campus of the University of Toronto is located in the heart of the city, and it is both an essential part of Toronto and a community in and of itself. Its population (there are roughly 50,000 students, professors, workers, and others on campus Sept–June) could form a small city—and if they did, it would be filled with historic buildings, innovative architecture, and gorgeous land-scaping. Fortunately, U of T is a public institution, so anyone can enjoy its beauty (few buildings are off limits). Since its founding in 1827, U of T—then called King's College—has been on the forefront in many fields. This was the place where insulin was discovered, where the electronic heart pacemaker was invented, where the first single-lung transplant took place, and where the gene responsible for cystic fibrosis was identified. But U of T is also on the cutting edge of design, and it's currently reinvesting its environment with the Open Space Master Plan (see www.utoronto.ca/openspace for details). The campus is

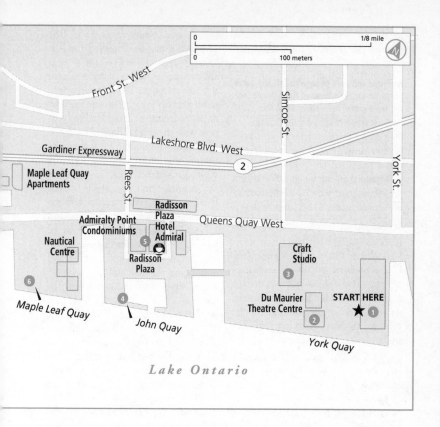

The map shows the following labels:

0 — 1/8 mile
0 — 100 meters

Front St. West

Simcoe St.

Lakeshore Blvd. West

Gardiner Expressway

2

York St.

Maple Leaf Quay Apartments

Rees St.

Radisson Plaza Hotel Admiral

Queens Quay West

Admiralty Point Condominiums

5

Nautical Centre

Craft Studio

3

Radisson Plaza

6

Du Maurier Theatre Centre

START HERE

★ 1

2

Maple Leaf Quay

4

John Quay

York Quay

Lake Ontario

so large that you could spend all day exploring it, but this walking tour will lead you to its highlights. See for your own eyes how a historic university is reshaping itself for the next century.

From the Queen's Park subway station, exit on the northwest corner of College Street and University Avenue. Look north and you'll see:

① Queen's Park

The rose-tinted sandstone-and-granite building that dominates the park is the seat of Ontario's provincial government. It's a stately sight, and the lush park that surrounds it is equally attractive. If the legislature is in session, you could go in to watch it in action.

Walk west along the north side of College Street. Look to your right at:

② The Leslie Dan Faculty of Pharmacy

This site is currently under construction, so what you see will depend on

the timing of your visit. But this C$70-million project, designed by Lord Norman Foster (the architect who created the Great Court at the British Museum, redeveloped Trafalgar Square, and reconstructed the Reichstag), promises to be dramatic.

Continue west on College Street. When you come to King's College Road, you'll see:

③ The Alumni Gates

Part of U of T's Open Space initiative is to make the university's entry points more distinctive. The Alumni Gates were a gift to the university from the alumni association in 2003, to mark the association's 100th anniversary. Two columns frame the south entryway and its view of the front of the campus, and a tree-lined boulevard leads north from here.

Turn right and walk through the Alumni Gates and north up the boulevard. As you walk you will see a yellow building, which is the:

④ Sandford Fleming Building
Named for the man who invented the worldwide system of Standard Time, this Edwardian building was built in 1907 and then rebuilt in 1977 after a fire. It's currently home to the Faculty of Applied Science and Engineering.

Next, on your left is:

⑤ Convocation Hall
Dating from 1907 just like its neighbor, U of T holds its graduation ceremonies here (it takes a couple of weeks each year to do them all). Many other special events take place here throughout the year. Archbishop Desmond Tutu has spoken here, as has Vaclav Havel.

In front of you is the green lawn of the front campus circle. Walk to the left around it. On your left will be:

⑥ Knox College
This 1915 building has been used in countless movies (*Good Will Hunting* was filmed on U of T's campus, for starters). It's not hard to see why—it's the perfect rendering of a neo-Gothic college. Step inside its sandstone walls to take in its intricate details (the Reading Room is the very best). Also, step into its quad—the hidden courtyard at its center.

Retrace your steps, turning left as you leave Knox College. Follow the front campus circle as it curves to the right and leads you to:

⑦ University College
UC, as it's known, was once an independent university, and it has one of the most fascinating histories in Toronto. Its foundation stone was laid without fanfare in October 1856—it was actually a secret, because the plan to create a nondenominational university had met with fierce opposition. The tremendous structure was built with great haste, and most of the

college was completed in 1857 (the 120-foot tower was finished the following year). UC wasn't just a great achievement in terms of construction but in purpose. Its first president wrote that UC would "enable the sons of the poorest man in the land to compete with the most affluent."

This unique building was designed using a mix of architectural styles by F.W. Cumberland. Take a close look at the columns and the windows and you'll see that no two are alike. UC was seriously damaged by an 1890 fire, and substantial segments of it had to be rebuilt. Step inside, turn right, and follow the hallway to its end; turn left and you'll pass the east staircase with its **coiled dragon** on the newel post (be sure to pet him for luck). Continue along the corridor until to reach the **UC quad.** There, you'll also find:

⑧ University Art Centre
This small but stunning gallery contains the **Malcove Collection,** which consists primarily of Byzantine art (p. 135). Lucas Cranach the Elder's 1538 painting *Adam and Eve* is also on display. The gallery also has a substantial Canadian collection, and its temporary gallery hosts various shows.

Walk back through the UC quad and into the building. Follow the corridor back to the east staircase. Pet the dragon again and walk out the east exit. If it's near lunchtime and your stomach is rumbling, this isn't a bad place to:

TAKE A BREAK
Your best bet for a leisurely lunch on campus is right in front of you: inside Hart House is the **Gallery Grill** (© 416/978-2445), a fine restaurant that is open from fall through spring. Its cooking is innovative, but its gorgeous setting makes it a good place to stop even just for tea (at last count there were more than 15 loose-leaf varieties here) or dessert. In summer you can count on the Arbor Room, a casual cafeteria-style restaurant, to be open; it's located in Hart House as well.

Walking Tour: University of Toronto

finish here

Bloor Street West

Bedford Rd.

Queen's Park

Bloor Street West

Sultan St.

St. Thomas St.

Devonshire Place

Charles Street West

St. Mary Street

Philosopher's Walk

Hoskin Avenue

Back Campus

St. George St.

Tower Rd.

QUEEN'S PARK

Queen's Park Crescent West

Queen's Park Crescent East

Emsley Pl.

St. Joseph Street

Harthouse Cir.

King's College Cir.

Front Campus

Wellesley St. West

Wellesley St. West

Provincial Legislature

Galbraith Rd.

St. George St.

King's College Rd.

Taddle Cd. Rd.

Grosvenor St.

Women's College Hospital

Grenville St.

Surrey Pl.

Beverley St.

Henry St.

McCaul St.

start here

College St.

University Avenue

0 · · · 1/8 mile

0 · · · 100 meters

N

1 Queen's Park
2 The Leslie Dan Faculty
   of Pharmacy
3 The Alumni Gates
4 Sandford Fleming Building
5 Convocation Hall
6 Knox College
7 University College
8 University Art Centre

9 Hart House
10 Soldiers' Tower
11 Trinity College
12 Royal Ontario Museum
13 Victoria College
14 Old Vic
15 Gardiner Museum of
   Ceramic Art
16 The Roof

Stepping outside of UC will bring you to Hart House Circle. Walk to the left and you'll reach:

⑨ Hart House

U of T's community center was conceived of by Vincent Massey, grandson of the industrialist Hart Massey. Vincent was a student at the university at the time, and while it took time for his plans to come to fruition—and eight years to build—Hart House opened on November 11, 1919. The Gothic Revival building contains reading rooms, a chapel, two dining spots, a billiards room, several club rooms, an interior courtyard, and the **Justina M. Barnicke Gallery** (p. 134). Wander through the building to see the Group of Seven paintings and other works of art.

Exit Hart House on its west side, close to the Justina M. Barnicke Gallery; turn right and walk north. Look back at Hart House to appreciate its:

⑩ Soldiers' Tower

The tower was added to the west end of Hart House between 1919 and 1924. Its arches are inscribed with the names of U of T alumni who died in both world wars. The tower itself houses a carillon with 51 bells, which are rung to mark special occasions.

Continue walking north till you reach the street. Cross Hoskin Avenue and you'll be standing in front of:

⑪ Trinity College

Appearances can be deceiving: the Tudor Gothic Trinity College looks like one of the oldest buildings in the city, but it was built in 1925. It has its own relaxing green quad, as well as an unusually grand **Anglican chapel,** which was designed by Sir Giles Gilbert Scott, who also created Liverpool Cathedral. (If you wish to see the chapel, you'll have to enter through the main entrance of the college; the outside door is locked as a rule.)

If you're facing Trinity College, turn right so that you're walking east along Hoskin. The street curves to the north to join Queen's

Park Crescent. Continue walking north. Ahead on your left is the:

⑫ Royal Ontario Museum

This Toronto treasure is currently being renovated, but many of its galleries are still open (p. 128). The ROM is adding six new crystal galleries designed by Daniel Libeskind, to the tune of C$200 million.

Before you reach the ROM you'll come to a TTC entrance; walk down the stairs, because this is the only way to cross Queen's Park here (you won't have to pay a fare). Resurface on the other side of Queen's Park. Charles Street is only a few steps north. Turn right on Charles, then turn right again into a laneway that brings you to:

⑬ Victoria College

Like University College, Victoria College was once a separate university (in some ways, it's still run as if it were; some of U of T's colleges are quite independent). The first thing you will notice is the stunning quad, which some regard as the most beautiful on campus. On your left is the new **Isabel Bader Theatre,** and on your right is **Emmanuel College,** a theological school of the United Church of Canada.

Continue following the laneway to:

⑭ Old Vic

The red-brick-and-sandstone Victoria College Building—known mainly by its nickname, Old Vic—is a masterpiece of Romanesque Revival architecture. It used to be called New Vic—when it opened in 1892, this was the new home of Victoria College, which had relocated to Toronto from Cobourg, Ontario. Walk around the entire building to appreciate its intricate architecture. Inside there's a bookstore.

Exit Old Vic from its main entrance, which is on its east side. Turn to your left and you'll find another laneway that leads directly up to Charles Street. Turn left on Charles and walk west to Queen's Park. Turn right, crossing Charles Street, and continue north on Queen's Park. The ROM is across the street on your left; on your right is the:

⑮ Gardiner Museum of Ceramic Art

Just like the ROM, the Gardiner is undergoing a major renovation. However, the museum will be closed for most of 2005.

Continue walking north; you will arrive at an intersection with Bloor Street West. Diagonally across from you, on the northwest corner, is the Park Hyatt. Cross to that corner; the entrance to the Park Hyatt is just a few steps north of the intersection. Turn left to enter the hotel; inside its South Tower, an elevator will take you up to:

⑯ The Roof

This elegant watering hole 18 stories up is one of the best places to get a

view of Toronto. If the weather is clement, head out to the balcony, which faces south and provides a spectacular view of the U of T campus.

TAKE A BREAK

For some light refreshment, stay a while at **The Roof**, which mixes some excellent and original cocktails. If you're hungry, there are many restaurants to choose from. **Sotto Sotto** (p. 105), **Boba** (p. 102), and **Jacques Bistro du Parc** (p. 104) are all a short walk away. Also nearby on Bloor Street West is **Greg's Ice Cream**.

WALKING TOUR 4   ST. LAWRENCE & DOWNTOWN EAST

Start:	Union Station.
Finish:	King subway station.
Time:	2 to 3 hours.
Best Time:	Saturday, when the St. Lawrence Market is in full swing.
Worst Time:	Sunday, when it's closed.

At one time, this area was at the center of city life. Today it's a little off-center, and yet it has some historic and modern architectural treasures, and a wealth of history in and around the St. Lawrence Market.

Begin at:

① Union Station

Check out the interior of this classical revival beauty, which opened in 1927 as a temple to and for the railroad. The shimmering ceiling, faced with vitrified Guastavino tile, soars 27m (89ft.) above the 79m-long (260-ft.) hall.

Across the street, at York and Front streets, stands the:

② Fairmont Royal York

The venerable railroad hotel is a longtime gathering place for Torontonians. It's the home of the famous Imperial Room cabaret and nightclub, which used to be one of Eartha Kitt's favorite venues. The hotel was once the tallest building in Toronto and the largest hotel in the British Commonwealth.

Check out the lobby, with its coffered ceiling and opulent furnishings. One floor up on the mezzanine is a new **gallery** of black-and-white photographs that cover the hotel's long and illustrious history.

As you leave the hotel, turn left and walk east on Front Street. At the corner of Bay and Front streets, look up at the stunning:

③ Royal Bank Plaza

The two triangular gold-sheathed towers rise 41 floors and 26 floors. A 40m-high (130-ft.) atrium joins them, and 150 pounds of gold enhances the mirrored glass. Webb Zerafa Menkes Housden designed the project, which was built between 1973 and 1977.

Cross Bay Street and continue east on Front Street. On the south side of the street is the impressive sweep of **One Front Street,** the main post office building (okay, not an exciting-sounding sight, but an attractive one).

On the north side of the street is the city's latest financial palace and most impressive architectural triumph, Bell Canada Enterprises':

④ BCE Place

Go inside to view the soaring galleria. Skidmore, Owings, and Merrill, with Bregman & Hamann, designed it in 1993. The twin office towers connect through a huge glass-covered galleria five stories high, spanning the block between Bay and Yonge streets. Designed by artist-architect Santiago Calatrava with Bregman & Hamann, it links the old Midland Bank building to the twin towers.

TAKE A BREAK
For an unusual dining experience, stop in at **BCE Place's Movenpick Marché** (© 416/366-8986), which turns diners into hunter-gatherers. Rather than waiting for table service, you forage for salads, pastas, and meat dishes at various counters. If you can't bear the thought of chasing down your grub, head across the courtyard to **Acqua** (© 416/368-7171) for Italian fare. The downstairs food court offers a variety of fast food and casual dining choices. If you prefer a deli sandwich, head for **Shopsy's,** 33 Yonge St. (© 416/365-3333; p. 101).

Back out on Front Street, turn left and continue to the northwest corner of Yonge and Front, stopping to admire the:

⑤ Bank of Montreal

The suitably ornate building (1885–86) held the most powerful Canadian bank of the 19th century, a force behind the colonial and federal governments. Inside, the banking hall rises to a beamed coffered ceiling with domed skylights of stained glass. It now houses the Stanley Cup and other hockey trophies, plus the **Hockey**

Hall of Fame (p. 144), another example of the city's genius for architectural adaptation. The exterior, embellished with carvings, porthole windows, and a balustrade, is a sight.

From here, you can look ahead along Front Street and see the weird mural by Derek M. Besant that adorns the famous and highly photogenic:

⑥ Flatiron or Gooderham Building (1892)

This building was the headquarters of George Gooderham, who had expanded his distilling business into railroads, insurance, and philanthropy. At one time his liquor business was the biggest in the British Empire, and he was also president of the Bank of Toronto. The five-story building occupies a triangular site, with the windows at the western edge beautifully curved and topped with a semicircular tower. The design is by David Roberts.

At the southwest corner of Yonge and Front streets, you can stop in at:

⑦ The Hummingbird Centre

The Hummingbird Centre sits across Scott Street from the **St. Lawrence Centre.** The former is home to the National Ballet of Canada and, at the moment, to the Canadian Opera Company (plans for a new opera house are tentative).

Continue east along Front Street to the:

⑧ Beardmore Building

At 35–39 Front St. E., this and the many other cast-iron buildings that line the street were the heart of the late-19th-century warehouse district, close to the lakefront and railheads. Now they hold stores like **Frida Crafts,** which sells imports from Guatemala, India, and Bangladesh, as well as jewelry, bags, candles, and other knickknacks; and **Mountain Equipment Co-op,** stocked with durable outdoor adventure goods. At no. 41–43, note the **Perkins Building,** and at no. 45–49, look for the

Walking Tour: St. Lawrence & Downtown East

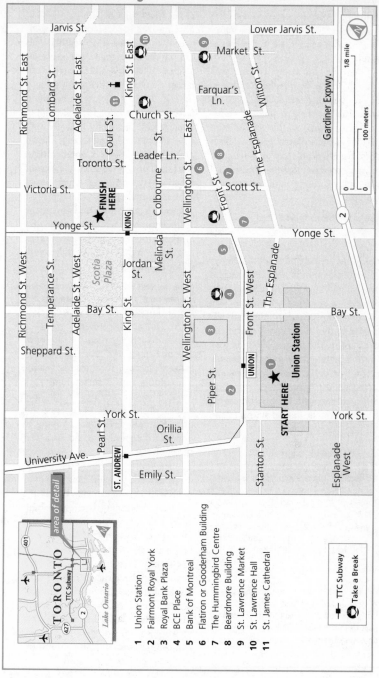

1/8 mile

100 meters

Jarvis St.

Lower Jarvis St.

Richmond St. East

Lombard St.

Adelaide St. East

King St. East

Market St.

Farquar's Ln.

Wilton St.

Gardiner Expwy.

Church St.

Court St.

Toronto St.

Leader Ln.

Colbourne St.

Wellington St. East

Front St.

Scott St.

The Esplanade

Victoria St.

FINISH HERE

Yonge St.

KING

Yonge St.

Richmond St. West

Temperance St.

Adelaide St. West

Scotia Plaza

Jordan St.

Melinda St.

Bay St.

King St.

Wellington St. West

Front St. West

The Esplanade

Bay St.

Sheppard St.

Piper St.

UNION

Union Station

START HERE

York St.

Pearl St.

Orillia St.

York St.

University Ave.

ST. ANDREW

Emily St.

Stanton St.

Esplanade West

1 Union Station
2 Fairmont Royal York
3 Royal Bank Plaza
4 BCE Place
5 Bank of Montreal
6 Flatiron or Gooderham Building
7 The Hummingbird Centre
8 Beardmore Building
9 St. Lawrence Market
10 St. Lawrence Hall
11 St. James Cathedral

TORONTO

Lake Ontario

area of detail

401

427

2

TTC Subway

TTC Subway
Take a Break

171

building with a totally cast-iron facade. The **Nicholas Hoare** bookstore, one of the coziest in the city, is at no. 45.

Continue browsing as you pass Church Street. **Wonderful & Whites,** 83 Front St., features delicate pieces—Victorian linens, lace, pillows, china, and glass. Some of the pieces even have beautiful, colorful patterns. Next door, **Ra** offers an array of Indian and other decorative accents—bedspreads and pillows, along with apparel and jewelry.

Now cross Market Street to the:

⑨ St. Lawrence Market

The old market building on the right holds this great market hall, which was constructed around the city's second city hall (1844–45). The elegant pedimented facade that you see as you stand in the center of the hall was originally the center block of the city hall. Today, the market abounds with vendors selling fresh eggs, Mennonite sausage, seafood, meats, cheeses, and baked goods. From Thursday to Saturday, in the north building across the street, a farmers' market starts at 5am.

☕ TAKE A BREAK
The most enjoyable places to stop are the stands offering fresh produce in the market itself. Other choices include **Le Papillon,** 16 Church St. (© 416/363-0838; p. 100), which features a raft of savory dessert crepes, and **HotHouse Cafe,** 35 Church St. (© 416/366-7800; p. 99).

Exit the market where you came in. Cross Wellington Street and cut through Market Lane Park and the shops at Market Square, past the north market building. Turn right onto King Street to:

⑩ St. Lawrence Hall

This was the focal point of the community in the mid–19th century. This hall was the site of grand city occasions, political rallies, balls, and entertainment. Frederick Douglass delivered an antislavery lecture; Jenny Lind and Adelina Patti sang in 1851 and 1860, respectively; General Tom Thumb appeared in 1862; and George Brown campaigned for Confederation. William Thomas designed the elegant Palladian-style building, which boasts a domed cupola.

Cross King Street and enter the 19th-century garden. It has a cast-iron drinking fountain for people, horses, and dogs, and flowerbeds filled with seasonal blooms.

If you like, rest on a bench while you admire the handsome proportions of St. Lawrence Hall and listen to the chimes of:

⑪ St. James Cathedral

Adjacent to the garden on the north side of King Street, this is one of my favorite places in Toronto. The beautiful building and its surrounding park make a serene setting to rest and gather one's thoughts—at least for now. A condo developer is hoping to build on the grounds of the park that surrounds St. James. Now *there* goes the neighborhood. Enjoy this beautiful oasis while you still can.

From here, you can view one of the early retail buildings that were built when King Street was the main commercial street. **Nos. 129–35** were originally an Army and Navy Store; cast iron, plate glass, and arched windows allowed the shopper to see what was available in the store. Also note nos. 111 and 125. The **Toronto Sculpture Garden,** 115 King St. (© 416/485-9658), is a quiet corner for contemplation.

WINDING DOWN
From St. James, the venerable **Le Royal Meridien King Edward,** 37 King St. E. (✆ 416/863-9700), is only a block away. You can stop for afternoon tea in the lobby lounge, or light fare or lunch in the **Café Victoria.** Both **La Maquette,** 111 King St. E. (✆ 416/366-8191), and **Biagio,** 157 King St. E. (✆ 416/366-4040), have appealing courtyards.

From St. James, go south on Church Street for 1 block and turn right into Colbourne Street. From Colbourne, turn left down Leader Lane to Wellington, where you can enjoy a fine view of the mural on the Flatiron Building and of the rhythmic flow of mansard rooflines along the south side of Front Street.

Turn right and proceed to Yonge Street, then turn right and walk to King Street to catch the subway to your next destination.

8

Shopping

Shopping in Toronto can be a kaleidoscopic experience. The *haute*-est international retailers—like Prada, Chanel, and Gucci—compete for attention with discount emporiums like Honest Ed's. Megastores dominate the landscape, yet boutiques are blossoming. And while foreign chains stake their claim in shopping arcades and malls, they stand shoulder to shoulder with homegrown talent.

The result of this chaos is a cornucopia of shops that fit a wide range of budgets and tastes. The bad news: While window-shopping is a laudable pastime, don't fool yourself that it will stop there . . . just be careful not to break the bank!

1 The Shopping Scene

While you may want to check out the impressive array of international retailers, it would be a mistake to overlook the locals. If your passion is fashion, do check out Canadian labels such as Lida Baday, Ross Mayer, Misura by Joeffer Caoc, Crystal Siemens, Brian Bailey, Mimi Bizjak, Mercy, Wolves, Linda Lundstrom, and Comrags.

Toronto also has a bustling arts-and-crafts community, with many galleries, custom jewelers, and artisans. Some of the best buys are on native and Inuit art. Artwork can be imported into the United States duty-free.

Stores usually open at around 10am from Monday to Saturday. Closing hours change depending on the day. From Monday to Wednesday, most stores close at 6pm; on Thursday and Friday, hours run to 8pm or 9pm; on Saturday, closing is quite early, usually around 6pm. Most stores are open on Sunday, though the hours may be restricted—11am or noon to 5pm is not unusual.

Almost every establishment accepts MasterCard and Visa, and a growing number take American Express. Many retailers accept U.S. cash, and the exchange rate tends to be a favorable one, especially downtown in the Eaton Centre area.

2 Great Shopping Areas

DOWNTOWN

CHINATOWN It's crowded and noisy, but don't let that put you off. Sure, there's the usual touristy junk, like cheapo plastic toys and jewelry, but the real Chinatown has a lot more to offer, including fine rosewood furniture, exquisite ceramics, and homeopathic herbs. Just don't try driving here: This is traffic purgatory, and best navigated on foot.

THE EATON CENTRE Okay, you're short on time, but you still want to fit in all your shopping. Where else can you go but the Eaton Centre? With more than 300 shops, including Browns, Danier, Birks, Nine West, La Vie en Rose, Femme de Carriere, Eddie Bauer, Banana Republic, Mendocino, Laura Secord, H&M, and Indigo, you'll be sure to find something.

Tips **Good to Know: Taxes & Rebates**

The provincial sales tax (PST) is 8%, and the national goods-and-services tax (GST) is 7%. Visitors can apply for a rebate of both when they leave the country. For details, see "Taxes" under "Fast Facts: Toronto," in chapter 3.

QUEEN STREET WEST   Queen Street West between University Avenue and Bathurst Street is rich with boutiques for both fashion and housewares, though there are a lot of familiar names thrown in the mix. Locals complain that this neighborhood isn't what it was before the Gap moved in, but it's still a great stomping ground for fashionistas in need of a fix.

THE UNDERGROUND CITY   Subterranean Toronto is a hive of shopping activity. While you won't find too many shops down here that don't have an aboveground location, the Underground City is a popular place in winter, and with those whose schedules don't allow them out of the Financial District.

WEST QUEEN WEST   Playing down its grittier roots, this hot new neighborhood has got the reputation for cutting-edge fashion that Queen Street West used to enjoy. The city has dubbed it the "Art & Design District." Starting at Bathurst Avenue and running west a few blocks past Ossington Avenue, this is where you'll find an incredible array of fashion talent, art galleries, and great new restaurants.

MIDTOWN

BLOOR STREET WEST   This strip of real estate, bordered by Yonge Street to the east and Avenue Road to the west, is where most of the top international names in fashion set up shop. If you're in the mood to see what Karl Lagerfeld is designing or to pick up a glittering bauble from Cartier or Tiffany, this is your hunting ground.

YORKVILLE   A far cry from its days as a hippie hangout and commune in the 1960s, this is now one of Toronto's best known—and most expensive—shopping neighborhoods. Little alleyways crisscross the streets, giving Yorkville a romantic, old-fashioned appeal. The shops here tend to be small boutiques that specialize, say, in beaded handbags or fine handmade papers. Bistros and cafes abound, giving rise to Yorkville's other pastime: people-watching.

3 Shopping A to Z

ANTIQUES

Toronto's antiques scene has exploded. Throw a stone in any direction and you're bound to hit an Edwardian console, or at least a classic Eames chair. For fine antiques, head north from Bloor Street along Avenue Road until you reach Davenport Avenue, or walk north on Yonge Street from the Rosedale subway station to St. Clair Avenue. Another top area is Mount Pleasant Road from St. Clair Avenue to Eglinton Avenue. For less pricey finds, head west on Queen Street to the Bathurst Street area. Merchandise at the Harbourfront Antique Market varies widely in quality and price.

Belle Epoque   If you're feeling pretty and looking for furniture to match, this attic-like shop is worth a look. The furnishings are luxurious, and some pieces would not be out of place at Versailles, gilt and all. Some reproductions mix with the real articles. 1066 Yonge St. © **416/925-0066.** Subway: Rosedale.

Constantine Interiors ⭑ Every item in this shop has been handpicked by its owner, Rita Tsantis. It's stocked with imposing wood furniture and delicate baubles. Be sure to check out the lighting selection—hand-painted Fortuny lamps are a house specialty—and gilt-trimmed glassware. 1110 Yonge St. ℂ 866/929-1177 or 416/929-1177. Subway: Rosedale.

Decorum Decorative Finds If you're going on an ocean voyage, can you resist a C$2,200 (US$1,540) vintage Louis Vuitton trunk? The wares here range from tables and chaise lounges to oil paintings and old books. All are top priced, but also top of the line. 1210 Yonge St. ℂ 416/966-6829. Subway: Summerhill.

Heritage Antique Market ⭑ *Finds* One Sunday each month, more than 60 antique dealers from Ontario and Québec descend on Bayview Village. Their wares include 19th- and 20th-century porcelains, jewelry, silver, furniture, and paintings. If you're in town when the market is, you're in luck. Be sure to call ahead or check the website for the schedule. At Bayview Village, 2901 Bayview Ave. (at Sheppard Ave.). ℂ 866/285-5515 or 416/483-6471. www.heritageantiqueshows.com. Subway: Bayview.

Horsefeathers! If your taste runs to English and French country-house styles, this emporium's for you. The 1,114-sq.-m (12,000-sq.-ft.) space boasts striking wooden pieces in walnut and mahogany that share the spotlight with tapestries and Persian carpets. A new, smaller outlet is at 1212 Yonge St. (ℂ **416/934-1771**). 630 Mount Pleasant Rd. ℂ **416/486-4555**. Subway: Eglinton, then no. 34 bus to Mount Pleasant.

L'Atelier This is about as glamorous as it gets. Napoleon III side tables share space with chrome bar stools and rococo Italian lamps. Many of the price tags hit four digits, but there are lovely accouterments for as little as C$10 (US$7). 1224 Yonge St. ℂ 416/966-0200. Subway: Summerhill.

Mostly Movables Inc Early- and mid-20th-century Canadian and European furnishings fill this shop. The pieces are generally in fine form, and the prices are somewhat lower than those at many Yorkville and Rosedale competitors. 1201 Bloor St. W. (3 blocks east of Lansdowne Ave.). ℂ 416/588-5545. Subway: Lansdowne.

Putti ⭑ Two generously proportioned rooms hold grand (and grandly priced) European treasures old and new: dining sets, armoires, cushions, and china. A recent addition is the floral department, which features both fresh and dried flowers. *Victoria* magazine has repeatedly featured this shop. 1104 Yonge St. ℂ 416/972-7652. Subway: Rosedale.

Whim Antiques The store is aptly named—whimsical it is. In business since 1973, it's filled with beautiful baubles, silverware, and decorative *objets,* and walking through it feels rather like being let loose in great-grandma's attic. 561 Mount Pleasant Rd. ℂ 416/481-4474. Subway: St. Clair, then Mount Pleasant bus to Belsize Ave.

Zig Zag This shop carries a mélange of styles, but the specialty is early Modernist pieces. The names to watch out for are Eames, Saarinen, Arne Jacobsen, and Warren Platner. There are some bargains, with excellent pieces in the C$200 to C$400 (US$140–US$280) range, with a few stellar finds that run as high as C$3,500 (US$2,450). 1142 Queen St. E. ℂ 416/778-6495. Subway: Queen, then any streetcar east to Coady Ave.

ART

Bau-Xi After viewing the masterworks at the Art Gallery of Ontario, you can head across the street and buy your own. Founded in 1965, Bau-Xi features

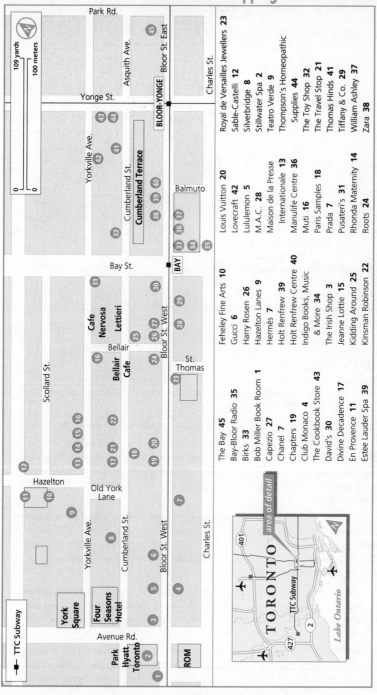

Midtown Shopping: Bloor/Yorkville

Royal de Versailles Jewellers **23**
Sable-Castelli **12**
Silverbridge **8**
Stillwater Spa **2**
Teatro Verde **9**
Thompson's Homeopathic
 Supplies **44**
The Toy Shop **32**
The Travel Stop **21**
Thomas Hinds **41**
Tiffany & Co. **29**
William Ashley **37**
Zara **38**

Louis Vuitton **20**
Lovecraft **42**
Lululemon **5**
M.A.C. **28**
Maison de la Presse
 Internationale **13**
Manulife Centre **36**
Muti **16**
Paris Samples **18**
Prada **7**
Pusateri's **31**
Rhonda Maternity **14**
Roots **24**

Feheley Fine Arts **10**
Gucci **6**
Harry Rosen **26**
Hazelton Lanes **9**
Hermès **7**
Holt Renfrew **39**
Holt Renfrew Centre **40**
Indigo Books, Music
 & More **34**
The Irish Shop **3**
Jeanne Lottie **15**
Kidding Around **25**
Kinsman Robinson **22**

The Bay **45**
Bay-Bloor Radio **35**
Birks **33**
Bob Miller Book Room **1**
Capezio **27**
Chanel **7**
Chapters **19**
Club Monaco **4**
The Cookbook Store **43**
David's **30**
Divine Decadence **17**
En Provence **11**
Estee Lauder Spa **39**

177

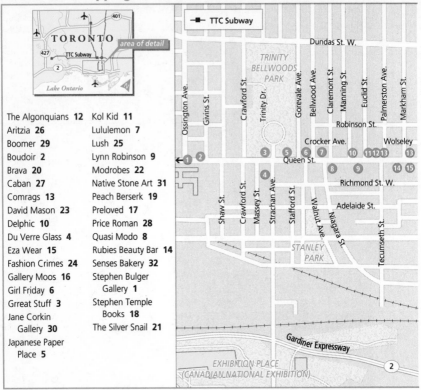

The Algonquians **12**
Aritzia **26**
Boomer **29**
Boudoir **2**
Brava **20**
Caban **27**
Comrags **13**
David Mason **23**
Delphic **10**
Du Verre Glass **4**
Eza Wear **15**
Fashion Crimes **24**
Gallery Moos **16**
Girl Friday **6**
Grreat Stuff **3**
Jane Corkin Gallery **30**
Japanese Paper Place **5**

Kol Kid **11**
Lululemon **7**
Lush **25**
Lynn Robinson **9**
Modrobes **22**
Native Stone Art **31**
Peach Berserk **19**
Preloved **17**
Price Roman **28**
Quasi Modo **8**
Rubies Beauty Bar **14**
Senses Bakery **32**
Stephen Bulger Gallery **1**
Stephen Temple Books **18**
The Silver Snail **21**

contemporary works by artists from across the country. **340 Dundas St. W. ℭ 416/977-0600. Subway: St. Patrick.**

Bay of Spirits Gallery Here you'll find works by native Indians from across Canada. Most of the collection focuses on the art of the Pacific Northwest, including totem poles, masks, prints, and jewelry. **156 Front St. W. ℭ 416/971-5190. Subway: Union.**

Eskimo Art Gallery This award-winning gallery has the largest collection of Inuit sculpture in Toronto. At any given time, it shows more than 500 pieces, with prices ranging from C$16 to C$22,000 (US$11–US$15,400). **12 Queens Quay W. (opposite Westin Harbour Castle). ℭ 800/800-2008 or 416/366-3000. Subway: Union, then LRT to Queens Quay.**

Feheley Fine Arts The Feheleys have been personally selecting every piece in their gallery for over 40 years, making this one of the most individualized collections of early and contemporary Inuit art anywhere. **14 Hazelton Ave. ℭ 416/323-1373. Subway: Bay.**

Gallery Moos German native Walter Moos has been a fixture on the Toronto art scene for more than 30 years. His gallery features top Canadian artists as well as international figures. **622 Richmond St. W. ℭ 416/504-5445. Subway: Osgoode, then any streetcar west to Bathurst St., and walk 1 block south.**

Jane Corkin Gallery ⭐ Most items here are historical and contemporary photographs from around the world. They include works by Cylla von Tiedemann, Irving Penn, and Herb Ritts. There is also a small collection of modernist painting and sculpture. 179 John St. © **416/979-1980.** Subway: Osgoode.

Kinsman Robinson Galleries The two stories of this Yorkville gallery display 20th-century figurative paintings, sculpture, and drawings. Artists represented include Stanley Cosgrove, Robert Katz, Esther Wertheimer, and Donald Liardi. Native Canadians Robert Davidson and Norval Morrisseau also exhibit their work here. There are a few paperworks by Zuniga, Braque, and Chagall, among others. 108 Cumberland St. © **800/895-4278** or 416/964-2374. Subway: Bay.

Olga Korper Gallery Established in 1973, this gallery houses contemporary Canadian and international works. Artists represented include Averbuch, John Brown, Sankawa, and the estate of Louis Comtois. 17 Morrow Ave. (off Dundas St. W.). © **416/538-8220.** Subway: Dundas West.

Ontario College of Art & Design Gallery *Finds* If you're interested in the work of an emerging generation of artists, check out the ongoing exhibitions at the OCAD. Students display sculpture, photography, painting, and multimedia installations. 285 Dundas St. W. © **416/977-6000.** Subway: St. Patrick.

Sable-Castelli This highly regarded gallery has been in business for more than 25 years. It represents contemporary American and Canadian artists,

including heavy hitters like Warhol and Oldenburg. 33 Hazelton Ave. $\textcircled{C}$ 416/
961-0011. Subway: Bay.

Sandra Ainsley $\star$ Specializing in glass sculpture, this renowned gallery represents more than 50 artists from across North America, including Dale Chihuly, Jon Kuhn, Peter Powning, Tom Scoon, Susan Edgerley, and David Bennett. The one-of-a-kind pieces have big price tags, but there are also some affordable items, such as paperweights, vases, and jewelry. In the Distillery Historic District, 55 Mill St. $\textcircled{C}$ 416/214-9490. Subway: King, then streetcar east to Parliament St.

Stephen Bulger Gallery This gallery displays contemporary Canadian and international photography; some of the artists represented include Diana Shearwood, Volker Seding, Lida Moser, and Vincenzo Pietropaolo. 1026 Queen St. W. $\textcircled{C}$ 416/504-0575. Subway: Osgoode, then streetcar west to Ossington Ave.

Susan Hobbs Gallery This small gallery, in an unprepossessing warehouse far from the Yorkville crowd, is a major player in Canadian contemporary art. Hobbs represents 11 of Toronto's best artists, including Ian Carr-Harris, Shirley Wiitasalo, Robin Collyer, and Sandra Meigs. 137 Tecumseth St. (at Queen St.). $\textcircled{C}$ 416/504-3699. Subway: Osgoode, then any streetcar west to Tecumseth St.

Ydessa Hendeles Art Foundation This is one of the most interesting contemporary art collections in the city. Hendeles features installations by international artists. Works on display include paintings, photography, and multimedia projects. 778 King St. W. $\textcircled{C}$ 416/603-2227. Subway: St. Andrew, then any streetcar west to Bathurst St.

AUDIOVISUAL & ELECTRONIC GOODS

Bay-Bloor Radio This 1,207-sq.-m (13,000-sq.-ft.) store carries all the latest and greatest audio equipment, from portable units to in-home theater systems. Manulife Centre, 55 Bloor St. W. $\textcircled{C}$ 416/967-1122. Subway: Bay.

Canadian Tire This is handyman heaven. The endless aisles overflow with gadgets for home, yard, office, car, and any place in between. This is where I head as Father's Day approaches. 839 Yonge St. $\textcircled{C}$ 416/925-9592. www.canadian tire.com. Subway: Yonge/Bloor.

Henry's $\star$ This bi-level shop deals in analog and digital photography. The first floor has electronic equipment, darkroom supplies, and a photo-processing lab. Upstairs, there's a wide selection of secondhand cameras and gear. 119 Church St. $\textcircled{C}$ 416/868-0872. Subway: Queen.

SpyTech James Bond wannabes, welcome. Entering Spy Tech is like having a free pass to Q's lab. Looking for a gadget to modify your telephone voice or a spook-worthy camera? You'll find it all here, though the price tags do get a little steep—all the way up to C$100,000 (US$70,000) for a bulletproof car. 2028 Yonge St. $\textcircled{C}$ 416/482-8588. Subway: Davisville.

BOOKS

Atticus Books Bookworms can while away hours in this crowded shop filled with secondhand scholarly tomes. It stocks many volumes of philosophy, psychology, and psychoanalysis. Antiquarian books and illuminated manuscripts are at the back of the store. 84 Harbord St. $\textcircled{C}$ 416/922-6045. Subway: Spadina, then walk south.

Ballenford Books on Architecture Interior designers, whether amateur or pro, will love this well-arranged store. The books cover everything from antique furniture to architectural theory, from urban design to landscaping. The shop also displays sketches and drawings by local architects. 600 Markham St. (south of Bloor St. W.). Ⓒ 416/588-0800. Subway: Bathurst.

Bob Miller Book Room   When I was a student at the University of Toronto, I would come into this academic bookstore looking for one text and end up browsing for ages. It stocks mainly literary fiction, humanities, and social sciences. Works in translation are carefully selected. 180 Bloor St. W., lower concourse. Ⓒ 416/922-3557. Subway: St. George.

Book City   All the books here are new, and many are discounted by 10% to 30%. There is also a good assortment of international magazines. Book City also has branches at 1430 Yonge St. (Ⓒ 416/961-1228), 1950 Queen St. E. (Ⓒ 416/698-1444), and 348 Danforth Ave. (Ⓒ 416/469-9997). 501 Bloor St. W. ⒸⒸ 416/961-4496. Subway: Bathurst.

Chapters ⭐   While the Chapters bookstores are now owned and operated by Indigo (see below), they retain their own unique charm. Eminently browse-worthy and well-stocked, Chapters boasts comfy chairs, a Starbucks cafe, and a host of free special events. Celebrity authors Sophia Loren and Sarah, Duchess of York, had their Toronto engagements here. There's another Chapters store at 142 John St. (Ⓒ 416/595-7349). The stores are open late, usually until 10 or 11pm on weeknights and midnight on weekends. 110 Bloor St. W. Ⓒ 416/920-9299. Subway: Bay.

The Cookbook Store   I call it food porn: lush, gooey close-ups of scallop ceviche and tiramisu. This store specializes in the kind of book that makes a gourmet's heart go pitter-patter. There are also tomes about wine, health, and restaurants. 850 Yonge St. Ⓒ 416/920-2665. www.cook-book.com. Subway: Yonge/Bloor.

David Mason   This charming used-book store is straight out of Dickens. It stocks many travel books, and a number of first editions of Canadian, American, and British works. The collections of 19th- and 20th-century literature are vast. 342 Queen St. W. Ⓒ 416/598-1015. Subway: Osgoode.

Glad Day Bookshop   This was the first gay-oriented bookstore in Canada, and it remains one of the best. The shelves hold a sizable collection of gay and lesbian fiction, biography, and history books, and the offerings have expanded to include magazines, CDs, videos, calendars, posters, and cards. 598A Yonge St., 2nd floor. Ⓒ 877/783-3725 or 416/961-4161. www.gladday.com. Subway: Wellesley.

Indigo Books Music & More ⭐   This Canadian-owned chain boasts an excellent selection of books, magazines, and videotapes. It has tables and chairs to encourage browsing, a cafe, and helpful staff. Best of all, there are special events (author visits, live performances, even seminars) almost daily. There are also events for kids. The store is a favorite with night owls—it's open until 11pm or midnight every day. There are branches at the Eaton Centre (Ⓒ 416/591-3622) and at 2300 Yonge St., at Eglinton Avenue (Ⓒ 416/544-0049). Manulife Centre, 55 Bloor St. W. Ⓒ 416/925-3536. www.indigo.ca. Subway: Yonge/Bloor or Bay.

Mabel's Fables ⭐   This charming shop is stocked with every book a child could possibly want—and a lot more. Offerings are grouped by age, going up to early adolescence. On weekends there are author visits and other special events. 662 Mount Pleasant. Ⓒ 416/322-0438. Subway: Eglinton, then no. 34 bus to Mount Pleasant, and walk 2 blocks south.

Nicholas Hoare   This shop has the cozy feel of an English library, with hardwood floors, plush couches, and a fireplace. There's an extensive selection of

Canadian and international fiction, as well as heavyweight art tomes and children's books. 45 Front St. E. ℂ **416/777-2665.** Subway: Union.

Open Air Books & Maps   This shop caters to nature lovers and ecology buffs. It carries a vast assortment of travel guidebooks and maps. 25 Toronto St. ℂ **416/ 363-0719.** Subway: King.

Seekers Books   New and old books about Eastern religion, mysticism, meditation, and the occult mix on the shelves. The focus is definitely New Age, but you'll find general-interest fiction and nonfiction, too. 509 Bloor St. W. ℂ **416/ 925-1982.** Subway: Bathurst.

Silver Snail ⭐   Remember those comic books you read as a kid? Well, they're all here, with adult-oriented comics like the *Sandman* series. You'll see a sizable section of imported editions, and posters and movie memorabilia, too. 367 Queen St. W. ℂ **416/593-0889.** Subway: Osgoode.

Steven Temple Books   If you're looking for a rare first edition of a 19th- or 20th-century literary work in English, be sure to visit this shop, which is open by appointment only. It also carries secondhand books about a variety of subjects. 489 Queen St. W., 2nd floor. ℂ **416/703-9908.** Subway: Osgoode, then any streetcar west.

University of Toronto Bookstore ⭐ *(Finds*   This is one of the best-stocked independent booksellers in town. They also host their own Reading Series, which has featured authors such as Ann-Marie MacDonald and Roddy Doyle; check the website for details about upcoming events. In the Koffler Centre, 214 College St. ℂ **416/978-7900.** www.uoftbookstore.com. Subway: Queen's Park.

The World's Biggest Bookstore ⭐   The debate about whether the World's Biggest is *really* the world's biggest rages on. Either way, the 27km (17 miles) of bookshelves do contain a good selection. Browsing is welcome, but the bright, bright lights are headache-inducing after a while. There are also software, video, and magazine departments. 20 Edward St. ℂ **416/977-7009.** Subway: Dundas.

CHINA, SILVER & GLASS

Bowring   This Canadian chain has an impressive pedigree that dates back to 1811. These days, they're known for their moderately priced ceramic dishes, decorative serveware, and crystal stemware. Personally, I stock up on their delicious candles and whimsical accessories (leopard-print napkins, anyone?). Eaton Centre. ℂ **416/596-1042.** www.bowring.com. Subway: Queen.

Du Verre   The store name is a bit of a misnomer. Gorgeous glassworks are on display, but they share this airy, open space with ceramics, wood and wrought-iron furniture, lamps, and candlesticks. 188 Strachan Ave. ℂ **416/593-0182.** Subway: Osgoode, then any streetcar west.

Muti   Murano glass designs and cheery ceramics from Italy dominate this store. Look a little closer and you'll find a few French tapestries and tablecloths, too. 88 Yorkville Ave. ℂ **416/969-0253.** Subway: Bay.

William Ashley ⭐ *(Value*   The last word in luxe, whether it be fine china, crystal, or silver. All of the top manufacturers are represented, including Waterford, Baccarat, Christofle, Wedgwood, and Lenox. Even if you're not in a buying mood, the detailed displays are fascinating. If you are in a buying mood, the prices are better than you'll find elsewhere. Manulife Centre, 55 Bloor St. W. ℂ **416/ 964-2900.** www.williamashley.com. Subway: Bay.

CIGARS & TOBACCO

Thomas Hinds   This is Havana heaven for the stogie set. Thomas Hinds carries a wide range of Cuban cigars and cigarillos, as well as pipes and the other smoking accouterments. Upstairs there's a lounge and humidor. 8 Cumberland St. ℂ 416/927-7703. Subway: Yonge/Bloor.

CRAFTS

The Algonquians ★   Ojibway-owned and -operated, this shop specializes in exquisite Native Canadian arts and crafts. The collection includes porcupine-quill jewelry, soapstone sculpture, Iroquois masks, prints, antique spearheads, and moccasins. 668 Queen St. W. ℂ 416/703-1336. Subway: Osgoode, then any streetcar west.

Arts on King   This 929-sq.-m (10,000-sq.-ft.) complex consists of boutiques selling original art, folk crafts, and furniture. Connected to it is the Wagner Rosenbaum Gallery, which exhibits work by new and established Toronto artists every month. 169 King St. E. ℂ 416/777-9617. Subway: King.

Art Zone   Sisters Jane and Kathryn Irwin own and operate this gallery-like space. Their main medium is stained glass, and their style is colorful and modern. They also carry a limited number of glass gift items, including bowls, trays, and sculptural objects. 592 Markham St. (south of Bloor St. W.). ℂ 416/534-1892. Subway: Bathurst.

Five Potters   Phone ahead for an appointment, and you're free to watch the ceramic artists—all women—at work. The pieces on display vary from functional to sculptural items. Prices range from C$15 to C$300 (US$11–US$210). 131A Pears Ave. ℂ 416/924-6992. Subway: St. George.

Frida *(Finds)*   Arts and crafts from Africa, Southeast Asia, and Latin America share space in this bi-level shop. It offers an assortment of colorful woven mats, clothes, carved statuettes, jewelry, and candelabra. 39 Front St. E. ℂ 416/366-3169. Subway: Union.

Native Stone Art   This shop houses the creations of native Indian artisans from across North America. There are Mohawk and Iroquois carvings, Cree moccasins, and Navajo, Zuni, and Hopi jewelry. The quality is very high. 2 McCaul St. (at Queen St. W.). ℂ 416/593-0924. Subway: Osgoode.

DEPARTMENT STORES

The Bay   The Hudson's Bay Company started out as a fur-trading business when the first French-speaking settlers came to Canada. Today, the Bay boasts excellent mid-range selections of clothing and housewares. It schedules weekend sales almost every week, though shoppers should be warned that winning the staff's attention requires patience. There are several locations around the city; addresses for the two best ones are listed here. (1) 176 Yonge St. (at Queen St.). ℂ 416/861-9111. Subway: Queen. (2) 2 Bloor St. E. (at Yonge St.). ℂ 416/972-3333. www. thebay.com. Subway: Yonge/Bloor.

Holt Renfrew   Designers such as Donna Karan, Christian Lacroix, and Yves St. Laurent figure in Holt Renfrew's four levels of merchandise. This is where you'll find the excellent Estée Lauder Spa; also a recent renovation created a beautiful space for the new Holt Renfrew Cafe (which is really a restaurant, not a cafe; see review page 104). The basement connects with an underground mall, and features a gourmet food department and a cafe (yes, this one really is a cafe). Holt Renfrew Centre, 50 Bloor St. W. ℂ 416/922-2333. www.holtrenfrew.com. Subway: Yonge/Bloor.

(*Value* **The Best Bargains**

Maybe you can't get something for nothing . . . but you can score some pretty fab finds on the cheap in Toronto. It's a treasure hunt of sorts, and the spoils are anything but certain, but when you find that perfect piece marked down to next-to-nothing, well, that just makes it all worthwhile. Many Toronto retailers, including luxurious Holt Renfrew, have their own outlet shops. Here's my own little black book of favorite foraging grounds. Happy hunting!

Dixie Outlet Mall   Ten minutes from Pearson International Airport is the answer to bargain-shoppers' prayers. It's hard to beat the Dixie Outlet Mall for number of bargains per square foot. There are more than 120 outlet shops here, including Femme de Carriere and choco-latier Laura Secord, so you're bound to find something. 1250 S. Service Rd., Mississauga. ℂ 905/278-7492. Gardiner Expressway/Queen Elizabeth Way (QEW) west to Dixie Rd. exit. Turn left, follow Dixie Rd. south to S. Service Rd.

Grreat Stuff   There's an awful lot of men's clothes packed into this small retail space, but if you're not troubled by claustrophobia, dig in for some amazing deals. Business casual is this shop's mainstay, though there are *grreat* prices on Italian silk ties and brand-name suits. 870 Queen St. W. ℂ 416/533-7680. Subway: Osgoode, then streetcar west to Shaw St.

Holt Renfrew Last Call   It might not be the most organized store you've laid eyes on, but what it lacks in tidiness it makes up for in bar-gains. The racks are laden with brands such as Donna Karan, Prada, and Versace, marked down to one-half to one-fifth of what they would normally cost. There have been rumors of Kate Spade handbags on sale here, but I have yet to arrive in time. May you have better luck. 370 Steeles Ave. W. ℂ 905/886-7444. Subway: Finch, then Steeles West bus.

Honest Ed's World Famous Shopping Centre (*Finds*   Ed's is a Toronto institution, framed with flashing red and yellow lights both outdoors *and* indoors. "Don't just stand there, buy something!" blurts out one brazen sign. This idiosyncratic store has a deal on everything from housewares to carpets, from clothing to sundries. Crazy-making as shopping here can be, the bargains are unbeatable—but be warned, the queues are, too. 581 Bloor St. W. ℂ 416/537-2111. Subway: Bathurst.

Sears   If you visited Toronto before 2000, you'll remember the gorgeous Eaton's department store, which anchored the Eaton Centre complex. Owned and operated by the Toronto-based Eaton family for more than a century, it closed in 1999. Sears Canada bought the Eatons name (minus the apostrophe) and opened this department store in its place. Now branded as a Sears store, it's more upscale than your average Sears. Eaton Centre. ℂ 416/343-2111. www.sears.ca. Subway: Dundas.

FASHION

Let's get this out of the way first: Toronto has all of the requisite big-name Euro-pean boutiques along Bloor Street West between Yonge Street and Avenue Road.

Marilyn's   Here's a rare thing: knockdown prices paired with attentive service. The specialty is Canadian fashions for women, from sportswear to glamorous gowns. There are also in-store seminars about fashion-forward topics like traveling with just one suitcase. 130 Spadina Ave. ℭ 416/504-6777. Subway: Spadina, then LRT to Queen St. W.

Paris Samples   This store snaps up designers' samples and marks them down 20% to 75%. The clothes range from wool pants to velvet dresses to micro-miniskirts. *One caveat:* The sizes are all under 14, and many clothes come only in the smallest sizes. 101 Yorkville Ave. ℭ 416/926-0656. Subway: Bay.

The Shoe Company   This is every foot fetishist's dream: great shoes for men and women from Unisa, Nine West, and others, marked down to unbeatable prices. There are lots of funky styles that won't be stylish for long, but it won't hurt your pocketbook to splurge. There are outlets around the city, including First Canadian Place. 711 Yonge St. ℭ 416/923-8388. Subway: Yonge/Bloor.

Tom's Place   After more than 40 years in business, Tom's Place looks sharper than ever. While the shop devotes an entire floor to women's wear, the best buys are in the men's department: You'll find brand-name merchandise by the likes of Armani and Valentino. Suits that cost C$495 to C$1,800 (US$347–US$1,260) elsewhere ring up for C$299 to C$850 (US$209–US$595) here. Tom's Place stocks sizes from 36 short to 50 tall. 190 Baldwin St. ℭ 416/596-0297. Subway: Spadina, then LRT to Baldwin St.

Winners   This northern outpost of the U.S.-owned T.J. Maxx chain offers great deals on clothes for men and women (think Jones New York, Tommy Hilfiger, and Earl Jeans), and top-name togs for the kiddies. There's also an ever-changing selection of housewares, cookware, linens, toiletries, and toys. The new 3,716-sq.-m (40,000-sq.-ft.) outlet at College Park is always packed, but its large, airy space is filled with deals. College Park. ℭ 416/598-8800; Subway: College. (The smaller but long-standing location in the Fashion District is another good bet. 57 Spadina Ave. ℭ 416/585-2052. Subway: Spadina, then LRT to King St. W.)

You'll find **Louis Vuitton** at no. 110, **Gucci** at no. 130, and **Chanel, Prada,** and **Hermès** bundled together at The Colonnade shopping arcade at no. 131. The listings below will focus primarily on shops that are unique to Toronto (with just a couple of exceptions). Also see the listings under "Shoes" and "Vintage Clothing," later in this chapter.

CHILDREN'S

Kids Cats & Dogs   Not just for kids—the shop carries its signature T-shirts, pajamas, and sweats in sizes from infant to adult. Everything, including knapsacks and comforters, sports a cat or dog motif. 508 Eglinton Ave. W. ℭ 416/484-1844. Subway: Eglinton.

Kol Kid *(Finds)*   West Queen West isn't just for grown-ups, you know. This charming boutique carries Canadian- and European-made clothing for kids, plus toys and furnishings. 670 Queen St. W. ✆ **416/681-0368.** Subway: Osgoode, then streetcar west to Palmerston Ave.

Lovechild   A favorite with tiny tots who are already developing fashion savvy, Lovechild offers a selection of groovy clothes in a rainbow of colors. 2523 Yonge St. ✆ **416/486-4746.** Subway: Eglinton.

Misdemeanors *(★)*   This is the juniors department of Pat Chorley's shop for grown-ups, Fashion Crimes (p. 188). Misdemeanors stocks the stuff that little girls' dreams are made of. In addition to gossamer gowns, there's a selection of flower-power home accents. 322½ Queen St. W. ✆ **416/351-8758.** Subway: Osgoode.

MEN'S & WOMEN'S

Club Monaco   This is Club Monaco's flagship store in Toronto. It's an airy, high-ceilinged space filled with casual wear and sportswear, with a smattering of work-ready clothes. It also has its own accessories and makeup lines. There are 19 other outlets around the city, including 403 Queen St. W. (✆ **416/979-5633**). 157 Bloor St. W. ✆ **416/591-8837.** www.clubmonaco.com. Subway: Museum.

H&M   The Swedish clothing giant finally made it to Toronto in 2004. This chain has a solid reputation for quickly knocking off fashions that sauntered down runways mere weeks before. The trade-off for the dirt-cheap prices on men's and women's clothing is that the quality is often somewhat ephemeral. But you weren't planning to wear that hot pink multiruffle miniskirt again next year, now were you? A multilevel store is slated to open at the **Eaton Centre** late in 2004. At Fairview Mall, 1800 Sheppard Ave. E. (at Don Mills). ✆ **416/497-7242.** Subway: Don Mills.

Hoax Couture Studio Boutique   The corset-topped dresses on display bring a Moulin Rouge cancan show to mind, but the shop's owners, Chris Tyrell and Jim Searle, design dramatic, playful clothes for men and women. Their starry client roster includes Diana Krall *and* Dennis Rodman. By appointment only. 163 Spadina Ave., 3rd floor. ✆ **416/597-8924.** Subway: Osgoode, then streetcar west to Spadina Ave.

The Irish Shop   If you're yearning for the Emerald Isle, you'll welcome the sight of lace shawls, linens, sweaters, and Celtic music, books, and giftware. There's also a selection of linen suits by Dublin designer Paul Costelloe. 150 Bloor St. W. ✆ **416/922-9400.** Subway: Bay.

Modrobes *(Value)*   Renowned for its comfy, casual clothing, Canadian-owned Modrobes got its start when its founder, Steven Debus, was still attending the university. Debus designed "exam pants"—trousers so comfy you could spend a day writing exams in them without your bum going numb. Today, the store's offerings include T-shirts, jackets, and hats. 239 Queen St. W. ✆ **416/597-9560.** www.modrobes.com. Subway: Osgoode.

Old Navy *(Overrated)*   The Gap's little brother hit Toronto like a hurricane when it opened in 2001. There are no longer queues to get into the store, but it remains incredibly popular—a fact that's an enduring mystery to me. Sure, the prices are reasonable, but the store is cramped and chaotic, and the product selection is much smaller than at its U.S. counterparts. Unless you've never been to an Old Navy outlet before, steer clear. Eaton Centre. ✆ **416/593-2551.** Subway: Dundas.

Roots   This is one Canadian retailer that seems to be universally loved. The clothes are casual, from hooded sweats to fleece jackets, and there's a good selection of leather footwear. Don't overlook the tykes' department, which has the same stuff in tiny sizes. Other locations include the Eaton Centre (© **416/593-9640**). 95A Bloor St. W. © **416/323-9512.** www.roots.ca. Subway: Bay.

Sim & Jones   Shop owners Pui Sim and Alarice Jones design clothes that move easily between a "smart casual" office environment and the smart chic of the latest bistro. The women's clothes are available in sizes 6 to 16. 388 College Street. © **416/920-2573.** Subway: Queen's Park, then streetcar to Borden St.

TNT Man/TNT Woman *Finds*   The acronym stands for "The New Trend," and this small chain offers just that, with fashions from Betsey Johnson and Plein Sud for les femmes, and Diesel and Iceberg Jean for les hommes. There are also locations uptown at 368 and 388 Eglinton Avenue. 87 Avenue Rd. © **416/975-1960** (men's shop) and **416/975-1810** (women's shop). Subway: Bay.

Zara *Value*   This Spanish retailer is renowned for transferring the latest looks into affordable fashions less than a month after they appear on the runway. This bi-level shop has a women's department at street level; the equally stylish men's shop is on the lower concourse. 50 Bloor St. W. © **416/916-2401.** www.zara.com. Subway: Bay.

MEN'S

Boomer *⚤*   Ever wonder where the Barenaked Ladies or Moist get the glad rags they wear in their videos? Look no farther than Boomer, a hip shop that stocks staples like Hugo Boss and Cinque, as well as the latest from Swedish trendsetter J. Linderberg. 309 Queen St. W. © **416/598-0013.** Subway: Osgoode.

Decibel   This trendy shop is a terrific spot to pick up the latest and greatest in casualwear. Labels range from well-known brands like Kenneth Cole to up-and-comers like Psycho Cowboy or Pusch (from Denmark and Calgary, respectively). 200 Queen St. W. © **416/506-9648.** Subway: Osgoode.

Delphic   Don't like trendy? Then don't shop here. If you do, you'll be confronted by fashion favorites like Evisu Jeans, which are imported from Japan. 706 Queen St. W. © **416/603-3334.** Subway: Osgoode, then streetcar west to Manning Ave.

Eza Wear *Finds*   West Queen West has more than its fair share of up-and-coming designers, and this is one example. Design duo Susanne Langlois and Erin Murphy make many of their cool clothes from hemp, which looks as elegant as linen. 695 Queen St. W. © **416/975-1388.** Subway: Osgoode, then streetcar west to Markham St.

Harry Rosen *⚤*   Designed like a minidepartment store, Harry Rosen carries the crème de la crème of menswear designers, including Hugo Boss, Brioni, and Versace. There's also a good selection of work-worthy footwear, and a famous "Great Wall of Shirts." 82 Bloor St. W. © **416/972-0556.** www.harryrosen.com. Subway: Bay.

Moores   There's something for everyone at this spacious shop. Most of the suits, sport coats, and dress pants are Canadian-made, and international designers like Oscar de la Renta are represented, too. Sizes run from extra short to extra tall and oversize. The prices tend to be reasonable, and bargains abound. 100 Yonge St. © **416/363-5442.** Subway: King.

WOMEN'S

Aritzia   This Vancouver retailer now has an outpost on Queen West (another one is set to open in the Eaton Centre). The clothes tend to be sporty and fun, though there are some sexy numbers by the hard-to-find French label Kookaï. 280 Queen St. W. © **416/977-9919.** Subway: Osgoode.

Comrags Designers Judy Cornish and Joyce Gunhouse create retro-inspired clothing that looks great on a variety of body types. 654 Queen St. W. © 416/360-7249. www.comrags.com. Subway: Osgoode, then streetcar west to Palmerston.

Ewanika *Finds* Little Italy is famous for its nightlife, but if you happen by during the day be sure to check out designer Trish Ewanika's boutique. Her tailored creations are perfect for women who don't like suits but want to look polished at work. 490 College St. © 416/927-9699. Subway: Queen's Park, then streetcar west to Palmerston Ave.

Fashion Crimes If Misdemeanors (p. 186) is a playground for little princesses, then Fashion Crimes is the stomping ground for their fairy godmothers. The glamorous dresses, designed by shop owner Pam Chorley, are a tribute to playful femininity. 322½ Queen St. W. © 416/351-8758. Subway: Osgoode.

Femme De Carriere ⭐ For a dose of Québecois savoir-faire, look no further than this elegant emporium. While the name translates into "career woman," the offerings range from shapely suits to evening-appropriate dresses and chic separates. There are branches in shopping centers around town, including First Canadian Place, Holt Renfrew Centre, Bayview Village, and Fairview Mall. Eaton Centre. © 416/595-0951. Subway: Queen.

Fresh Baked Goods *Finds* Surprise, this *isn't* a bakery. Owner Laura Jean "the knitting queen" features a line of flirty knitwear made of cotton, mohair, wool, or lace. This is a favorite haunt of the celebrity set—stars like Neve Campbell drop by when they're in town. The staff is friendly and incredibly helpful; if you like a sweater but not its buttons, they will sew on different ones from their sizeable collection free of charge. They also do custom orders. 274 Augusta Ave. © 416/966-0123. www.freshbakedgoods.com. Subway: Spadina, then LRT to Baldwin St., and walk 2 blocks west.

F/X The significance of the name is clear from the start: This is dressing for dramatic effect. Funkier pieces from the prêt-à-porter collections of Vivienne Westwood and Anna Sui are at the back of the store. There are also cutting-edge shoes and boots, a makeup collection, and candy. 152 Spadina Ave. © 416/703-5595. Subway: Spadina, then LRT to Queen St. W.

Girl Friday *Finds* Local designer Rebecca Nixon creates feminine dresses, suits, and separates for her shop under the name Girl Friday. The store also carries pieces from hip labels Nougat and Dish, but I come here for Nixon's elegant but affordable pieces. 740 Queen St. W. © 416/364-2511. www.girlfridayclothing.com. Subway: Osgoode, then streetcar west to Claremont St.

Jeanne Lottie ⭐ Can you make a fashion statement with a handbag? Canadian designer Jane Ip thinks so—and she's made a convert out of me. Purses for all occasions, from zebra-patterned boxy bags for day to glittering sequin-encrusted numbers for a night out, fill her boutique. Prices are surprisingly low, with most offerings in the C$50 to C$80 (US$35–US$56) range. There are also beaded shoes and sparkly accessories. 106 Yorkville Ave. © 416/975-5115. www.jeanne lottie.com. Subway: Bay.

Linda Lundstrom Lundstrom has been designing women's clothing since the early 1970s. Her distinctive brand of sportswear incorporates native Canadian art and themes. The famous La Parka coat is still a bestseller. 136 Cumberland St. © 416/927-9009. Subway: Bay.

Lululemon ⭐ Yoga devotees will be delighted by this West Queen West shop. In addition to the house label's nicely designed workout wear you'll find Ayurvedic skin care products by Christy Turlington, yoga mats, and other accessories. The newest outpost is at 130 Bloor St. W. (ℂ **416/964-9544**). 734 Queen St. W. ℂ **416/703-1399**. www.lululemon.com. Subway: Osgoode, then streetcar west to Claremont St.

Maxi Boutique Homegrown talent takes center stage here, with designs from Lida Baday, Ross Mayer, and Misura by Joeffer Caoc. There's a full complement of suits, separates, and eveningwear. 575 Danforth Ave. ℂ **416/461-6686**. Subway: Pape.

Peach Berserk ⭐ *Finds* Toronto designer (and local legend) Kingi Carpenter creates dramatically printed silk separates, dresses, and coats. But don't look for demure florals—prints range from bold martini glasses to the ironic "Do I Look Fat in This?" logo. 507 Queen St. W. ℂ **416/504-1711**. www.peachberserk.com. Subway: Osgoode, then streetcar west to Spadina.

Price Roman ⭐ The husband-and-wife team of Derek Price and Tess Roman produces sleek, tailored clothes with a sultry edge. They are rightly famous for their special occasion dresses. 267 Queen St. W. ℂ **416/979-7363**. Subway: Osgoode.

Rhonda Maternity For the last of the red-hot mamas, there's this glamorous boutique. The stylish suits, sweater sets, and sportswear are this store's exclusive designs. 110 Cumberland St. ℂ **416/921-3116**. Subway: Bay.

FOOD

The Big Carrot Who says health food can't be fun? This large-scale emporium stocks everything from organic produce to vitamins to all-natural beauty potions. Stop in at the cafe for a vegetarian snack or light meal. 348 Danforth Ave. ℂ **416/466-2129**. www.thebigcarrot.ca. Subway: Chester.

The Bonnie Stern School Crammed to the rafters with cooking accouterments (such as stovetop grills) and exotic books, this store also features the raw ingredients you need to produce fine cuisine. It carries top-notch olive oil, balsamic vinegar, Asian sauces, and candied flower petals. If you take a course or seminar, you get a 10% discount on everything you buy. 6 Erskine Ave. ℂ **416/484-4810**. www.bonniestern.com. Subway: Eglinton.

Global Cheese Shoppe ⭐ *Value* Cheese, glorious cheese. More than 150 varieties are available, from mild boccocini to the greenest of Gorgonzola, and the staff is generous with samples. 76 Kensington Ave. ℂ **416/593-9251**. Subway: Spadina, then LRT to Baldwin Ave.

House of Tea Visitors to this shop can drink in the heady scent of more than 150 loose teas. And the selection of cups, mugs, and tea caddies runs from chic to comical. 1017 Yonge St. ℂ **416/922-1226**. Subway: Rosedale.

Pusateri's *Finds* The Pusateri's store up at Lawrence and Avenue Road is a Toronto institution—and a delight for gourmets—but because of its out-of-the-way location, I haven't recommended it for visitors. Now that problem has been solved: In 2003, Pusateri's opened a gorgeous new store on Yorkville Avenue at the corner of Bay Street. The quality is as high as ever, though some of the offerings differ from the uptown shop—for example, travelers will appreciate the excellent prepared meals that can be eaten on the go. 57 Yorkville Ave. ℂ **416/785-9100**. www.pusateris.com. Subway: Bay.

Senses Bakery ⭐   The pastries and chocolates here are simply exquisite. At one time you would have had to stop by the Soho Metropolitan Hotel to stock up; now there's an outpost at Bayview Village (2901 Bayview Ave. at Sheppard, ℂ416/227-9149) as well as the 35-seat Queen Street cafe. 2 Queen St. E., unit 106. ℂ 416/364-7303. www.senses.ca. Subway: St. Andrew.

Simone Marie Belgian Chocolate   All of the rich truffles, colorful almond dragées, and fruit jellies in this shop are flown in from Belgium. If you're going to splurge, you may as well do it in style. 126A Cumberland St. ℂ 416/968-7777. Subway: Bay.

Sugar Mountain Confectionery   Remember Pez, candy necklaces, and lollipop rings? Sugar Mountain carries the tooth-aching sweets of youth, several of which have been elevated to cult status. Teens are drawn to this store, but the biggest customers are nostalgic boomers. 320 Richmond St. W. ℂ 416/204-9544. Subway: Osgoode.

GIFTS & MORE

B&J Trading *Finds*   I've always wanted to be one of those people who can wrap up gifts with style. Unfortunately I never learned how, but that no longer matters since I discovered B&J in Chinatown. This store stocks a wide assortment of goods, but their claim to fame is the gift prep department. They've got unusual wrapping papers, bows, and bags—but best of all, they have beautiful presentation boxes that could almost be gifts themselves. 378 Spadina Ave. ℂ 416/586-9655. Subway: Spadina, then streetcar south to Nassau St.

French Country ⭐ *Finds*   Owner Viola Jull spent several years living in France, and she re-creates a Parisian atmosphere in her shop. Many items are unique, including painted lampshades, antique silver, and framed prints. There are also a few gourmet food products and hand-milled soaps. 6 Roxborough St. W. ℂ 416/944-2204. Subway: Rosedale.

Ice   This small store is a big lure for visiting celebs. Do the Bliss Spa and Philosophy skin-care lines draw them in? Maybe it's the eye-catching T-shirts or the fab costume jewelry. 163 Cumberland St. ℂ 416/964-6751. Subway: Bay.

Japanese Paper Place   The Japanese have elevated papermaking to an art form. In addition to being popular with artists, this shop has all the boxes, papers, and handmade cards you could ever need to create exquisite gift-wrappings. Better yet, it also stocks instruction books! 887 Queen St. W. ℂ 416/703-0089. www.japanesepaperplace.com. Subway: Osgoode, then any streetcar west to Ossington Ave.

Legends of the Game   This collectibles store, just 2 blocks north of Sky-Dome, houses memorabilia of Babe Ruth, Wayne Gretzky, Muhammad Ali, and Michael Jordan, among others. There are trading cards, team jerseys, and other souvenirs. 322A King St. W. ℂ 416/971-8848. Subway: St. Andrew.

Oh Yes, Toronto   Looking for souvenirs for the folks back home? Oh Yes, Toronto stocks no end of Hogtown knickknacks, as well as quality T-shirts and sweatshirts. There's another outlet at Queens Quay West (ℂ 416/203-0607). Eaton Centre. ℂ 416/593-6749. Subway: Dundas or Queen.

HEALTH & BEAUTY

Elizabeth Milan Hotel Day Spa ⭐   Even if you don't have time for the spa, you will appreciate the well-stocked shop in its foyer. Elizabeth Milan carries one of the widest arrays of imported beauty products I've ever seen, including

Dermologica, Yonka, Gehwol, and the perennial favorite from France, Decleor. Fairmont Royal York, 100 Front St. W. © 416/350-7500. www.elizabethmilanspa.com. Subway: Union.

Holt Renfrew   Sure, it's a department store—but one where the lion's share of the newly renovated first floor is dedicated to beauty. The famous faces—Chanel, Estée Lauder, Lancome—are all there, but so are a slew of other brands including Stila, Jo Malone, Laura Mercier, DuWop, and Nars. Holt Renfrew Centre, 50 Bloor St. W. © 416/922-2333. www.holtrenfrew.com. Subway: Yonge/Bloor.

Lush   This clever U.K.-based emporium looks like a gourmet grocery store. The heady scent of perfumes is the giveaway. Lush stocks a selection of fizzy bath bombs, skin lotions and potions, and aromatherapy-oriented items. All products are sold by weight. 312 Queen St. W. © 416/599-5874. www.lush.com. Subway: Osgoode.

M.A.C. ★   This makeup line used to be a trade secret among models and actors, though the word has been out for a while. (The company was founded in Toronto and is now owned by Estée Lauder.) M.A.C.'s flagship store is perpetually packed, especially on weekends, but if you call ahead you can schedule an appointment for a makeup lesson. The C$25 (US$18) charge is entirely redeemable in product. In addition to cosmetics, the store carries skin- and hair-care supplies. 89 Bloor St. W. © 416/929-7555. www.maccosmetics.com. Subway: Bay.

Noah's *Value*   This is a mecca for health nuts. Noah's boasts aisle after aisle of vitamins and dietary supplements, organic foods and "natural" candies, skin-care and bath products, and books and periodicals. The staff is well informed and helpful. There's a smaller but more centrally located outlet at 667 Yonge St. (at Bloor; © 416/969-0220). 322 Bloor St. W. © 416/968-7930. Subway: Spadina.

Rubies Beauty Bar   This tiny shop carries beauty and bath products by Canadian brands you've probably never heard of before, such as Silk Road and Cake, but they all smell gorgeous. Rubies also sells some clothing and lingerie. 715 Queen St. W. © 416/601-6789. Subway: Osgoode, then streetcar west to Bathurst.

Thompson's Homeopathic Supplies *Finds*   This is just like an old-fashioned apothecary, with endless rows of potions behind a wooden counter. It has a homeopathic remedy for everything from the common cold to dermatitis to conjunctivitis. The staff is friendly and knowledgeable. 844 Yonge St. © 416/922-2300. Subway: Yonge/Bloor.

HOUSEWARES & FURNISHINGS

The Art Shoppe   This is one of the prettiest stores in the city, with top-notch furniture arranged into suites of rooms. A wide range of styles is on display, from gilty baroque to streamlined Art Deco. The price tags are high, but the store is well worth browsing. 2131 Yonge St. © 416/487-3211. www.theartshoppe.com. Subway: Eglinton.

Caban   Club Monaco's foray into the world of home decor has been a slam-dunk. This bi-level ode to loft living features clean-lined furnishings, table settings and accessories—all for reasonable prices. 262 Queen St. W. © 416/596-0386. www.caban.com. Subway: Osgoode.

Elte Carpet & Home   With 12,077 sq. m (130,000 sq. ft.) of showroom space, Elte has room for a lot more than rugs. This megastore is divided into boutiques where big names like Ralph Lauren and Calvin Klein flog their home-design lines. History-spanning reproductions abound, and there are a few antiques finds, too. 80 Ronald Ave. (just west of Dufferin St.). ℂ 416/785-7885. Subway: Eglinton W., then any westbound bus to Ronald Ave.

En Provence   Anyone who has been carried away by reading about the south of France—think of Peter Mayle's *A Year in Provence*—will feel right at home here. It stocks brightly colored dinnerware, printed bed linens, and wrought-iron furniture. 20 Hazelton Ave. ℂ 416/975-9400. Subway: Bay.

Kitchen Stuff Plus ⟨Value⟩   This housewares shop sells brand-name goods from the likes of Umbra at discount prices. It offers a good selection of picture frames, wine racks, area rugs, candles, painted ceramics, and kitchen accessories. 703 Yonge St. ℂ 416/944-2718. www.kitchenstuffplus.com. Subway: Yonge/Bloor.

Nestings ⟨★⟩   This terrific shop delivers comfort and style in equal measure. Many of the items, from ornate iron kettles to tassel-trimmed ottomans, hark back to a more glamorous age. There's also **Nestings Kids** at 418 Eglinton Ave. (ℂ 416/322-0511; Subway: Eglinton, then walk west to Avenue Rd.). 1609 Bayview Ave. ℂ 416/932-3704. Subway: Eglinton, then no. 34 bus to Bayview.

Quasi-Modo Modern Furniture   With offerings for both home and office, this shop showcases some of the best of streamlined 20th-century design. Many of the items are European imports, like the tables and chairs by Sweden's Bruno Mathsson; other furnishings are from lines such as Knoll, Kartell, and Flou. 789 Queen St. W. ℂ 416/366-8370. Subway: Osgoode.

Tap Phong Trading Co. ⟨Finds⟩   If you have only a few minutes in Chinatown, spend them here. You'll find beautiful hand-painted ceramics, earthenware, dec-orative items, kitchen utensils, and small appliances. Best of all, just about every-thing is inexpensive and of reliable quality. 360 Spadina Ave. ℂ 416/977-6364. Subway: Spadina, then LRT to Baldwin St.

Teatro Verde ⟨★⟩   Life is drama, so why shouldn't the items you fill your home with be dull? That seems to be the question at Teatro Verde, where even table coasters are things of great beauty. Hazelton Lanes. ℂ 416/966-2227. www.teatro verde.com. Subway: Bay.

UpCountry ⟨★⟩   This Canadian company made its reputation with upscale Arts-and-Crafts and mission-style home furnishings. The offerings at its flagship Toronto shop have expanded to include modern and contemporary furniture as well as vintage metal pieces. The sizable selection of decorative touches includes globes and pottery, and now inhabits a separate location at 16 Eastern Ave. (at Trinity St.; ℂ 416/367-3906). 214 King St. E. ℂ 416/777-1700. www.upcountry.ca. Subway: King.

JEWELRY

Birks ⟨★⟩   This Canadian institution, founded in 1879, is synonymous with top quality. Among the silver, crystal, and china is an extensive selection of top-qual-ity jewelry, including exquisite pearls and knockout diamond engagement rings (the diamonds themselves were mined in northern Canada). There's even a chil-dren's section, filled with keepsake gifts like Royal Doulton Bunnykins china and whimsical picture frames by Nova Scotia's Seagull Pewter. My personal favorite is the showcase of antique estate jewelry. There's a smaller branch at the Eaton Centre (ℂ 416/979-9311). Manulife Centre, 55 Bloor St. W. ℂ 416/922-2266. www.birks.com. Subway: Bay.

Experimetal   Some of proprietor Anne Sportun's sterling silver, gold, and platinum creations have won design awards. She will also fashion custom engagement and wedding bands. Also on display are pieces by other North American jewelers. 588 Markham St. (south of Bloor St. W.). © 416/538-3313. www.experimetal.com. Subway: Bathurst.

Mink *Finds*   In gangster-speak, a "mink" is a sexy woman—exactly the type who would love the fabulous fakes at this boutique. Many of the necklaces, bracelets, and rings are Canadian-designed, but a few are Euro imports. 550 College St. © 416/929-9214. Subway: Queen's Park, then streetcar west to Euclid Ave.

Royal de Versailles Jewellers   This European-style shop carries an eye-catching assortment of pearls, gold, and platinum. The designs range from classic to funkier, playful styles. There are also watches by the likes of Piaget, Cartier, Rolex, and Tag Heuer, as well as a Bulgari boutique. 101 Bloor St. W. © 416/967-7201. Subway: Bay.

Silverbridge   Most of the necklaces, bracelets, rings, and earrings here are fashioned of silver, and the sensibility is modern. Most of the designs are the work of Costin Lazar, and they are produced in Toronto; Lazar will also take on custom work. There are also a few pieces in 18-karat gold and platinum, as well as watches by Georg Jensen and Ole Mathiesen. 162 Cumberland St. © 416/923-2591. www.silverbridge.com. Subway: Bay.

Tiffany & Co.   Diamonds are still a girl's best friend at this Art Deco–style shop. Precious gems and designs by Elsa Peretti and Paloma Picasso are on the first level; the second floor holds silver jewelry, stationery, and housewares. 85 Bloor St. W. © 416/921-3900. www.tiffany.com. Subway: Bay.

LEATHER GOODS

Danier *Value*   This Canadian chain carries suede and leather coats, suits, pants, and skirts at reasonable prices. Not-uncommon sales knock the prices down 20% to 50%. Eaton Centre. © 416/598-1159. www.danier.com. Subway: Queen.

Taschen!   Exclusive designer handbags, luggage, wallets, and other accessories are mainstays here. Many are European imports, and quality is high. 162 Cumberland St. © 416/961-3185. Subway: Bay.

LINGERIE

La Senza *Value*   This Montréal-based chain carries moderately priced but eye-catching bra-and-panty sets and naughty-looking nighties. There are also plush unisex robes and patterned boxers. An assortment of slippers, candles, bath mousse, and picture frames rounds out the offerings. Holt Renfrew Centre, 50 Bloor St. W. © 416/972-1079. www.lasenza.com. Subway: Yonge/Bloor.

La Vie en Rose   You'll find quite the eclectic collection of undies here, from sensible cotton briefs to maribou-trimmed teddies, retro PJs to up-to-the-minute cleavage enhancers. The items at the front of the store are inexpensive; the farther back you go, the pricier it gets. Eaton Centre. © 416/595-0898. Subway: Queen.

Linea Intima *Finds*   While there's no shortage of fabulous undergarments at this boutique, the real reason to visit is owner Liliana Mann's encyclopedic knowledge of what suits the female form. This extends to prosthetics and bras that are designed for women who have had mastectomies. 1925 Avenue Rd. © 416/416-780-1726. www.lineaintima.com. Subway: York Mills, then bus west along Wilson Ave. to Avenue Rd. and walk 6 blocks south to Brooke Ave.

MAGAZINES & NEWSPAPERS

Great Canadian News Company　This small shop has a great selection, with more than 2,000 magazines filling its shelves, but not a comfortable place for a lengthy browse. BCE Place, 30 Yonge St. (at Front St.). ℂ 416/363-2242. Subway: Union.

Maison de la Presse Internationale ✦　Although this store fills up fast on weekends, drawing expats and locals alike, it's still a great place to while away an hour. The many international magazines and newspapers are as current as you'll find. 102 Yorkville Ave. ℂ 416/928-2328. Subway: Bay.

MALLS & SHOPPING CENTERS

Atrium on Bay　This two-level complex has more than 60 shops selling clothing, jewelry, furniture, and more. Bay and Dundas sts. ℂ 416/980-2801. Subway: Dundas.

Bayview Village ✦ *Finds*　Think that you hate malls? Visit this one before you swear off. Elegantly designed and moderately sized, Bayview Village is home to several independent boutiques as well as some chain stores (such as the best Chapters bookstore in the city). It's also a place to come for excellent food: the Oliver & Bonacini restaurant is here (p. 113), and so is a tiny outpost of the Senses Bakery. 2901 Bayview Ave. (at Sheppard Ave.). ℂ 416/226-0404. Subway: Bayview.

College Park　This shopping center has been under renovation forever, but some new sections are now complete, including the giant new Winners store (see "The Best Bargains" on p. 184). 444 Yonge St. ℂ 416/597-1221. Subway: College.

Eaton Centre ✦　It's odd that one of urban Toronto's main attractions is a mall—but, oh, what a mall. More than 285 shops and restaurants spread over four levels in the Eaton Centre, which takes up 2 entire city blocks. 220 Yonge St. ℂ 416/598-2322. www.torontoeatoncentre.com. Subway: Dundas or Queen.

Fairview Mall　This massive shopping complex with its 260 stores has been around for years, but until the Sheppard subway line opened up, it wasn't easily accessible by public transit. Now that the subway brings you right to the door, you can easily shop at Toronto's first H&M store, as well as The Bay, Sears, Birks, Femme de Carriere, La Senza, Harry Rosen, and Danier. 1800 Sheppard Ave E. ℂ 416/491-0151. www.fairviewmall.com. Subway: Don Mills.

First Canadian Place ✦　A piece of the labyrinth of the underground city, this complex houses 120 shops and restaurants. It also stages free noontime events each week, with performances as diverse as Opera Atelier's Handel recital and the dancing monks of the Tibetan Drikung Monastery. There are also ongoing art exhibitions. King and Bay sts. ℂ 416/862-8138. Subway: King.

Hazelton Lanes ✦　A byword for elegance and extravagance, Hazelton is a two-level complex with about 90 shops. The charming courtyard at the center transforms into an ice-skating rink in winter. 55 Avenue Rd. ℂ 416/968-8602. www.hazeltonlanes.com. Subway: Bay.

Holt Renfrew Centre　Anchored by the chic Holt Renfrew department store, this small underground concourse is more down to earth. It connects with the Manulife Centre and the Hudson's Bay Centre. 50 Bloor St. W. ℂ 416/923-2255. Subway: Yonge/Bloor.

Manulife Centre ✦　More than 50 posh shops—including William Ashley, Indigo Books Music & More, and a top-notch LCBO outlet—occupy this complex. The Manulife connects to the Holt Renfrew Centre underground. 55 Bloor St. W. ℂ 416/923-9525. Subway: Bay.

> **Tips Same Time Next Year**
>
> In addition to the post-holiday sales at most shops, there are some don't-miss special sales that locals have penned into their calendars. Sale locations are often scattered around the city, so call each store for details and exact dates.
>
> - **MAY:** The **Fashion Design Council of Canada** hosts a clearance sale of top-name Canadian designer wear at the Design Exchange, 234 Bay St. ℂ **416/977-6184.**
> - **JULY:** Many retailers host semiannual sales that cut prices by as much as 50%. Some of the best are at **The Art Shoppe,** 2131 Yonge St., ℂ **416/487-3211** (p. 191); **Holt Renfrew,** 50 Bloor St. W., ℂ **416/ 922-2333** (p. 183); and **Elte Carpet & Home,** 80 Ronald Ave., ℂ **416/785-7885** (p. 191).
> - **OCTOBER:** The **Old Clothing Show & Sale** should really be called the New *and* Old Clothing Show, because there's almost as much new clothing here as there is vintage wear. Exhibition Place, ℂ **416/ 410-1310.**
> - **NOVEMBER:** Fine china and crystal retailer **William Ashley's** (p. 182) annual warehouse sale is one of the season's most eagerly anticipated events; call ℂ **416/964-2900** for information. The **One-of-a-Kind Craft Show & Sale** brings about 400 craft artists under one roof at Exhibition Place, and the prices are often better than you'll find in shops; call ℂ **416/960-3680.** The **Fashion Design Council of Canada** hosts another designer clearance sale this month, in case you missed the one in May (see above).

Queen's Quay Terminal   This is waterfront shopping at its best, with more than 30 shops and cafes. Queen's Quay caters to tourists—you'll find some unique items, but the prices tend to be moderate to high. 207 Queens Quay W. ℂ 416/203-0510. www.queens-quay-terminal.com. Subway: Union, then LRT to Queens Quay.

Royal Bank Plaza   Part of Toronto's underground city, the Royal Bank Plaza connects to Union Station and to the Royal York Hotel. Its 60-plus outlets include a variety of shops, two full-service restaurants, and a food court. The building above it is worth a look, too. Bay and Front sts. ℂ 416/974-5570. Subway: Union.

Scarborough Town Centre   This is a megamall to rival the Eaton Centre; if you're staying on the city's eastern fringe, you can't miss it. It has more than 200 shops, including branches similar to those at the Eaton Centre. Hwy. 401 and McCowan Ave. ℂ 416/296-0296. Subway: Scarborough Town Centre.

Village by the Grange   Cheek-by-jowl to the Art Gallery of Ontario, the Grange contains more than 40 shops. Its International Food Market has decent Middle Eastern and Asian selections. 122 St. Patrick St. ℂ 416/598-1414. Subway: St. Patrick.

MARKETS

Kensington Market ⟨★⟩   This neighborhood has changed dramatically in the past 40 years. Originally a Jewish community, it now borders on Chinatown. It contains several Asian herbalists and grocers, as well as West Indian and Middle Eastern shops. Kensington Avenue has the greatest concentration of vintage clothing stores in the city. For a full description, see "Walking Tour 1: China-town & Kensington Market," in chapter 7. Along Baldwin, Kensington, and Augusta aves. No phone. Subway: Spadina, then LRT to Baldwin St. or Dundas St. W.

St. Lawrence Market   This market is a local favorite for fresh produce, and it even draws people who live a good distance away. Hours are Tuesday through Thursday from 9am to 7pm, Friday from 8am to 8pm, and Saturday from 5am (when the farmers arrive) to 5pm. See p. 145 in chapter 6 for a complete description. 92 Front St. E. ℭ 416/392-7219. www.stlawrencemarket.com. Subway: Union.

MUSIC

HMV   This is the flagship Toronto store of the British chain. (You'll find smaller outlets throughout the city.) The selection of pop, rock, jazz, and classical music is large. Best of all, you can listen to a CD before you buy it. 333 Yonge St. ℭ 416/596-0333. Subway: Dundas.

The Music Store   On the Toronto Symphony Orchestra's home turf, this attractive shop includes several TSO CDs in its collection of classical and choral music. Roy Thomson Hall, 60 Simcoe St. ℭ 416/593-4822. Subway: St. Andrew.

Sam the Record Man   I, like most Torontonians, still have a soft spot for Sam's, though it is but a shadow of its former glory. The store—beloved by Canadian artists like Joni Mitchell, Rush, Liona Boyd, and the Guess Who because it has always promoted homegrown talent—has gone through rough times of late, and large sections of the store now lie empty. 347 Yonge St. ℭ 416/977-4650. Subway: Dundas.

SEX TOYS

Lovecraft ⟨★⟩   Believe it or not, Lovecraft—which marks its 33rd anniversary in 2005—is downright wholesome. Sure, there are the requisite bad-girl (and -boy) lingerie and toys, but much of the shop stocks joke gifts, T-shirts with suggestive slogans, and an impressive collection of erotic literature (no porn mags). The staff is friendly and the atmosphere playful. 27 Yorkville Ave. ℭ 877/923-7331 or 416/923-7331. Subway: Bay.

SHOES

Browns ⟨★⟩   To treat your feet to fabulous footwear by Manolo Blahnik, Prada, or Ferragamo, beat a path to this newly renovated shop for men and women; while you're there, check out Browns own house label, which is well-designed *and* less pricey. There's also a selection of leather handbags. Browns has several branches around the city. Eaton Centre. ℭ 416/979-9270. www.brownsshoes.com. Subway: Queen.

Capezio   Whether you're looking for the perfect pair of ballet slippers or an up-to-the-minute design from Steve Madden or Guess, you'll find it here. All the shoes and other leather goods are for women. 70 Bloor St. W. ℭ 416/920-1006. Subway: Bay.

David's   For serious shoppers only. This high-end store stocks elegant footwear for men and women—from Bruno Magli, Bally, and Sonia Rykiel, as

well as the store's own collection—but prices are accordingly steep. 66 Bloor St. W.
© 416/920-1000. Subway: Bay.

Mephisto These shoes are made for walking—particularly because they're made from all natural materials. Devotees of this shop, now in its third decade, swear that it's impossible to wear out Mephisto footwear. 1177 Yonge St. © 416/968-7026. Subway: Summerhill.

Petit Pied ★ For especially tiny tootsies, check out this elegant shop. Petit Pied carries children's shoes for newborns to adolescents. Many of the brands are European, including Minibel and Elefanten, but there are also sporty designs from Nike and Reebok. 890 Yonge St. © 416/963-5925. Subway: Rosedale.

TOYS

George's Trains Everything the young (or young at heart) could want to spruce up a model train set is here, including tracks, stations, and scenic backdrops. There are wooden trains as well as train kits. 510 Mount Pleasant Rd. © 416/489-9783. www.georgestrains.com. Subway: Davisville, then no. 11 or 28 bus to Mount Pleasant, and walk 1 block north.

Kidding Awound *Finds* Wind-up gadgets are the specialty here—there are hundreds to choose from. There are also some antique toys (which you won't let the kids near) and gag gifts. 91 Cumberland St. © 416/926-8996. Subway: Bay.

The Little Dollhouse Company ★ This toy store isn't really for kids. It's beloved by adults in search of miniature tea services and wicker furniture. It also sells nine different dollhouse kits, from a stately Victorian mansion to a ranch bungalow. 612 Mt. Pleasant Rd. © 416/489-7180. www.littledollhousecompany.com. Subway: Eglinton, then no. 34 bus east to Mount Pleasant, and walk 2 blocks south.

Science City ★ Kids and adults alike will love this tiny store filled with games, puzzles, models, kits, and books—all related to science. Whether your interest is astronomy, biology, chemistry, archaeology, or physics, you'll find something here. Holt Renfrew Centre, 50 Bloor St. W. © 416/968-2627. Subway: Yonge/Bloor.

Top Banana Fun for kids—and their parents. The toys range from Thomas the Tank Engine to Stomp Rockets. There are also games and books galore. 639 Mount Pleasant Rd. © 416/440-0111. Subway: Eglinton, then no. 34 bus east to Mount Pleasant, and walk 2 blocks south.

The Toy Shop This double-decker shop carries toys, many of them educational, from around the world. It also stocks a good selection of books, games, and videos. 62 Cumberland St. © 416/961-4870. Subway: Bay.

TRAVEL GOODS

Tilley Endurables *Value* The Tilley hat may not be Canada's greatest style moment, but it certainly is one of the most recognizable. The hats, belts, socks, and other travel gear are all well made, and they really will endure. Note that Tilley has branched out into travel underwear (they admit that "sexy they may not be," but claim that two sets of their underclothes will get you around the world—*now* I'm curious). Queens Quay, 207 Queens Quay W. © 416/203-0463. www.tilley.com. Subway: Union, then LRT to Queens Quay.

The Travel Stop *Finds* If an item is made in travel size, The Travel Stop stocks it. Offerings include steamers and hair dryers, travel guides, and luggage. There's also a travel agency at the back of the store. 130 Cumberland St. © 416/961-6088. www.thetravelstop.com. Subway: Bay.

VINTAGE CLOTHING

Asylum Secondhand jeans and vintage dresses line the racks in this Kensington Market stalwart. Bargains turn up in odd places, like the Anne Klein scarf at the bottom of a C$1 (US70¢) bin. There's also an assortment of toys and candy. 42 Kensington Ave. © 416/595-7199. Subway: Spadina, then LRT to Baldwin St.

Boudoir ★ *Finds* From the moment I stepped inside and smelled the wafting perfume, I was seduced. This sexy shop is a treasure trove: The fabulous frocks, vintage dressing tables and lounges, gilded mirrors, and glittering baubles create a setting that's fit for a queen (fortunately the prices are down-to-earth). In the evening, you can stop by for a cocktail (the back room is actually a *licensed* lounge). 990 Queen St. W. © 416/535-6600. Subway: Osgoode, then streetcar west to Ossington.

Brava ★ This shop is a favorite among local stylists, who pick up everything from cashmere sweaters to evening wraps for ladies, and printed shirts to golf pants for gents. 483 Queen St. W. © 416/504-8742. Subway: Osgoode, then streetcar west to Spadina.

Courage My Love *Value* With its mix of vintage clothing and new silver jewelry, Courage is a Kensington Market favorite. Dresses run from '50s velvet numbers to '70s polyester, and almost everything costs less than C$25 (US$18). There's also a good selection of tweedy jackets and starchy white shirts. The owners' cat makes an occasional furtive appearance. 14 Kensington Ave. © 416/979-1992. Subway: Spadina, then LRT to Dundas St. W.

Divine Decadence The price tags at this glamorous shop are sky-high, but the dresses are so beautiful and well-maintained that I almost think of Divine Decadence as a couture museum. Take a look for yourself at the Lanvins and Balenciagas of years gone by. 136 Cumberland St. © 416/324-9759. Subway: Bay.

Ex-Toggery This is a consignment shop with outlets around the city. Items don't last long, particularly because the price drops every week. Scour the racks for designer names like Versace and Donna Karan. There are also a variety of vintage items on display, from clothing to accessories. 115 Merton St. © 416/488-5393. www.extoggery.com. Subway: Davisville.

The Paper Bag Princess *Finds* Toronto isn't known as Hollywood North for nothing. L.A. has had a Paper Bag Princess boutique for several years, but only recently did its owner, Toronto native Elizabeth Mason, decide to open up a location in her hometown. This store is a treasure trove, and its boudoir-like setting makes it a sexy place to shop. The mint-condition Chanel and Pucci outfits cost a bundle, but what else would you expect? 287 Davenport Rd. © 416/925-2603. www.paperbagprincess.com. Subway: Bay.

Preloved ★ This isn't a traditional vintage store, because the classic clothes here have been repurposed. The pieces really are one-of-a-kind: The shop's owners breathe new life into cast-off jeans and T-shirts by adding unique details like vintage lace. The roster of celeb fans includes Alanis Morissette. 613 Queen St. W. © 416/504-8704. Subway: Osgoode, then streetcar west to Bathurst.

WINE

In Ontario, Liquor Control Board of Ontario (LCBO) outlets and small boutiques at upscale grocery stores sell wine; no alcohol is sold at convenience stores. The best deals are on locally produced wines—especially the ice wine, a sweet dessert wine that has won awards the world over. There are LCBO outlets all over the city, and prices are the same at all of them. The loveliest shop is at the **Manulife Centre,** 55 Bloor St. W. (© **416/925-5266**). Other locations are at 20 Bloor St. E. (© **416/368-0521**), the Eaton Centre (© **416/979-9978**), and Union Station (© **416/925-9644**). See www.lcbo.com for information about products and special in-store events.

Vintages stores have a different name, but they're still LCBO outlets. Check out the one at Hazelton Lanes (© **416/924-9463**) and at Queens Quay (© **416/864-6777**).

9

Toronto After Dark

Toronto may not have a reputation for being a city that never sleeps, but it does have a vital and varied nightlife scene. It's a mecca for top-notch theater—you can sometimes see Broadway shows before they reach Broadway. The Toronto Symphony Orchestra is world renowned, and the city's many dance and music venues host the crème de la crème of international performers. Some of the best entertainment is in Toronto's comedy clubs, which have served as training grounds for stars such as Jim Carrey, Mike Myers, Dan Aykroyd, and John Candy.

The nightclub scene moves at a frenetic pace. Martini bars are perennially popular, though lower-key pool bars are in vogue, too.

MAKING PLANS For listings of local performances and events, check out *Where Toronto* (www.where.ca/toronto) and *Toronto Life* (www.torontolife.com), as well as the *Toronto Star* (www.thestar.com). For up-to-the-minute lists of hot-ticket events, check out the free weeklies *Now* and *Eye,* available around town in newspaper boxes, and at bars, cafes, and bookstores. The city website **www.toronto.com** also boasts lengthy lists of performances. Events of particular interest to the gay and lesbian community are listed in *Xtra!* (www.xtra.ca), another free weekly available in newspaper boxes and many bookstores.

GETTING TICKETS For almost any theater, music, or dance event, you can buy tickets from **Ticketmaster** (© 416/870-8000; www.ticketmaster.ca). There's a service charge on every ticket (not just every order) sold over the phone. To avoid the charge, head to a ticket center. They're scattered throughout the city; call the information line for the lengthy list of locations.

1 The Performing Arts

Toronto's arts scene offers something for everyone year-round. The city's arts institutions are widely renowned, and many top-notch international performers pass through town.

THEATER

While it may seem that Toronto favors big-budget musicals—*The Producers* and *Mamma Mia!* have both made a big splash here—there are many excellent smaller companies, too. Many of the smaller troupes have no permanent performance space, so they move from venue to venue.

The best time to capture the flavor of Toronto's theater life is during the **Fringe Festival** (© 416/534-5919; www.fringefestival.com), usually held for 12 days starting in late June or early July. In July and August, try to catch the **Dream in High Park** (© 416/368-3110; www.canstage.com). It mounts stunning productions of Shakespearean or Canadian plays from the CanStage company in an outdoor setting.

(*Value* Discount Tickets

Want to take in a show, but don't want to spend a bundle on it? Drop by the **T.O. Tix booth** ★ (© **416/536-6468**, ext. 40), which sells half-price day-of-performance tickets. The booth is currently located in the Yonge-Dundas Square, which is just across the street from the Eaton Centre. T.O. Tix accepts cash, Visa, and MasterCard, and all sales are final. The booth is open Tuesday through Saturday from noon to 7:30pm; it's closed Sunday and Monday (tickets for performances on those days are sold on Sat).

LANDMARK THEATERS & PERFORMANCE VENUES

Canon Theatre ★   The Canon has had a tumultuous history. It got its start as the Pantages Theatre in 1920 as a vaudeville-cum-motion-picture theater. It was billed as the largest cinema in Canada with its 3,373 seats, and its opulent design (by the famous theater architect Thomas Lamb) was widely admired. However, the theater's fortunes sank in 1929—not because of the stock market crash, but because its owner was embroiled in a legal battle. RKO Pictures snapped up the Pantages, renamed it the Imperial, and used it exclusively as a movie house. Eventually the gorgeous space was carved into six cinemas. It was rescued and dramatically renovated by the Livent production company, which poured C$18 million (US$13 million) into the work. Livent also brought back its original name, and the new 2,250-seat Pantages Theatre was home for many years to the lavish Andrew Lloyd Webber show *The Phantom of the Opera*. But after Livent collapsed, the theater went dark for a long time. Fortunately, its current owners—who have renamed it the Canon—have turned over the theater's management and programming to Mirvish Productions (owned by "Honest Ed" Mirvish, who has done more to revitalize Toronto's theater scene than anyone). The Canon is currently home to *The Producers*. 244 Victoria St. © **416/364-4100** or 416/872-1212. www.onstagenow.com. Tickets C$51–C$93 (US$36–US$65). Subway: Dundas.

The Distillery Historic District ★★   This was once the home of the Gooderham-Worts Distillery, which was Canada's largest distilling company in the 19th century. The 45-building complex is an outstanding example of industrial design from the Victorian age. In 2003 it was reinvented as the Distillery Historic District, which includes galleries, restaurants, and shops. The district also houses three performing arts venues, and the Dancemakers and the Native Earth troupes now perform here. 55 Mill St. © **416/367-1800**. www.thedistillerydistrict.com. Tickets C$15–C$40 (US$11–US$28). Subway: King, then streetcar east to Parliament St.

The Elgin and Winter Garden Theatre Centre ★   These landmark theaters first opened their doors in 1913, and today they vie with the Royal Alex and the Princess of Wales Theatre for major shows and attention. Recent productions have included *The Full Monty* and the South African *Umoja: The Spirit of Togetherness,* which celebrates that nation's musical heritage.

Both the Elgin and the Winter Garden have been restored to their original gilded glory at a cost of C$29 million (US$20 million). They are the only double-decker theaters in Toronto. The downstairs Elgin is larger, seating 1,500 and featuring a lavish domed ceiling and gilded decoration on the boxes and proscenium. Hand-painted frescoes adorn the striking interior of the 1,000-seat Winter Garden. Suspended from its ceiling and lit with lanterns are more than 5,000

Downtown After Dark

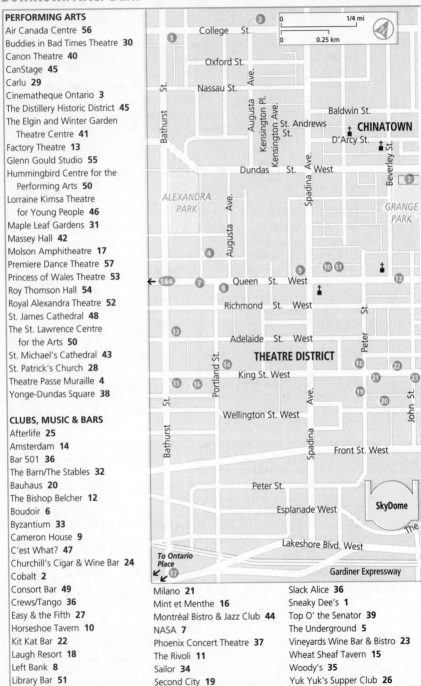

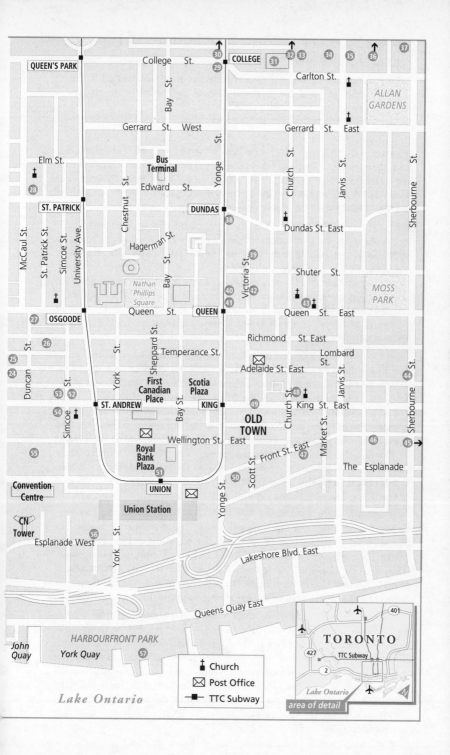

> (*Tips* **Farther Afield**
>
> Don't forget that two major theater festivals—the **Shaw Festival** in Nia-gara-on-the-Lake and the **Stratford Festival** in Stratford—are only an hour or two away. See chapter 10 for details.

branches of beech leaves, which have been preserved, painted, and fireproofed. Both theaters offer everything from Broadway musicals and dramas to concerts and opera performances, and are favorite venues of the Toronto International Film Festival. 189 Yonge St. ⓒ **416/872-5555** for tickets, or 416/314-2901 for tour info. Tickets C$20–C$85 (US$14–US$60). Subway: Queen.

Princess of Wales Theatre This spectacular 2,000-seat state-of-the-art facil-ity was built for the production of *Miss Saigon,* with a stage large enough to accommodate the landing of the helicopter in that production. More recently it was home to *The Lion King,* and at press time it is where the wildly popular Toronto production of *Hairspray* is playing. Frank Stella, who painted 929 sq. m (10,000 sq. ft.) of colorful murals, decorated the exterior and interior walls. People in wheelchairs have access to all levels of the theater (not the norm in Toronto). 300 King St. W. ⓒ **416/872-1212.** www.onstagenow.com. Tickets C$21–C$116 (US$15–US$81). Subway: St. Andrew.

Royal Alexandra Theatre ★★ When shows from Broadway migrate north, they usually head for the Royal Alex. Subscription buyers often snap up tickets, so your best bet is to call or order tickets online ahead of time. Recent shows here have included *Mamma Mia!,* the ABBA-inspired musical.

The 1,495-seat Royal Alex is a magnificent spectacle. Constructed in 1907, it owes its current health to discount-store czar and impresario Ed Mirvish, who refurbished it (as well as the surrounding area) in the 1960s. Inside, it's a riot of plush reds, gold brocade, and baroque ornamentation. Avoid the second balcony and the seats "under the circle," which don't have the greatest sight lines. 260 King St. W. ⓒ **800/461-3333** for tickets, or 416/872-1212. www.onstagenow.com. Tickets C$26–C$94 (US$18–US$66). Subway: St. Andrew.

The St. Lawrence Centre for the Arts For 3 decades, the St. Lawrence Centre has presented top-notch theater, music, and dance performances. The Bluma Appel Theatre is home to the CanStage company, and the smaller Jane Mallet Theatre features the Toronto Operetta Theatre Company, among others. This is a popular spot for lectures, too. 27 Front St. E. ⓒ **800/708-6754** or 416/366-7723. www.stlc.com. Tickets C$20–C$70 (US$14–US$49). Mon night pay what you can. Senior and student discounts may be available 30 min. before performance. Subway: Union.

Toronto Centre for the Arts Built in 1993, this gigantic complex is home to the North York Symphony and the Amadeus Choir. It's also the Toronto base of the Royal Opera Company, a group that is devoted to staging operas with tra-ditional sets, costumes, and staging. It contains several performance venues. The 1,850-seat Apotex Theatre has featured award-winning musicals such as *Sunset Boulevard* and *Ragtime;* the 1,025-seat George Weston Recital Hall books music events. The complex also includes a 250-seat studio theater and an art gallery. 5040 Yonge St. ⓒ **416/733-9388.** www.tocentre.com. Tickets C$15–C$75 (US$11–US$53). Sub-way: North York Centre.

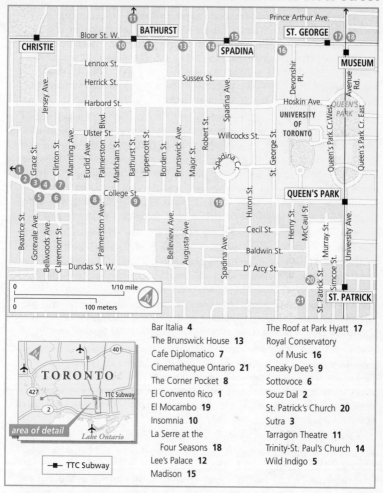

Bar Italia **4**
The Brunswick House **13**
Cafe Diplomatico **7**
Cinematheque Ontario **21**
The Corner Pocket **8**
El Convento Rico **1**
El Mocambo **19**
Insomnia **10**
La Serre at the
Four Seasons **18**
Lee's Palace **12**
Madison **15**

The Roof at Park Hyatt **17**
Royal Conservatory
of Music **16**
Sneaky Dee's **9**
Sottovoce **6**
Souz Dal **2**
St. Patrick's Church **20**
Sutra **3**
Tarragon Theatre **11**
Trinity-St. Paul's Church **14**
Wild Indigo **5**

THEATER COMPANIES & SMALLER THEATERS

Buddies in Bad Times Theatre ⚐ Established in 1979, this "gay, lesbian and queer" theater company produces edgy and provocative new Canadian works. Their work is not for everyone (the list of upcoming productions identifies shows that are "not for the faint of heart," and they mean it), but Buddies produces shows that you simply won't see anywhere else. The theater also stages Canadian adaptations of some well-known works, such as Ibsen's *Hedda Gabler*. American Sky Gilbert has helped build the theater's cutting-edge reputation. 12 Alexander St. ✆ 416/975-8555. www.buddiesinbadtimestheatre.com. Tickets C$10–C$25 (US$7–US$18); some performances are pay-what-you-can. Subway: Wellesley.

CanStage ⚐⚐ The CanStage company performs an eclectic variety of Canadian and international plays. Recent productions include *Urinetown, The Glass Menagerie,* and the late Pulitzer Prize–winning author Carol Shield's *Larry's Party.* They perform at the St. Lawrence Centre, seating 500 to 600, and the Berkeley Theatre, a more avant-garde, intimate space.

CanStage also presents open-air summer theater—traditionally Shake-speare—in High Park. It's known as the **Dream in High Park.** The company plans to focus more on Canadian-written works in the near future. Berkeley Theatre, 26 Berkeley St., and St. Lawrence Centre, 27 Front St. E. © **416/368-3110.** www.canstage. com. Tickets C$20–C$69 (US$14–US$48). Mon night pay what you can. Senior and student discounts may be available 30 min. before performance. Subway: Union for St. Lawrence Centre. King, then any streetcar east to Berkeley St. for Berkeley Theatre.

Factory Theatre ⚐   Since it opened in 1970, the Factory Theatre has focused on presenting Canadian plays, from political dramas to over-the-top comedies. The 2004–05 season marks the theater's 35th anniversary, and the season promises to be the most fascinating yet. Performances showcase up-and-coming scribes as well as established playwrights. George F. Walker started his career at the Factory, and two of his top works—*Adult Entertainment* and *The End of Civilization*—will be revived in 2005. 125 Bathurst St. © **416/504-9971.** www.factory theatre.ca. Tickets C$10–C$30 (US$7–US$21). Subway: St. Andrew, then any streetcar west.

Lorraine Kimsa Theatre for Young People ⚐⚐ *Kids*   Toronto's such a theater town that even tiny tots (and the rest of the family) get their own performance center. The always-enjoyable Lorraine Kimsa Theatre (formerly known as the Young Peoples Theatre) mounts whimsical productions such as *Jacob Two-Two Meets the Hooded Fang* (by the late great Mordecai Richler), and children's classics such as *Pinocchio* and *The Miracle Worker.* This theater company is particularly committed to diversity in its programming and in its artists. 165 Front St. E. © **416/862-2222.** www.lktyp.ca. Tickets C$14–C$28 (US$9.80–US$20). Subway: Union.

Native Earth Performing Arts Theatre   This small company is dedicated to performing works that express and dramatize the native Canadian experience. Playwright Thomson Highway, who authored *Dry Lips Oughta Move to Kapuskasing,* was one of the company's founders. Performing at the Case Goods Theatre in the Distillery Historic District, 55 Mill St. © **416/367-1800.** www.nativeearth.ca. Tickets C$10–C$25 (US$7–US$18).

Tarragon Theatre ⚐   The Tarragon Theatre opened in 1971. It produces original works by such famous Canadian literary figures as Michel Tremblay, Michael Ondaatje, and Judith Thompson, and an occasional classic or off-Broadway play. It's a small, intimate theater. 30 Bridgman Ave. (near Dupont and Bathurst sts.). © **416/531-1827,** or 416/536-5018 for administration. www.tarragontheatre.com. Tickets C$10–C$33 (US$7–US$23). Sun pay what you can. Subway: Bathurst.

Theatre Passe Muraille   This theater started in the late 1960s, when a pool of actors began experimenting and improvising original Canadian material. It continues to produce innovative, provocative theater by such contemporary Canadian playwrights as John Mighton, Daniel David Moses, and Wajdi Mouawad. There are two stages—the Mainspace seats 220, the more intimate Backspace, 70. 16 Ryerson Ave. © **416/504-7529.** www.passemuraille.on.ca. Tickets C$16–C$35 (US$11–US$25) Subway: Osgoode, then any streetcar west to Bathurst.

Toronto Truck Theatre   The Toronto Truck Theatre is the home of Agatha Christie's *The Mousetrap,* now in its 29th year. It's Canada's longest-running show—and it shows no signs of losing steam. 94 Belmont St. © **416/922-0084.** Tickets C$16–C$45 (US$18–US$32). Subway: Rosedale.

DINNER THEATERS

Famous People Players Dinner Theatre ⚐   This group mounts unique, visually fantastic "black light" shows. Famous People Players is renowned not just for the quality of its shows, but also for bringing out the creative potential in performers with disabilities. The price of the show includes a four-course dinner and backstage tour. 110 Sudbury St. ℰ **888/453-3385** or 416/532-1137. www.fpp.org. Dinner and show C$40 (US$28) adults, seniors, and children 13 and over, C$27 (US$19) children 12 and under. Subway: Osgoode, then any streetcar west to Dovercourt.

Medieval Times Dinner & Tournament *Kids*   Milord and Milady welcome you to their castle, where you'll be brought a cutlery-free meal by "serving wenches," view knights on horseback, and witness medieval games in the company of 1,000 of your closest friends. Adults may have trouble getting into the spirit of things, but it's always a hit with kids. Exhibition Place. ℰ **416/260-1234.** www.medievaltimes.com. Tickets C$66 (US$46) adults, C$46 (US$32) children 12 and under. Subway: Bathurst, then Bathurst streetcar south to Exhibition Place (last stop).

Mysteriously Yours   After 12 years at the Fairmont Royal York, the show has gone uptown. The action at this interactive whodunit gets under way around dessert time. Actors are scattered at tables around the room, and guests try to solve the crime with the aid of a detective who leads the investigation. 2026 Yonge St. ℰ **800-668-3323** or 416/486-7469. www.mysteriouslyyours.com. Dinner and show C$48–C$75 (US$34–US$53); show only C$35–C$45 (US$25–US$32). Subway: Davisville.

MAJOR CONCERT HALLS & AUDITORIUMS

In addition to the Elgin and Winter Garden Theatres, the Toronto Centre for the Arts, the Distillery Historic District, and the St. Lawrence Centre, these are the city's top performance venues.

The Carlu ⭐   Toronto welcomed the return of the Carlu in 2003. Located on the seventh floor of College Park, it was considered one of the grandest concert halls in Canada when it opened in 1931; like so many other venues in Toronto, the Carlu was shuttered in the 1970s. Now the 1,200-seat concert hall is back in favor, and its architecture is believed to be one of the best surviving examples of Art Moderne in the world (it was created by Jacques Carlu, the architect also responsible for New York's Rainbow Room). Unfortunately, the Carlu's revival coincided with the SARS outbreak, so the theater has had a slow start. College Park, 444 Yonge St., 7th Floor. ℰ **416/410-8727** for theater, or 416/870-8000 for tickets. www.thecarlu.com. Tickets C$30 (US$21) and up. Subway: College.

Glenn Gould Studio ⭐   This 340-seat radio concert hall offers chamber, jazz, and spoken-word performances. Its name celebrates the great, eccentric Toronto pianist whose life was cut short by a stroke in 1982. 250 Front St. W. ℰ **416/ 205-5555.** www.glenngouldstudio.cbc.ca. Tickets C$20–C$75 (US$14–US$36). Subway: Union.

Hummingbird Centre for the Performing Arts   If you visited Toronto before 1997, you might remember this as the O'Keefe Centre. It became famous in 1974 when Mikhail Baryshnikov defected after performing here. Since then, Hummingbird Communications has invested in renovations and refurbishing. This 3,223-seat center is still the home of the National Ballet of Canada; the Canadian Opera Company also performs here, though it will have its own opera house in 2006. 1 Front St. E. ℰ **416/872-2262.** www.hummingbirdcentre.com. Tickets C$40–C$125 (US$28–US$88). Subway: Union.

Massey Hall   This landmark building is one of Canada's premier music venues. The 2,800 seats aren't the most comfortable, but the flawless acoustics will make you stop squirming. The music performances run from classical to pop to rock to jazz, with recent stops by the likes of Diana Krall, Jewel, Prince, and

Pink. This is also a popular stop for lectures. 178 Victoria St. ℂ **416/593-4822.** www.masseyhall.com. Tickets C$25–C$100 (US$18–US$70). Subway: King.

Premiere Dance Theatre   This hall, specifically designed for dance performances, is where you can catch Toronto's leading contemporary dance companies. Toronto Dance Theatre and the Danny Grossman Dance Company perform here. Queen's Quay Terminal, 207 Queens Quay W. ℂ **416/973-4000.** www.harbour frontcentre.com. Tickets C$30–C$95 (US$21–US$67). Subway: Union, then LRT to York Quay.

Roy Thomson Hall ⭐   This stunning concert hall is home to the Toronto Symphony Orchestra, which performs here from September to June, and to the Toronto Mendelssohn Choir. Since it opened in 1982, it has also played host to an array of international musical artists, including Cecilia Bartoli, the late Ray Charles, Ravi Shankar, and Aretha Franklin. The hall was designed to give the audience a feeling of unusual intimacy with the performers—none of the 2,812 seats is more than 33m (108 ft.) from the stage. The hall closed for 5 months in 2002 for an extensive acoustic enhancement project that also increased the size of the stage. 60 Simcoe St. ℂ **416/593-4822.** www.roythomson.com. Tickets C$25–C$120 (US$18–US$84). Subway: St. Andrew.

Yonge-Dundas Square ⭐   Toronto's open-air entertainment venue is located across the street from the Eaton Centre. It opened with a splashy concert that drew 55,000 people in May 2003. Summer is its liveliest season: events include a Tuesday-night film series, and a Summer Serenades series featuring local musicians. When not in use for events, Yonge-Dundas is a public square where you can stroll or sit by its fountains. Year-round, this is home to the T.O. Tix discount tickets booth. Yonge and Dundas, southeast corner. ℂ **416/979-9960.** www. ydsquare.ca. Free admission. Subway: Dundas.

CLASSICAL MUSIC & OPERA

In addition to the major musical venues mentioned above, visitors can check to see what's playing at churches around town. Possibilities include **Trinity-St. Paul's Church,** 427 Bloor St. W. (ℂ **416/964-6337**), the home of the Toronto Consort, performers of early music; **St. Patrick's Church,** Dundas and McCaul streets (ℂ **416/483-0559**); and **St. James's Cathedral,** King Street East and Jarvis Street, where the Orpheus Choir sings. The **University of Toronto** (ℂ **416/978-3744** for the box office) offers a full range of instrumental and choral concerts and recitals in Walter Hall and the Macmillan Theatre. It's also worth checking out who's performing at the **Royal Conservatory of Music,** 273 Bloor St. W. (ℂ **416/408-2825**).

If you're a fan of new music, look out for the **Sonic Boom concert series** (ℂ **416/944-3100**), which produces new opera and other contemporary music.

Canadian Opera Company ⭐⭐   Canada's largest opera company, the sixth largest in North America, was founded in 1950. At the moment, it is staging its productions at the Hummingbird Centre from September to April, but it will have its own home in the fall of 2006, when the Four Seasons Centre for the Performing Arts will open. The Canadian Opera Company is currently in the process of staging the most ambitious work in opera, Wagner's monumental *Ring Cycle.* Four different directors are helming each of the operas: Atom Egoyan directed *Die Walküre,* which was presented first; Francois Girard will direct *Siegfried* during the 2005 season; and Tim Albery will take on *Götterdammerung* in early 2006. The first opera in the cycle, *Das Rheingold,* will be presented last, in the fall of 2006, and it will inaugurate the new opera house. 227 Front St. E.

C 416/872-2262 or 416/363-6671. www.coc.ca or www.ringcycle.ca. Tickets C$38–C$135 (US$27–US$95). Subway: Union.

Tafelmusik Baroque Orchestra *⭐* This internationally acclaimed group plays baroque compositions by the likes of Handel, Bach, and Mozart on authentic period instruments. Visiting musicians frequently join the 19 permanent performers. It gives a series of concerts at **Trinity/St. Paul's United Church,** 47 Bloor St. W., and stages other performances in Massey Hall and the Toronto Centre for the Arts (p. 204). 427 Bloor St. W. *C* 416/964-6337. www.tafel musik.org. Tickets C$15–C$65 (US$11–US$46). Subway: Yonge/Bloor for Trinity/St. Paul's; King for Massey Hall; North York Centre for Toronto Centre for the Arts.

Toronto Mendelssohn Choir *⭐* This world-renowned group first performed in Massey Hall in 1895; it now calls Roy Thomson Hall home. Its repertoire ranges from Verdi's *Requiem,* Bach's *St. Matthew Passion,* and Handel's *Messiah* to the soundtrack of *Schindler's List.* 60 Simcoe St. *C* 416/598-0422. www.tmchoir.org. Tickets C$29–C$90 (US$20–US$63). Subway: St. Andrew.

Toronto Symphony Orchestra The symphony performs at Roy Thomson Hall from September to June. Its repertoire ranges from classics to jazzy Broadway tunes to new Canadian works. In June and July, the symphony puts on free concerts at outdoor venues throughout the city. 60 Simcoe St. *C* 416/593-4828. www.tso.on.ca. Tickets C$15–C$75 (US$11–US$53). Subway: St. Andrew.

POP & ROCK MUSIC VENUES

Everyone comes to Toronto—even Madonna, who ran into some trouble with the obscenity police a while back. Tickets are available through **Ticketmaster** (*C* 416/870-8000). In addition to the previously mentioned **Hummingbird Centre** and **Massey Hall,** these are the major pop and rock music venues.

Air Canada Centre Better known as a sports venue (it's home to the Maple Leafs and the Raptors), the Air Canada Centre also hosts popular musical acts. Neil Young has performed here, as have Ozzy Osbourne, Justin Timberlake, and Mariah Carey. 40 Bay St. (at Lakeshore Blvd). *C* 416/815-5500. www.theaircanadacentre. com. Subway: Union, then LRT to Queens Quay.

Kingswood Music Theatre From May to September, Kingswood's open-air theater plays host to diverse, top-notch talent. Don Henley, the Beach Boys, the Scorpions, Barry Manilow, and Public Enemy have all played here. The bandshell is covered, but the lawn seats aren't—so beware in bad weather. Paramount Canada's Wonderland, 9580 Jane St., Vaughn. *C* 905/832-8131. Subway: Yorkdale or York Mills, then GO Express Bus to Wonderland. By car: Take Yonge St. north to Hwy. 401 and go west to Hwy. 400. Go north on Hwy. 400 to Rutherford Rd. exit and follow signs. From the north, exit at Major Mackenzie.

Molson Amphitheatre *⭐* This is a favorite summer spot because you can listen to music by the side of Lake Ontario. Most of the seating is on the lawn, and it's usually dirt-cheap. Ontario Place, 955 Lakeshore Blvd. W. *C* 416/314-9900. www.ontario place.com. Subway: Bathurst, then Bathurst streetcar south to Exhibition Place (last stop).

SkyDome The biggest venue in the city, SkyDome is where the biggest acts usually play. Ticket prices frequently rise into the stratosphere. This venue is about as intimate as a parking lot. If you're seated in the 400 (Upper SkyBox) or 500 (SkyDeck) levels, you'll be watching the show on the JumboTron, unless you bring your binoculars. And remember to steer clear of the seats next to the JumboTron, or you won't see anything at all. 1 Blue Jays Way. *C* 416/341-3663. www.skydome.com. Subway: Union.

DANCE

Dancemakers   Artistic director Serge Bennathan's nine-person company has gained international recognition for its provocative mix of stylized physical movement and theater. One of the best-known works in its repertoire is *Sable/Sand,* which won a Dora Award for choreography. Performing at the Case Goods Theatre in the Distillery Historic District, 55 Mill Street. ✆ 416/367-1800. www.dance makers.org. Tickets C$20–C$35 (US$14–US$25).

Danny Grossman Dance Company   The choreography of this local dance favorite is noted for its athleticism, theatricality, humor, and passionate social vision. The company performs both new works and revivals of modern-dance classics. Refreshing, fun, and exuberant. Performing at Premiere Dance Theatre, Queen's Quay Terminal, 207 Queens Quay W. ✆ 416/973-4000. Office: 511 Bloor St. W. ✆ 416/ 408-4543 or 416/531-5268. www.dgdance.org. Tickets C$22–C$38 (US$15–US$27).

National Ballet of Canada ★★   Perhaps the most beloved and famous of Toronto's cultural icons is the National Ballet of Canada. English ballerina Celia Franca launched the company in Toronto in 1951, and served as director, principal dancer, choreographer, and teacher. Over the years, the company has achieved great renown.

The company performs at the Hummingbird Centre in the fall, winter, and spring; tours internationally; and makes summer appearances before enormous crowds at the open theater at Ontario Place. Its repertoire includes the classics and works by Glen Tetley *(Alice),* Sir Frederick Ashton, and Jerome Robbins. James Kudelka, who has created *The Miraculous Mandarin, The Actress,* and *Spring Awakening,* was appointed artist-in-residence in 1991. Performing at Hummingbird Centre for the Performing Arts, 1 Front St. E. (✆ 416/872-2262), and Ontario Place, 955 Lakeshore Blvd. W. Office: 157 King St. E. ✆ 416/366-4846. www.national.ballet.ca. Tickets C$26–C$114 (US$18–US$80).

Toronto Dance Theatre   The city's leading contemporary-dance company burst onto the scene in 1972, bringing an inventive spirit and original Canadian dance to the stage. Director Christopher House joined in 1979 and has contributed more than 35 new works to the repertoire, including *Severe Clear* and the critically acclaimed *Nest.* Performing at Premiere Dance Theatre, Queen's Quay Terminal, 207 Queens Quay W. ✆ 416/973-4000. Office: 80 Winchester St. www.tdt.org. Tickets C$17–C$38 (US$12–US$27).

2 The Club & Music Scene

COMEDY CLUBS

Toronto must be one heck of a funny place. That would explain why a disproportionate number of comedians, including Jim Carrey and Mike Myers, hail from here. This is one true Toronto experience you shouldn't miss.

The Laugh Resort   If you get your kicks from incisive humor with occasional dashes of social commentary, this is your place. Gilbert Gottfried, Paula Poundstone, Ray Romano, and George Wallace have performed here. Most of the acts are stand-up solos, though there are sometimes inspired improvs, too. At the Holiday Inn on King, 370 King St. W. ✆ 416/364-5233. www.laughresort.com. Tickets C$7–C$18 (US$4.90–US$13). Subway: St. Andrew.

The Rivoli ★   While the Riv is well known for its music performances and poetry readings, the Monday night ALT.COMedy Lounge is its biggest draw. It features local and visiting stand-ups, and is best known as the place where the

> **Tips Good to Know: Nightlife**
>
> The drinking age in Ontario is 19, and most establishments enforce the law. Expect long queues on Friday and Saturday after 10pm at clubs in the downtown core. Bars and pubs that serve drinks only are open Monday through Saturday from 11am to 2am. Establishments that also serve food are open Sunday, too. If you're out at closing time, you'll find the subway shut down, but special late-night buses run along Yonge and Bloor streets. Major routes on streets such as College, Queen, and King operate all night. To find out what's on, see "Making Plans," earlier in this chapter.

Kids in the Hall got their start. Shows take place in the intimate 125-seat back room. See p. 97 in chapter 5 for a restaurant review. 332 Queen St. W. ✆ 416/597-0794. www.altcomedylounge.com. Pay-what-you-can admission. Subway: Osgoode.

Second City ★ This was where Mike Myers, otherwise known as Austin Powers, received his formal—and improvisational—comic training. Over the years, the legendary Second City has nurtured the likes of John Candy, Dan Aykroyd, Bill Murray, Martin Short, Andrea Martin, and Eugene Levy. It continues to turn out talented young actors. The scenes are always funny and topical, though the outrageous post-show improvs usually get the biggest belly laughs. Next door is the **Tim Simms Playhouse** (✆ **416/343-0022**), an intimate space that features fledgling local stand-up talent. 56 Blue Jays Way. ✆ 800/263-4485 or 416/343-0011. www.secondcity.com. Dinner and show from C$35 (US$25); show only C$13–C$25 (US$9.10–US$18). Reservations required. Subway: St. Andrew.

Yuk Yuk's Superclub Yuk Yuk's is Canada's original home of stand-up comedy. Comic Mark Breslin founded the place in 1976, inspired by New York's Catch a Rising Star and Los Angeles's Comedy Store. Some famous alumni include Jim Carrey, Harland Williams, Howie Mandel, and Norm MacDonald. Other headliners have included Jerry Seinfeld, Robin Williams, and Sandra Bernhard. Monday is new talent night, and Tuesday is all improv. There's another Yuk Yuk's in **Mississauga,** not far from Pearson International Airport (✆ **905/434-4985**). 224 Richmond St. W. ✆ 416/967-6425. www.yukyuks.com. Dinner and show from C$25 (US$18); show only C$5–C$15 (US$3.50–US$11). Subway: Osgoode.

COUNTRY, FOLK, ROCK & REGGAE

C'est What? About as cozy as the basement of a historic warehouse can be, this casual spot attracts young and old alike. It offers 28 draft beers and a broad selection of single malts. Half pub and half performance space, C'est What? has played host to the likes of Jewel, the Barenaked Ladies, and Rufus Wainwright before they hit the big time. If the nightly acoustic music doesn't suit, check out the abundant board games. 67 Front St. E. ✆ 416/867-9499. www.cestwhat.com. Cover C$2–C$10 (US$1.40–US$7). Subway: Union.

El Mocambo ★ This rock-'n'-roll institution was where the Rolling Stones rocked in the '70s, Elvis Costello jammed in the '80s, and Liz Phair mesmerized in the '90s. It has played peek-a-boo in recent years—it regularly closes and reopens. At the moment its usual Spadina Avenue digs are open again. In fact, they've been renovated and they have a new sound system. This is the Lazarus of the Toronto music scene. 464 Spadina Ave. ✆ 416/968-2001. Cover C$5–C$15 (US$3.50–US$11). Subway: Spadina, then streetcar south to College St.

The Horseshoe Tavern   This old, traditional venue has showcased the sounds of the decades: blues in the '60s, punk in the '70s, New Wave in the '80s, and everything from ska to rockabilly to Celtic to alternative rock in the '90s. It's the place that launched Blue Rodeo, the Tragically Hip, the Band, and Prairie Oyster, and staged the Toronto debuts of the Police and Hootie & the Blowfish. It attracts a cross section of 20- to 40-year-olds. 368 Queen St. W. ℭ **416/598-4753.** Cover from C$10 (US$7) for special concerts. Subway: Osgoode.

Lee's Palace   Versailles this ain't. Still, that hasn't deterred the crème de la crème of the alternative music scene. The Red Hot Chili Peppers, the Tragically Hip, and Alanis have performed here. Despite the graffiti grunge, Lee's does boast the best sight lines in town. The audience is young and rarely tires of slam dancing in the mosh pit in front of the stage. 529 Bloor St. W. ℭ **416/532-1598.** www.leespalace.com. Cover C$2–C$20 (US$1.40–US$14). Subway: Bathurst.

Phoenix Concert Theatre   One of the oldest dance halls in Toronto, the Phoenix attracts an all-ages, all-races crowd that includes straights and gays. As a rock venue, it showcases such artists as Screaming Headless Torsos and Patti Smith. On the weekends, it gets the crowds dancing with a mixture of retro, Latin, alternative, and funk. Thursday is gay night. 410 Sherbourne St. ℭ **416/323-1251.** Cover C$5–C$15 (US$3.50–US$11). Subway: College, then any streetcar east to Sherbourne St.

The Rivoli ★   Currently this is the club for an eclectic mix of performances, including grunge, blues, rock, jazz, comedy, and poetry reading. Holly Cole launched her career here, Tori Amos made her Toronto debut in the back room, and the Kids in the Hall still consider it home (see "Comedy Clubs," above). Shows begin at 8pm and continue until 2am. Upstairs, there's a billiards room and espresso bar. 332 Queen St. W. ℭ **416/597-0794.** Cover C$5–C$15 (US$3.50–US$11). Subway: Osgoode.

The Underground   Located in the basement of the Drake Hotel, this venue was designed with flexibility in mind. It's a good thing too, because the performers who appear here range from local and visiting musical acts to burlesque artists. At the Drake Hotel, 1150 Queen St. W. ℭ **416/531-5042.** Cover C$2–C$15 (US$1.40–US$11). Subway: Osgoode, then streetcar west to Beaconsfield.

JAZZ, RHYTHM & BLUES

In addition to the clubs listed below, check out **www.tojazz.com** for the latest listings.

Montréal Bistro & Jazz Club ★   Here's a great two-for-one deal. Top performers like Oscar Peterson (still performing after his stroke in 1993), Molly Johnson, Ray McShann, and George Shearing perform in a small room lit by rose-tinted lamps; the neighboring room (see p. 100 in chapter 5) is a Québecois eatery that features *tourtière* and smoked-meat sandwiches. 65 Sherbourne St. ℭ **416/363-0179.** www.montrealbistro.com. Cover C$8–C$20 (US$5.60–US$14). Subway: King, then any streetcar east to Sherbourne St.

Reservoir Lounge   This perennial favorite is a modern-day speakeasy. The cramped space—it seats only 100—is below street level, yet feels intimate rather than claustrophobic. Live jazz, whether Dixieland, New Orleans, or swing, belts out 6 nights a week. The epicenter for the swing dance craze in Toronto, this is still the place to watch glam hepcats groove. 52 Wellington St. E. ℭ **416/955-0887.** www.reservoirlounge.com. Cover C$5–C$7 (US$3.50–US$4.90). Subway: King.

The Rex   This watering hole has been drawing jazz fans since it first opened in 1951. Admittedly the decor hasn't changed much since the old days, but the sounds you'll find here are cutting edge. The Rex lures top local and international talent; Tuesday is the weekly jam night. 194 Queen St. W. ℂ 416/598-2475. Cover up to C$8 (US$5.60). Subway: Osgoode.

Southern Po Boys This new restaurant and club bills itself as the "Mardi Gras of the North." The menu is strictly rich Southern fare, and the sounds are bluesy and soulful. 159 Augusta St. ℂ 416/993-6768. Cover C$2–C$5 (US$1.40–US$3.50). Subway: Spadina, then LRT south to Dundas.

Top O' the Senator ⭐ Upstairs from the Torch bistro (see p. 98 in chapter 5) and the Senator Diner, this is one of the classiest jazz joints in town. Top performers, such as vocalist Molly Johnson and sax goddess Jane Bunnett, have graced the long, narrow space. Leathery couches and banquettes add to the lounge-lizard ambience. The third-floor humidor has a premium collection of Cuban smokes. 249 Victoria St. ℂ 416/364-7517. www.thesenator.com. Cover C$8–C$10 (US$5.60–US$7). Subway: Dundas.

DANCE CLUBS

Dance clubs come and go at an alarming pace—the hottest spot can close or turn into a decidedly unhip place almost overnight—so keep in mind that some of the spots listed below may have disappeared or changed entirely by the time you visit. Some things stay constant, though. Most clubs don't have much of a dress code, though "no jeans" rules are not uncommon. The clubs here are reasonably sure bets, but naturally the list won't include the hot spots that will have opened by the time you get to town. Be sure to check out the club listings in the free weekly *Now* or at www.martiniboys.com or www.torontolife.com for the latest and greatest.

Several primarily gay and lesbian clubs attract a sizable hetero contingent; one notable destination is **El Convento Rico** (p. 219).

Afterlife Formerly the Limelight, this is truly the club that won't die. People have been coming in from the suburbs forever to dance, play pool, and lounge, and they show no signs of stopping. No jeans. 250 Adelaide St. W. ℂ 416/593-6126. Cover C$5–C$10 (US$3.50–US$7). Subway: St. Andrew.

Bauhaus The unfinished metal-and-rivet decor gives this space an industrial feel. A young PVC-clad crowd dances to R&B and soul on the first floor, and to house and hip-hop on the second. 31 Mercer St. ℂ 416/977-9813. www.bauhaus nightclub.com. Cover C$10–C$15 (US$7–US$11). Subway: St. Andrew.

Berlin As sophisticated and soigné as it tries to be—it has a smashing dining room and Tuesday-night salsa lessons—Berlin is best known as an upscale meat market. A perennial favorite in the Young and Eligible—oops, Yonge and Eglinton—neighborhood, the crowd is a little older (late-20s–mid-40s) than at most of the downtown clubs. As the club's cheesy but memorable ad goes, this is where "man meets woman, not boy meets girl." Consider yourself warned. 2335 Yonge St. ℂ 416/489-7777. Cover C$10 (US$7). Subway: Eglinton.

The Docks ⭐ This vast waterfront party is a complex that books live entertainers like James Brown, Blue Rodeo, and the Pointer Sisters. The dance club boasts more than a dozen bars, the latest in lighting, and other party effects. Thursday night is foam fun (that is, beer). There's a restaurant and a full raft of sports facilities, too. 11 Polson St. (off Cherry St.). ℂ 416/461-DOCKS. Subway: Union, then taxi (about C$7/US$4.90) to Lakeshore Blvd. E. and Cherry St.

Easy & the Fifth This is the place to come if you're looking for a sophisticated crowd. The music is less frenzied, and you might even manage a conversation. The dance area is a loftlike space. In the back, there's a cigar bar furnished with Oriental rugs and comfortable armchairs, plus two pool tables. The dress code in effect is "smart casual" (collared shirts, no jeans or caps). 225 Richmond St. W. ⓒ 416/979-3000. Cover C$10–C$14 (US$7–US$9.80). Subway: Osgoode.

Indian Motorcycle Café and Lounge It's got a bar, pool tables, and a dance floor—who could ask for anything more? When the 20- and 30-something patrons tire of dancing to R&B and rock, they take refuge on one of the several comfy couches in the bar. 355 King St. W. ⓒ 416/593-6996. Subway: St. Andrew.

NASA Space cadets, unite: house music plays in a "Jetsons"-like futuristic space. The crowd here is too young to have seen *2001: A Space Odyssey* the first time around, but video screens offer glimpses. If you think a theme bar sounds like fun, this is your place; if you've been there and done that, go elsewhere. 609 Queen St. W. ⓒ 416/504-8356. Cover C$10 (US$7). Subway: Osgoode.

Sneaky Dee's Pool tables and Mexican food complement alternative rock spun by a DJ in the club upstairs until 1:30am. Downstairs, the bar is open until 3am on weekdays, 5am on weekends. 431 College St. ⓒ 416/603-3090. Subway: Queen's Park, then any streetcar west to Bathurst St.

3 The Bar Scene

The current night scene encompasses a flock of attractive bistros with billiard tables. You can enjoy cocktails, a reasonably priced meal, and a game of billiards in comfortable, aesthetically pleasing surroundings. The cigar bar is still in vogue, and most clubs have a humidor for the stogie set. Unlike dance clubs, the bars and lounges in Toronto are a pretty stable bunch.

BARS & LOUNGES

Boudoir ⚡ *Finds* Yes, Boudoir is a shop (p. 198), but its back room is a cocktail lounge. As retro-sexy as the vintage store it's attached to, the bar offers beauty treatments while you sip. Manicures and martinis actually go very well together, darlings. 990 Queen St. W. ⓒ 416/535-6600. Subway: Osgoode, then streetcar west to Ossington.

Cobalt Note to the Beautiful People: when you come to Toronto, this is where you'll want to spend your evenings. The level of attitude here may amuse some and annoy others, but the cocktails really are delicious (try the Jubilee). 426 College St. ⓒ 416/923-4456. Subway: Queen's Park.

Eau As noted in the dining review in chapter 5 (p. 86), Eau is a stylish place, and it's definitely a see-and-be-seen spot. The cocktail menu is astonishingly overpriced for Toronto: One martini—"the-big-eau," which mixes vodka, champagne, and ice wine—costs C$18 (US$13). Frankly, it wasn't one of the better martinis I've had. On the other hand, the setting is gorgeous and the service is excellent. 609 King St. W. ⓒ 416/203-9399. Subway: St. Andrew.

Laide ⚡ The name is a double entendre, and it won't be the only one you encounter at this sexy bar. Retro erotica images and a stripper's pole with a Use at Your Own Risk caveat help set the scene. Ooh, baby. 138 Adelaide St. E. ⓒ 416/850-2726. Subway: King.

Cueing Up

It's not hard to find a bar or a restaurant with a token pool table—it's a must-have accessory in some quarters—but real shark shops aren't so easy to come by. If you have a serious pool habit, try one of the following clubs.

Academy of Spherical Arts Okay, maybe this isn't your typical pool hall, but it has a great pedigree: The 465-sq.-m (5,000-sq.-ft.) space used to house billiard manufacturer Brunswick. Now it looks more like a turn-of-the-20th-century gentlemen's club (there are even a few antique pool tables). This is a popular celebrity-sighting spot, and the likes of Kevin Bacon, Minnie Driver, Dennis Hopper, and Lennox Lewis have been known to drop by. (Because the Academy hosts private parties, always call to make sure it's open.) 38 Hanna St. ✆ 416/532-2782. Subway: St. Andrew, then streetcar west along King St. to Atlantic Ave. and walk 1 block south.

Bar Italia & Billiards Downstairs, a young, trendy, good-looking crowd quaffs drinks or coffee and snacks on Italian sandwiches. Upstairs, guys and gals gather 'round the six pool tables. This scene is strictly for the flirtatious—serious game-players should go elsewhere. 582 College St. ✆ 416/535-3621. Subway: Queen's Park, then any streetcar west to Clinton St.

Charlotte Room *Billiards Digest* has called the Charlotte Room one of the 10 best billiard rooms in North America. It feels like an old-boys' club. In addition to the 10 tables, there's a pub-grub menu and, on occasion, live jazz music. 19 Charlotte St. ✆ 416/598-2882. Subway: St. Andrew.

The Corner Pocket Smack-dab in the middle of trendy Little Italy, there's The Corner Pocket. Unpretentious and low-key, the hall has 17 billiard tables (and one foosball table, in case you're interested). The big-screen television is always tuned to sports. 722 College St. ✆ 416/928-3540. Subway: Queen's Park, then any streetcar west to Crawford St.

Left Bank The lower-level bar at the Left Bank restaurant is a perennial favorite. It's especially inviting in winter, when the fire warms folks playing billiards or lolling on the comfortable banquettes. 567 Queen St. W. ✆ 416/504-1626. Subway: Osgoode, then any streetcar west to Bathurst.

Lobby ✦ *(Finds)* You'd be forgiven for mistaking this lounge for a gallery—because really, it's both. The airy white-on-white setting is opulent, and the crowd is dressed to match. The gallery features the work of up-and-coming local artists. 21 Avenue Rd. ✆ 416/964-0411. Subway: Bay or Museum.

Madison ✦ Affectionately known as the Maddy, this is a popular Annex bar. The crowd, which includes many students from nearby U of T, fills every floor and terrace. The newest development is the billiard room, with 10 tables. Everyone in the friendly crowd seems to know everyone else. 14 Madison Ave. ✆ 416/927-1722. Subway: Spadina.

Mint et Menthe ✦ Strictly for the been-there-done-that types, this lounge serves up excellent cocktails to a 30-something crowd. The setting is a little on the antiseptic side—white walls, white floors, white furniture—but the sexy music and communal couches give this bar some heat. 325 King St. W. ℭ **416/ 599-9909.** Subway: St. Andrew.

Panorama From this 51st-floor perch above Bloor and Bay, visitors can see north and south for 241km (149 miles)—at least on a clear day. Go for the lit skyline and the Latin music. Arrive early if you want a window seat. In the Manulife Centre, 55 Bloor St. W. ℭ **416/967-0000.** Subway: Bloor/Yonge.

The Pilot This watering hole dates to the early years of World War II. Regulars who go way back mix with a suited-up after-work crowd. It's an unpretentious place with pool tables and a wonderful rooftop patio. 22 Cumberland St. ℭ **416/923-5716.** Subway: Yonge/Bloor.

Shark City Forget *Jaws*—the sharks here sport well-cut suits and smoke Havanas. When not busy striking a pose, the young, uptown crowd shoots some pool at the basement tables. There's also a restaurant with basic pizza and pasta offerings and a small patio. 117 Eglinton Ave. E. ℭ **416/488-7899.** Subway: Eglinton.

Souz Dal ✩ Located in Little Italy, Souz Dal stands out. It's dark and intimate, painted deep purple and mustard, and decorated in exotic Moroccan fashion. Kilims adorn the walls; the bar is fashioned out of copper. Candles light the small, trellised patio. There's a great selection of martinis and margaritas, as well as tropical drinks, like the Havana (rum, guava juice, and lime). Thursday is acid-jazz night. 636 College St. ℭ **416/537-1883.** Subway: Queen's Park, then any streetcar west to Grace St.

Sutra ✩ *Finds* This intimate Little Italy bar has a subtly sexy vibe. The long slim space somehow manages not to feel claustrophobic. The heady cocktail of soft jazz music and champagne-infused drinks will leave you shaken and stirred. 612 College St. ℭ **416/537-8755.** Subway: Queen's Park, then any streetcar west to Clinton St.

PUBS & TAVERNS

Allen's Allen's sports a great bar that offers more than 80 beer selections and 164 single malts. Guinness is the drink of choice on Tuesday and Saturday nights, when folks reel and jig to the Celtic-Irish entertainment. 143 Danforth Ave. ℭ **416/463-3086.** Subway: Broadview.

The Amsterdam ✩ This brewpub is a beer-drinker's heaven, serving more than 200 labels as well as 30 types on draft. By 8pm the tables in the back are filled, and the long bar is jammed. In summer the patio is fun, too. 600 King St. W. (at Portland St.). ℭ **416/504-6882.** Subway: St. Andrew, then any streetcar west.

The Bishop and the Belcher This British-style pub offers 14 drafts on tap and a decent selection of single malts. The classic pub fare includes bangers and mash, shepherd's pie, and a ploughman's lunch. 361 Queen St. W. ℭ **416/591-2352.** Subway: Osgoode.

The Brunswick House This cavernous room, affectionately known as the Brunny House, is a favorite with University of Toronto students. Waiters carry trays of frothy suds between the Formica tables. Impromptu dancing to background music and pool and shuffleboard playing drown out the sound of at least two of the large-screen TVs, if not the other 18. This is an inexpensive place to down some beer. Upstairs, there's live-broadcast thoroughbred and harness racing from international tracks, including Hong Kong. 481 Bloor St. W. ℭ **416/ 964-2242.** Subway: Spadina or Bathurst.

Cameron House   Old and new hippies hang in the front room, with its rococo bar. Local bands try out in the back room. On Sunday, the Cameron serves an amazingly good brunch. 408 Queen St. W. ℭ 416/703-0811. Subway: Osgoode.

Dora Keogh Irish Pub ⚑   Created by the same crew that devised the perennially popular Allen's, Dora Keogh is an unusually elegant pub. The evening brings music, with local fiddlers and vocalists strutting their stuff; famous fiddler Natalie McMaster has been known to join in, as have various members of the Irish group the Chieftains. 141 Danforth Ave. ℭ 416/778-1804. Subway: Broadview.

Hotel Bars

Just as some of the best restaurants in the city are in hotels, so are some of the most charming watering holes. While I'm all for heading out and experiencing what a city has to offer, don't overlook these options in your home away from home.

Accents   This romantic wine bar offers many selections by the glass. The lighting is flattering, and a pianist provides jazz background music throughout the evening. Given how popular the Sutton Place is with the Hollywood glitterati, it's no surprise to see stars pass through the bar. At the Sutton Place Hotel, 955 Bay St. ℭ 416/924-9221. Subway: Museum or Wellesley.

The Consort Bar   This is a wonderfully clubby, old-fashioned bar. Not only does it boast comfortable wing chairs, but also its 2.5m-high (8-ft.) windows onto the street afford excellent people-watching. The suited-up crowd is generally more corporate than romantic—with some sweet exceptions. At Le Royal Meridien King Edward, 37 King St. E. ℭ 416/863-9700. Subway: King.

The Library Bar   This intimate, wood-paneled bar is the best place in the city to order a top-quality martini, which is served in a generous "fishbowl" glass. With its leopard-print couches and wingback chairs, it has an old-fashioned, almost colonial feel. I think it's one of the most romantic settings in town. At the Fairmont Royal York, 100 Front St. W. ℭ 416/863-6333. Subway: Union.

The Lounge   When the Drake Hotel opened in 2004, it was an immediate hit. No place in this West Queen West space is as perennially packed as its ground-floor lounge. The wallpaper looks not unlike a Rorschach test, which should make for interesting conversation over martinis. At the Drake Hotel, 1150 Queen St. W. ℭ 416/531-5042. Subway: Osgoode, then streetcar west to Beaconsfield.

The Roof   Author Mordecai Richler called this the only civilized spot in Toronto. It's an old literary haunt, with comfortable couches in front of a fireplace, and excellent drinks. The walls sport caricatures of members of Canada's literary establishment. The James Bond martini— vodka with a drop of lillet—is my personal favorite. The view from the outdoor terrace is one of the best in the city. At the Park Hyatt Toronto, 4 Avenue Rd. ℭ 416/924-5471. Subway: Museum or Bay.

The Rebel House ★   The youngish crowd here dresses in designer sportswear. This neighborhood pub draws them in with its impressive selection of microbrews and reasonably priced grub. 1068 Yonge St. ✆ 416/927-0704. Subway: Rosedale.

The Unicorn   This Celtic pub is named for the Irish Rovers song. Along with the usual pub staples, there's Irish stew and a great list of imported dark ales. It's a fun, relaxed place to unwind. 175 Eglinton Ave. E. ✆ 416/482-0115. Subway: Eglinton.

Wheat Sheaf Tavern   Designated a historic landmark, this is the city's oldest tavern—it's been in operation since 1849. For fans, eight screens show great moments in sports. The jukebox features 1,200 choices, and there are two pool tables and an outdoor patio. 667 King St. W. ✆ 416/504-9912. Subway: St. Andrew, then any streetcar west to Bathurst St.

WINE BARS

Centro   Upstairs is the gorgeous dining room (see p. 111 in chapter 5); downstairs is the upscale wine bar. A well-dressed crowd drops by for the convivial atmosphere, the gourmet pizzas and pastas, and the extensive selection of wines, which includes more than 600 varieties from around the globe. 2472 Yonge St. ✆ 416/483-2211. Subway: Eglinton.

Sottovoce ★   The name (which translates as "very softly") must be an inside joke, because the decibel level here is outrageous. This wine bar is still a great find, not least because it serves truly inspired focaccia sandwiches and salads. 595 College St. ✆ 416/536-4564. Subway: Queen's Park, then any streetcar west to Clinton St.

4 The Gay & Lesbian Scene

Toronto's large, active gay and lesbian community has created a varied nightlife scene. At some nightspots, such as the **Phoenix Concert Theatre,** one night a week is gay night (in this case, Thurs). See "Country, Folk, Rock & Reggae," earlier in this chapter.

Bar 501   This bar is popular with gay men for its Sunday evening drag shows, which often attract crowds that watch from the sidewalk through the large front window. There's also Saturday afternoon bingo with the infamous Sister Bedelia. 501 Church St. ✆ 416/944-3272. Subway: Wellesley.

The Barn/The Stables   This is one of the city's oldest gay bars. The male-only crowd keeps the second-story dance floor jammed. There are afternoon underwear parties on Sunday, and sex videos, too. The favored look is denim with occasional ranch-style allusions (you'll see a few spurs). There's also an on-site leather shop selling fetish gear and clothing. 418 Church St. ✆ 416/977-4702. Subway: College.

Byzantium ★★ _Value_   An attractive but low-key bar-restaurant, Byzantium attracts an affable gay and straight crowd. The cocktails are both excellent and reasonably priced (you must try either the Red Velvet or the Black Orchid; either is C$7/US$4.90). You can follow drinks with dinner in the adjacent dining room, where the cooking is top-notch. 499 Church St. ✆ 416/922-3859. Subway: Wellesley.

Crews/Tango   Located in a renovated Victorian house, this two-in-one club boasts a large outdoor patio. Crews is a gay bar for men, and it is known for its pubby atmosphere and its drag shows, which start at 11pm on Wednesday through Sunday. The adjoining Tango bar draws a lesbian crowd. It hosts Tuesday- and Thursday-night karaoke; on Friday and Saturday nights, the women head for the dance floor. 508 Church St. © 416/972-1662. Subway: Wellesley.

El Convento Rico ★★ *Finds*   The Latin beat beckons one and all—straight, gay, and otherwise—to this lively club. If you don't know how to samba, you can pick up the basics at the Friday- and Sunday-night dance lessons, but if you don't learn, no one on the jam-packed dance floor will notice. There's a substantial hetero contingent that comes out just to watch the fabulous drag queens—and don't be surprised if you encounter a bachelorette party in progress. 750 College St. © 416/588-7800. www.elconventorico.com. Cover C$5 (US$3.50) or less. Subway: Queen's Park, then streetcar west.

Foxy's & Coyote's ★   This a very popular lesbian bar. It's in the same space that the longtime favorite Pope Joan was in, but Foxy's is under new management and its ambience is different. Think less cozy, more sexy. The main floor has the martini bar; upstairs is the main dance floor as well as a pool table and games area. 547 Parliament St. (at Winchester St.). © 416/929-1695. Subway: Wellesley, then any streetcar east to Parliament St., and walk 2 blocks south.

Sailor   This bar is attached to Woody's (see below), but has a livelier atmosphere; unlike Woody's, you won't see many women here. Every Thursday there's a Best Chest competition, and on Sunday the draw is the drag show. In the evening, a DJ spins an assortment of dance and alternative tunes. 465 Church St. © 416/972-0887. Subway: Wellesley.

Slack Alice   This incredibly popular bar draws a gay and lesbian crowd, with more than a few straights. The menu features home-style comfort food; on weekend evenings, a DJ gets the crowd on its feet. 562 Church St. © 416/969-8742. Subway: Wellesley.

Woody's ★   A friendly, popular local bar, Woody's attracts mainly men but welcomes women; the crowd is a mix of gay and hetero. It's a popular meeting spot, especially for weekend brunch. 467 Church St. (south of Wellesley St.). © 416/972-0887. www.woodystoronto.com. Subway: Wellesley.

Zelda's ★ *Finds*   This is a don't-miss spot in Toronto's Gay Village. Yes, the queues can be long—but when you get inside, it will be worth it. Zelda's has great food and a great sense of humor—hopefully you'll be there for one of the many theme nights (love those nurse outfits). 542 Church St. © 416/922-2526. Subway: Wellesley.

5 Cinemas & Movie Houses

There is no shortage of movie theaters—in fact, monster megaplexes are the rage at the moment. Check *Now, Eye,* www.toronto.com, or one of the daily newspapers for listings. *One caveat:* The Eaton Centre has lots of movies playing, but its theaters are maybe three times the size of a suburban living room. That's just not good.

Carlton Cinemas   Home to the subtitled set, the Carlton plays films—many of them superb—that frequently don't see the light of day anywhere else. Many of the offerings originate in France, Italy, Russia, or China; there's also a smattering of independent North American films. Buy tickets early on weekends. 20 Carlton St. © 416/598-2309. Tickets C$10 (US$7). Tues discounts. Subway: College.

Sweet Treats: Toronto's Dessert Cafes

Nightlife doesn't have to mean high culture, barhopping, or anything in between. It doesn't even mean you have to stop eating. Here are some of the city's most agreeable places to satisfy a sweet tooth and do some people watching.

Caffe Demetre In the heart of Greektown on the Danforth, Demetre is known for its Old World ambience as well as its sweets: Belgian waffles, oversize sundaes, cakes, tortes, and baklava. It's popular at all hours of the evening with a casual crowd, and on weekends it draws families. Closing time is midnight Sunday through Thursday, and 3am Friday and Saturday. 400 Danforth Ave. ℰ **416/778-6654**. Subway: Broadview.

Desserts by Phipps The cafe serves salads and sandwiches, but the decadent desserts draw the crowds. Cappuccino chiffon cake is a direct hit, as are the moist but not gooey apple confections. 420 Eglinton Ave. W. ℰ **416/481-9111**. Subway: Eglinton.

Dufflet Pastries ★ On menus around town, you'll sometimes see mention of "desserts by Dufflet." *Divine* is the word that best applies to these confections. Owner Dufflet Rosenberg bakes some of the most delectable tortes, tarts, and pastries in the city. The problem is deciding where to start. Chocolate raspberry truffle? Cappuccino dacquoise? Your call. There are a few selections for people with gluten or nut allergies, and the cafe also serves light fare. 787 Queen St. W. ℰ **416/504-2870**. www.dufflet.com. Subway: Osgoode, then any streetcar west to Euclid Ave.

Cinematheque Ontario This organization shows the best in contemporary cinema. The programs include directors' retrospectives, plus new films from France, Germany, Japan, Bulgaria, and other countries that you won't find in the first-run theaters around town. Screenings at Art Gallery of Ontario, 317 Dundas St. W. (between McCaul and Beverley sts.). Office: 2 Carlton St. ℰ **416/967-7371** or 416/923-3456 (box office). Tickets C$10 (US$7) adults, C$5.50 (US$3.85) seniors and students. Subway: St. Patrick.

The Docks ★ *Kids* Feeling nostalgic for the 1950s? This vast entertainment complex on the waterfront has its own drive-in movie theater. It has a 500-car capacity, and it screens double features of current blockbusters during the summer. Show up around 8:30pm to get a prime spot to park. 11 Polson St. (off Cherry St.). ℰ **416/461-DOCKS**. Tickets: C$13 (US$9.10) adults, C$6.50 (US$4.55) seniors, C$4 (US$2.80) children 12 and under. Subway: Union, then taxi (about C$7/US$4.90) to Lakeshore Blvd. E. and Cherry St.

Paramount *Kids* It's a giant megaplex, true, but it's a really nice one. If you're going to see a blockbuster, it may as well be on a giant screen in a theater with plush comfy seats, right? 259 Richmond St. W. ℰ **416/368-6089**. Tickets C$12 (US$8.40). Tues discounts. Subway: Osgoode.

6 Coffeehouses

While Starbucks has certainly staked out territory in Toronto, the Canadian chain the **Second Cup** is holding its ground. It offers a full range of flavored

Greg's Ice Cream ★★ *Finds*　One taste of Greg's homemade ice cream will turn you into an addict. (I should know—I've been one since high school!) Different flavors are available each day, and the staff is generous about handing out samples. It's hard for me to pick one favorite flavor, but the roasted marshmallow would definitely be up there. 200 Bloor St. W. *©* 416/961-4734. Subway: Museum or St. George.

Just Desserts　This cafe stays open practically around the clock on weekends for those in need of a sugar fix. Around 40 desserts are available—as many as 12 different cheesecakes, 10 or so pies, plus an array of gâteaux, tortes, and meringues. All cost around C$6 (US$4.20). 555 Yonge St. (at Wellesley). *©* 416/963-8089. Subway: Wellesley.

Senses Bakery ★★ *Finds*　It's always seemed strange to me that the Eaton Centre lacked a good cafe. Well, now there's one just across the street. There is some light, lunch-appropriate food here too, but the real draw is the divine collection of pastry confections and chocolates. 2 Queen St. E. *©* 416/364-7303. Subway: Queen.

Sicilian Ice Cream Company　This old-fashioned ice-cream parlor is Toronto's top purveyor of Italian *gelati*. The wonderful patio is open in the summer. 712 College St. *©* 416/531-7716. Subway: Queen's Park, then streetcar west.

coffees and espresso varieties, plus cakes, muffins, croissants, and gift items. Another chain, **Timothy's,** invites you to pour your own selection from about 10 varieties. My favorite coffeehouses are all independents, though.

Cafe Diplomatico ★　One of the oldest cafes in Toronto, this Little Italy gem has mosaic marble floors, wrought-iron chairs, and an extra-large sidewalk patio. Many longtime area residents get their caffeine fix here in the morning; the patio attracts a trendier crowd. 594 College St. *©* 416/534-4637. Subway: Queen's Park.

Daily Express Café　Near the student ghetto in the Annex neighborhood, this lively cafe draws most of its crowd from the nearby University of Toronto. 280 Bloor St. W. *©* 416/944-3225. Subway: St. George.

Future Bakery　This rambling cafe attracts an artsy crowd with fine breads and a selection of coffees. Would-be writers scribble away in well-lit corners. 483 Bloor St. W. *©* 416/922-5875. Subway: Spadina.

Gypsy Co-Op　Coffee is not the only king here. Many teas and herbal infusions (for everything from stress to colds and flu) are available, as are super-rich brownies. 815 Queen St. W. *©* 416/703-5069. Subway: Osgoode, then any streetcar west to Manning.

Lettieri ★　The house rule is that after 7 minutes, a pot of coffee is no longer fresh. This place takes the bean seriously. In addition to the wide range of coffees, there are focaccia sandwiches, tarts, cookies, and pastries. 94 Cumberland St. *©* 416/515-8764. Subway: Bay.

10

Side Trips from Toronto

Here's a classic good news/bad news situation: Some of the greatest attractions in this region are within a 2-hour drive of Toronto. They're easily accessible, which is a good thing, but if you're trying to shoehorn all of the sights into a short stay . . . you've got some serious choices to make. This chapter describes the three best—the theater town of Stratford, the wine region of Niagara-on-the-Lake, and the golf/spa/sailing resort retreat of the Muskokas—as well as the less well-known city of Hamilton.

For information about the areas surrounding Toronto, contact **Tourism** **Ontario** (© **800/ONTARIO** or 416/314-0944; www.travelinx.com), or visit the travel center in the Eaton Centre on Level 1 at Yonge and Dundas streets. It's open Monday through Friday from 10am to 9pm, Saturday from 9:30am to 6pm, and Sunday from noon to 5pm. Another good resource is the **Southern Ontario Tourism Organization** (© **800/267-3399** or www.soto.on.ca), which has a travel-planning booklet, an e-mail newsletter, and an informative website.

1 Stratford ⭐

145km (90 miles) NW of Toronto

The Stratford Festival has humble roots. The idea of a theater was launched in 1953 when director Tyrone Guthrie lured the great Sir Alec Guinness to the stage here. Whether Sir Alec knew the "stage" was set up in a makeshift tent is another question, but his acclaimed performance gave the festival the push—and press—it needed to become an annual tradition. Since then the Stratford Festival has grown to become one of the most famous in North America, and its four theaters (no more tents!) have put this charming and scenic town on the map. While visitors will notice the Avon River and other sights named in honor of the Bard, they may not realize that Stratford has another claim to fame. It's home to one of Canada's best cooking schools, which makes dining at many of the spots in town a delight.

> **Tips** **A Helpful Planning Tool**
>
> Each week **Outside Toronto** (www.outsidetoronto.com) suggests things to see and do within a 2-hour drive of the city: antiques shows, farmers' markets, recreational events. The "Places to Go" section directs you to museums, festivals, and charming little towns. The site provides maps, too.

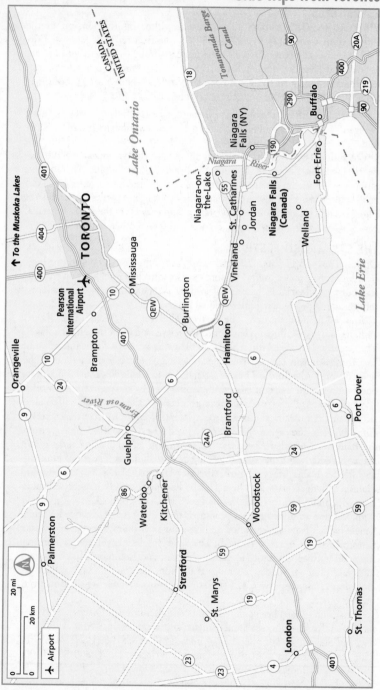

ESSENTIALS

VISITOR INFORMATION For first-rate visitor information, go to the **Information Centre** (© 519/273-3352) by the river on York Street at Erie. From May to early November, it's open Sunday through Wednesday from 9am to 5pm, and Thursday through Saturday from 9am to 8pm. At other times, contact **Tourism Stratford,** 47 Downie St., Stratford, ON N5A 1W7 (© **800/561-SWAN** or 519/271-5140; www.city.stratford.on.ca).

GETTING THERE Driving from Toronto, take Highway 401 west to Interchange 278 at Kitchener. Follow Highway 8 west onto Highway 7/8 to Stratford.

VIA Rail (© **800-VIA-RAIL** or 416/366-8411; www.viarail.ca) operates several trains daily along the Toronto–Kitchener–Stratford route. The toll-free number works within North America; if you're traveling from overseas, you can book your rail travel in advance through one of Via's general sales agents. There's a long list of local agents on www.viarail.ca, and they cover the U.K., Australia, New Zealand, Hong Kong, Japan, France, and several other countries.

THE STRATFORD FESTIVAL ☆

On July 13, 1953, *Richard III,* starring Sir Alec Guinness, was staged in a huge tent. From that modest start, Stratford's artistic directors have built on the radical, but faithfully classic, base established by Tyrone Guthrie to create a repertory theater with a glowing international reputation.

Stratford has four theaters. The **Festival Theatre,** 55 Queen St., in Queen's Park, has a dynamic thrust stage (a modern re-creation of an Elizabethan stage). The recently renovated **Avon Theatre,** 99 Downie St., has a classic proscenium. The **Tom Patterson Theatre,** Lakeside Drive, is an intimate 500-seat theater. The newest venue—the **Studio Theatre** (attached to the Avon Theatre)—opened its doors in 2002; the 278-seat space will be used for new and experimental works.

World famous for its Shakespearean productions, the festival also offers classic and modern theatrical masterpieces. Recent productions have included *My Fair Lady, The Hunchback of Notre Dame,* and *The King and I.* Offerings from the Bard have included *Romeo and Juliet, Richard III,* and *The Taming of the Shrew.* Sir Alec wasn't the company's only famous alumnus: The list of luminaries includes Dame Maggie Smith, Sir Peter Ustinov, Alan Bates, Christopher Plummer, Irene Worth, and Julie Harris. Present company members include Tom McCamus, Cynthia Dale, Colm Feore, and Lucy Peacock.

In addition to attending plays, visitors may enjoy the "Celebrated Writers Series," which features renowned authors (some of whom have penned works performed at the Stratford Festival). The list of speakers has included Margaret Atwood, Michael Ondaatje, Joyce Carol Oates, and Rohinton Mistry. All lectures take place on Sunday mornings at the Tom Patterson Theatre or the Studio Theatre, and they cost C$24 (US$17) per person; tickets are available from the box office.

The season usually begins in May and continues through October, with performances Tuesday through Sunday nights and matinees on Wednesday, Saturday, and Sunday. Ticket prices range from C$39 to C$100 (US$27–US$70), with special prices for students and seniors. For tickets, call © **800/567-1600;** visit www.stratfordfestival.ca; or write to the Stratford Festival, P.O. Box 520, Stratford, ON N5A 6V2. Tickets are also available in the United States and Canada at Ticketmaster outlets. The box office opens for mail and fax orders in late January; telephone and in-person sales begin in late February.

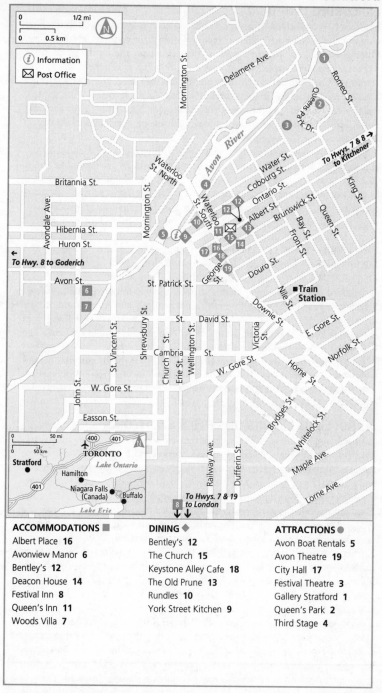

0 1/2 mi
0 0.5 km

ⓘ Information
✉ Post Office

Romeo St.
Delamere Ave.
Queens Pk.
Mornington St.
Avon River
To Hwys. 7 & 8 to Kitchener
Water St.
Cobourg St.
Ontario St.
Albert St.
Brunswick St.
King St.
Britannia St.
Waterloo St. North
Waterloo St. South
Mornington St.
Avondale Ave.
Hibernia St.
Huron St.
← To Hwy. 8 to Goderich
Bay St.
Queen St.
Front St.
Douro St.
Nile St.
■ Train Station
Avon St.
St. Patrick St.
George St.
Downie St.
E. Gore St.
Norfolk St.
Shrewsbury St.
St.
David St.
St. Vincent St.
St.
Church St.
Erie St.
Wellington St.
Victoria St.
W. Gore St.
Home St.
Cambria
St.
John St.
W. Gore St.
Easson St.
Railway Ave.
Dufferin St.
Brydges St.
Whitelock St.
Maple Ave.
Lorne Ave.
To Hwys. 7 & 19 to London

0 50 mi
0 50 km
400 401
TORONTO
Lake Ontario
Stratford
Hamilton
401
Niagara Falls (Canada)
Buffalo
Lake Erie

ACCOMMODATIONS ■
Albert Place **16**
Avonview Manor **6**
Bentley's **12**
Deacon House **14**
Festival Inn **8**
Queen's Inn **11**
Woods Villa **7**

DINING ◆
Bentley's **12**
The Church **15**
Keystone Alley Cafe **18**
The Old Prune **13**
Rundles **10**
York Street Kitchen **9**

ATTRACTIONS ●
Avon Boat Rentals **5**
Avon Theatre **19**
City Hall **17**
Festival Theatre **3**
Gallery Stratford **1**
Queen's Park **2**
Third Stage **4**

EXPLORING THE TOWN

Stratford has a wealth of attractions that complement the theater offerings. It's a compact town, easily negotiable on foot. Within sight of the Festival Theatre, **Queen's Park** has picnic spots beneath tall shade trees and by the Avon River. There are also some superb dining and good shopping prospects.

Past the Orr Dam and the 90-year-old stone bridge, through a rustic gate, lies a very special park, the **Shakespearean Garden.** In the formal English garden, where a sundial measures the hours, you can relax and contemplate the herb and flower beds and the tranquil river lagoon, and muse on a bust of Shakespeare by Toronto sculptor Cleeve Horne.

If you turn right onto Romeo Street North from highways 7 and 8 as you come into Stratford, you'll find the **Gallery Stratford,** 54 Romeo St. (✆ **519/271-5271;** www.gallerystratford.on.ca). It's in a historic building on the fringes of Confederation Park. Since it opened in 1967, it has mounted fine Canadian-focused shows, often oriented to the theater arts. Its hours change with the seasons, but mid-May through late September it's open from 9am to 5pm (call ahead for hours for other times of year). Admission is approximately C$8 (US$5.60) for adults, C$6 (US$4.20) for seniors and students 12 and up, and free for children 11 and under. Admission prices change with the special exhibits on display, and are usually discounted during fall and winter.

Stratford is a historic town, dating to 1832. Ninety-minute **guided tours of Stratford** take place Monday through Saturday in July and August, and on Saturday only in May, June, September, and October. They leave at 9:30am from the visitor's booth by the river, and are free of charge (call ahead to confirm). The visitor's booth also has maps available for self-guided tours.

Paddleboat, kayak, and canoe rentals are available at the **Boathouse,** behind and below the information booth. It's open daily from 9am until dusk in summer. Contact **Avon Boat Rentals,** 40 York St. (✆ **519/271-7739**). There's also a boat, the **Juliet III,** which offers scenic half-hour tours.

A COUPLE OF EXCURSIONS FROM STRATFORD

Only half an hour or so from Stratford, the twin cities of **Kitchener** and **Waterloo** have two drawing cards: the **Farmer's Market** and the famous 9-day **Oktoberfest.** The cities still have a German-majority population (of German descent, and often German speaking), and many citizens are Mennonites. On Saturday starting at 6am, you can sample shoofly pie, apple butter, kochcase, and other Mennonite specialties at the market in the Market Square complex, at Duke and Frederick streets in Kitchener. For additional information, contact the **Kitchener–Waterloo Area Visitors and Convention Bureau,** 2848 King St. E., Kitchener, ON N2A 1A5 (✆ **519/748-0800;** www.kw-visitor.on.ca). It's open from 9am to 5pm weekdays only in winter, daily in summer. For Oktoberfest information, check out www.oktoberfest.ca, call ✆ **888/294-HANS** or 519/570-HANS, or write to **K-W Oktoberfest,** P.O. Box 1053, 17 Benton St., Kitchener, ON N2G 4G1.

Eight kilometers (5 miles) north of Kitchener is the town of **St. Jacobs.** It has close to 100 shops in venues such as a converted mill, silo, and other factory buildings. For those interested in learning more about the Amish-Mennonite way of life, the **Meetingplace,** 33 King St. (✆ **519/664-3518**), shows a short film about it (daily in summer, weekends only in winter). Ironically enough, there's also a **St. Jacobs Outlet Mall** (surely not run by the Amish!), filled with discounted Levi's jeans, Paderno cookware, Liz Claiborne and Jones New York

---

Finds **An Open-Air Art Gallery**

Museums are grand, but who wants to spend a glorious summer day indoors? Thanks to the **Art in the Park** (© **519/272-0429**; www.artinthe parkstratford.com), you can have both. On Wednesdays, Saturdays, and Sundays from June through September, regional artists gather at Lakeside Drive and Front Street and put on a show from 9am to 5pm, weather permitting. The artists and artisans work in various media, so you'll find paintings, sculptures, ceramics, jewelry, and glass, among other things. While many of the works are for sale, this isn't just a market: the artists are selected through a juried process, and they are required to demonstrate their medium as part of their display.

---

clothing, Cadbury's chocolate, and Royal Doulton giftware. It's located at 25 Benjamin Road, and it's open Monday through Friday from 9:30am to 9pm, Saturday 8:30am to 6pm, and Sunday noon to 5pm (closed Jan 1 and Dec 25). Call © **519/888-0138** for more information.

WHERE TO STAY

When you book your theater tickets, you can book your accommodations at no extra charge. Options range from guest homes for as little as C$40 (US$28) to first-class hotels charging more than C$125 (US$88). Call the **Stratford Festival Accommodation Bureau** at © **800/567-1600** for information (note that some accommodations are only open to festival-goers, and these can only be booked through the Accommodation Bureau). You can also get information about where to stay from **Tourism Stratford** at © **800/561-SWAN.** Rooms in Stratford are most expensive in June, July, and August; it's easier to get a discount from fall to spring.

HOTELS & MOTELS

Albert Place Around the corner from the Avon Theatre, the Albert Place has large rooms with high ceilings. Furnishings are simple and modern. Some units have separate sitting rooms. Rates include coffee, tea, and doughnuts served in the lobby in the early morning.

23 Albert St., Stratford, ON N5A 3K2. © 519/273-5800. Fax 519/273-5008. 34 units. C$90–C$125 (US$63–US$88) double; C$165 (US$116) suite. Rates include small breakfast. MC, V. Pets accepted. **Amenities:** Restaurant; dry cleaning. *In room:* A/C, TV.

Bentley's *Finds* This inn enjoys an excellent location at the center of town. The soundproof rooms are luxurious duplex suites with efficiency kitchens. Period English furnishings and attractive drawings, paintings, and costume designs on the walls make for a pleasant ambience. Five units have skylights. The adjoining British-style pub, also called Bentley's, is popular with festival actors (see "Where to Dine," below).

99 Ontario St., Stratford, ON N5A 3H1. © 800/361-5322 or 519/271-1121. www.bentleys-annex.com. 13 units. Apr–mid-Nov C$160 (US$112) double; mid-Nov–June C$80 (US$56) double. Extra person C$20 (US$14). AE, DC, MC, V. Free parking. **Amenities:** Pub. *In room:* A/C, TV, kitchen, fridge, coffeemaker, hair dryer.

Festival Inn The Festival Inn sits outside town off highways 7 and 8, on 8 hectares (20 acres) of landscaped grounds. This is the largest full-service hotel in

Stratford. The place has an Old English air, with stucco walls, Tudor-style beams, and high-backed red settees in the lobby. Tudor style prevails throughout the large, motel-style rooms. All have wall-to-wall carpeting, matching bedspreads, floor-to-ceiling drapes, and reproductions of old masters on the walls. Some units have charming bay windows with sheer curtains, and all rooms in the main building, north wing, and annex have refrigerators. The indoor pool has an outdoor patio.

1144 Ontario St. (P.O. Box 811), Stratford, ON N5A 6W1. ✆ **800/463-3581** or 519/273-1150. Fax 519/273-2111. www.festivalinnstratford.com. 182 units. C$135–C$205 (US$95–US$144) double. Extra person C$10 (US$7). Winter discounts (about 30%) available. AE, DC, MC, V. Free parking. **Amenities:** Dining room; coffee shop; indoor pool; Jacuzzi; sauna. In room: A/C, TV, fridge, coffeemaker.

The Queen's Inn   The Queen's Inn occupies one of the best locations in Stratford—it's right in the town center. The historic building is about a century and a half old, but the guest rooms have a fresh look every year, after the owners use the winter months for refurbishing. The English-style Boar's Head Pub is on the premises; there's also a restaurant, Henry's, that serves breakfast, lunch, and dinner during the summer (winter hours limited and variable). Breakfast is included in the room rates.

161 Ontario St., Stratford, ON N5A 3H3. ✆ **800/461-6450** or 519/271-1400. Fax 519/271-7373. www.queensinnstratford.ca. 32 units. Mid-Apr to mid-Nov C$85–C$130 (US$60–US$91) double, C$165–C$225 (US$116–US$158) suite; mid-Nov to mid-Apr 16 C$69 (US$48) double, from C$85 (US$60) suite. Rates include breakfast. AE, DC, MC, V. Free parking. Pets accepted. **Amenities:** Restaurant; pub; business center; limited room service; babysitting; same-day dry cleaning. In room: A/C, TV, hair dryer.

BED & BREAKFASTS

For more information on the bed-and-breakfast scene, contact **Tourism Stratford,** 47 Downie St., Stratford, ON N5A 1W7 (✆ **800/561-SWAN** or 519/271-5140; www.city.stratford.on.ca). The office is open Monday through Friday from 9am to 5pm. There are also extensive bed-and-breakfast listings on www.bbcanada.com.

Avonview Manor   In a 1916 Edwardian house on a quiet street, Avonview Manor offers attractive individually furnished rooms. Three have queen-size beds; the suite contains four singles, a sitting room, and a private bath. Breakfast is served in a bright dining room that overlooks the garden. Guests have the use of a kitchen. The living room is very comfortable, particularly in winter, when guests can cozy up in front of the stone fireplace. Smoking is allowed only on the porch. There's also an in-ground pool and Jacuzzi.

63 Avon St., Stratford, ON N5A 5N5. ✆ **519/273-4603.** www.bbcanada.com/avonview. 4 units, 2 with private bathroom. C$90–C$110 (US$63–US$77) double; C$120–C$160 (US$84–US$112) suite. Rates include full breakfast. No credit cards; personal checks accepted. Street parking. **Amenities:** Outdoor pool; Jacuzzi; sauna. In room: A/C; no phone.

Deacon House ⭐   This is a great location, within walking distance of everything. Dianna Hrysko and Mary Allen have restored Deacon House, a shingle-style structure built in 1907. Rooms are decorated in country style, with iron-and-brass beds, quilts, pine hutches, oak rockers, and rope-style rugs. The comfortable living room holds a fireplace, TV, wingback chairs, and a sofa. The main-floor guest kitchen is a welcome convenience, as is the second-floor sitting and reading room. The entire house is nonsmoking, but allergy sufferers should know that there are pets in the house.

101 Brunswick St., Stratford, ON N5A 3L9. ✆ **877/825-6374** or 519/273-2052. Fax 519/273-3784. www.bbcanada.com/1152.html. 6 units. C$110–C$140 (US$77–US$98) double. Extra person C$35 (US$25). Rates include full breakfast. Off-season packages available. MC, V. Free parking. In room: A/C, hair dryer, no phone.

Woods Villa ★ This handsome 1870 house is home to Ken Vinen, who collects and restores early "musical amusement devices" from phonographs to vintage jukeboxes; the 30 pieces around the house are all in working order. Five rooms have fireplaces, and the handsome suite boasts a canopy bed. Rooms are large and offer excellent value, and there is more emphasis on customer service than you'd normally expect at a B&B. Morning coffee is delivered to your room, followed by breakfast prepared to order and served in the dining room. There's an attractively landscaped outdoor pool and terrace. House policies are no smoking, no children, and no pets (there are several birds, including cockatoos and macaws, in residence).

62 John St. N., Stratford, ON N5A 6K7. © 519/271-4576. www.woodsvilla.orc.ca. 6 units. C$195–C$250 (US$137–US$175) double. Rates include full breakfast. MC, V. Street parking. Children not allowed. **Amenities:** Outdoor pool. *In room:* A/C, TV, hair dryer, iron.

A NEARBY PLACE TO STAY & DINE

Langdon Hall ★★ This elegant house stands at the head of a curving, tree-lined drive. Eugene Langdon Wilks, a great-grandson of John Jacob Astor, completed it in 1902. It remained in the family until 1987, when its transformation into a small country-house hotel began. Today, its Langdon Hall is a Relais & Châteaux property, and its 81 hectares (200 acres) of lawns, gardens, and woodlands make for an ideal retreat. The main house, of red brick with classical pediment and Palladian-style windows, has a beautiful symmetry. Throughout, the emphasis is on comfort rather than grandiosity. The luxurious on-site spa offers a complete range of treatments. Most rooms surround the cloister garden. Each is individually decorated; most have fireplaces. The furnishings consist of handsome reproduction antiques, mahogany wardrobes, ginger-jar porcelain lamps, and armchairs upholstered with luxurious fabrics. The property has a croquet lawn and cross-country ski trails.

The light, airy dining room serves fine regional cuisine. Main courses run C$22 to C$32 (US$15–US$22). Tea is served on the veranda, and there's a bar.

R.R. 3, Cambridge, ON N3H 4R8. © 800/268-1898 or 519/740-2100. Fax 519/740-8161. www.langdonhall. ca. 49 units. C$259–C$699 (US$181–US$489) double. Rates include full breakfast. Spa packages from C$180 (US$126). AE, DC, MC, V. Free parking. From Hwy. 401, take exit 275 south, turn right onto Blair Rd., follow signs. Pets accepted. **Amenities:** Dining room; bar; outdoor pool; tennis courts; health club; spa; Jacuzzi; sauna; concierge; business center; 24-hr. room service; babysitting; dry cleaning; billiard room. *In room:* A/C, TV, dataport, coffeemaker, hair dryer, iron.

WHERE TO DINE
VERY EXPENSIVE

The Church ★★ CONTINENTAL The Church is simply stunning. The organ pipes and the altar of the 1873 structure are intact, along with the vaulted roof, carved woodwork, and stained-glass windows. You can sit in the nave or the side aisles and dine to appropriate sounds—usually Bach. Fresh flowers and elegant table settings further enhance the experience.

In summer, there's a special four-course prix-fixe dinner menu for C$95 (US$67), or C$130 (US$91) if paired with wine; an a la carte menu is also available. Appetizers might include asparagus served hot with black morels in their juices, white wine, and cream; or sauté of duck foie gras with leeks and citron, mango, and ginger sauce. Among the short selection of entrees, you might find Canadian caribou with port and blackberry sauce and cream-braised cabbage with shallots and glazed chestnuts, or lobster salad with green beans, new potatoes, and truffles scented with caraway. Desserts are equally exciting—try charlotte of white chocolate mousse with summer fruit and dark chocolate sauce.

The upstairs Belfry is a popular pre- and post-theater gathering place and is open for lunch and dinner.

To dine here during the festival, make reservations as soon as you buy your tickets. In the off season, call ahead; hours vary, and the restaurant is closed from late December through mid-April.

70 Brunswick St. (at Waterloo St.). © **519/273-3424**. www.churchrestaurant.com. Reservations required. Main courses C$38–C$62 (US$27–US$43). AE, DC, MC, V. The Church: Tues–Sat 5pm–8:30pm; Sun 11:30am–1:30pm; off-season hours vary. The Belfry: Tues–Sat 11:30am–midnight; off-season hours vary.

EXPENSIVE

The Old Prune ✪ CONTINENTAL   Situated in a lovely Edwardian home, the Old Prune has three dining rooms and an enclosed garden patio. Former Montréalers, the proprietors demonstrate Québec flair in both decor and menu. The menu changes constantly because the dishes are based on what's fresh and what's in season (much of the produce comes from the region's organic farms). Appetizers might include outstanding house-smoked salmon with lobster potato salad topped with Sevruga caviar, or refreshing tomato consommé with saffron and sea scallops. Among the main courses, you might find Perth County pork loin grilled with tamari and honey glaze and served with shiitake mushrooms, pickled cucumbers, and sunflower sprouts; steamed bass in Napa cabbage with curry broth and lime leaves; or rack of Ontario lamb with smoky tomatillo-chipotle pepper sauce. Desserts, such as rhubarb strawberry Napoleon with vanilla mousse, are always inspired. There is also a vegetarian prix-fixe menu.

151 Albert St. © **519/271-5052**. www.oldprune.on.ca. Reservations required. 3-course prix-fixe dinner C$66 (US$46); lunch main courses C$10–C$17 (US$7–US$12); dinner main courses C$19–C$33 (US$13–US$23). AE, MC, V. Wed–Sun 11:30am–1pm; Tues–Sat 5–9pm; Sun 5–7:45pm. Call for winter hours.

Rundles ✪ INTERNATIONAL   Rundles provides a premier dining experience in a serene dining room overlooking the river. Proprietor Jim Morris eats, sleeps, thinks, and dreams food, and chef Neil Baxter delivers the exciting, exquisite cuisine to the table. The prix-fixe dinner offers palate-pleasing flavor combinations. Appetizers might include shaved fennel, arugula, artichoke, and Parmesan salad or warm seared Québec foie gras. Among the five main dishes might be poached Atlantic salmon garnished with Jerusalem artichokes, wilted arugula, and yellow peppers in a light carrot sauce; or pink roast rib-eye of lamb with ratatouille and rosemary aioli. My dessert choice would be glazed lemon tart and orange sorbet, but hot mango tart with pineapple sorbet is also a dream.

9 Cobourg St. © **519/271-6442**. www.rundlesrestaurant.com. Reservations required. 3-course prix-fixe dinner C$68 (US$48), "gastronomic" prix-fixe dinner C$78 (US$55). AE, DC, MC, V. Apr–Oct Wed and Sat–Sun 11:30am–1:15pm, Tues 5–7pm, Wed–Sat 5–8:30pm, Sun 5–7pm. Closed Nov–Mar.

MODERATE

Keystone Alley Cafe ✪ CONTINENTAL   The food here is better than the fare at some pricier competitors. Theater actors often stop in for lunch—perhaps a sandwich, like the maple-grilled chicken-and-avocado club, or a main dish like cornmeal-crusted Mediterranean tart. At dinner, entrees range from breast of Muscovy duck with stir-fried Asian vegetables and egg noodles in honey-ginger sauce, to escalopes of calves' liver accompanied by garlic potato purée and creamed Savoy cabbage with bacon. The short wine list is reasonably priced.

34 Brunswick St. © **519/271-5645**. www.keystonealley.com. Reservations recommended. Main courses C$17–C$27 (US$12–US$19). AE, DC, MC, V. Mon–Sat 11:30am–2:30pm; Tues–Sat 5–9pm.

INEXPENSIVE

Bentley's CANADIAN/ENGLISH   Bentley's is *the* local watering hole, and a favorite theater company gathering spot. The popular pastime is darts, but you can also watch TV. In summer you can sit on the garden terrace and enjoy the light fare—grilled shrimp, burgers, gourmet pizza, fish and chips, shepherd's pie, and pasta dishes. The dinner menu features more substantial fare, including lamb curry, sirloin steak, and salmon baked in white wine with peppercorn-dill butter. The bar offers 16 drafts on tap.

99 Ontario St. © 519/271-1121; www.bentleys-annex.com. Reservations not accepted. Main courses C$9–C$18 (US$6.30–US$13). AE, DC, MC, V. Daily 11:30am–1am.

York Street Kitchen ECLECTIC   This small restaurant is a fun, funky spot that serves reasonably priced, high-quality food. You can come here for break-fast burritos and other morning fare, and for lunch sandwiches, which you build yourself by choosing from a list of fillings. In the evenings, expect to find com-fort foods like meat loaf and mashed potatoes or barbecued chicken and ribs.

41 York St. © 519/273-7041. www.yorkstreetkitchen.com. Reservations not accepted. Main courses C$8–C$17 (US$5.60–US$12). AE, V. Apr to early Oct daily 8am–8pm; mid-Oct to Mar daily 8am–3pm. Closed Dec 24–Jan 5.

2 Niagara-on-the-Lake & Niagara Falls

130km (81 miles) SE of Toronto

Only 1½ hours from Toronto, Niagara-on-the-Lake is one of the best-preserved and prettiest 19th-century villages in North America. Handsome clapboard and brick period houses border the tree-lined streets. It's the setting for one of Canada's most famous events, the **Shaw Festival.** The town is the jewel of the **Ontario wine region.**

Less than a half-hour drive from Niagara-on-the-Lake is **Niagara Falls,** which was for decades the region's honeymoon capital (I say this in an attempt to explain its endless motels—each with at least one suite that has a heart-shaped pink bed). While the falls are a majestic sight, I have my reservations about the town, espe-cially since the casino opened. My advice would be to stay at an inn in Niagara-on-the-Lake and come to Niagara Falls for a day trip. By the way, the drive along the **Niagara Parkway** is a delight: With its endless parks and gardens, it's an oasis for nature-lovers. (See "Along the Niagara Parkway," later in this chapter.)

ESSENTIALS

VISITOR INFORMATION   The **Niagara-on-the-Lake Chamber of Commerce,** 153 King St. (P.O. Box 1043), Niagara-on-the-Lake, ON L0S 1J0 (© **905/468-4263;** www.niagaraonthelake.com), provides information and can help you find accommodations. It's open Monday through Friday from 9am to 5pm, and Saturday and Sunday from 10am to 5pm.

For Niagara Falls travel information, contact **Niagara Falls Tourism** at (© **800/56-FALLS;** www.discoverniagara.com), or the **Niagara Parks Commission,** Box 150, 7400 Portage Rd. S., Niagara Falls, ON L2E 6T2 (© **905/356-2241;** www.niagaraparks.com). **Information centers** are open daily in summer from 9am to 6pm at Table Rock House and the Maid of the Mist Plaza.

GETTING THERE   Niagara-on-the-Lake is best seen by **car.** From Toronto, take the Queen Elizabeth Way (signs read QEW) to Niagara via Hamilton and St. Catharines, and exit at Highway 55. The trip takes about 1½ hours.

Amtrak and **VIA** (© 416/366-8411) operate **trains** between Toronto and New York, but they only stop in Niagara Falls and St. Catharine's, not Niagara-on-the-Lake. Call © **800/361-1235** in Canada or **800/USA-RAIL** in the United States. From either place, you'll need to rent a car. Rental outlets in St. Catharines include **National Tilden,** 162 Church St. (© **905/682-8611**), and **Hertz,** 404 Ontario St. (© **905/682-8695**). In Niagara Falls, **National Tilden** is at 4523 Drummond Rd. (© **905/374-6700**).

THE SHAW FESTIVAL

The Shaw celebrates the dramatic and comedic works of George Bernard Shaw and his contemporaries. From April to October, the festival offers a dozen plays in the historic **Court House,** the exquisite **Shaw Festival Theatre,** and the **Royal George Theatre.** Some recent performances have included *Hay Fever, The House of Bernarda Alba, Chaplin,* and Shaw's *Caesar and Cleopatra.*

Free chamber concerts take place Sunday at 11am. Chats introduce performances on Friday evenings in July and August, and question-and-answer sessions follow Tuesday evening performances.

The Shaw announces its festival program in mid-January. Tickets are difficult to obtain on short notice, so book in advance. Prices range from C$26 to C$75 (US$18–US$53). For more information, contact the **Shaw Festival,** P.O. Box 774, Niagara-on-the-Lake, ON L0S 1J0 (© **800/511-7429** or 905/468-2172; www.shawfest.com).

EXPLORING THE TOWN

Niagara-on-the Lake is small, and most of its attractions are along one main street, making it easy to explore on foot.

SIGHTS

Fort George National Historic Site ★ *Kids* It's easy to imagine taking shelter behind Fort George's stockade fence and watching for the enemy from across the river—even though today there are only condominiums on the opposite riverbank.

The fort played a central role in the War of 1812: it was headquarters for the British Army's Centre Division. The division was comprised of British regulars, local militia, Runchey's corps of former slaves, and aboriginal forces. The fort was destroyed by American artillery fire in May 1813. After the war it was partially rebuilt, but it was abandoned in 1828 and not reconstructed until the 1930s. You can view the guardroom (with its hard plank beds), the officers' quarters, the enlisted men's quarters, and the sentry posts. The self-guided tour includes interpretive films. Those who believe in ghosts take note: The fort is one of Ontario's favorite "haunted" sites.

Niagara Pkwy. © **905/468-6614;** www.parkscanada.ca or www.friendsoffortgeorge.ca. Admission C$8 (US$5.60) adults, C$7 (US$4.90) seniors, C$5 (US$3.50) children 6–16, free for children 5 and under, C$25 (US$18) family (2 adults, 2 children). Apr 1–Oct 31 daily 10am–5pm.

Niagara Historical Society Museum More than 20,000 artifacts pertaining to local history make up this collection. They include many possessions of United Empire Loyalists who first settled the area at the end of the American Revolution. It's interesting, but then again I'm a history geek. If you're like me, allow 1½ hours for your visit.

43 Castlereagh St. (at Davy). © **905/468-3912.** Admission C$5 (US$3.50) adults, C$3 (US$2.10) seniors, C$2 (US$1.40) students with ID, C$1 (US70¢) children 5–12. May–Oct daily 10am–5pm; Mar–Apr and Nov–Dec daily 1–5pm; Jan–Feb Sat–Sun 1–5pm.

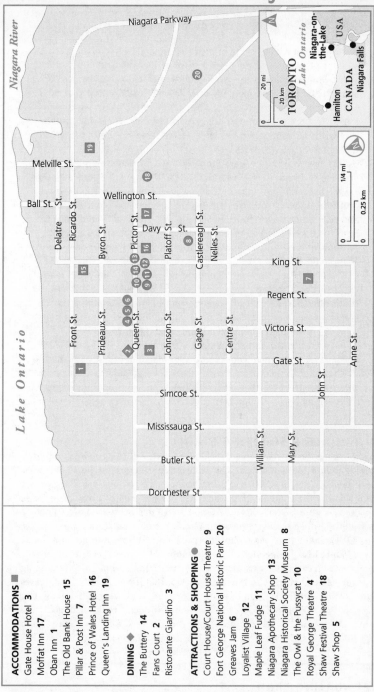

Niagara River

Niagara Parkway

Lake Ontario

Lake Ontario

Niagara-on-the-Lake

USA

TORONTO

Niagara Falls

Hamilton

CANADA

20 mi

20 km

1/4 mi

0.25 km

Melville St.

Ball St.   St.

Wellington St.

Delatre

Ricardo St.

Byron St.

Picton St.

Davy

Platoff St.

St.

Castlereagh St.

Nelles St.

King St.

Regent St.

Victoria St.

Gate St.

Front St.

Prideaux St.

Queen St.

Johnson St.

Gage St.

Centre St.

William St.

Mary St.

John St.

Anne St.

Simcoe St.

Mississauga St.

Butler St.

Dorchester St.

ACCOMMODATIONS ■
Gate House Hotel **3**
Moffat Inn **17**
Oban Inn **1**
The Old Bank House **15**
Pillar & Post Inn **7**
Prince of Wales Hotel **16**
Queen's Landing Inn **19**

DINING ◆
The Buttery **14**
Fans Court **2**
Ristorante Giardino **3**

ATTRACTIONS & SHOPPING ●
Court House/Court House Theatre **9**
Fort George National Historic Park **20**
Greaves Jam **6**
Loyalist Village **12**
Maple Leaf Fudge **11**
Niagara Apothecary Shop **13**
Niagara Historical Society Museum **8**
The Owl & the Pussycat **10**
Royal George Theatre **4**
Shaw Festival Theatre **18**
Shaw Shop **5**

Touring Niagara-on-the-Lake Wineries

Visiting a local winery is one of the loveliest (and tastiest) ways to pass an hour or two in this region. For maps of the area and information about vintners, contact the **Wine Council of Ontario,** 110 Hanover Dr., Suite B-205, St. Catharines, ON L2W 1A4 (© **888/5-WINERY** or 905/ 684-8070; www.wineroute.com). The wineries listed below are close to the town of Niagara-on-the-Lake. Tours are free. Prices for tastings vary with the winery and the wine you're sampling, and usually run C$3 to C$10 (US$2.10–US$7).

Take Highway 55 (Niagara Stone Rd.) out of Niagara-on-the-Lake, and you'll come to **Hillebrand Estates Winery** (© **905/468-7123;** www.hillebrand.com), just outside Virgil. It's open year-round, plays host to a variety of special events (including a weekend concert series), and even offers bicycle tours. Hillebrand's Vineyard Café, with views of both the barrel-filled cellar and the Niagara Escarpment, is a delightful spot for lunch or dinner. Winery tours start on the hour daily from 10am to 6pm.

If you turn off Highway 55 and go down York Road, you'll reach **Château des Charmes,** west of St. David's (© **905/262-5202;** www. chateaudescharmes.com). The winery was built to resemble a French manor house, and its architecture is unique in the region. One-hour tours are given daily. Open from 10am to 6pm year-round.

To reach the **Konzelmann Winery,** 1096 Lakeshore Rd. (© **905/935-2866;** www.konzelmannwines.com), take Mary Street out of Niagara-on-the-Lake. This vintner is famous for its award-winning ice wines. It offers tours from May to late September, Monday through Saturday.

A NOSTALGIC SHOPPING STROLL

A stroll along the town's main artery, Queen Street, will take you by some entertaining, albeit touristy, shops. The **Niagara Apothecary,** at no. 5 (© **905/ 468-3845**), dates to 1866. Gold-leaf script marks its original black-walnut counters and the contents of the drawers, and the original glass and ceramic apothecary ware is on display. At no. 13 is the **Scottish Loft** (© **905/ 468-0965**), which is filled with tartans, Celtic memorabilia, candy, books, CDs, and DVDs (aside from the tartans, the products hail from England and Wales, too). **Maple Leaf Fudge,** no. 14 (© **905/468-2211**), offers more than 20 varieties that you can watch being made on marble slabs. At no. 16 is a charming toy store, **The Owl and the Pussycat** (© **905/468-3081**). At no. 35 is **Greaves Jam** (© **905/468-7331**), run by fourth-generation jam makers. **Irish Design** at no. 38 (© **905/468-7233**) sells hand-knit sweaters, traditional gold and silver jewelry, and other treasures from the Emerald Isle. The **Shaw Shop** (© **800/511-7429**), no. 79, next to the Royal George Theatre, carries GBS memorabilia and more. There's also a Dansk outlet and several galleries selling contemporary Canadian and other ethnic crafts.

JET-BOATING THRILLS

Jet boat excursions leave from the dock across from 61 Melville St. at the King George III Inn. Don a rain suit, poncho, and life jacket, and climb aboard. The boat takes you out onto the Niagara River for a trip along the stonewalled canyon to the whirlpool downriver. The ride starts slow but gets into turbulent water. Trips, which operate from May to October, last an hour and cost C$54 (US$38) for adults, and C$44 (US$31) for children 13 and under. Reservations are required. Call the **Whirlpool Jet Boat Company** at © 888/438-4444 or 905/468-4800, or visit www.whirlpooljet.com.

WHERE TO STAY

In summer, hotel space is in high demand, but don't despair if you're having trouble nailing down a room. Contact the Chamber of Commerce, which provides an accommodations-reservations service. Note that several of the hotels in town are owned by the same company, Vintage Inns (the company is famous for buying upscale properties and making them even more luxurious). However, there are 120 bed-and-breakfasts around town to choose from, too. The **Niagara-on-the-Lake Chamber of Commerce** (© 905/468-4263; www. niagaraonthelake.com) provides information about them and can help you find a place to stay.

IN TOWN
Expensive

Gate House Hotel ⭐ Unlike many of the Canadiana-influenced lodgings in town, the Gate House Hotel is decorated in cool, clean-lined Milanese style. Guest rooms have a marbleized look, and are accented with ultramodern black lamps, block marble tables, leatherette couches, and bathrooms with sleek Italian fixtures. The effect is quite glamorous. Ristorante Giardino, one of the best places to dine in town, is in the hotel.

142 Queen St. (P.O. Box 1364), Niagara-on-the-Lake, ON L0S 1J0. © 905/468-3263. www.gatehouse-niagara.com. 10 units. C$145–C$230 (US$102–US$161) double. AE, MC, V. Free parking. **Amenities:** Restaurant; concierge. *In room:* A/C, TV, hair dryer.

Oban Inn ⭐ In a prime location overlooking the lake, the Oban Inn is a lovely place to stay. It's in a charming white Victorian house with a green dormer-style roof and windows, plus a large veranda. (The house is a re-creation of the original 1824 structure, which burned down in 1992.) The gorgeous gardens are the source of the bouquets throughout the house. Downstairs is a piano bar with leather Windsor-style chairs and a fireplace.

Each of the comfortable rooms is unique. They are furnished with antique reproductions—cornhusk four-poster beds with candlewick spreads, ginger-jar lamps, and club-style sofas. It's all very homey and old-fashioned.

160 Front St. (at Gate St.), Niagara-on-the-Lake, ON L0S 1J0. © 888/669-5566 or 905/468-2165. www. vintageinns.com. 22 units. From C$225 (US$158) double. Packages available. AE, DC, DISC, MC, V. Free parking. **Amenities:** Piano bar; lounge; access to nearby health club; bike rental; babysitting. *In room:* A/C, TV, dataport, hair dryer, iron.

Pillar & Post Inn The discreetly elegant Pillar & Post is a couple of blocks from the maddening crowds on Queen Street. In recent years it has been transformed into one of the most sophisticated accommodations in town, complete with a spa that offers the latest in deluxe treatments and a Japanese-style warm mineral-spring pool, complete with cascading waterfall (spa packages are available). The light, airy lobby boasts a fireplace, lush plantings, and comfortable seating. The style is classic Canadiana: The spacious rooms all contain old-fashioned furniture, Windsor-style chairs, a pine cabinet (with a color TV tucked inside), and historical engravings. In the back, there's a secluded pool.

Some rooms facing the outdoor pool on the ground level have bay windows and window boxes.

48 John St. (at King St.), Niagara-on-the-Lake, ON L0S 1J0. © **888/669-5566** or 905/468-2123. Fax 905/468-1472. www.vintageinns.com. 123 units. From C$225 (US$158) double; from C$425 (US$298) suite. AE, DC, MC, V. Free parking. **Amenities:** 2 dining rooms; wine bar; indoor and outdoor pools; spa; Jacuzzi; sauna; bike rental; concierge; business center; dry cleaning. *In room:* A/C, TV, dataport, minibar, hair dryer, safe.

Prince of Wales Hotel & Spa ★★   The Prince of Wales is the most luxurious hotel in the district. This place has it all: a central location across from the lovely gardens of Simcoe Park; full recreational facilities, including an indoor pool; a luxurious spa; lounges, bars, and restaurants; and attractive rooms, beautifully decorated with antiques or reproductions. It has a lively atmosphere yet retains the elegance and charm of a Victorian inn. Bathrooms have bidets, and most rooms have minibars. The hotel's original section was built in 1864; in 1999, the hotel was renovated and restored to its original glory. All rooms are nonsmoking.

6 Picton St., Niagara-on-the-Lake, ON L0S 1J0. © **888/669-5566** or 905/468-3246. Fax 905/468-5521. www.vintageinns.com. 114 units. From C$225 (US$158) double. Packages available. AE, DC, DISC, MC, V. Valet parking C$5 (US$3.50), free self-parking. Pets accepted. **Amenities:** Dining room; cafe; bar; lounge; indoor pool; health club; spa; Jacuzzi; bike rental; concierge; business center; 24-hr. room service; massage; dry cleaning. *In room:* A/C, TV, dataport, hair dryer, iron, safe.

Queen's Landing Inn   Overlooking the river and within walking distance of the theaters, the Queen's Landing Inn is a modern, Georgian-style mansion. Half the rooms have fireplaces, and 32 contain fireplaces and Jacuzzis. The spacious rooms are comfortably furnished with half-canopy or brass beds, wingback chairs, and large desks. This hotel attracts a business-oriented crowd, in part because of its excellent conference facilities, which include 20 meeting rooms.

155 Byron St., at Melville St., (P.O. Box 1180), Niagara-on-the-Lake, ON L0S 1J0. © **888/669-5566** or 905/468-2195. www.vintageinns.com. 144 units. From C$225 (US$158) double; from C$425 (US$298) suite. AE, DC, DISC, MC, V. Free parking. **Amenities:** Dining room; lounge; indoor pool; health club; Jacuzzi; sauna; bike rental; concierge; business center; 24-hr. room service; babysitting; dry cleaning. *In room:* A/C, TV, dataport, minibar, hair dryer, iron, safe.

White Oaks Conference Resort & Spa   Not far from Niagara-on-the-Lake, White Oaks is a sports enthusiast's paradise. Across from the resort is the Royal Niagara golf course, which consists of three 9-hole courses that are meant to be played in combinations (it's like having three different 18-hole courses). In 2000, the resort added a full-service luxury spa, which has become one of its main attractions. It's entirely possible to arrive here, be caught in a flurry of athletic activity all weekend, and not set foot outside the resort. The rooms are well designed, and they have oak furniture, vanity sinks, and niceties like a phone in the bathroom. Suites have brick fireplaces, marble-top desks, Jacuzzis (some heart-shaped), and bidets. All of the guest rooms have been soundproofed. *One caveat:* The Superior rooms, which are the least expensive, are on the tiny side, at about 34 sq. m (370 sq. ft.) on average, and the decor is bland. The Tower rooms, which are one tier up, are much nicer.

The long list of spa treatments for men and women includes facials, massages, body wraps, and manicures. Some of the less orthodox therapies include reiki (a Japanese massage to "align your energy field"), and Danse de la Mains, a massage choreographed to music and performed by two therapists.

Taylor Rd., Niagara-on-the-Lake, ON L0S 1J0. © **800/263-5766** or 905/688-2550. Fax 905/688-2220. www.whiteoaksresort.com. 220 units. July–Aug from C$160 (US$112) double, C$190 (US$133) suite. Off-season discounts available. AE, DC, MC, V. Free parking. From QEW, exit at Glendale Ave. **Amenities:** Restaurant/wine bar; outdoor terrace cafe; coffee shop; 8 tennis courts; 5 squash courts; 2 racquetball courts; health club; spa; sauna; bike rental; children's center; concierge; business center; massage. *In room:* A/C, TV, dataport, hair dryer.

Moderate

Moffat Inn *Value*   This is a fine budget-conscious choice in a convenient location. Most rooms contain brass-framed beds and furnishings in traditional-style wood, wicker, and bamboo. Each has a teakettle and supplies. Eight rooms have fireplaces. Free coffee is available in the lobby. There's also a restaurant, Tetley's, which serves fondue, steaks, and sushi. *One caveat:* If you have trouble climbing stairs, this hotel would not be a good choice; most of the guest rooms are on the second floor and there is no elevator (there's no porter to handle luggage, either).

60 Picton St. (at Queen St.), Niagara-on-the-Lake, ON L0S 1J0. © **905/468-4116.** www.moffatinn.com. 22 units. Apr 15–Oct and late Dec C$99–C$179 (US$69–US$125) double; Nov to mid-Dec and Jan–Apr 14 C$79–C$149 (US$55–US$104) double. AE, MC, V. Free parking. **Amenities:** Restaurant; bar; access to nearby health club. *In room:* A/C, TV, dataport, coffeemaker, hair dryer.

The Old Bank House ✯   Beautifully situated down by the river, this two-story Georgian was built in 1817 as the first branch of the Bank of Canada. In 1902 it hosted the Prince and Princess of Wales, and today it is a charming bed-and-breakfast inn. Several tastefully decorated units have private entrances; one is the charming Garden Room, which also has a private trellised deck. Several of the rooms have private balconies. Eight units have a refrigerator and coffee or tea supplies. The most expensive suite accommodates five in two bedrooms. The extraordinarily comfortable sitting room (open to all guests) holds a fireplace and eclectic antique pieces.

10 Front St. (P.O. Box 1708), Niagara-on-the-Lake, ON L0S 1J0. © **877-468-7136** or 905/468-7136; www.oldbankhouse.com. 9 units. C$115–C$225 (US$81–US$158) double; C$230 (US$161) 2-bedroom suite. Rates include breakfast. AE, MC, V. Free parking. **Amenities:** Jacuzzi. *In room:* A/C, no phone.

ALONG THE WINE ROAD

Inn on the Twenty and the Vintage House ✯   On the grounds of the Cave Spring Cellars, one of Niagara's best wineries, these modern accommodations consist entirely of handsome suites. Each has an elegantly furnished living room with a fireplace, and a Jacuzzi in the bathroom. Seven are duplexes—one of them, the deluxe loft, has two double beds on its second level—and five are single-level suites with high ceilings. All of the suites are nonsmoking. The inn's eatery, On the Twenty Restaurant & Wine Bar (p. 239), is across the street. Its spa offers a full range of services for men and women, and it offers special packages for couples. Next door to the inn is the **Vintage House,** an 1840 Georgian mansion; it contains three suites, all with private entrances, for those who want to feel that they're in a secluded hideaway.

3845 Main St., Jordan, ON L0R 1S0. © **800/701-8074** or 905/562-5336. www.innonthetwenty.com. 30 units. From C$221 (US$155) suite; winter discounts available. AE, DC, MC, V. Free parking. From QEW, take Jordan Rd. exit south; at first intersection, turn right onto 4th Ave., then right onto Main St. **Amenities:** Restaurant; nearby golf course; health club; concierge. *In room:* A/C, TV, dataport, coffeemaker, hair dryer, iron.

WHERE TO DINE
IN TOWN

In addition to the listings below, don't forget the dining rooms at the **Pillar & Post, Queen's Landing,** and the **Prince of Wales,** all listed above.

The stylish **Shaw Cafe and Wine Bar,** 92 Queen St. (© **905/468-4772**), serves lunch and light meals, and has a patio. The **Epicurean,** 84 Queen St. (© **905/468-3408**), offers hearty soups, quiches, sandwiches, and other fine dishes in a sunny Provence-inspired dining room. Service is cafeteria style. Half a block off Queen Street, the **Angel Inn,** 224 Regent St. (℄ **905/468-3411**), is a delightfully authentic English pub. For an inexpensive down-home breakfast, go to the **Stagecoach Family Restaurant,** 45 Queen St. (℄ **905/468-3133**). It also serves basic family fare, such as burgers, fries, and meat loaf, but doesn't accept credit cards. **Niagara Home Bakery,** 66 Queen St. (℄ **905/468-3431**), is the place to stop for chocolate-date squares, cherry squares, croissants, cookies, and individual quiches.

The Buttery CANADIAN/ENGLISH/CONTINENTAL   The Buttery has been a dining landmark for years. At its weekend Henry VIII feasts, "serving wenches" bring food and wine while "jongleurs" and "musickers" entertain. The meal consists of "four removes"—courses involving broth, chicken, roast lamb, roast pig, sherry trifle, syllabub, and cheese, all washed down with a goodly amount of wine, ale, and mead.

The tavern menu features spareribs, 8-ounce New York strip, shrimp in garlic sauce, and such English pub fare as lamb curry and steak, kidney, and mushroom pie. On the dinner menu, I highly recommend rack of lamb or shrimp curry. Finish with mud pie or Grand Marnier chocolate cheesecake. You can take home fresh baked goods—pies, strudels, dumplings, cream puffs, or scones.

19 Queen St. ℄ **905/468-2564**. Reservations strongly recommended; required for Henry VIII feast. Henry VIII feast C$49 (US$34); tavern main courses (available Tues–Sun 11am–5pm, all day Mon) C$9–C$16 (US$6.30–US$11); dinner main courses C$26 (US$18). MC, V. Apr–Nov daily 11am–11pm; Dec–Mar Sun–Thurs 11am–7:30pm. Afternoon tea year-round daily 2–5pm.

Fans Court CHINESE   This comfortable spot, decorated with fans, cushioned bamboo chairs, and round tables spread with golden tablecloths, serves some of the best food in town. In summer, there's outdoor dining in the courtyard. The cuisine is primarily Cantonese and Szechuan. The menu includes Singapore beef, moo shu pork, Szechuan scallops, and lemon chicken.

135 Queen St. ℄ **905/468-4511**. Reservations recommended. Main courses C$13–C$20 (US$9.10–US$14). AE, MC, V. Tues–Sun noon–9pm.

Ristorante Giardino ⭐ NORTHERN ITALIAN   On the ground floor of the Gate House Hotel is this sleek, ultramodern restaurant, with a gleaming marble-top bar and brass accents throughout. The food is Northern Italian with fresh American accents. Main courses might include baked salmon seasoned with olive paste and tomato concasse, veal tenderloin marinated with garlic and rosemary, and braised pheasant in juniper-berry-and-vegetable sauce. There are several pasta dishes, plus such appealing appetizers as medallions of langostine garnished with orange and fennel salad. Desserts include a fine tiramisu, and *panna cotta* with seasonal berries.

In the Gate House Hotel, 142 Queen St. ℄ **905/468-3263**. www.gatehouse-niagara.com. Main courses C$25–C$40 (US$18–US$28). AE, MC, V. May–Sept daily 11:30am–2:30pm and 5–10pm; Oct–Apr daily 5:30–9pm.

IN NEARBY VIRGIL, ST. CATHARINES & WELLAND

Café Garibaldi ⭐ ITALIAN   This relaxed spot is a favorite among locals. It serves Italian staples such as zuppa di pesce and veal scalloppine; homemade lasagna is the most requested dish. The wine list features the local vintners' goods and some fine bottles from Italy.

375 St. Paul St., St. Catharines. ℄ **905/988-9033**. Reservations recommended for dinner. Main courses C$13–C$27 (US$9.10–US$19). AE, DC, MC, V. Tues–Sat 11:30am–2:30pm and 5–10pm. From QEW, exit at Ontario St., follow DOWNTOWN sign to St. Paul St. and turn left.

Rinderlin's CONTINENTAL   An intimate town-house restaurant, Rinderlin's has evolved from a traditional French restaurant to one with a Continental flair. On the dinner menu, you might find sautéed shrimps and scallops in medium-hot curry sauce on a bed of basmati rice; roast pork tenderloin with honey-mustard-bacon sauce; herb polenta with grilled bell pepper, eggplant, and zucchini; and local venison with wild mushrooms and game sauce. There are also several vegetarian options. Desserts are seasonal—one favorite is the white chocolate torte flavored with brandy and served with raspberry sauce.

24 Burgar St., Welland. ℂ **905/735-4411.** Reservations recommended. Main courses C$21–C$30 (US$15–US$21). AE, DC, MC, V. Mon–Fri 11:30am–1:30pm; daily 6–8pm. From QEW, take Hwy. 406 to Burgar St. exit, turn left.

Wellington Court ★★ CONTINENTAL   In an Edwardian town house with a flower trellis, the three candlelit dining rooms here are adorned with mirrors, lithographs, and photographs. The menu features daily specials along with such items as beef tenderloin in shallot-and-red-wine reduction, roasted breast of chicken on gingered plum preserves, and grilled sea bass with cranberry vinaigrette. Not surprisingly, given the location, the wine list is full with excellent Niagara bottles.

11 Wellington St., St. Catharines. ℂ **905/682-5518.** Reservations recommended. Main courses C$22–C$35 (US$15–US$25). MC, V. Tues–Sat 11:30am–2:30pm and 5–9:30pm. From QEW, exit at Lake St., turn left, follow to Wellington Ave., turn left, follow for 1 block, turn right.

ALONG THE WINE ROAD

Hillebrand's Vineyard Café ★ CONTINENTAL   This dining room is light and airy, and its floor-to-ceiling windows offer views over the vineyards to the distant Niagara Escarpment, or of wine cellars bulging with oak barrels. The food is excellent. The seasonal menu might feature such dishes as poached Arctic char with shellfish ragout, or prosciutto-wrapped pheasant breast atop linguine tossed with mushrooms, roasted eggplant, and shallot. The starters are equally luxurious. Try roasted three-peppercorn pear served warm with salad greens, pine nuts, and Parmesan slivers, or spiced goat cheese and grilled portobello "sandwich" with walnuts and endive. In case the food isn't enticing enough (and it should be), the restaurant also hosts special events throughout the year, many featuring jazz musicians.

Hwy. 55, between Niagara-on-the-Lake and Virgil. ℂ **905/468-7123.** www.hillebrand.com. Reservations strongly recommended. Main courses C$25–C$40 (US$18–US$28). AE, MC, V. Daily noon–11pm (closes earlier in winter).

Mark Picone at Vineland Estates ★★ CONTINENTAL   This inspired eatery serves some of the most innovative food along the wine trail. On warm days you can dine on a deck under a spreading tree, or stay in the airy dining room. Start with a plate of seasoned mussels in a ginger broth. Follow with a Canadian Angus tenderloin with a risotto of truffles and morel mushrooms, or go for pan-seared sweetbreads with a celeriac and potato mash and confit of mushrooms glazed with ice wine. For dessert, there's a wonderful tasting plate of Canadian farm cheeses, including Abbey St. Benoit blue Ermite; for sweettooths, there's a hard-to-resist maple-walnut cheesecake in a biscotti crust.

3620 Moyer Rd., Vineland. ℂ **888/846-3526** or **905/562-7088.** www.vineland.com. Reservations strongly recommended. Main courses C$25–C$40 (US$18–US$28). AE, MC, V. Daily noon–2:30pm and 5:30–9pm.

On the Twenty Restaurant & Wine Bar ★ CANADIAN   This restaurant is a favorite among foodies. The gold-painted dining rooms cast a warm glow.

The cuisine features ingredients from many producers, giving On the Twenty a small-town feel. Naturally, there's an extensive selection of Ontario wines, including some wonderful ice wines to accompany such desserts as lemon tart and fruit cobbler. On the Twenty Restaurant is associated with the Inn on the Twenty (p. 237), across the street.

At Cave Spring Cellars, 3836 Main St., Jordan. © 905/562-7313. www.innonthetwenty.com. Reservations recommended. Main courses C$22–C$40 (US$15–US$28). AE, DC, MC, V. Daily 11:30am–3pm and 5–10pm.

ALONG THE NIAGARA PARKWAY ★

The Niagara Parkway, on the Canadian side of the falls, is a gem. Unlike the American side, it abounds with natural wonders, including vast expanses of parkland. You can drive along the 56km (35-mile) parkway all the way from Niagara-on-the-Lake to Niagara Falls on the parkway, taking in attractions en route. Here are the major ones, listed in the order that you'll encounter them:

- The **White Water Walk,** 4330 River Rd. (© **905/374-1221**): The scenic boardwalk runs beside the raging white waters of the Great Gorge Rapids. Stroll along and wonder how it must have felt to challenge this mighty torrent, where the river rushes through the narrow channel at an average speed of 35kmph (22 mph). Admission is C$7.50 (US$5.25) for adults, C$6.50 (US$4.55) for children 6 to 12, free for children 5 and under.

- The **Whirlpool Aero Car** (© **905/354-5711**): This red-and-yellow cable-car contraption whisks you on a 1,097m (3,600-ft.) jaunt between two points in Canada. High above the Niagara Whirlpool, you'll enjoy excellent views of the surrounding landscape. Admission is C$10 (US$7) for adults, C$6 (US$4.20) for children 6 to 12, free for kids 5 and under. Open daily May to the third Sunday in October. Hours are from 10am to 4:30pm.

- The **Niagara Parks Botanical Gardens and School of Horticulture** (© **905/356-8119**): Stop here for a free view of the vast gardens and a look at the **Floral Clock,** which contains 25,000 plants in its 12m-diameter (40-ft.) face. The new **Butterfly Conservatory** is also in the gardens. In this lush tropical setting, more than 2,000 butterflies (50 international species) float and flutter among such nectar-producing flowers as lantanas and pentas. The large bright blue luminescent Morpho butterflies from Central and South America are particularly gorgeous. Interpretive programs and other presentations take place in the auditorium and two smaller theaters. The native butterfly garden outside attracts the more familiar swallowtails, fritillaries, and painted ladies. Admission is C$10 (US$7) for adults, C$6 (US$4.20) for children 6 to 12, free for children 5 and under. The school opens at 9am daily. It closes at 8pm in May and June; 9pm in July and August; 6pm in March, April, September, and October; and 5pm from November through February. It's closed December 25.

- **Queenston Heights Park:** This is the site of a famous War of 1812 battle, and you can take a walking tour of the battlefield. Picnic or play tennis (for C$6/US$4.20 per hour) in the shaded arbor before moving to the **Laura Secord Homestead,** Partition Street, Queenston (© **905/262-4851**). This heroic woman threaded enemy lines to alert British authorities to a surprise attack by American soldiers during the War of 1812. Her home contains a fine collection of Upper Canada furniture from the period, plus artifacts recovered from an archaeological dig. Stop at the candy shop and ice-cream parlor. Tours run every half-hour. Admission is C$3.50 (US$2.45). Open late May through Labour Day weekdays from 9am to 3:30pm and weekends from 11am to 5pm.

- Fruit farms, like **Kurtz Orchards** (© 905/468-2937), and wineries such as the **Inniskillin Winery,** Line 3, Service Road 66 (© **905/468-3554** or 905/468-2187): You'll find peaches, apples, pears, nectarines, cherries, plums, and strawberries at Kurtz; you can tour the 32 hectares (80 acres) on a tractor-pulled tram. Inniskillin is open daily from 10am to 6pm June through October, and Monday through Saturday from 10am to 5pm November through May. The self-guided free tour has 20 stops that explain the winemaking process. A free guided tour, offered daily in summer and Saturday only in winter, begins at 2:30pm.
- **Old Fort Erie,** 350 Lakeshore Rd., Fort Erie (© 905/871-0540): It's a reconstruction of the fort that was seized by the Americans in July 1814, besieged later by the British, and finally blown up as the Americans retreated across the river to Buffalo. Guards in period costume stand sentry duty, fire the cannons, and demonstrate drill and musket practice. Open daily from 10am to 6pm from the first Saturday in May to mid-September, and weekends only to Canadian Thanksgiving (U.S. Columbus Day). Admission is C$7.50 (US$5.25) for adults, C$4.50 (US$3.15) for children 6 to 16, free for children 5 and under.

SEEING NIAGARA FALLS

You simply cannot come this far and not see the falls, which are the seventh natural wonder of the world. The most exciting way to do that is from the decks of the **Maid of the Mist** ✦✦, 5920 River Rd. (© **905/358-5781;** www.maid ofthemist.com). The sturdy boat takes you right in—through the turbulent waters around the American Falls, past the Rock of Ages, and to the foot of the Horseshoe Falls, where 34.5 million imperial gallons of water tumble over the 54m-high (176-ft.) cataract each minute. You'll get wet, and your glasses will mist, but that won't detract from the thrill. Boats leave from the dock on the parkway just down from the Rainbow Bridge. Trips operate daily from mid-May to mid-October. Fares are C$13 (US$9.10) for adults, and C$8 (US$5.60) for children 6 to 12, free for children 5 and under.

Go down under the falls using the elevator at **Table Rock House,** which drops you 46m (151 ft.) through solid rock to the tunnels and viewing portals of the **Journey Behind the Falls** (© 905/354-1551). You'll receive—and appreciate—a rain poncho. Admission is C$10 (US$7) for adults, C$6 (US$4.20) for children 6 to 12, free for children 5 and under.

You can ride the external glass-fronted elevators 159m (522 ft.) to the top of the **Skylon Tower Observation Deck,** 5200 Robinson St. (© **905/356-2651;** www.skylon.com). The observation deck is open daily from 8am to midnight from June to Labour Day; hours vary in other seasons, so call ahead. Adults pay

---

Moments The Falls by Night

Don't miss seeing the falls after dark. Twenty-two xenon gas spotlights, each producing 250 million candlepower of light, illuminate them in shades of rose pink, red magenta, amber, blue, and green. Call © **800/ 563-2557** (in the U.S.) or 905/356-6061 for schedules. The show starts around 5pm in winter, 8:30pm in spring and fall, and 9pm in summer. In addition, from July to early September, free fireworks start at 10pm every Friday.

C$9.50 (US$6.65), seniors C$8.50 (US$5.95), children 12 and under C$5.50 (US$3.85). There is a revolving restaurant here but be warned that it's something of a tourist trap, with a C$25 (US$18) minimum per adult charge at lunch and a C$37 (US$26) minimum charge at dinner (there is a separate menu for kids). Also there's a C$2 (US$1.40) per-person fee just for the elevator ride to the restaurant. Do the math and you'll see that it adds up to a pretty expensive proposition for a family to eat here.

For a different view of Niagara Falls, stop by the **IMAX Theater,** 6170 Buchanan Ave. (© **905/358-3611;** www.imaxniagara.com). You can view the raging, swirling waters in *Niagara: Miracles, Myths, and Magic,* shown on a six-story-high screen. Admission is C$12 (US$8.40) for adults and students, C$9.50 (US$6.65) for seniors, C$8.50 (US$5.95) for children 4 to 12. I have to say that I consider this a lot of money to pay for a movie that is only 45 minutes long. Still, I'm an IMAX fan, and I have to admit the film looks great; also, if you see a second feature, it will only cost C$5.85 (US$4.10) per person.

The falls are also exciting in winter, when the ice bridge and other formations are quite remarkable.

WHERE TO STAY & DINE NEAR THE FALLS

While Niagara-on-the-Lake is a far more scenic and charming option, you may find yourself staying overnight in Niagara Falls. One good hotel bet is the **Sheraton on the Falls,** 5875 Falls Ave. (© **888/229-9961** or 905/374-4445), which offers rooms with a truly gorgeous view; many have balconies. Rates start around C$120 (US$84) in the winter and C$200 (US$140) in summer for a double

A Family Adventure

If you're looking for something to keep the kids amused, visit **MarineLand** ✦, 7657 Portage Rd. (© **905/356-9565;** www.marineland canada.com). At the aquarium-theater, King Waldorf, the walrus mascot, presides over performances by killer whales, dolphins, and sea lions. Friendship Cove, a 4.5-million-gallon breeding and observation tank, lets the little ones see killer whales up close. Another aquarium features displays of freshwater fish. At the small wildlife display, children enjoy petting and feeding the deer and seeing bears and Canadian elk.

Marineland also has theme-park rides, including a roller coaster, a Tivoli wheel (a fancy Ferris wheel), Dragon Boat rides, and a fully equipped playground. The big thriller is Dragon Mountain, a roller coaster that loops, double-loops, and spirals through 305m (1,000 ft.) of tunnels. There are three restaurants, or you can picnic.

In summer, admission is C$33 (US$23) for adults and children 10 and over, C$28 (US$20) for seniors and children 5 to 9, and free for children 4 and under. Open daily July and August from 9am to 6pm; mid-April to mid-May and September to mid-October from 10am to 4pm; and mid-May to June from 10am to 5pm. Closed November through April. Rides open in late May and close the first Monday in October. In town, drive south on Stanley Street and follow the signs; from the QEW, take the McCleod Road exit.

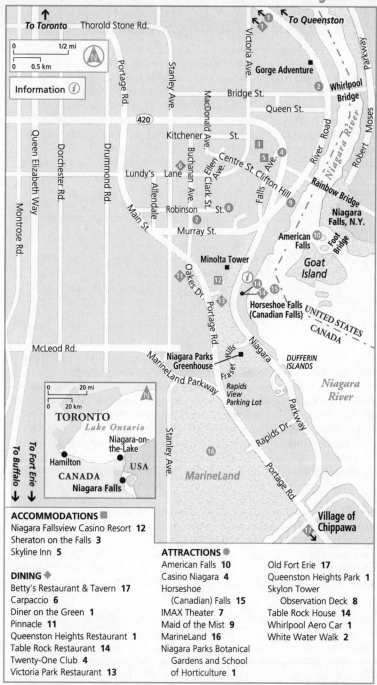

Niagara Parkway Commission Restaurants

The Niagara Parkway Commission has commandeered the most spectacular scenic spots, where it operates reasonably priced dining outlets. They serve traditional family-style food at lunch and dinner, and do not accept reservations. **Table Rock Restaurant** (© **905/354-3631**) and **Victoria Park Restaurant** (© **905/356-2217**), on the parkway right by the falls, are both pleasant, if crowded. **Diner on the Green** (© **905/ 356-7221**) is also on the parkway, at the Whirlpool Golf Course near Queenston. It's very plain.

The star of the Niagara Parkway Commission's eateries is **Queenston Heights,** 14275 Niagara Pkwy. (© **905/262-4274**). Set in the park among firs, cypresses, silver birches, and maples, the open-air balcony affords a magnificent view of the lower Niagara River and the rich fruit-growing land through which it flows. Or you can sit under the cathedral ceiling in a room where the flue of the stone fireplace reaches to the roof. Dinner options might include fillet of Atlantic salmon with Riesling-chive hollandaise, prime rib, or grilled pork with apples and cider–Dijon mustard sauce. Afternoon tea is served from 3 to 5pm in the summer. If nothing else, go for a drink on the deck and enjoy the terrific view.

---

room. If you're more interested in gambling than a view, check out **The Skyline Inn,** 5685 Falls Ave. (© 800/263-7135 or 905/374-4444), which is right by Casino Niagara. Rates here start at C$75 (US$53) per night. The newest place to stay is the luxurious **Niagara Fallsview Casino Resort,** 6380 Fallsview Blvd. (© 888/FALLSVUE; http://discoverniagara.com/fallsviewcasino), which opened in June 2004. It boasts its own 18,580-sq.-m (200,000-sq.-ft.) casino, a performing arts theater, a spa, and 10 dining spots. Its 368 rooms start at C$179 (US$125) for a double.

Dining is not one of Niagara Falls's strengths. It's not that you can't find any restaurants—the town is full of them. But it's a challenge to find good food that doesn't cost a small fortune. One interesting option is the **Pinnacle,** 6732 Oakes Dr. (© 905/356-1501), which offers a Continental menu and a remarkable view from the top of the Minolta Tower. **Carpaccio,** 6840 Lundy's Lane (© 905/371-2063), is surrounded by fast-food outlets, but its fine Italian cooking makes it a gastronomic oasis. Over at Casino Niagara, the **Twenty-One Club,** 5705 Falls Ave. (© 905/374-3598), is pricey but delicious. **Betty's Restaurant & Tavern,** 8921 Sodom Rd. (© 905/295-4436), is an inexpensive spot that serves up hearty portions of comfort food.

3 The Muskoka Lakes

Just a 90-minute drive north of Toronto, the Muskoka region has been a magnet for visitors since the 19th century. While the area proved futile for farming (it's located on the Canadian Shield, where you need only dig a foot or two in some places to come up against sheets of granite), its more than 1,600 lakes, unspoiled wilderness and laid-back attitude made it an excellent place for a retreat. In the past decade, Muskoka's charms have expanded to include excellent golf courses,

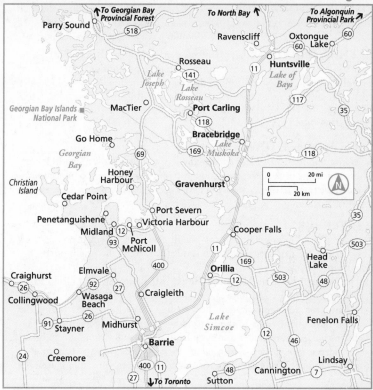

soothing spas, and top-notch restaurants. While the region is at its most popular in summer, when families congregate at the resorts and Hollywood celebrities like Goldie Hawn and Tom Hanks lounge at their lakefront "cottages," this is a great area to visit at any time of the year.

Once accessible only by the water, Muskoka is still a boater's dream. The region also has several towns of note: Gravenhurst, Bracebridge, Port Carling, Huntsville, and Bala. Located a few kilometers apart, these communities date back to the 1850s, when logging was Muskoka's primary industry. Filled with historic sites and more modern attractions, it's well worth devoting a day or two to explore them (fortunately, they are all easily reachable by car these days).

ESSENTIALS

GETTING THERE   You can drive from the south via Highway 400 to Highway 11, from the east via highways 12 and 169 to Highway 11, and from the north via Highway 11. It's about 160km (99 miles) from Toronto to Gravenhurst, 15km (9 miles) from Gravenhurst to Bracebridge, 25km (16 miles) from Bracebridge to Port Carling, and 34km (21 miles) from Bracebridge to Huntsville. **VIA Rail** (© **416/366-8411;** www.viarail.ca) services Gravenhurst, Bracebridge, and Huntsville from Toronto's Union Station. There is also an airport about 18km (11 miles) from Gravenhurst, which is used mainly for small aircraft. There are several other landing strips, and a helicopter-landing pad at the Deerhurst Resort in Huntsville.

VISITOR INFORMATION   For information on the region, contact **Muskoka Tourism,** on Highway 11 at Severn Bridge, R.R. 2, Kilworthy, ON P0E 1G0 (© **800/267-9700** or 705/689-0660; www.muskoka-tourism.on.ca).

GETTING AROUND   While you won't need a car if you plan to stay close to your resort while you're here (an entirely reasonable proposition), you will need a car if you're planning to do a lot of sightseeing in the area. You could take the train to Bracebridge, then rent a car at **Budget,** 1 Robert Dollar Dr. (© **705/ 645-2755**). There's also a **National** car rental center in Huntsville on Howland Dr. (© **705/787-1111**).

EXPLORING THE TOWNS

Both Gravenhurst and Huntsville are lovely towns that are well worth a visit. They are scenic but they also have enough shops, restaurants, and public spaces to make them interesting. Unless you have kids, there's not much of a reason to linger in Bracebridge.

GRAVENHURST

Gravenhurst is Muskoka's first town—the first you reach if you're driving from Toronto and the first to achieve town status (in 1887 at the height of the log- ging boom).

The **Norman Bethune Memorial House** is the restored 1890 birthplace of Dr. Norman Bethune, 235 John St. N. (© **705/687-4261**). In 1939, this sur- geon, inventor, and humanitarian died tending the sick in China during the Chinese Revolution. Tours of the historic house include a modern exhibit on Bethune's life. A visitor center displays gifts from Chinese visitors and an orien- tation video is shown. In summer, the house is open daily from 10am to 4pm from June through October, weekdays only from 1pm to 4pm from November through May. Admission is C$3.50 (US$2.45) adults and C$2 (US$1.40) for children 6 to 16, free for children 5 and under.

Sailing is one of Muskoka's greatest summer pleasures. Gravenhurst is home to the Muskoka Fleet, which includes a lovingly restored coal-powered 1887 steamship, the **RMS *Segwun.*** There are a variety of cruising options available, such as the 1-hour tour (C$14/US$9.80 adults, C$7.50/US$5.25 children), a 2-½-hour lunch cruise (C$43/US$30 adults, C$28/US$20 children), and a 4-hour late-afternoon tour of **Millionaire's Row** (C$40/US$28 adults, C$31/US$22 children), where you can be dazzled by the real estate as well as the natural beauty of the region. Advance reservations are required for all of the tours; call © **705/687-6667** or visit www.muskokafleet.com for more information.

Year-round, there are theater performances at the **Gravenhurst Opera House** (© **705/687-5550**), which celebrates its 104th anniversary in 2005. In summer only, there are shows at the **Port Carling Community Hall** (© **705/765- 5221**). For either, tickets usually cost between C$15 and C$30 (US$11–US$21).

BRACEBRIDGE: SANTA'S WORKSHOP

Halfway between the equator and the North Pole, **Bracebridge** bills itself as Santa's summer home, and **Santa's Village** (© **705/645-2512;** www.santas village.ca) is an imaginatively designed fantasyland full of delights: pedal boats and bumper boats on the lagoon, a roller-coaster sleigh ride, a Candy Cane Express, a carousel, and a Ferris wheel. At Elves' Island, kids can crawl on a sus- pended net and over or through various modules—the Lunch Bag Forest, Cave Crawl, and Snake Tube Crawl. Rides, water attractions, and roving entertainers are all part of the fun. Mid-June through Labour Day, it's open daily from 10am to 6pm. Admission is C$19 (US$13) ages 5 and up and C$14 (US$9.80) for seniors and children 2 to 4, free for children under 2.

PORT CARLING

As waterways became the main means of transportation in the region, **Port Carling** grew into the hub of the lakes. It became a boat-building center when a lock was installed connecting Lakes Muskoka and Rosseau, and a canal between Lakes Rosseau and Joseph opened all three to navigation. The **Muskoka Lakes Museum** on Joseph Street (© **705/765-5367**) captures the flavor of this era. July and August, it's open Monday through Saturday from 10am to 5pm and Sunday noon to 4pm; June, September, and October, hours are Tuesday through Saturday from 10am to 4pm and Sunday from noon to 4pm. Admission is C$3 (US$2.10) adults and C$2 (US$1.40) seniors and students. At press time, it's closed for renovation and expansion, but it will be open for the 2005 summer season.

HUNTSVILLE

Since the late 1800s, lumber has been the name of the game in Huntsville, and today it's Muskoka's biggest town, with major manufacturing companies. You can see some of the region's early history at the **Muskoka Heritage Place,** which includes **Muskoka Pioneer Village,** 88 Brunel Rd., Huntsville (© **705/789-7576;** www.muskokaheritageplace.org). It's open daily from 11am to 4pm from mid-May to mid-October. Admission is C$10 (US$7) adults and C$7 (US$4.90) children 3 to 12; free for children 2 and under. Muskoka Heritage Place also features the **Portage Flyer Steam Train.** Once part of the world's smallest commercial railway, it ran from 1904 till 1958. Now it has been reborn as a tourist attraction, and you can ride its scenic route from Tuesday through Saturday for C$5 (US$3.50) for adults and C$3 (US$2.10) for kids.

Robinson's General Store on Main Street in Dorset (© **705/766-2415**) is so popular it was voted Canada's best country store. Wood stoves, dry goods, hardware, pine goods, and moccasins—you name it, it's here.

WHERE TO STAY

Muskoka is famous for its lakes, but its resorts are renowned, too. While I normally like to wander from place to place when I travel to a particular area, I honestly think I could just stay put at one of the resorts here and be completely entertained for a week. There are also bed-and-breakfast and country-inn choices aplenty. Contact **Muskoka Tourism** (© **800/267-9700** or 705/689-0660; www.muskoka-tourism.on.ca) or the **Muskoka Bed and Breakfast Association,** 175 Clairmont Rd., Gravenhurst, ON P1P 1H9 (© **705/687-4511;** www.bbmuskoka.com).

RESORTS

Deerhurst Resort ★★★ **Kids**   The Deerhurst first opened its doors to guests in 1896, but its greatest expansion has occurred in the past 2 decades. Even more recently, a C$30-million renovation that ended in late 2002 really enhanced the property. This stunning resort complex now rambles over 320 hectares (800 acres), and it boasts an array of amenities that boggles the mind: two 18-hole golf courses (part of the Muskoka Golf Trail) and a golf academy; a full-service Aveda spa; seemingly endless miles of nature trails for hiking (or snowmobiling or cross-country skiing in winter); canoeing, kayaking, and all manner of water sports; an ambitious musical revue than runs all summer; and horseback riding. (Note that most of the activities, including golf, spa, and skiing, are available to visitors not staying at the resort.)

Fun Fact **The Shania Connection**

The Deerhurst has many charms to recommend it, and whether or not you stay there you must check out its excellent song-and-dance stage show. Now in its 24th year, it's famous in part because the phenomenally talented Shania Twain performed in it for 3 years (1988–1990). Twain has kept up her connection with the Deerhurst since, even having her wedding there. In 2002 she brought Katie Couric and a film crew from CNN to reminisce about her days on its stage. Twain continues to visit the resort—and when she does, she always checks out the show. Every summer the show is different, but it is always a pleasure to see.

The accommodations here are spread out among several buildings on the property. They range from high-ceilinged hotel rooms in the Terrace and Bayshore buildings to fully appointed one-, two-, or three-bedroom suites, many with fireplaces and/or whirlpools. The suites come with all the comforts, including CD players, TVs, and VCRs; some have full kitchens with microwaves, dishwashers, and washer/dryers. The most expensive suites are the three-bedroom units on the lake. One major draw is the top-notch Aveda spa, which has some of the most talented therapists I've ever encountered. The Deerhurst is an excellent spot for a family vacation, though it's also very popular with conference groups. The separate buildings make it easy to cater to each.

1235 Deerhurst Dr., Huntsville, ON P1H 2E8. (℃) **800/461-4393** or 705/789-6411. Fax 705/789-2431. www. deerhurstresort.com. 388 units. Summer from C$229 (US$160) double; from C$259 (US$181) suite; rest of the year from C$139 (US$97) double, from C$169 (US$118) suite. AE, DC, DISC, MC, V. Free parking. Take Canal Rd. off Hwy. 60 to Deerhurst Rd. **Amenities:** 2 restaurants; 2 bars; 2 indoor pools and 3 outdoor pools; tennis courts; 2 18-hole golf courses; indoor sports complex, 3 squash courts, racquetball court; spa; 11 Jacuzzis; sauna; children's programs; concierge; business center; limited room service; laundry service; dry cleaning. *In room:* A/C, TV, dataport, minibar, hair dryer.

Delta Grandview Resort ⭐ *(Kids)* If the Deerhurst is for the folks on the fast track, the Delta Grandview is for those looking for a more measured pace. This smaller resort retains the natural beauty and contours of the original farmstead even while providing the latest resort facilities. Eighty accommodations are traditional hotel-style rooms, but most units are suites in a series of buildings, some down beside the lake and others up on the hill with a lake view. All are spectacularly furnished. Each executive suite contains a kitchen, a dining area, a living room with a fireplace and access to an outside deck, a large bedroom, and a large bathroom with a whirlpool bath. The main dining room, the Rosewood Inn, is located in one of the resort's original buildings and overlooks Fairy Lake. Snacks are served in summer at the Dockside Restaurant right on the shores of the lake. In summer, the free Kidzone program provides supervision—and plenty of fun—for kids 4 to 12 from 8am to 4pm. That way, adults can spend the day on the Mark O'Meara golf course.

939 Hwy. 60, Huntsville, ON P1H 1Z4. (℃) **877/472-6388** or 705/789-4417. Fax 705/789-6882. 200 units. Summer from C$170 (US$119) double; rest of the year from C$100 (US$70) double. AE, MC, V. Free parking. **Amenities:** 2 restaurants; indoor and outdoor pools; 18-hole and 9-hole golf courses; 3 tennis courts; health club; children's programs; babysitting. *In room:* A/C, TV.

Taboo Resort ⭐⭐⭐ *(Kids)* Located near the town of Gravenhurst in the southern Muskoka region, Taboo stands out for its sleek sophistication in a bucolic setting. Known until May 2003 as Muskoka Sands, the resort's new name may conjure up images of a hedonistic adults-only retreat. The truth is anything but: Taboo is a family-friendly zone, with a kids' club that schedules activities for every day of the week during the high season in summer. But the fact that the resort is so willing to take care of the children means that many adults can soak up spa treatments or dine at one of the on-site restaurants without a second thought.

Taboo is best known for its golf course, which Mike Weir (Canada's top PGA ranked golfer) named his home course in June 2002. The course is a major stop on the Muskoka Golf Trail. There's also the Golf Academy for those who want to improve their game. Another reason to come to Taboo is the excellent dining. The resort has indulged gourmets by creating two entirely different restaurants: Wildfire (p. 251), a serious innovator that pairs up Canadian ingredients and Asian cooking techniques, and the Winewood, which elegantly serves up more traditional fare.

One of my favorite things about Taboo is that every single room, large and small alike, has its own deck or balcony. While all of the sophisticated offerings at the resort are excellent, nothing beats taking in the utterly serene and beautiful setting it enjoys.

Muskoka Beach Rd., R.R. 1, Gravenhurst, ON P1P 1R1. ℂ 800/461-0236 or 705/687-2233. Fax 705/687-7474. www.tabooresort.com. 157 units. Summer from C$295 (US$207) double, from C$410 (US$287) suite; rest of the year from C$150 (US$105) double, from C$210 (US$147) suite. AE, MC, V. Free parking. **Amenities:** 3 restaurants; bar; 3 outdoor and 1 indoor pool; 2 golf courses (18-hole and 9-hole); 5 tennis courts; squash court; health club; spa (in-room treatments also available); Jacuzzi; sauna; children's programs; game room; concierge; business center; limited room service; laundry service; dry cleaning. In room: A/C, TV, hair dryer.

Tamwood Resort (Kids) A great choice for families, Tamwood Lodge is a moderate-size log lodge on Lake Muskoka, 10km (6 miles) west of town. The main lodge has 35 units, all simply but nicely decorated, and there are a few cottages. The four deluxe loft accommodations are stunningly appointed in pine, and each features two bedrooms with skylights, plus a loft area, two baths, an efficiency kitchen, and a living room with a Franklin stove and a balcony from which you can dive into Lake Muskoka. Three new waterfront units come with fireplaces. Knotty-pine furnishings and large granite fireplaces imbue the lounge and main dining room with character. The resort offers a wealth of activities, including fishing, tennis, volleyball, badminton, and shuffleboard, plus free water-skiing and boating, and all the winter sports imaginable. There's also lots of organized family fun, including baseball games, marshmallow roasts, and bingo.

Hwy. 118, R.R. 1, Bracebridge, ON P1L 1W8. ℂ 800/465-9166 or 705/645-5172. www.tamwoodresort.com. 35 units. From C$130 (US$91) per person. MC, V. Free parking. **Amenities:** Indoor pool; nearby golf course; 3 tennis courts; spa; watersports equipment/rentals; children's programs; game room. In room: A/C, TV, fridge.

Windermere House Resort (★) The appearance is a little bit deceiving: The Windermere looks like a striking 1870s stone-and-clapboard turreted mansion. In fact, the building was destroyed by fire in 1996 and rebuilt, according to its original design, in 1997. It overlooks well-manicured lawns that sweep down to Lake Rosseau. Out front stretches a broad veranda furnished with Adirondack chairs and geranium-filled window boxes. Rebuilding allowed the guest rooms to enjoy modern conveniences (including air-conditioning), while retaining a traditional, homey look. Most of the rooms have gorgeous views (the best look over the lake), and a few have balconies or walkout decks.

Off Muskoka Rte. 4 (P.O. Box 68), Windermere, ON P0B 1P0. ℂ 800/461-4283 or 705/769-3611. Fax 705/769-2168. www.windermerehouse.com. 78 units. From C$170 (US$119) double. Rates include breakfast. Weekly rates also available. AE, MC, V. Free parking. **Amenities:** Restaurant; lounge; outdoor pool; golf course; tennis courts; children's programs; limited room service; laundry service; dry cleaning. *In room:* A/C, TV, minibar.

COUNTRY INNS

Inn at the Falls 🌟 *Finds*   This attractive "inn" is actually a group of seven Victorian houses on a quiet cul-de-sac overlooking Bracebridge Falls and the Muskoka River. The inviting gardens are filled with delphiniums, peonies, roses, and spring flowers, plus there's an outdoor heated pool. The guest rooms are individually decorated, with antiques and English chintz. Some units have fireplaces, Jacuzzis, and balconies; others have views of the falls. The Fox & Hounds is a popular local gathering place at lunch or dinner. In winter, the fire crackles and snaps, but in summer the terrace is filled with flowers and umbrella-shaded tables. The more elegant Carriage Room serves upscale Continental fare.

1 Dominion St., P.O. Box 1139, Bracebridge, ON P1L 1V3. 🄯 877/645-9212 or 705/645-2245. Fax 705/645-5093. www.innatthefalls.net. 42 units. From C$100 (US$70) double; from C$195 (US$137) suite. Extra person C$16 (US$11). Rates include breakfast. AE, DC, MC, V. Free parking. **Amenities:** 2 restaurants; outdoor pool; nearby golf course. *In room:* TV.

Severn River Inn *Value*   The Severn River Inn (19km/12 miles north of Orillia and 14km/9 miles south of Gravenhurst) occupies a 1906 building that has served as a general store, post office, telephone exchange, and boardinghouse. The guest rooms are individually furnished with pine and oak pieces, brass beds, floral-patterned fabrics, flouncy pillows, and quilts. The suite contains a sitting room and the original old bathtub and pedestal sink (this is the only room with a bathtub—the others all have showers only). The intimate restaurant, with a

---

The Rocky Road for Golfers

If you're been longing for a golf getaway, Muskoka is your perfect place to be. The region's resorts boast beautifully designed courses, created by the likes of Nick Faldo, Mike Weir, and Mark O'Meara. The greens here truly are different. Muskoka is located on the **Canadian Shield**, a bedrock layer just a few feet below the surface. The granite proved to be a millstone for farmers who tried to work the land, but it makes an excellent setting for golfers. The landscape is filled with natural rock outcroppings, and the golf courses take full advantage. Not only does the locale make for a stunning landscape, but it heightens the challenge. Add in the primeval forests and plenty of water, and you'll understand why the term "magical" is so often applied to Muskoka.

Some of the area's top-rated golf courses—such as the Deerhurst Highlands, Mark O'Meara Course at Grandview, and Taboo—have banded together to create the Muskoka Golf Trail. These design-your-own package plans allow you to stay at one resort but golf at the others (otherwise competition for tee times can be tough). Call 🄯 800/465-3034 or 905/755-0999, or visit www.muskokagolftrail.com for details. For general information about all of the courses in Muskoka, visit www.golfinmuskoka.com, www.teeingitup.com/ontario, or www.muskoka-tourism.on.ca.

Victorian ambience, is candlelit at night. In summer, the screened-in porch and outdoor patio overlooking the river are favored dining spots. The menu features contemporary Continental cuisine.

Cowbell Lane off Hwy. 11 (P.O. Box 100), Severn Bridge, ON P0E 1N0. ℂ **705/689-6333**. Fax 705/689-2691. www.severnriverinn.com. 10 units. From C$70 (US$49) double; from C$120 (US$84) suite. Rates include breakfast. MC, V. Free parking. **Amenities:** Restaurant; lounge; nearby golf course. *In room:* A/C.

WHERE TO DINE
VERY EXPENSIVE

Wildfire ✸✸✸ *Finds* FUSION/INTERNATIONAL   It's strange to think that some Torontonians are coming to Muskoka to eat, given the big city's impressive culinary pedigree. But chef Michael Pataran has cooked at two of Toronto's most famous kitchens—Monsoon (p. 87) and Rain (p. 91)—so perhaps it's no wonder that this elegant and dramatic new restaurant is attracting gourmets from far and wide. Wildfire does have an a la carte menu, but roughly two-thirds of its diners choose one of the chef's "Faith" tasting menus. These 4-, 5-, and 11-course experiences put the diner completely in the chef's capable hands: They don't list the beautifully presented dishes, in part because Pataran believes people shouldn't make blanket statements like "I don't eat seafood." Think that you could never enjoy caribou, salmon tartare, or eel? Think again, because it's almost impossible to resist these culinary masterpieces. Rest assured, you'll love 'em all. The restaurant's floor-to-ceiling windows face west, so that you can take in the glorious sunset over the lake.

Muskoka Beach Rd., R.R. 1, Gravenhurst, ON P1P 1R1. ℂ **705/687-2233**. www.tabooresort.com. Reservations strongly recommended. Main courses C$29–C$41 (US$20–US$29); tasting menus start at C$80 (US$56). AE, DC, MC, V. Daily 6–10pm.

EXPENSIVE

Eclipse ✸✸ CANADIAN/INTERNATIONAL   Recently renovated and remodeled, Eclipse remains a Muskoka favorite. With an expansive lake view, this spacious dining room with a soaring ceiling of Douglas fir beams is a blend of fine dining and casual Muskoka charm. Open for breakfast, lunch, and dinner, the restaurant has a lengthy menu, so it's relatively easy to please different tastes; there are also many vegetarian options. My favorite appetizer is the baked phyllo pastry filled with forest mushrooms and goat cheese, but the Sizzle—the signature dish—is the most popular (tiger shrimp sautéed in garlic, dried chiles and white wine and baked under mozzarella). Entrees run the gamut from breast of pheasant filled with wild rice and cranberries, to a rack of lamb rubbed with fresh herbs and sourdough crumbs and served with apple-maple compote. The wine list is just as interesting as the menu. There are 175 selections, which sounds daunting, though the well-informed staff are ready to help you navigate through it.

1235 Deerhurst Dr., Huntsville, ON P1H 2E8. ℂ **705/789-6411**. www.deerhurstresort.com. Reservations recommended. Main courses C$27–C$32 (US$19–US$22). AE, DC, MC, V. Daily 7–11am and 5–11pm.

3 Guys and a Stove ✸ INTERNATIONAL   The name might sound casual—and the atmosphere is indeed unpretentious—but the cooking is very fine. This is a family restaurant (with a special menu for kids), but the gourmet quotient is high. The curried pumpkin and sweet potato soup is an absolute must-have when it's on the menu; the spicy chicken stew is another surefire winner.

143 Hwy. 60, Huntsville. ℂ **705/789-1815**. Main courses C$15–C$25 (US$11–US$18). AE, MC, V. Daily 11am–9:30pm.

Rest, Relax, Recharge

Northern Ontario is deservedly famous for its outdoor activities, from skiing to boating, and from hiking to biking. But a growing segment of the tourist trade in these parts is coming for another reason altogether: spas. Getting away from it all in these parts no longer automatically means going on an ice fishing expedition; It could just as easily involve a hot rock massage (one of the latest trends). The spas listed below aren't targeted at women—the number of men going to spas has increased exponentially, so spas are offering almost all of their services to both sexes. For more information, including a free directory, contact the **Spas Ontario** association at ℂ **800/990-7702,** or visit the website at www.spasontario.com. Two of the best are at resorts:

Deerhurst Resort (p. 247): The Deerhurst thoughtfully provides children's programs, so you can drop off the tykes before you go for your aromatherapy massage or Ancient Dead Sea Mud Wrap (in fact, there is a special Couple's De-Stressor package . . .). The emphasis here is on total relaxation, and with all of the delicious Aveda products and scents, it's impossible to resist. The Deerhurst was one of the founding members of Spas Ontario, and the standards at the spa are excellent. The highly trained therapists are particularly talented at working out those inevitable golf-induced kinks.

Taboo Resort (p. 248): This is the choice for those who want to lie in the lap of luxury—and get a Swedish or reflexology massage while they're at it. The name of the newly built spa is Indulgence, which seems terribly appropriate. The list of services is comprehensive, and includes facials, manicures, pedicures, waxing, and of course massage. There are also several tempting body treatments, such as the Cranberry-Maple Body Polish, which includes a maple-sugar exfoliating scrub, a cranberry-infused whirlpool bath, and a rubdown with cranberry moisturizer (mmm . . .).

MODERATE

Blondie's ⭐ *Finds*   This small family-run restaurant is a rare find in Muskoka. While the menu has plenty of comfort foods—think fish and chips, prime rib, eggs Benedict, and smoked-meat sandwiches—there's also more exotic fare, such as sushi and a variety of seafood dishes. Blondie's is also the official caterer to the Gravenhurst Opera House. The setting is like a country kitchen, with its round wooden tables and cheery decorations, and the service is just as warm.

151 Brock St., Gravenhurst. ℂ **705/687-7756.** Reservations recommended for dinner. Main courses C$10–C$20 (US$7–US$14). MC, V. Mon–Tues 9:30am–3pm; Wed–Sat 9:30am–8pm.

4 Hamilton

75km (47 miles) SW of Toronto

On a landlocked harbor spanned at its entrance by the Burlington Skyway's dramatic sweep, Hamilton has long been nicknamed "Steeltown" for its industrial roots. Since the early 1990s however, Hamilton has been making a name for

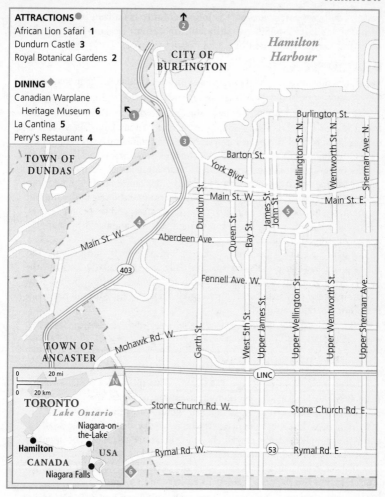

ATTRACTIONS ●
African Lion Safari **1**
Dundurn Castle **3**
Royal Botanical Gardens **2**

DINING ◆
Canadian Warplane
  Heritage Museum **6**
La Cantina **5**
Perry's Restaurant **4**

CITY OF
BURLINGTON

*Hamilton
Harbour*

Burlington St.

TOWN OF
DUNDAS

Barton St.

York Blvd.

Wellington St. N.
Wentworth St. N.
Sherman Ave. N.

Main St. W.

Main St. E.

Dundurn St.

Queen St.

Bay St.

James St.
John St.

Aberdeen Ave.

Main St. W.

403

Fennell Ave. W.

West 5th St.

Upper James St.

Upper Wellington St.

Upper Wentworth St.

Upper Sherman Ave.

Garth St.

TOWN OF
ANCASTER

Mohawk Rd. W.

LINC

0   20 mi
0   20 km

TORONTO
Lake Ontario

Niagara-on-
the-Lake

Hamilton

USA

CANADA
Niagara Falls

Stone Church Rd. W.

Stone Church Rd. E.

Rymal Rd. W.

53

Rymal Rd. E.

6

itself with its ever-expanding list of attractions. It takes less than an hour to drive here from Toronto, and it's well worth a day trip for the whole family.

ESSENTIALS

VISITOR INFORMATION   The Tourism Hamilton Information Centre has been relocated to 34 James St. S., 8th Floor, Hamilton, ON L8P 2X8 (© **800/ 263-8590** or 905/546-2666; www.hamiltonundiscovered.ca). It has a wealth of information about what to see and do, as well as where to dine and sleep. Its year-round hours run from Monday through Friday from 9am to 5pm.

GETTING THERE   Hamilton is easy to get to by car. From Toronto, take the Queen Elizabeth Way (signs read QEW) to Hamilton. The drive will take about an hour.

   GO (Government of Ontario) Transit is a commuter train that connects Toronto and Hamilton. Call © **800/438-6646** or 416/869-3200 for information, or check out www.gotransit.com. The **John C. Munro Hamilton International Airport** (© 905/679-8359; www.hamiltonairport.com) has long been popular with cargo carriers and is now a hub for WestJet.

WHAT TO SEE & DO

Hamilton's downtown core is best explored on foot, though you may want a car to visit attractions in the outlying areas.

African Lion Safari ★   Just a half-hour drive northwest of Hamilton, you'll find a mirror image of a traditional zoo: At the African Lion Safari, visitors remain caged in their cars or in a tour bus while the animals roam wild and free. The 300-hectare (750-acre) wildlife park contains rhinos, cheetahs, lions, tigers, giraffes, zebras, vultures, and many other species. In addition to the safari, the cost of admission covers other attractions like the cruise aboard the African Queen, during which a tour guide will take you around the lake and point out local inhabitants like spider monkeys, crested macaques, and ring-tailed lemurs. There's also a train that will take you through a forest populated by snapping turtles, among other wildlife.

The park has three baby Asian elephants: Samson, Albert, and George. And the elephant-bathing event, which occurs daily, will particularly fascinate the kids. There's also a Pets' Corner filled with frisky otters and pot-bellied pigs. There are several play areas for children as well, including the Misumu Bay water park (bring bathing suits!).

Safari Rd, Cambridge. © 800/461-WILD or 519/623-2620. www.lionsafari.com. Admission C$24 (US$17) adults, C$21 (US$15) seniors, C$19 (US$13) children 3–12, free for children 2 and under; rates are discounted in spring and fall. Late June to Labour Day daily 10am–5:30pm; late Apr to mid-June and early Sept to early Oct daily 9am–4pm. Closed mid-Oct to mid-Apr.

Canadian Warplane Heritage Museum   This interactive museum charts the course of Canadian aviation from the beginning of World War II to the present. Visitors can climb into the cockpits of World War II trainer crafts or a CF-100 jet fighter. The most popular attractions are the flight simulators, which allow aspiring pilots to test their flight skills. There are also short documentary films, photographs, and other memorabilia. The aircraft on display include rarities like the Avro Lancaster bomber and the deHavilland Vampire fighter jet. The collection also includes a variety of military and transport craft.

9280 Airport Rd. (at the John C. Munro Hamilton International Airport), Mount Hope. © 877/347-3359 or 905/670-3347. www.warplane.com. Admission C$10 (US$7) adults, C$8 (US$5.60) seniors and youths 8–18, free for children 7 and under; family admission for 2 adults and 2 youths is C$30 (US$21). Daily 9am–5pm. Closed Jan 1, Dec 25.

Dundurn Castle   The castle affords a glimpse of the opulent life as it was lived in this part of southern Ontario in the mid–19th century. Sir Allan Napier Mac-Nab, prime minister of the United Provinces of Canada in the mid-1850s and a founder of the Great Western Railway built it between 1832 and 1835; Queen Victoria knighted him for the part he played in the Rebellion of 1837. The 35-plus-room mansion has been restored and furnished in the style of 1855. The gray stucco exterior, with its classical Greek portico, is impressive enough, but inside, from the formal dining rooms to Lady MacNab's boudoir, the furnishings are rich. The museum contains a fascinating collection of Victoriana. In December, the castle is decorated splendidly for a Victorian Christmas.

The **Hamilton Military Museum** is on the grounds of Dundurn Castle. For those who are interested, it traces Canadian military history from the War of

1812 through World War I. Admission is included when you buy a ticket for Dundurn Castle.

Dundurn Park, York Blvd. (C) **905/546-2872**. Admission C$10 (US$7) adults, C$8 (US$5.60) seniors and students with ID, C$5 (US$3.50) children 6–14, free for children 5 and under. Victoria Day to Labour Day daily 10am–4pm; the rest of the year, Tues–Sun noon–4pm. Closed Jan 1, Dec 25–26.

Royal Botanical Gardens ⭐ Situated just north of the city, the Royal Botanical Gardens spreads over 1,214 glorious hectares (2,999 acres). The Rock Garden features spring bulbs in May, summer flowers in June to September, and chrysanthemums in October. The Laking Garden blazes during June and July with irises, peonies, and lilies. The arboretum fills with the heady scent of lilac from the end of May to early June, and the exquisite color bursts of rhododendrons and azaleas thereafter. The Centennial Rose Garden is at its best late June through mid-September.

The gardens host many festivals during the year, including the Mediterranean Food & Wine Festival in February, the popular Ontario Garden Show in early April, the Tulip Festival in May, the Rose Society Show in June, and the Japanese Flower Society Show in September.

Should you work up an appetite while strolling the grounds, there are several on-site dining options, including the Gardens Café, which is open year-round, and the Rock Garden Tea House or the Turner Pavilion (both open throughout the summer).

680 Plains Rd. W., Burlington (C) **905/527-1158**. www.rbg.ca. Admission C$15 (US$11) adults, C$12 (US$8.40) seniors and children 13–17, C$3 (US$2.10) children 5–12, free for children 4 and under. Daily 9:30am–dusk. Closed Jan 1, Dec 25.

WHERE TO STAY

Because Hamilton is so close to Toronto, it's easy to make a day trip here and back, rather than pulling up stakes and spending the night here. However, if you do want to stay in the area, several well-known chains have hotels here, including **Sheraton** ((C) **800/514-7101** or 905/529-5515), **Ramada** ((C) **800/2RAMADA** or 905/528-3451), and **Comfort Inn** ((C) **877/424-6423** or 905/560-4500).

WHERE TO DINE

The suggested restaurants in St. Catharine's and Welland, such as **Café Garibaldi, Wellington Court,** and **Rinderlin's** (p. 238, 239, and 239), are just a short drive away from Hamilton. However, Hamilton has a few restaurants worth checking out, too.

La Cantina ⭐ ITALIAN This is really two restaurants in one: There's a formal dining room, which serves up elegant plates like veal scaloppini in a dry Marsala sauce, and seared ostrich medallions cooked with pinot noir; equally elegant pasta plates include rotini with ham and peppers in a vodka sauce. Then there's the casual pizzeria, which serves up more than 20 varieties of pizza, ranging from the traditional Quattro Stagione (four seasons) with prosciutto, artichokes, olives, and mozzarella, to the unusual Gamberi, which is topped with shrimp, smoked, salmon, olives, eggplant, and pesto. This is a very popular spot, so try to make a reservation or arrive early, especially at lunch. If you're very lucky, you might just secure a seat in the restaurant's garden patio.

60 Walnut St. S. (C) **905/521-8989**. Reservations recommended. Main courses C$10–C$26 (US$7–US$18). AE, MC, V.

Perry's Restaurant INTERNATIONAL   This casual family-style restaurant has a large menu that has something for everyone. It borrows from a range of cuisines, including Italian, French, Mexican, Greek, and American. Offerings include chicken souvlakia, rack of ribs, hearty sandwiches, and fish and chips. There are also lighter options such as salads, soups, and chicken fingers. There's a sunny patio at the front of the restaurant, too.

1088 Main St. W. *Ⓒ* **905/527-3779.** Main courses C$6–C$13 (US$4.20–US$9.10). MC, V. Daily 11:30am–1am.

Appendix:
Toronto in Depth

In less than 300 years, Toronto has grown from a trading post to a vibrant international capital. Read on to get a sense of how it happened.

1 History 101

FROM FUR TRADING POST TO MUDDY YORK

As in most cities, the influences of geography, trade, and communications shaped Toronto and its history. Although the city today possesses a downtown core, it also sprawls across a large area—a gift of geography, for there are no physical barriers to stop it. When European settlement began, the broad plain rising from Lake Ontario to an inland ridge of hills (around today's St. Clair Ave.), and stretching between the Don River in the east and the Humber in the west, made the location ideal.

Native Canadians had long stopped here—at the entrance to the Toronto Trail, a short route between the Lower and Upper lakes. In 1615, French fur trader Etienne Brûleé was the first European to travel the trail. It wasn't until 1720 that the French established the first trading post, known as Fort Toronto, to intercept the furs that were being taken across Lake Ontario to New York State by English rivals. Fort Rouille, built on the site of today's CNE grounds, replaced the trading post in 1751. When the 1763 Treaty of Paris ended the Anglo-French War after the fall of Québec, French rule in North America effectively ended, and the city's French antecedents were all but forgotten.

Only 32km (20 miles) across the lake from the United States, Toronto has always been affected by what happens south of the border. When the

Dateline

- **1615** Etienne Brûleé travels the Toronto Trail. "Toronto" is derived from a Huron term for "place of meeting."
- **1720** France establishes post at Toronto.
- **1751** French build Fort Rouille.
- **1759** Fort Rouille burned during British conquest.
- **1763** Treaty of Paris effectively ends French rule in Canada.
- **1787** Lord Dorchester, British governor of Québec, purchases land from Scarborough to Etobicoke from the Mississauga tribe.
- **1793** Governor of Upper Canada, Col. John Simcoe, arrives and names settlement York. It becomes capital of Upper Canada.
- **1796** Yonge Street laid out, a 53km (33-mile) oxcart trail.
- **1812–15** War of 1812, between United States and England, uses Canada as a battleground. In 1813, Americans invade, blow up Fort York, and burn Parliament buildings. In 1814, U.S. troops are driven out of Canada.
- **1820s** Immigration of Nonconformists and Irish Catholics fosters reform politics.
- **1828** Erie Canal extended to Oswego on Lake Ontario.
- **1830s** Orange Order becomes prominent influence in politics.
- **1832–34** Cholera epidemics.
- **1834** City named Toronto; City Council replaces magistrates; William Lyon Mackenzie becomes first mayor.

continues

American Revolution established a powerful, potentially hostile new nation, Toronto's location became strategically more important, or so it seemed to John Graves Simcoe. He was lieutenant governor of the newly formed province of Upper Canada, which had been established in 1791 to administer the frontiers—from Kingston and Quinte's Isle to Windsor and beyond—settled largely by Loyalists fleeing the Revolution. To Simcoe, Toronto was more defensible than Fort Niagara and a natural arsenal for Lake Ontario, which also afforded easy access to Lake Huron and the interior.

The governor had already purchased a vast tract of land from the Mississauga tribe for the paltry sum of £1,700 (US$2,600), plus blankets, guns, rum, and tobacco. In 1793, Lieutenant Governor Simcoe, his wife, Elizabeth, and the Queen's Rangers arrived. Simcoe ordered a garrison built, renamed the settlement York, and laid it out in a 10-block rectangle around King, Front, George, Duke, and Berkeley streets. Beyond stretched a series of 40-hectare (100-acre) lots from Queen to Bloor, which were granted to mollify government officials, who resented having to move to the mosquito-plagued, marshy outpost. Its muddiness was prodigious, and in fact a story is told of a fellow who saw a hat lying in the middle of a street, went to pick it up, and found the head of a live man submerged below it! In 3 short years a small hamlet had grown, and Simcoe had laid out Yonge Street—then a 53km (33-mile) oxcart trail. Four years later the first Parliament meeting confirmed York as the capital of Upper Canada.

FROM MUDDY YORK TO THE FAMILY COMPACT

The officials were a more demanding and finicky lot than the sturdy frontier farmers, and businesses sprang up to serve them. By 1812, the population had grown to 703 and included a

- 1837 Former mayor Mackenzie leads rebellion sparked by economic downturn.
- 1840s–50s Mass Irish immigration.
- 1841 Act of Union establishes the United Province of Canada, with Kingston as ruling seat; Toronto loses status as a capital.
- 1843 The university, King's College, opens.
- 1844 City Hall built. George Brown founds the *Globe*.
- 1849 Great fire destroys much of city. Anglican King's College converts to secular University of Toronto.
- 1851 Population 30,000 (33% Irish). Anglican Trinity College founded. St. Lawrence Hall built.
- 1852 Toronto Stock Exchange opens. Grand Trunk Railroad charted, linking Québec, Montréal, Toronto, Guelph, and Sarnia.
- 1853 St. James Cathedral completed.
- 1858 Storm creates the Toronto Islands.
- 1861 Horse-powered street railway runs along Yonge to Yorkville.
- 1867 Canadian Confederation; Toronto becomes capital of new province of Ontario.
- 1868 Canada First movement begins.
- 1869 Eaton's department store opens.
- 1871 Population 56,000.
- 1872 Simpson's department store opens.
- 1876 John Ross Robertson starts *Evening Telegram*, which wields influence for next 90 years.
- 1886 Provincial parliament buildings erected in Queen's Park.
- 1893 First Stanley Cup played.
- 1896 *Maclean's* newsmagazine started.
- 1901 Population 208,000.
- 1903 The dramatic short film *Hiawatha* is the first movie made in Canada.
- 1904 Great Fire burns much of downtown.
- 1906 First autos produced by Canada Cycle and Motor Company. Toronto Symphony founded.
- 1907 Bell strike broken. Royal Alexandra opens. The Lord's Day Act forbids all public activity except churchgoing on Sunday.

brewer-baker, blacksmith, watchmaker, chair-maker, apothecary, hatter, and tailor.

During the War of 1812, despite initial victories at Queenston and Detroit, Canada was under siege. In April 1813, 14 ships carrying 1,700 American troops invaded York, blew up the incomplete fort, burned the Parliament buildings, and carried off the mace (which was not returned until 1934). The British general burned a 30-gun warship, the *Sir Isaac Brock,* which was under construction, and retreated, leaving young John Strachan to negotiate the capitulation. This event did much to reinforce the town's pro-British, anti-American attitude—a feeling that persists to some extent to this day. In retaliation for the burning of Fort York, some Canadians went to Washington and torched the American president's residence. (The Americans later whitewashed it to hide the charred wood—hence, the White House.)

A conservative pro-British outlook permeated the official political oligarchy that dominated York, a group dubbed the Family Compact. Many of the names on street signs, subway stops, and maps derive from this august group of early government officers and their families. Among them were William Jarvis, a New England Loyalist who became provincial secretary; John Beverley Robinson, son of a Virginia Loyalist, who became attorney general at age 22 and later chief justice of Upper Canada; and Scottish-educated Dr. John Strachan, a schoolmaster who became an Anglican rector and, eventually, the most powerful figure in York. Anglo-Irish Dr. William Warren Baldwin, doctor, lawyer, architect, judge, and parliamentarian, laid out Spadina Avenue as a thoroughfare leading to his country house; the Boultons were prominent lawyers, judges, and politicians—Judge D'Arcy Boulton built a mansion,

1909 Florence Nightingale Graham drops out of nursing school in Toronto, changes her name to Elizabeth Arden, and founds the first cosmetics empire.

1911 Founding members of the Group of Seven meet at the Toronto Arts and Letters Club.

1912 Garment workers' strike broken. Royal Ontario Museum founded.

1914 New Union Station built.

1914–18 World War I; 70,000 Torontonians enlist, and 13,000 die.

1920 The Art Gallery of Toronto mounts the first Group of Seven exhibit.

1921 Population 521,893.

1922 University of Toronto researchers Frederick Banting and Charles Best discover insulin.

1923 Dr. Banting is awarded the Nobel Prize in medicine. Parliament passes the Chinese Exclusion Act. Ernest Hemingway moves to Toronto to become a reporter for the *Star.*

1930s The Great Depression; thousands go on relief.

1931 Maple Leaf Gardens built as home base for the Maple Leafs.

1938 Toronto native Joseph Shuster creates *Superman.*

1939 Canada enters World War II; thousands of troops leave from Union Station.

1940–45 Toronto functions as war supplier.

1947 Cocktail lounges approved.

1950 Sunday sports allowed.

1951 Population 31% foreign-born.

1954 Metro created; Toronto becomes a model for urban consolidation. Toronto native Marilyn Bell, 16, becomes first person to swim across Lake Ontario. In October, Hurricane Hazel kills 83 people in Toronto.

1959 York University, Toronto's second major institution of higher education, opens.

1960 Movies are shown in Toronto on Sunday for the first time.

1961 Population 42% foreign-born.

1963 Ryerson Polytechnic University founded.

continues

the Grange, which later became the core of the art museum and still stands today.

These men, extremely conscious of rank, were conformist, conservative, pro-British, Tory, and Anglican. Their power was broken only later in the 19th century, as a larger and more diverse population gave reformers a chance to challenge their control. But even today, their influence lingers in the corporate world, where a handful of companies and individuals control 80% of the companies on the Toronto Stock Exchange.

THE EARLY 1800s—CANAL, RAILROAD & IMMIGRATION

The changes that eventually diluted their control began in the early 19th century. During the 1820s, 1830s, and 1840s, immigrants—Irish Protestants and Catholics, Scots, Presbyterians, Methodists, and other Nonconformists—poured in to settle the frontier farmlands. By 1832 York had become the largest urban community in the province, with a population of 1,600. Already well established commercially as a supply center, York enjoyed another boost when the Erie Canal was extended to Oswego on Lake Ontario, giving it direct access to New York, and the Welland Canal was built across the Niagara Peninsula, allowing access to Lake Erie and points beyond. In 1834, the city was incorporated and York became Toronto, a city bounded by Parliament Street to the east, Bathurst to the west, the lakefront to the south, and 400 yards north of the current Queen Street (then called Lot) to the north. Outside this area—west to Dufferin Street, east to the Don River, and north to Bloor Street—lay the "liberties," out of which the city would later carve new wards. North of Bloor, local brewer Joseph Bloor and Sheriff Jarvis were already drawing up plans for the village of Yorkville.

■ **1965** New City Hall at Nathan Phillips Square is unveiled. Canada and the United States sign the Autopact, creating boom times in Toronto and nearby Oshawa.

■ **1966** U.S. draft dodgers start fleeing to Canada; many settle in Toronto.

■ **1970s** Influx of immigration from Asia, Africa, India, Pakistan, the Caribbean, and Latin America.

■ **1974** Mikhail Baryshnikov defects from the USSR during a trip to Toronto.

■ **1975** Toronto International Film Festival founded. CN Tower becomes the world's tallest freestanding structure.

■ **1980s** Creation and expansion of the Greater Toronto area, including nearby cities of Hamilton and Oshawa.

■ **1981** Population 3,898,933.

■ **1984** City's 150th anniversary.

■ **1989** SkyDome opens, drawing wide criticism of its C$570-million (US$399-million) cost.

■ **1992** Residents of Toronto Islands win 40-year struggle to retain their homes. Blue Jays win World Series for the first time.

■ **1993** Blue Jays repeat as World Series champions.

■ **1995** Progressive Conservative Government elected in Ontario.

■ **1996** Population 4,263,757. *Fortune* magazine names Toronto best city in the world to live and work in. University of Toronto professor John Polanyi wins Nobel Prize in Chemistry.

■ **1997** Protests in Queen's Park target social service cuts and the passage of Bill 103, creating a megacity.

■ **1998** Toronto becomes a megacity anyway.

■ **1999** Researchers at McMaster University in Hamilton discover unusual characteristics of Einstein's brain. The new Air Canada Centre becomes home to the Maple Leafs and the Raptors.

■ **2001** Toronto loses its bid to host the 2008 Olympics to Beijing.

■ **2002** Toronto hosts the first World Youth Day ever held in Canada; the event includes a visit by Pope John Paul II.

As more immigrants arrived, the population grew more diverse, and demands arose for democracy and reform. Among the reformers were such leaders as Francis Collins, who launched the radical paper *Canadian Freeman* in 1825; lawyer William

▪ **2003** Toronto gains several new attractions, including the Distillery Historic District, the Yonge-Dundas Square, and the Carlu Theatre. Toronto tourism drops due to the SARS scare. Same-sex marriage is legalized in Ontario in June.

Draper; and, perhaps most famous of all, fiery William Lyon Mackenzie, who was elected Toronto's first mayor in 1834.

Mackenzie had started his *Colonial Advocate* to crusade against the narrow-minded Family Compact, calling for reform and challenging their power to such an extent that some of them dumped his presses into the lake. By 1837, Mackenzie, undaunted, was calling for open rebellion.

A severe depression, financial turmoil, and the failure of some banks all contributed to the 1837 Rebellion, one of the most dramatic events in the city's history. On December 5, the rebels, a scruffy bunch of about 700, gathered at Montgomery's Tavern outside the city (near modern-day Eglinton Ave.). Led by Mackenzie on a white mare, they marched on the city. Two days later the city's militia, called out by Sheriff Jarvis, scattered the rebels at Carlton Street. Both sides then turned and ran. Reinforcements arrived, pursued the rebels, and bombarded the tavern with cannonballs. Mackenzie fled to the United States, and two other leaders—Lount and Matthews—were hanged. Their graves are in the Necropolis cemetery.

Between 1834 and 1884 the foundations of an industrial city were laid: Toronto gained water works, gas, and public transportation. Many municipal facilities were built, including a city hall, the Royal Lyceum Theatre (1848) on King near Bay, the Toronto Stock Exchange (1852), St. Lawrence Hall (1851), an asylum, and a jail.

During the 1850s the building of the railroads accelerated the economic pace. By 1860, Toronto was at the center of a railroad web. It became the trading hub for lumber and grain imports and exports. Merchant empires were founded, railroad magnates emerged, and institutions like the Bank of Toronto were established.

Despite its growth and wealth, Toronto still lagged behind Montréal, which had twice Toronto's population in 1861. But Toronto increasingly took advantage of its superior links to the south, and that edge eventually helped it overtake its rival. Under the Confederation of 1867, the city was guaranteed another advantage: As the capital of the newly created Ontario, Toronto, in effect, controlled the minerals and timber of the north.

During this mid-Victorian period the growth of a more diverse population continued. In 1847, Irish famine victims began flooding into Toronto, and by 1851 and 1852 the Irish-born were the city's largest single ethnic group. While many of them were Ulster Protestants who did not threaten the Anglo-Protestant ascendancy, the newcomers were not always welcomed—a pattern that repeated whenever a new immigrant group threatened to change the shape and order of society. As the gap between the number of Anglicans and Catholics closed, sectarian tensions increased, and the old-country Orange and Green conflicts flared into mob violence.

LATE- & HIGH-VICTORIAN TORONTO

Between 1871 and 1891 the city's population more than tripled, shooting from 56,000 to 181,000. The burgeoning urban market helped spawn two great

Toronto retailers—Timothy Eaton and Robert Simpson—who moved to Toronto from Ontario towns to open stores at Queen and Yonge streets in 1869 and 1872, respectively. Eaton developed his reputation on fixed prices, cash sales only, and promises of refunds if the customer wasn't satisfied—all unique gambits at the time. Simpson copied Eaton and competed by providing better service, such as two telephones to take orders instead of one. Both enterprises developed into full-fledged department stores, and both entered the mail-order business, conquering the country with their catalogs.

The business of the city was business, and amassing wealth was the pastime of such figures as Henry Pellatt, stockbroker, president of the Electrical Development Company, and builder of Casa Loma; E. B. Osler; George Albertus Cox; and A. R. Ames. Although these men were self-made entrepreneurs, not Family Compact officials, they formed a traditional socially conservative elite, linked by money, taste, investments, and religious affiliation. And they were staunchly British. They and the rest of the citizens celebrated the Queen's Jubilee in 1897 with gusto, and gave Toronto boys a rousing send-off to fight in the Boer War in 1899. The prominent businessmen also had a fondness for clubs—the Albany Club for the Conservatives, and the National Club for the Liberals. As in England, their sports clubs (notably the Royal Yacht Club, the Toronto Cricket Club, the Toronto Golf Club, and the Lawn Tennis Club) carried a certain cachet.

The boom spurred new commercial and residential construction. Projects included the first steel-frame building—the Board of Trade Building (1889) at Yonge and Front—George Gooderham's Romanesque-style mansion (1890) at St. George and Bloor (now the York Club), the provincial parliament buildings in Queen's Park (1886–92), and the city hall (1899) at Queen and Bay. Public transit improved, and by 1891 the city had 109km (68 miles) of tracks for horse-drawn cars. Electric lights, telephones, and electric streetcars appeared in the 1890s.

FROM 1900 TO 1933

Between 1901 and 1921 the population more than doubled, climbing from 208,000 to 521,893. The economy continued to expand, fueled by the lumber, mining, wholesale, and agricultural machinery industries, and after 1911 by hydroelectric power. Toronto began to seriously challenge Montréal. Much of the new wealth went into construction, and three marvelous buildings from this era can still be seen today: the Horticultural Building at the Exhibition Grounds (1907), the King Edward Hotel (1903), and Union Station (1914–19). Most of the earlier wooden structures had been destroyed in the Great Fire of 1904, which wiped out 5.6 hectares (14 acres) of downtown.

The booming economy and its factories attracted a wave of new immigrants—mostly Italians and Jews from Russia and Eastern Europe—who settled in the city's emerging ethnic enclaves. By 1912, Kensington Market was well established, and the garment center and Jewish community were firmly ensconced around King and Spadina. Little Italy clustered around College and Grace. By 1911 more than 30,000 Torontonians were foreign-born, and the slow march to change the English character of the city had begun.

It was still a city of churches worthy of the name "Toronto the Good," with a population of staunch religious conservatives, who barely voted for Sunday streetcar service in 1897 and in 1912 banned tobogganing on Sunday. As late as 1936, 30 men were arrested at the lakeshore resort of Sunnyside because they exposed their chests—even though the temperature was 105°F (41°C)! In 1947, cocktail lounges were approved, but it wasn't until 1950 that playing sports on Sunday became legal.

Increased industrialization brought social problems, largely concentrated in Cabbagetown and the Ward, a large area that stretched west of Yonge and north of Queen. Here, poor people lived in crowded, wretched conditions: Housing was inadequate, health conditions poor, and rag-picking, or sweatshop labor, the only employment.

As industry grew, unionism also increased, but the movement, as in the United States, failed to organize politically. Two major strikes—at Bell in 1907 and in the garment industry in 1912—were easily broken.

The larger, wealthier city also became an intellectual and cultural magnet. Artists like Charles Jefferys, J. H. MacDonald, Arthur Lismer, Tom Thomson, Lawren Harris, Frederick Varley, and A. Y. Jackson, most associated with the Group of Seven, set up studios in Toronto. Their first group show opened in 1920. Toronto also became the English-language publishing center of the nation, and national magazines like *Maclean's* (1896) and *Saturday Night* were launched. The Art Gallery of Ontario, the Royal Ontario Museum, the Toronto Symphony Orchestra, and the Royal Alexandra Theatre all opened before 1914.

Women advanced, too, at the turn of the 20th century. In 1880, Emily Jennings Stowe became the first Canadian woman authorized to practice medicine. In 1886, the University of Toronto admitted women. Clara Brett Martin was the first woman admitted to the law courts. The women's suffrage movement gained strength, led by Dr. Stowe, Flora McDonald Denison, and the Women's Christian Temperance Union.

During World War I, Toronto sent 70,000 men to the trenches; about 13,000 were killed. At home, the war had a great impact economically and socially: Toronto became Canada's chief aviation center; factories, shipyards, and power facilities expanded to meet the needs of war; and women entered the work force in great numbers.

After the war the city took on much more of the aspect and tone that characterize it today. Automobiles appeared on the streets—the Canadian Cycle and Motor Company had begun manufacturing them in 1906 (the first parking ticket was given in 1908), and one or two skyscrapers appeared. Although 80% of the population was of British origin, ethnic enclaves were clearly defined.

The 1920s roared along, fueled by a mining boom that saw Bay Street turned into a veritable gold-rush alley where everyone was pushing something hot. The Great Depression followed, inflicting 30% unemployment in 1933. The only distraction from its bleakness was the opening of Maple Leaf Gardens in 1931. Besides being an ice-hockey center, it also was host to large protest rallies during the Depression, and later such diverse entities as the Jehovah's Witnesses, Billy Graham, the Ringling Bros. Circus, and the Metropolitan Opera.

As in the United States, hostility toward new immigrants was rife during the '20s. It reached a peak in 1923, when the Chinese Exclusion Act was passed, banning Chinese immigration. In the 1930s, antagonism toward Jews intensified. Signs such as NO JEWS, NIGGERS, OR DOGS were posted occasionally at Balmy and Kew beaches. In August 1933, the display of a swastika at Christie Pits caused a battle between Nazis and Jews.

AFTER WORLD WAR II

In 1939, Torontonians again rallied to the British cause, sending thousands to fight in Europe. At home, plants turned out fighter bombers and Bren guns, and people endured rationing—one bottle of liquor a month, and limited supplies of sugar and other staples—while they listened to the war-front news delivered by Lorne Greene.

Already prosperous by World War II, Toronto continued to expand during the 1940s. The suburbs alone added more than 200,000 to the population between 1940 and 1953. By the 1950s, the urban area had grown so large, disputes between city and suburbs were so frequent, and the need for social and other services was so great that an effective administrative solution was needed. In 1953, the Metro Council, composed of equal numbers of representatives from the city and the suburbs, was established.

Toronto became a major city in the 1950s, with Metro providing a structure for planning and growth. The Yonge subway opened, and a network of highways was constructed. It linked the city to the affluent suburbs. Don Mills, the first new town, was built between 1952 and 1962; Yorkdale Center, a mammoth shopping center, followed in 1964. American companies began locating branch plants in the area, fueling much of the growth.

The city also began to loosen up. While the old social elite (still traditionally educated at Upper Canada College, Ridley, and Trinity College) continued to dominate the boardrooms, politics, at least, had become more accessible and fluid. In 1954, Nathan Phillips became the first Jewish mayor, signifying how greatly the population had changed from the days when immigrants were primarily British, American, or French. In 1947, the Chinese Exclusion Act of 1923 was repealed, opening the door to relatives of Toronto's then small Chinese community. After 1950, the door swung open further. Germans and Italians were allowed to enter, adding to the communities that were already established; then, under pressure from the United Nations, Poles, Ukrainians, Central European and Russian Jews, Yugoslavs, Estonians, Latvians, and other East Europeans poured in. Most arrived at Union Station, having journeyed from the ports of Halifax, Québec City, and Montréal. At the beginning of the 1950s, the foreign-born were 31% of the population; by 1961, they were 42%, and the number of people claiming British descent had fallen from 73% to 59%. The 1960s brought an even richer mix of people—Portuguese, Greeks, West Indians, South Asians, Chinese, Vietnamese, and Chilean refugees—changing the city's character forever.

In the 1960s, the focus shifted from the suburbs to the city. People moved back downtown, renovating the handsome brick Victorians so characteristic of today's downtown. Yorkville emerged briefly as the hippie capital—the Haight-Ashbury of Canada. Gordon Lightfoot and Joni Mitchell sang in the coffeehouses, and antiwar protests took over the streets. Perhaps the failure of the experimental, alternative Rochdale College in 1968 marked the demise of that era. By the mid-1970s, Yorkville had been transformed into a village of elegant boutiques and galleries and high-rent restaurants, and the funky village had moved to Queen Street West.

In the 1970s, Toronto became the fastest-growing city in North America. For years the city had competed with Montréal for first-city status, and now the separatist issue and the election of the Parti Québecois in 1976 hastened Toronto's dash to the tape. It overtook Montréal as a financial center, boasting more corporate headquarters. Its stock market was more important, and it remained the country's prime publishing center. A dramatically different city hall opened in 1965, a symbol of the city's equally new dynamism. Toronto also began reclaiming its waterfront, with the development of Harbourfront. The city's new power and wealth came alive in new skyscrapers and civic buildings—the Toronto Dominion, the 72-story First Canadian Place, Royal Bank Plaza, Roy Thomson Hall, the Eaton Centre, the CN Tower—all of which transformed the 1930s skyline into an urban landscape worthy of world attention.

Unlike the rapid building of highways and other structures completed in the 1950s, these developments were achieved with some balance and attention to the city's heritage. From the late '60s to the early '80s, citizens fought to ensure that the city's heritage was saved and that development was not allowed to continue as wildly as it had in the '50s. The best examples of the reform movement's success were the stopping of the proposed Spadina Expressway in 1971 and the fight against several urban renewal plans.

During the 1970s, the provincial government also helped develop attractions that would polish Toronto's patina and lure visitors: Ontario Place in 1971, Harbourfront in 1972, and the Metro Zoo and the Ontario Science Centre in 1974. Government financing also supported the arts and helped turn Toronto from a city with four theaters in 1965 to one boasting more than 40 today.

2 Toronto Today

Toronto's growth has continued steadily since the 1970s, though the past several years have been a tumultuous time for the city. The merger of its separate municipalities, rapid population growth, and provincial government budget-slashing have all had a serious impact on the life of the city. Toronto has few friends in the provincial government (perhaps because its citizens vote against it whenever given the opportunity). In addition to forcing the megacity merger through, the Conservative provincial government (or "Tories") cut social spending. The most frequent complaint heard in Toronto is that the city's municipal taxes aren't reinvested in its infrastructure, but end up being funneled to less populous parts of the province. Sadly the city's homeless problem only seems to be growing rather than improving. Ontario elected a new Liberal government in the fall of 2003, but they don't seem to be doing any more for the city than the Tories did.

But it has also been a boom time for Toronto, with the opening of new attractions such as the Distillery Historic District; the renovation and expansion of institutions such as the Royal Ontario Museum and the Art Gallery of Ontario; the construction of a long-awaited opera house; the introduction of a third subway line; and a burgeoning dining and entertainment scene. The downtown core is thriving, and the energy is driving its development west into previously neglected areas. Toronto is still the city of choice for arriving immigrants: 300,000 Hong Kong émigrés have joined Toronto's Chinese community, and there have been influxes from Somalia, Eastern Europe, India, Pakistan, and Central America. Neighborhoods around town preserve these cultures. While their influence is strong in many areas, it is perhaps most visible to a short-term visitor in the city's diverse dining options and in Toronto's many cultural festivals.

In 2001, Toronto made a Herculean effort to convince the International Olympic Committee that it would make the perfect host city for the 2008 Games, but it lost out to Beijing. Local wags claimed that Toronto was being "strongly encouraged" to go after the 2012 Games. However, the fact that Vancouver won the 2010 Winter Games has likely quashed that dream for now. Fortunately, the local government is considering the implementation of some of the terrific plans that were drawn up to win over the IOC. Watch for further development along the waterfront. Undoubtedly Toronto's energy will be channeled in new and interesting directions.

Index

See also Accommodations and Restaurant indexes, below.

ACCOMMODATIONS

RESTAURANTS

Frommer's Complete Guides

The only guide independent travelers need to make smart choices, avoid rip-offs, get the most for their money, and travel like a pro.

Frommer's
Southeast Asia
With Coverage of the Best Temples and Beaches

Frommer's

WILEY

Travel Tip: He who finds the best hotel deal has more to spend on facials involving knobbly vegetables.

Hello, the Roaming Gnome here. I've been nabbed from the garden and taken round the world. The people who took me are so terribly clever. They find the best offerings on Travelocity. For very little cha-ching. And that means I get to be pampered and exfoliated till I'm pink as a bunny's doodah.

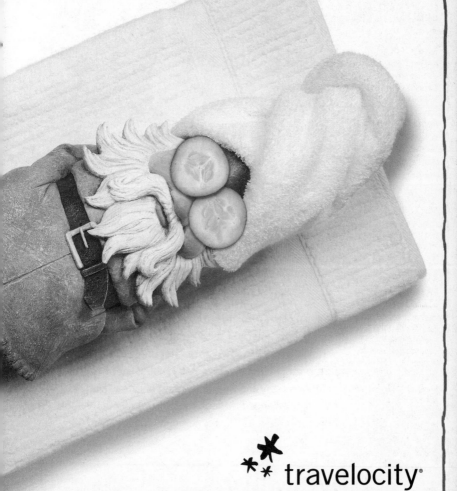

travelocity

1-888-TRAVELOCITY / travelocity.com / America Online Keyword: Travel

Travel Tip: Make sure there's customer service for any change of plans — involving friendly natives, for example.

One can plan and plan, but if you don't book with the right people you can't seize le moment and canoodle with the poodle named Pansy. I, for one, am all for fraternizing with the locals. Better yet, if I need to extend my stay and my gnome nappers are willing, it can all be arranged through the 800 number at, oh look, how convenient, the lovely company coat of arms.

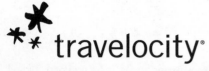

travelocity®

Travel Tip: He who finds the best hotel deal has more to spend on facials involving knobbly vegetables.

Hello, the Roaming Gnome here. I've been nabbed from the garden and taken round the world. The people who took me are so terribly clever. They find the best offerings on Travelocity. For very little cha-ching. And that means I get to be pampered and exfoliated till I'm pink as a bunny's doodah.

travelocity®

1-888-TRAVELOCITY / travelocity.com / America Online Keyword: Travel